Media, Crime, and Criminal Justice

Media, Crime, and Criminal Justice

Images, Realities, and Policies

FOURTH EDITION

RAY SURETTE
University of Central Florida

Australia • Brazil • Japan • Korea • Mexico • Singapore • Spain • United Kingdom • United States

WADSWORTH
CENGAGE Learning™

Media, Crime, and Criminal Justice: Images, Realities, and Policies, Fourth Edition
Ray Surette

Acquisitions Editor: Carolyn Henderson Meier

Assistant Editor: Erin Abney

Editorial Assistant: John Chell

Marketing Manager: Michelle Williams

Marketing Assistant: Jillian Myers

Marketing Communications Manager: Laura Localio

Content Project Management: PreMediaGlobal

Creative Director: Rob Hugel

Art Director: Maria Epes

Print Buyer: Linda Hsu

Rights Acquisitions Account Manager, Text: Don Schlotman

Rights Acquisitions Account Manager, Image: Don Schlotman

Production Service: PreMediaGlobal

Text Designer: PreMediaGlobal

Photo Researcher: PreMediaGlobal

Cover Designer: Riezebos Holzbaur/Christopher Harris

Cover Image: © Luc Latulippe/Corbis

Compositor: PreMediaGlobal

For product information and technology assistance, contact us at **Cengage Learning Customer & Sales Support, 1-800-354-9706**.
For permission to use material from this text or product, submit all requests online at **www.cengage.com/permissions**.
Further permissions questions can be e-mailed to **permissionrequest@cengage.com**.

Library of Congress Control Number: 2010930049

Student Edition:

ISBN-13: 978-0-495-80914-2

ISBN-10: 0-495-80914-4

Wadsworth
20 Davis Drive
Belmont, CA 94002-3098
USA

Cengage Learning is a leading provider of customized learning solutions with office locations around the globe, including Singapore, the United Kingdom, Australia, Mexico, Brazil, and Japan. Locate your local office at **www.cengage.com/global**.

Cengage Learning products are represented in Canada by Nelson Education, Ltd.

To learn more about Wadsworth, visit **www.cengage.com/wadsworth**

Purchase any of our products at your local college store or at our preferred online store **www.cengagebrain.com**.

Printed in the United States of America
2 3 4 5 6 7 13 12

To my wife Susan and my children Jennifer, Paul, and Tim

About the Author

Ray Surette   has a doctorate in criminology from Florida State University and is a Professor of Criminal Justice at the University of Central Florida. His crime and media research interests revolve around the media's effects on perceptions of crime and justice, criminogenic media, and criminal justice policies. He has published numerous articles and books on media, crime, and criminal justice topics and is internationally recognized as a scholar in the area. He has published research on the development of public information officers in criminal justice agencies, crime and justice infotainment programming, copycat crime, the effects of news coverage of celebrity trials on similarly charged non-publicized trials and on police recruits, the effects of news coverage of corrections on municipal jail population trends, media oriented terrorism, and the use of computer-aided camera surveillance systems in law enforcement. He is currently working on a book on copycat crime as well as studying the use of camera surveillance systems by law enforcement in neighborhoods and other public areas and the relationship between media and criminal justice policy support.

Brief Contents

FOREWORD   xiii
PREFACE   xv

1   Predators, Pictures, and Policy   1

2   Social Constructionism   29

3   Crime and Criminality   52

4   Crime Fighters   84

5   The Courts   105

6   Corrections   132

7   Crime Control   155

8   The Media and Criminal Justice Policy   180

9   Media and Crime and Justice in the Twenty-First Century   200

GLOSSARY   219
NOTES   226
REFERENCES   247
INDEX   269

Contents

FOREWORD   xiii
PREFACE   xv

1   Predators, Pictures, and Policy   1
Media and Criminal Justice: A Forced Marriage   1
The Blurring of Fact and Fiction   4
A Brief History of Crime-and-Justice Media   5
   Print Media   6
   Sound Media   10
   Visual Media   11
   New Media   13
Types of Content   15
   Entertainment   15
   Advertising   16
   News   16
   Infotainment   19
Crime and Justice as a Mediated Experience   24
Chapter Summary   27
Writing Assignments   28
Suggested Readings   28

2   Social Constructionism   29
The Social Construction of Crime and Justice   29
The Sources of Social Knowledge   30

Experienced Reality   31

Symbolic Reality   31

Socially Constructed Reality   32

The Social Construction Process and the Media   32

The Concepts of Social Constructionism   34

Claims Makers and Claims   34

Frames   37

Narratives   41

Symbolic Crimes   42

Ownership   43

The Social Construction Process in Action   44

Social Construction of Road Rage   45

Reconstruction of Driving Under the Influence   45

Competing Constructions of the Arrest of Rodney King   46

Social Constructionism and Crime and Justice   48

Chapter Summary   50

Writing Assignments   50

Suggested Readings   51

3   Crime and Criminality   52

Criminals, Crimes, and Criminality   52

Criminals   53

Predatory Criminality   54

Crime Victims   55

Crimes   57

White-Collar Crime   58

Criminological Theories and the Media   61

Criminality in Today's Media   64

Criminogenic Media   66

Violent Media and Aggression   67

Media and Criminal Behavior   69

Copycat Crime   70

Media-Oriented Terrorism   77

Criminogenic Infotainment   79

Chapter Summary   81

Writing Assignments   82

Suggested Readings   82

4   Crime Fighters   84

Law Enforcement: A House Divided   84

Media Constructs of Professional Soldiers in the War on
Crime   86

Lampooned Police   86

G-Men and Police Procedurals   87

Cops   90

Police as Infotainment: "Who you gonna call?"   92

*Dusting for Saliva: The CSI Effect, Forensic Science, and Juror
Expectations   95*

Police and the Media   97

Media Constructs of Citizen Soldiers in the War on Crime   99

Private Investigators   99

Private Citizens   99

Professional Versus Citizen Crime Fighters   101

Chapter Summary   103

Writing Assignments   104

Suggested Readings   104

5   The Courts   105

Media, Infotainment, and The Courts   105

Courts, Attorneys, and Evidence   106

Crime-Fighting Attorneys   107

Female Attorneys   108

Media Trials   109

Media Trial Effects   110

Merging Judicial News with Entertainment   114

Live Television in Courtrooms   117

Pretrial Publicity, Judicial Controls, and Access   119

Pretrial Publicity   119

Judicial Mechanisms to Deal with Pretrial Publicity   121

Media Access to Government Information   125

Reporters' Privilege and Shield Laws   125

The Courts as Twenty-First-Century Entertainment   126

Chapter Summary   130

Writing Assignments   131

Suggested Readings   131

6 Corrections 132

Historical Perspective   132

Sources of Correctional Knowledge   135

    Prison Films   135

    Correctional Television and Infotainment   138

    Corrections in the News   140

Corrections Portraits and Stereotypes   148

    Prisoners   149

    Correctional Institutions   150

    Correctional Officers   150

The Primitive "Lost World" of Corrections   151

Chapter Summary   153

Writing Assignments   153

Suggested Readings   154

7 Crime Control 155

Media and Crime Control   155

    Public Service Announcements Join the War on Crime   156

    Victimization-reduction Ads   159

    Citizen-cooperation Ads   160

Case Processing Using Media Technology   163

    Judicial System Use   163

    Law Enforcement Use   165

Surveillance   166

    History and Issues   167

    Benefits and Concerns of Increased Surveillance   171

    Balancing Police Surveillance and Public Safety   174

1984: An Icon Before its Time   176

Chapter Summary   178

Writing Assignments   178

Suggested Readings   179

8 The Media and Criminal Justice Policy 180

Slaying Make-Believe Monsters   180

Media Crime-and-Justice Tenets   181

    The Backwards Law   182

    Media's Crime-and-Justice Ecology   184

Immanent Justice Rules the Media   *186*

Technology Enhances Crime Fighting   187

Real-World Crime and Justice Problems   *188*

Criminal Justice Policy and Media Research   189

Crime on the Public Agenda   *189*

Beliefs and Attitudes about Crime   *190*

Crime-and-Justice Policies   *191*

The Social Construction of Crime-and-Justice Policy   195

Chapter Summary   198

Writing Assignments   199

Suggested Readings   199

9   Media and Crime and Justice in the Twenty-First Century   200

Crime-and-Justice Media Messages   200

Media Anticrime Efforts   *202*

Two Postulates of Media and Crime and Justice   *204*

Expanded Public Access to Criminal Justice Procedures   *206*

Mediated Reality   *207*

The Future of Crime-and-Justice Reality   209

Spectacles   *209*

Surveillance   *211*

Mediated Criminal Justice   213

What You Have Learned   215

Chapter Summary   217

Writing Assignments   218

Suggested Readings   218

GLOSSARY   219
NOTES   226
REFERENCES   247
INDEX   269

Foreword

Everyone who studies crime and justice shares a sense of frustration about the way media depictions dominate the common viewpoint on crime and criminal justice, often in ways that distort reality. The television show *CSI*, for example, is great entertainment but hardly fits the way 99 percent of crimes are solved. So-called real police stories follow some officers as they go about their duties, but even though the film is real, the portrait of police work that results is distorted by the focus on chase scenes and angry encounters. Judge Judy bears little resemblance to actual judges in demeanor or behavior. The Practice always presents cases with some sort of twist, but such cases are the exception rather than the rule. The nightly news covers crime with an eye to generating high ratings, not great insight. American culture has an affinity for crime as a source of stimulation and even entertainment, but the result is that what we think we know about crime and justice from the way our media portray it often corresponds poorly to the everyday reality of crime and justice.

For those who are professionals in the business of criminal justice—those who wish to reform or improve justice practices and crime prevention effectiveness—the media portrayals are often an impediment. It is not so much that the media get it wrong as that they focus on aspects of crime and justice that are, in the scheme of things, not so important. Of course we all want to apprehend serial killers and stop predatory sex offenders, but they are uncommon in the life of the justice system. The more pressing themes of improving the effectiveness of treatment programs, youth prevention systems, crime control strategies, and so forth can get lost in the way the media focus on images of crime that are much more engrossing to the everyday citizen.

It is, therefore, with extraordinary pleasure that I welcome the fourth edition of Ray Surette's *Media, Crime, and Criminal Justice* to the Wadsworth Contemporary Issues in Crime and Justice Series. Created to provide detailed and effective exposure of important or emerging issues and problems that ordinarily receive insufficient attention in traditional textbooks, the series also provokes thought and changes perceptions by challenging us to become more sophisticated consumers of crime-and-justice knowledge. Its titles seek to expose myths about crime and justice, deepen understandings of the nature of crime and the processes of justice, and inspire new perspectives on these topics.

For those who seek a book that will make you an informed student of crime-and-justice policy and practice, you could not do better than the one you are now holding. Professor Surette is an astute student of popular culture, the social power of symbols, and the effect of media on public imagination. In this book, he provides a detailed examination of the ways that media coverage affects our popular understanding of justice. The results are sometimes subtle and sometimes blatant. For example, the way the nightly news covers crime creates a subtle bias on the part of the public that our cities are dangerous and that the justice system is incapable of protecting innocents. By contrast, the way punishment is covered creates a much less subtle bias that our system of justice is lenient. Both of these biases are partly right, but mostly wrong. And the reality—much more complex than the public perception—is often not widely understood.

Surette writes about every aspect of crime and justice. The book opens with a thorough and authoritative description of the way our "realities" about crime and justice are constructed from social sources of knowledge. It is this fact that makes the media portrayal of crime and justice so important, because media are among the most powerful sources of social information. The book then considers in turn the three main agencies of criminal justice: the police, the courts, and corrections, with a chapter devoted to each topic. The final chapters consider the broader problem of crime prevention and criminal justice policy in the context of a media-dominated social construction of crime.

In the end, this is a book that helps us to rethink crime by offering a critical perspective on how we go about understanding it. Crime is not popular culture, and criminal justice is not entertainment. On the contrary, crime is a crucial social problem rooted in related social problems such as inequality and poverty. Criminal justice is a key function of the state that is less powerful with regard to our safety than we might like but more important to our everyday rights than we would ordinarily think.

This is an important book, a book that carves out new areas for thinking and challenges the popular mind-set about crime and justice. I commend it to you.

Todd R. Clear
Series Editor

Preface

The fourth edition of *Media, Crime, and Criminal Justice* is written for undergraduate criminal justice students. It is my belief that to understand contemporary crime and justice, students have to understand the role the media play in the life cycle of criminal justice issues and policies. Maturing in a culture where crime and justice media content is pervasive, students are naturally attracted to a course that helps them understand the media ocean they swim in. They also bring a priceless enthusiasm and interest in the subject. This revised fourth edition taps into that enthusiasm and employs an expanded number of recent and visual examples to connect the material to the students' lives. While engaging them, this book helps students to become critical media consumers and insightful observers of the ongoing relationship between media, crime, and justice. After finishing the book, students who previously had not considered the linkages between the media, crime, and justice will be unable to sit through a crime show or newscast without a thoughtful reaction and recognition of the underlying processes that generate the crime and justice media they receive and the criminal justice policies they experience.

The knowledge covered in this text is drawn from criminal justice, criminology, sociology, political science, law, public administration, journalism, medicine, psychology, and communication research. Sources include traditional academic and professional journals as well as numerous pop-culture media such as magazines, newspapers, music, video-games, films, and Internet sites. As an undergraduate introductory text, the fourth edition serves as an entrée to the research questions and social concerns without the weight of extensive graduate level coverage of statistics and research designs. The book discusses the vast and disparate research but does not go into methodological, measurement, or statistical issues in great depth. Instead, the discussions provide basic understandings of the theoretical ideas and concepts that frame the research, the major findings that have been generally accepted by researchers in the field, the issues that are still under debate, and the questions that remain unaddressed.

Massively covered criminal trials, advances in media technology, new types of media content—and new ways of delivering the content—are especially important in the construction of crime-and-justice reality and continually increase the impact of media on crime and justice. However, most people interact with the media as passive consumers. They are conditioned to receive the media knowledge without considering where this information comes from, what effect it has on their attitudes and perceptions, or how it affects society. This book encourages readers to ask questions about the media such as why certain images of crime are linked together in newscasts, why similar crimes will be sensationalized in one instance and given scant attention in another, and why some explanations of crime and some criminal justice policies are forwarded in the media over others.

The fourth edition serves as a main text in a media, crime, and justice course and as a supplementary work in courses where the instructor wishes to feature connections between media, crime, and justice. It is a particularly useful supplementary text for "introduction to criminal justice," "introduction to law enforcement," "criminal justice policy," "victimization," and "crime prevention" courses. The text can be used by students with and without substantial backgrounds in communications, journalism, criminal justice, law, and the additional disciplines that make up this inherently interdisciplinary subject.

ORGANIZATION

Organized into nine chapters, the book follows the content and influence of the media from the committing of crime through the sequential components of the criminal justice system as typically covered in undergraduate criminal justice courses. Within this organization, the connection between media and criminal justice policy is a running theme. The book makes that point that pervasive media images of predatory criminals work as steering currents on our criminal justice policy. Each chapter includes discussions of how media renditions affect a particular area of criminal justice policy. Recognition of this policy linkage is vital because the media determine in important ways what behaviors we criminalize, how we approach crime control, how we handle criminal cases, how we sentence convicted offenders, and what correctional conditions and programs we create. In addition, the media's portraits of crime and justice sway the public's beliefs and expectations, as well as the demands placed upon the system. In a very real way the media construct our crime-and-justice reality and derived criminal justice policy.

Below is a summary of each chapter:

- **Chapter 1, Predators, Pictures, and Policy** The first chapter serves as an introduction to the media, crime, and justice relationship and provides historical and conceptual overviews. Differing types of media and of content are introduced and defined, and the argument for the importance of studying the relationship between media crime and justice is made. Discussions of crime and justice as a mediated experience are included.

- **Chapter 2, Social Constructionism** To help students understand how the media relate to crime and justice, the book employs the theoretical perspective of social constructionism and devotes an entire chapter to its ideas and concepts. The demonstration of how social constructionism works in the crime and justice realm is the chapter's goal. The chapter provides crime-and-justice social construction applications within discussions of "road rage," "killer drunks," and the "Rodney King arrest" and other more recent examples.

- **Chapter 3, Crime and Criminality** This chapter covers the "criminological theory" that one finds in media content. It discusses how crime, criminals, and explanations of criminality are portrayed in the media and how these media portraits can be criminogenic and related to real-world criminal behavior. Copycat crime and media-orientated terrorism are discussed in detail.

- **Chapter 4, Crime Fighters** This chapter focuses on the media portrait of crime fighting. Describing the professional sworn law enforcement officers and the civilian crime fighters found in the media, the chapter contrasts the images of crime fighters in their media constructed worlds to the real world of law enforcement. Material on the unique nature of the portrait of policing found in the infotainment media and a "CSI" effect is also included.

- **Chapter 5, The Courts** This chapter covers the judicial system as portrayed in the media, focusing on the media co-optation of the courts as infotainment vehicles within massively covered "media trials." In addition to discussions of long-standing issues like pre-trial publicity, courtroom control of news media, and reporter access to proceedings and offenders, discussions on new media and the public image of courtrooms and male and female attorneys are included.

- **Chapter 6, Corrections** Chapter 6 covers the media portrait of correctional institutions, correctional officers, and prisoners. A discussion that reviews the limited sources of knowledge the public has regarding corrections and the implications of this limitation on the social construction of corrections and correctional policy is included. The stereotypes of prisoners, correctional officers, and correctional institutions found in the media are discussed. In addition, material on the interactions between terrorism, corrections, and the media is included.

- **Chapter 7, Crime Control** In this chapter, how criminal justice practitioners increasingly use media venues and media technology to reduce crime, gather information, patrol communities, deter offenders, and process cases is discussed. The recent explosive expansion of camera-based public surveillance systems (CCTV surveillance) is discussed in depth. Sections on Madison Avenue–style anticrime advertisements and the judicial use of cameras and videotapes in court proceedings are also included.

- **Chapter 8, The Media and Criminal Justice Policy** Chapter 8 provides both an overview of the media content of crime and justice and details the explicit connections the content has to criminal justice policy. The chapter explores the two main tenets of crime-and-justice media that have direct implications for criminal justice policy: the backwards law and the operation of immanent justice in crime-and-justice media content. Discussions of the research on media effects on the public's beliefs and attitudes about crime and justice, the rank of crime and justice on the public agenda, and direct and indirect media effects on criminal justice policy are included.

- **Chapter 9, Media, Crime, and Justice in the Twenty-first Century**, The final chapter distills the main points of the book and offers projections about the future of the media, crime, and justice relationship as the impact of new communication media makes itself fully felt. Designed and offered not as serious prophecies but as platforms to launch discussion, forecasts are developed of what readers might find over the next decades using two opposing worst-case scenarios. In scenario 1, "Spectacles," totally free-wheeling interactive, instant infotainment driven media dominates in a society having little social control on the media. In scenario 2, "Surveillance," strict social control on the media exists with rigid restrictions on crime-and-justice content along with extensive media-based anticrime and public surveillance efforts. The lessons of each scenario and the new media age of "criminal justice pixel policy" are discussed.

NEW FOR THE FOURTH EDITION

The primary difference between the third and fourth editions of *Media, Crime, and Criminal Justice* is that in the fourth edition recent examples are plentiful and material covering contemporary media and crime issues, particularly new communication media, are emphasized. Entire sections of chapters are devoted to new topics including the CSI effect; the production of crime news; the dynamics of copycat crime; the effect of video games; celebrity crime news; terrorism and the media; the impact of new personal and mobile media, public space surveillance, and memorial criminal justice policies; and mediated criminal justice. Every chapter has had its text thoroughly edited, revised, and updated and has new and updated photos.

- New material in Chapter 1 include new boxes on Amber Alerts and the death of Michael Jackson; updated video game, reality TV, and comic book images; new discussions of the creation of crime news and new media; and revised updated tables, figures, and boxes on the history of media, crime, and justice and the contemporary crime-and-justice-mediated experience.

- New to Chapter 2 are boxes on Tiger Woods' car accident and adultery, politician crime claims, and the 9/11 terrorist attacks as symbolic crimes. Revised and new passages on the concepts of social constructionism are included. DUI, road rage, and Rodney King as examples of social constructionism theory applied to crime and justice have been revised.

- Chapter 3 has new discussions of crime victims and white-collar crime added and new material on Martha Stewart, the D.C. snipers case, and Grand

Theft Auto and copycat crime. The discussions of criminogenic media and copycat crime have been substantially expanded with additional examples and figures included.

- New to Chapter 4 are a revised box and a separate expanded in-text discussion on the CSI effect. In addition, revised material on the differences between media-portrayed police and real-world police officers and a new box on crime fighting and terrorism in contemporary media appear.

- Additions to Chapter 5 includes new material on media trials. One is a revised box on the seminal media trial of O. J. Simpson. Boxes on the Italian murder trial of U.S. college student Amada Knox and on the CourtTV (aka TruTV) network are available as well. New and updated images for all boxes are added. A revised updated table of media trial examples now includes the Bernie Madoff Ponzi scam, Kobe Bryant sexual assault, Khalid Shaikh Mohammed terrorist, and the Scott Peterson and Dennis Rader murder trials.

- Chapter 6 has new boxes on the growth of incarceration rates in the United States and media developments; Paris Hilton's jail term; terrorism, corrections, and the media; and new media and corrections. Revised and new passages on infotainment and corrections; prison films and correctional news; and the media portraits of female inmates, correctional institutions and officers are included.

- New material in Chapter 7 includes a new box on anticrime Internet Web sites and a new box on profiling and camera surveillance. A revised box on daily life in a surveillance society is also found. A new passage on the judicial use of media technology is included as well as an expanded and revised discussion of surveillance.

- New to Chapter 8 are boxes on Megan's Law and memorial criminal justice policy and the news value of celebrity crimes. Revised boxes discuss "Three Strikes and You're Out" and a new figure details the media role in the social construction of criminal justice policy. An extensively revised, substantially expanded discussion of the tenets of crime and justice found in the media and their connection to criminal justice policies is included.

- Chapter 9 has a discussion of new media—the new communication and interactive media devices that are changing when and how individuals gather media content. Associated new boxes on twitter activity by jurors affecting trials, virtual reality–linked crimes, and YouTube and justice are included.

LEARNING TOOLS

Each chapter is supplemented with a number of learning tools. Chapters begin with a listing of chapter objectives that target the themes running through each chapter. Each chapter ends with a set of learning tools:

- A bulleted chapter summary which restates and re-emphasizes the main points of each chapter.

- A set of writing assignments related to each chapter's content for students to extend the lessons of each chapter to outside of the classroom.

- A list of suggested additional readings that explore the main themes of the chapter in additional depth and can be used as entrées into the literature for term paper assignments.

Additional imbedded chapter learning features are:

- Boxes containing supplemental media-based examples to demonstrate concepts and points from each chapter and to highlight connections between what students are reading in the text and what they are seeing, hearing, and reading in their daily lives.

- Photos to link chapter concepts and themes to visual imagery.

- Bold faced in-text key terms which link to an end-of-book glossary.

Lastly, the fourth edition includes:

- An updated bibliography and end-of-book footnotes.

- A separate Instructor's Manual with chapter overviews, question pools with objective, short-answer and essay items, and lists of Internet sites and popular music for each chapter is available.

ANCILLARIES

Instructor's Resource Manual with Test Bank. The manual includes learning objectives, key terms, a detailed chapter outline, media activities, and a test bank. Each chapter's test bank contains questions in multiple-choice and true-false formats, with a full answer key. The test bank is coded to the learning objectives that appear in the main text, and includes the page numbers in the main text where the answers can be found.

ACKNOWLEDGMENTS

I would first like to thank the individuals at Wadsworth who contributed to the development and production of this book. Carolyn Henderson-Meier provided encouragement and support and was especially helpful in the transition from the third to the fourth edition. I would also like to thank our Content Project Manager, Remya Divakaran for her help and patience. Megan Lessard diligently acquired the photographs assisted in obtaining permissions. PreMediaGlobal created the artwork and graphics. I am also grateful to Gail Humiston, University of Central Florida Doctoral candidate in Public Affairs who prepared the Instructor's Manual. I thank all of them for their patience and professionalism.

Also deserving thanks are the reviewers, both those who reviewed and offered suggestions in response to the third edition and those who reviewed drafts of the fourth edition. I extend my sincere appreciation, for the final work is much improved and strengthened due to their suggestions.

Finally, my family deserves special thanks. My wife Susan and my three children Jennifer, Paul, and Tim provide continual love and understanding. Without them, my own socially constructed reality would be uninspired.

Ray Surette
Orlando, Florida

1

Predators, Pictures, and Policy

CHAPTER OBJECTIVES

After reading Chapter 1, you will

- Understand the relationship of media to crime and criminal justice
- Appreciate how criminal justice policy is impacted by the media
- Know the history of crime-and-justice media
- Understand the basic differences between the types of media
- Understand how different media content is related to media crime and justice portraits

MEDIA AND CRIMINAL JUSTICE: A FORCED MARRIAGE

Why should one study crime, justice, and the media? There is one good reason and many secondary ones. Before we explore those reasons, try a quick experiment. Pick up today's newspaper and look at the local television schedule. Note the number of shows that deal with committing, solving, or fighting crime. Next turn to the movie listings and do the same. Check out an Internet news site and count the number of crime-and-justice stories. Do the same with the evening's televised local and national news programs. If you subscribe to any magazines, check their contents for articles that are crime or justice related. If you are reading a novel, is a crime or a criminal an important element of the story? Count how many of your e-mails, mobile communications, or blog postings refer to crime or criminal trials. Write down the names of five people you can think of who received a lot of publicity within the past two years. How many of the five were connected to a crime, investigation, or trial? Finally, note what people talked about at work or school yesterday and today. How often are crimes and justice issues discussed?

I'm willing to bet that much of your television and movies, your written and TV news, your pleasure reading, your Internet content, your electronic communications, and your personal conversations involve crime-and-justice issues. In fiction and fact, crimes, criminals, investigations, and trials course through our media.[1] At the most basic level, crime, justice, and the media have to be studied together because in twenty-first-century America they are inseparable, wedded to each other in a forced marriage. They cohabitate in an unavoidable raucous and riotous relationship.

How did the marriage come about? Crime and justice has always provided a substantial portion of the media's raw material. Criminal trials and heinous crimes, along with their victims, investigators, judges, attorneys, and citizens provide the popular crime-and-justice stories, which are packaged and marketed. The images, ideas, and narratives that dominate the media influence how people think about crime and justice. The behaviors we think should be criminalized; who we feel should be punished; what the punishments should be; and how we think the police, judges, attorneys, correctional officers, criminals, and victims should act are all influenced by the media portraits of crime and justice.[2] Compounding these influences, the technological ability of media to gather, recycle, and disseminate information has never been faster or broader, and mass media has never been more diverse. More crime-and-justice media content is available to more people via more avenues and in more formats today than ever before. A flood of technologies—from **personal digital assistant devices** (**PDAs**), to cable television and satellite networks, to VCRs, to the Internet, to electronic games, to virtual reality devices—create a fast-paced hyperactive media. This new high-speed media world dominated by entertainment values and visual images is a special concern in the area of crime and justice.[3]

However, the fact that a contentious relationship exists between media and criminal justice is not the most important reason to study crime and the media. The most important effect of this marriage is on criminal justice policy. The media have had important effects on criminal justice policy in America for a long time. For example, the book *Uncle Tom's Cabin* had an effect on slave laws in the mid-1800s, the film *I Am a Fugitive from a Chain Gang* affected U.S. correctional practices in the 1930s, and movies and books like the *Silence of the Lambs* influenced policies aimed at a "rampant" serial killer threat in the 1980s. That ability has risen to new heights. Today we live in a criminal justice policy era where media renditions frequently drive crime-and-justice practices at blinding speed.[4] The media and criminal justice policy link is easily seen in **memorial criminal justice policies**, which are named for individuals, usually victims (see Box 1.1). We have Megan's Law and Amber Alerts due to massive publicity of a heinous crime and its innocent victim.[5] Even when not named after an individual, much of our criminal justice policy exists because of the impact of high-profile crimes being co-opted as symbols for specific policy campaigns.[6] The "Three Strikes and You're Out" legislation that followed the co-optation of the kidnapping and murder of twelve-year-old Polly Klaas in California in the late 1990s is a classic example of this media-driven policy process.[7] Today no politician can be "soft" on crime. It was not that long ago that crime was seen as a local problem

Box 1.1   Memorial Criminal Justice Policy—Amber Alerts

Nine-year-old Amber Hagerman was abducted in 1996 while bike riding near her home in Arlington, Texas. Her body was found four days later in a ditch with her throat slashed. The Amber Hagerman Child Protection Act was signed into law by President Clinton three years later creating America's Missing Broadcast Emergency Response (AMBER) Alert system to solicit citizen tips and interrupt in-progress child kidnappings (Miller, Griffin, Clinkinbeard & Thomas 2009). Other memorial crime control–targeted legislation includes "Megan's Law," requiring community notification of sex offenders residing locally; "Jessica's Law," requiring long prison terms and lifetime monitoring for sexual crimes against children; "Carlie's Law" for quicker revocation of federal probationers; and the "Adam Walsh Child Protection and Safety Act," which authorized the creation of a nationwide sex offender database (Griffin & Miller 2008 pp. 161–162).

AP Photo/Ric Francis

and a state-level policy issue. But in today's media environment, the public expects national policies addressing local street crime, neighborhood school violence, municipal police needs, and lower-court criminal proceedings.

That local criminal justice issues are seen as needing national policy responses is due to the national character of the media–criminal justice marriage. Contemporary media cover local crime through a national lens where a neighborhood crime is portrayed as an example of society-wide failures. In addition to raising selected local crimes to national prominence, local crime is portrayed in the media as being beyond the ability and resources of local criminal justice. The solutions to crime painted as sensible are given a punitive federal orientation. "What must the nation do about crime?" is the question of the day rather than "What does my community need to do about crime and other connected social problems?" Hence, the most important reason for examining the often unhappy media–criminal justice marriage is that it ultimately determines how we react to crime and how we spend our tax dollars. As a result current criminal justice policy is another commodity governed by what is newsworthy and salable via the media—what fits the needs of the media and voters.[8]

Although most important in terms of actual social impact, the media–criminal justice policy connection is not seen by the public as the most significant media effect on crime and justice. The public worries most about a set concerns more visible in the media. These concerns—media-orientated terrorist events, copycat crime, coverage of media trials, and media-linked social violence—provide secondary reasons for studying the media, crime, and justice. The criminal justice policies we support and pursue due to the media ultimately affect these worrisome but secondary issues as well. These are all significant issues, which will be discussed in depth, but the media's most significant impact is on how we spend our taxes, what and who we criminalize, and how we deal with offenders.

THE BLURRING OF FACT AND FICTION

What is the state of the media–criminal justice marriage today? First, everyone appears to be wedded to the media in some fashion. Whether measured in terms of Internet hours, television programs viewed, movie attendance, music downloads, or the popularity of video games, the exposure to media is enormous. Today, virtually everyone is an audience member of some form of media. In a basic way, media provide the broadly shared, common knowledge in our society independent of occupation, education, and social status. The knowledge acquired via mass media is generally perceived as less important and more transient, but also as more entertaining and enjoyable. When compared to religious information or institutional histories, which can extend for centuries, media-generated knowledge has a shorter life span, usually not exceeding a generation. Indeed, generations are often defined and—particularly true for popular music—can be distinguished by the media that is current during their youth.

With technological progress and broadening media reach, concerns began to grow. In addition to worries about direct criminogenic media effects on copycat crime and media-oriented terrorism, concern that the extracts of reality the media create were unduly influencing the public's view of reality grew.[9] The reason for increased concern is that media snapshots of reality present a specific, narrow slice of the world that has been chosen, reshaped, and marketed to the public.[10] Although the bulk of media content is recognized by the public as unrealistic and heavily edited, continued exposure to media content ultimately influences one's view of reality, and this influence increases in areas where alternate sources of information are less available. Such is the case for crime and justice and, like candy to cavities, a diet heavy on media will corrode your perception of reality. Within this media-generated perception of crime-and-justice reality, a core set of images, headed by the image of a predatory violent stranger, is exploited by both the media and criminal justice policy makers.[11]

The contemporary media serve as an accelerating and expanding knowledge circulatory system; quickly moving ideas, images, and information. An important development is the looping of media content. **Looping** results when events and information are repeatedly cycled and recycled through the media into the culture to reemerge in new contexts.[12] For example, a police car chase video cycles from courtroom evidence to local news footage, to infotainment program content, to a clip inserted in a comedy movie, to sundry Internet Web sites. This continuous looping and reformatting of content results in the blurring of fact and fiction. People come to believe fictional events are real, that real events didn't happen, and hybrid—part real, part fiction—events flourish. Such effects are common in the crime-and-justice arena.[13] Many believe, for example, that Hannibal Lector is a real serial killer and Jack the Ripper is fictional, and real events such as the Kennedy assassination become hopelessly confounded in a blur of factual and fictional portrayals. In an odd way, people no longer trust the news (which is supposed to be true) but seem to be more willing to believe entertainment and infotainment media (which don't try to be truthful). Thus many do not believe the news reports regarding the conclusions of the Warren Commission Report on the Kennedy assassination but do believe a commercial movie, *JFK*, about it.[14]

In the end, the direction of influence between crime and justice on one side and media on the other is a two-way street—the mass media influence crime and justice, and crime-and-justice events become grist for the media.[15] In addition to the myriad entertainment products that deal in crime and justice, the media and media technology are simultaneously perceived as both a major cause of crime and violence and a powerful potential solution to crime. While blaming the media for many social ills, we also look to the media to help reduce violence and drug use, deter crime, and bolster the image of the criminal justice system. In law enforcement we look to the media to aid in criminal investigations, manhunts, and street and vehicle patrols. In the courts, we look for assistance in processing criminal cases, reducing case backlogs, conducting trials, presenting testimony and evidence, and deciding guilt. In corrections, we look to media images for our perception of correctional institutions, programs and personnel, and to enhance security and surveillance. The media–criminal justice marriage is truly a love-hate relationship, and as far as criminal justice policy is concerned, it is the most important relationship that exists. To understand both the historical development and the future of crime and justice in America, one must take into account the influences of the media and understand how crime-and-justice events become popular media products. Gaining that understanding is the basic goal of this book.

A BRIEF HISTORY OF CRIME-AND-JUSTICE MEDIA

A necessary step in exploring the relationship between the media and crime and justice is to first look at the basic structure of the media in America. The media can be thought of as roughly structured along two dimensions: types of media and types of content. Four types of media are found in the United States: print, sound, visual, and new media. As shown in Table 1.1, each media type has enjoyed dominance during a historic period. Of course, all types are still found today, and new media often combine print, sound, and visuals in new ways. Table 1.1 also reflects the historic trend in the evolution of media to include more information, which is more easily accessed, and which today makes the mediated experience similar to actual experience.[16] Each media type's relationship to crime and justice can be understood through a brief history.

Print Media

Print was the first medium to generate a mass market, usually dated as beginning in the 1830s with the emergence of the U.S. penny press daily newspapers. One of the first such newspapers, the *New York Sun*, began to include a daily police-court news column in 1833 and experienced a notable circulation boost.[17] Other penny dailies followed suit, and human-interest crime stories quickly became a staple of these inexpensive, popular newspapers. These early papers portrayed crime as the result of class inequities and often discussed justice as a process manipulated by the rich and prominent. They frequently contained due process arguments and advocated due process reforms while presenting individual crimes as examples of larger social and political failings.[18] Helped by the success of the penny press, a market for weekly crime magazines followed. By the twentieth century, magazines focusing on crime, sex scandals, corruption, sports, glamour, and show business all flourished.[19] Providing an early model for contemporary news and modern television programs, mass marketing, and consumption of crime infotainment was born.

Detective and Crime Thrillers.   The two most popular print-based crime genres to emerge in nineteenth-century print media were detective and crime thriller magazines and "dime" novels. Significant social concerns with the popular media also originated with these products. Both were escapist literature, and by the latter half of the nineteenth century, they described crime as originating in individual personality or moral weakness rather than being due to broader social forces. By downplaying wider social and structural explanations of crime found in the earlier penny press newspapers, these novels helped reinforce the existing social order—the status quo. In addition, the "heroic" detectives in these works closely resembled the criminals they apprehended—calculating and often odd loners.[20] The portraits of crime and justice produced during this time are surprisingly similar to those found today; both present images that reinforce the status quo; promote the impression that competent, often heroic individuals are pursuing and capturing criminals, and encourage the belief that criminals can be readily recognized and crime ultimately curtailed through aggressive law enforcement efforts.

Comic Books.   Marketed to both children and adults, one of the more socially influential print media to develop in the twentieth century was the comic book. From their beginning, comic books featured crime-fighting policemen, private detectives, and costumed superheroes. Combining pop art with printed texts,

T A B L E 1.1   Crime-and-Justice Media History

Sound Media Dominate

Antiquity	Theater, folktales, and myths	Limited access and distribution to local audiences so that content effects are not extensive and media experience is clearly different from real life. Urban legends are a contemporary example.
1200–1500s	Ballads	Popular songs forward the criminal as celebrity and aid in the development of a pop culture focus on criminality. Hip-hop music provides contemporary examples.

Print Media Dominate

1400–1700s	Pamphlets and broadsheets	The historical roots of today's crime and justice infotainment programming. Crime news reach is wider though still limited to comparatively small audiences. Gallows sermons were a popular criminal justice example.
1830s	Penny press	Crime news begins to reach large markets and become a central feature of news. First mass-marketed media.
1880s	Dime novels	Detective and crime novels marketed to divergent audiences. The profit in entertainment crime media is recognized and exploited for the first time.
1890s	Yellow journalism	News media makes significant shift to become mass infotainment media. Dramatization of crimes and criminals in infotainment formats encouraged.

Visual Media Dominate

1910s	Commercial film introduced	Beginning of media audience homogenization via shared content that is consumed regardless of gender, language, race, religion, or social status. The beginning of everyone having access to similar information about the world.
1920s	Commercial radio networks	Modern programming and economic structure of for-profit media established as an unchallenged assumption. First in-home electronic delivery of media content, which eases access for children and allows media for the first time to circumvent traditional socialization efforts of parents, schools, and religion. Children can now learn about the world directly from the media without having to leave their living room or learn to read.
1930s	Film dominates	U.S. commercial film industry is the dominant media and its crime and justice content comes under criticism. Social concerns arise about the glorification of crime and criminals and copycat effects of movies. First serious research of media effects and censorship efforts by government.

(continued)

TABLE 1.1   Crime-and-Justice Media History (Continued)

1930–1940s	Comic books peak	Comic books fill a reality-defining niche for crime and justice and are read by both adults and children. Violent and graphic content generates public crusades against comics as corruptors of youth and demonstrates the structure of the argument that subsequent attacks on other media such as pop music and video games will take.
1950s	Television	In-home, electronic live visual media quickly dominate and forces other media forms to change. Everyone can now easily see and access the same information about the world. Crime programming becomes a major portion of total content.
1970s	Cable television	Content choices expand enormously. Movement from broadcasting to large audiences assumed to be homogenous to narrowcasting to small heterogeneous audience segments with focused content interests such as sports, cooking, or crime. More graphic content becomes easily available for home consumption.
New Media Arrive		
1980s	Videocassette recorders	Decision of where to consume content begins to move from producers to consumers with unedited home access to films.
	Electronic games	First interactive media where consumer has a role in content development. Consumers begin process of becoming collaborative content authors such as deciding which crime and justice role to assume—criminal or crime fighter—and determining final story outcome.
1990s	Computer games and Internet	Electronic access to information goes global and the development of a digital reality begins to take form.
2000 to present	Virtual reality devices	Media and computer-augmented experiences begin to supplant real world experiences for consumers. Much of the world is experienced solely through media devices and content. Fast-paced media-driven crime-and-justice policy era emerges.

comic books have constructed some of the more sophisticated images and analyses of crime and justice found in the media.[21] Evolving out of the newspaper-based comic strips of the 1890s and combined with the twentieth-century pulp magazine market, comic books first appeared in the 1930s. In addition to fictional comic stories, reality-crime comics appeared in 1942, featuring stories about actual criminals and their crimes. These criminal point-of-view comics became the most popular comic book genre between 1947 and 1954.[22] Similar to contemporary popular music and video games, comic books regularly underwent

© EC Comics, 1954

As this 1954 comic book cover illustrates, a morbid interest in heinous crimes
and their exploitation can be found in many time periods and many types of media.

periods of public concern and attack, the strongest coming in the late 1940s and
early 1950s. The outcry and criticisms resulted in a self-adopted industry code that
banned torture, sadism, and detailed descriptions of crimes. Comic books enjoyed
great popularity, particularly with young males into the 1980s because they filled a
media void. Comics could present criminals, heroes, and crime-fighting action

beyond the technical and censored limits of radio, film and television. Today comic books have declined in popularity as electronic video games have gained in popularity. But comic books persist as part of the **multimedia web**, and their crime-and-justice portrayals still prosper via licensing deals that span films, video games, toys, food, cartoons, and television shows.

The primary difference between contemporary print media in its varied forms and contemporary electronic media is not found in their constructed images of crime and justice but in audience access and social penetration of their content. From the late-nineteenth-century media dominated by print to the contemporary media dominated by electronically delivered visual images, the constructed messages of crime and justice have remained relatively constant. To access print media, the consumer needs to be literate, gain access to the materials, and make a clear decision to use or not use them. Exposure to their content has therefore always been less "mass" and more selective. Exposure to the modern, electronically dominated mass media images and messages, on the other hand, is difficult to avoid. The first medium to have an omnipresent capability was audio, and it was distributed via radio broadcast networks.

Sound Media

First delivered and mass-marketed via radio networks, pure audio media have evolved from vinyl records to 8-track tapes, to compact discs, to MPI files, and other digital forms. Sound media are obviously neither print nor visual, but they bridge the two by delivering information in a linear fashion akin to print while evoking mental images and emotions analogous to visuals. In the 1920s, radio networks dominated as the home entertainment and information medium.[23] Despite coexisting with film, radio portrayals of criminality were different. The primary difference being, of course, that violence could only be heard, not seen. Their impact should not be underestimated however. As Orson Wells discovered after his 1938 *War of the Worlds* radio broadcast caused social panic, for some, "hearing is believing."

Radio.   Together with films, radio imagery established the business framework that television would subsequently exploit. Exemplified by coverage of the *Hindenburg* explosion and disaster, the Lindbergh baby kidnapping trial, and the Scopes "monkey" evolution trial, radio established itself as the first live, on-the-scene news reporting medium. The television news format of 30- to 60-second news spots presented within established categories (the world, the nation, sports, weather, economics, crime, and so forth) originated with radio programming. Within these news categories, the industry use of "news themes" was created in which coverage of a particular type of crime would prevail. The news would give a type of crime saturation coverage for a short time and then turn to something new. Together with the producers of the film industry's newsreels, which brought weekly visual coverage of news to the public, radio producers created the style that television would embellish: short-term, visceral, emotional news coverage of discrete "crime events."

On the entertainment side, radio drama, particularly at its height during the 1930s and 1940s, included a substantial and popular—though never a dominant—proportion of crime-fighting, detective, and suspense programming.[24] During this time, a number of classic programs such as *The Shadow, Sherlock Holmes,* and *True Detective* could be heard. Other "Radio Noir" programs, as they came to be termed, gave the culture a host of private detectives including Nick Carter and Philip Marlowe, wise-cracking tough guys who disdained the police. Radio crime programming also included hardened federal agents and reality programming. One popular early show, *Gang Busters,* which began in 1935, is the forerunner of current crime stoppers and *Most Wanted*–style programming. The best known of the early radio crime shows was *Dragnet,* which made a successful transition to television in the 1950s and established the format for the 1950s television docudramas based on police procedures and investigations.

The suspense programming found in radio also foretold the more graphic visual effects found in today's media. Unrestrained by concerns about offensive pictures, radio was able to conger up mental images via sound effects that could not be shown in films of the time. These gristly sound effects preceded today's graphic visual special effects—sizzling bacon for an electric chair execution, life-savers crushed between teeth for bones being snapped, chopped cabbages for heads being severed, and wet noodles squished with a bathroom plunger for the eating of human flesh. Collectively, radio crime-and-justice programming provided the models for modern day crime-and-justice reality programming, the contemporary stereotypes of criminals and criminal justice, the heavy emphasis on law enforcement activities over other segments of the criminal justice system, and the exploitation of sensational heinous crimes. All aspects of contemporary crime-and-justice media that are berated today are traceable to early radio. Not surprisingly, television programmers borrowed heavily from this tested and popular set of narratives in developing their crime programming in the 1950s.

Visual Media

Film.   It was films at the beginning of the twentieth century that first provided the media with the ability to blanket all of society. The movie industry nationalized media content by making its content available to every social, economic, and intellectual stratum. Initially silent and inexpensive, the movies did not even require a common language, as radio programming did. The images were universally available and widely consumed, and film rapidly came to reflect and shape American culture. By 1917, the U.S. motion picture industry was established as the premier commercial entertainment form in the world. By the 1930s, two of every three Americans attended a movie weekly.[25] With their immense popularity, the movies were the first modern mass media, and their emergence heralded the creation of a twentieth-century mass culture that crossed geographic, economic, and ethnic lines. As both a social event and a source of social information, movies were the first medium able to bypass the traditional socializing agents of church, school, family, and community and directly reach individuals with information and images.

Though not every movie, television show, or radio program produced during a particular time frame portrayed the same crime-and-justice theme, dominant themes have been identified with certain periods.[26] Beginning with films and carried on in radio dramas, the first media criminals were descendants of Western outlaws, but unlike the "bandit heroes" and other gang members of Western dime novels, early film criminals were usually portrayed as urban citizens. Most of these early twentieth-century portraits depicted ruthless crooks engaged in corrupt business practices in the pursuit of wealth, a motif that has remained popular to this day. Also common in film plots between 1910 and 1920 were nostalgic portrayals of a simple youthful criminality, reflecting street gang experiences among working-class immigrants. Such films reflected the social impact of large immigrations into the United States during the early part of the twentieth century. From the 1920s to the 1950s, the media criminal slowly evolved from an early-twentieth-century immigrant into a sullen returning World War I veteran, again transformed in the 1930s into a high-rolling bootlegger and Depression-era gunman, and finally into a modern corporate or syndicate executive-gangster. In the 1940s, depictions of violence, terrorism, and murder also became more graphic as gangsters, policemen, and detectives (many now with weapon fetishes) became more violent and less distinguishable from one another.[27] Following World War II, the new visual medium of television came on the scene and combined characteristics of both film and radio to quickly become the dominant media.

Television.   Introduced between 1948 and 1951, television soon replaced radio as the prime home entertainment medium, forcing the movie industry to restructure and driving radio dramas into history.[28] Television was not just radio and newspapers with pictures, it was an entirely new medium that fundamentally influenced the shape and content of all media and in doing so helped create a new and different society.[29] Television's growth and public acceptance was phenomenal, and the existing business models for commercial radio facilitated television's emergence. Because the nature and needs of the market dominated programming decisions from the beginning, television programming has always aimed at attracting and holding large audiences. Borrowing its basic themes and programming ideas from film, radio, and stage, and reformatting them in broadly palatable, noncontroversial products, television quickly came to be described as a vast wasteland of recycled, mediocre programs. Despite the critics, Americans embraced television. In 1977, the number of television sets to Americans reached a 1-to-1 ratio and has never declined.[30] Although computer, videogame, and DVD screens now compete for viewer attention, television viewing remains an important activity for most Americans.[31]

In creating content, television executives found a gold mine in crime programming. Although television was modeled after radio, crime was never a dominant part of radio programming, but crime and justice was a substantial portion of programming and the amount devoted was a social concern from television's inception.[32] Crime shows became a staple of prime time television entertainment in the late 1950s. Prompted by the success of adult Westerns and later by a program called The Untouchables, crime shows accounted for around one-third of all prime time shows from 1959 to 1961.[33] This trend leveled off during the 1960s but began to increase again during the early 1970s until it reached a peak in 1975, when almost 40 percent of the three then dominant networks' prime time schedules contained shows focusing on crime and law enforcement.[34]

While the major television networks periodically de-emphasize crime programming, the total amount of crime-and-justice programming available via television is greater than ever with crime themes found across all types of programming. Special programming such as movies shown on television, miniseries, program promotions, syndicated programs, and local, satellite, and cable network programming all contain significant proportions of crime-related content.[35] Collectively, these varied sources of new and recycled programming make crime and violence a significant element of television content.

New Media

In addition to the traditional print, sound, and visual media, we have today new digital interactive media exemplified by the Internet, electronic games, and PDAs. New media allow for faster and broader communications and encourage the merging and looping of content between media.[36] The globalization of information has resulted, and the social reconstruction of crime news and crimes have followed suit.[37] Significant differences between new media and traditional media make the new media less focused on large, passive, heterogeneous audiences. First, they target small homogenous audiences that have a special interest in a narrow type of content. This characteristic was first developed in the traditional media of radio where you find jazz, classical, and classic rock stations and in specialized magazines like *True Detective*. Described as **narrowcasting** as opposed to broadcasting, the key is that new media do not try to attract everyone but instead target a small but loyal audience that shares a content interest. The effect of this approach is readily apparent on the Internet where one can find a large number of highly focused, narrow content dedicated Web sites. A subject search of the best-known serial killers, for example, will produce a number of such dedicated sites.

The second characteristic is the **on-demand** nature of the new media, which means that the delivery of content is controlled and determined to a much greater degree by the consumer. First available for music via phonographs and records, the invention of the VCR was the major technological breakthrough that allowed consumers of visual media content to determine the time and place of consumption. Today a number of commercial products allow selective use of television shows, movies, music, and games. People with a special interest in shows about criminal forensics can have those programs automatically recorded for subsequent viewing at their discretion. Except perhaps for live events that one wants to experience in real time, little media content must be consumed at a particular time and in a particular place today.

The third characteristic that is most unique to the new media is that of **interactivity**.[38] The new media allow the consumer to be an active participant in the development of the content. Interactivity is most apparent in the realm of video games where the electronic content is immediately determined by the actions of

D. Hurst/Alamy

The newest addition to crime and media concerns is the interactive nature of realistic virtual reality video games. In these games, players participate in violent acts and are rewarded for them within the game.

the players. Whether a victim is killed or spared, a crime solved or not, a criminal caught or escaped is not predetermined by a story author but is post-determined by gamers.[39] In addition, chat rooms, blogs, and Internet sites all allow Web surfers to create and influence the news content they consume.[40]

New media have hypothesized criminogenic effects when they provide avatar–like criminal models to copy and stimulate interpersonal communications about crime.[41] For example, a rap song can generate interpersonal conversations that encourage vandalism or violence within youth gangs or new media communications such as blogs, Twitter, and e-mails can encourage imitation among geographically separated terrorist groups. The Internet is seen as a particularly powerful criminogenic influence due to it having both mass and interpersonal elements. As part way between mass media and interpersonal communication, the Internet provides a unique one-to-many communication avenue.[42] It provides word-of-mouth communication with global reach. Where real world criminogenic instructors are not available, the Internet can substitute with interpersonal communications and deliver detailed how-to crime information.[43]

The social significance of these characteristics is that the new media moves the audience from passive media customers to active media co-producers.[44] Combined with computers to generate virtual realities, new media experiences are the closest to actual experienced reality available. For crime and justice, this means that media consumers can experience committing a murder rather than just observing one, help to catch an offender rather than just watch over the shoulder of a crime fighter, and determine guilt or innocence of the defendant rather than just follow a trial.[45] A candidate copycat offender can search out like-minded role models and interact with them on a personal level while anonymously learning crime techniques. With the technology of new media, crime and justice media has passed from passive audience consumption to active audience participation.

TYPES OF CONTENT

In addition to the different types of media, four basic types of content appear throughout the media. Figure 1.1 portrays the basic media content areas: advertising, news, entertainment, and infotainment. As shown, today advertising content overlays and infiltrates all other content, and infotainment has emerged to create a niche between news and entertainment. Traditionally, news, entertainment, and advertising were sufficient to define the media content landscape, but today infotainment is a significant addition. With content looping, the movement of information and images into and between the four media content areas today can be rapid and multidirectional, and the boundaries between media areas are porous and increasingly blurred. The explosion of infotainment media vehicles means that one can be hard pressed to decide which of the four content categories some recent media products fit into.

Entertainment

Entertainment is escapism. It involves all of the media content that is not forwarded as reflecting any specific reality or real event. Entertainment content is popular because it provides a pleasurable escape from reality. Its narratives engage

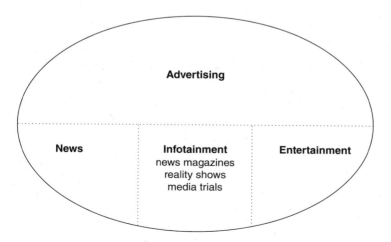

F I G U R E 1.1 Types of Media Content

and transport. Entertainment provides views of realities that cannot be otherwise seen and describes experiences that will not be personally experienced via mediated events that do not happen. In the entertainment world of crime and justice, you will see impossible crimes, fights, and adventures by people with abilities that no humans possess. The entertainment products of the media are best thought of as play, and crime-and-justice stories have been estimated to account for about one-fourth of all entertainment output.[46]

Advertising

Advertising is work. It is the lifeblood of the mass media. Advertising can be conceived as all of the media content purposely geared to persuade monetary decisions. Traditionally distinct from other content, the boundary between advertising and the rest of mass media has dissolved. One now commonly sees product placements in films, news stories produced by corporate public relations offices, and infomercials disguised as talk and news shows. The sole media realm found to be comparatively low on crime and violence, advertising has become a pervasive, multiavenue, continuous media campaign interwoven into and throughout other media content.

News

News has been marketed as true, current, and objective information about significant world events. As such, it plays a strong role in one's perception of reality and deserves an extended discussion. Contemporary news is essentially voyeurism. In crime-and-justice news, you are usually informed about real events and real people, but these events are often rare and distant. They display the lives of people caught up in extreme circumstances, involving bizarre crimes, spectacular trials, and extraordinary situations. News provides filtered, molded snippets of the abnormal criminal events of the world for voyeuristic consumption. Crime-and-justice news today is an escape from the normal via a construction of the unusual. The amount of contemporary news has markedly expanded due to the increased number of media outlets. For its part, crime news has been "social control" news, and is often reported with accompanying information about law enforcement efforts and new social control policies such as curfews or crack downs.[47] A crime news story normally unfolds in three segments.[48] It begins with an announcement that a crime has occurred. The viewer is then visually or verbally transported to the scene of the crime. Finally, the focus shifts to the identity and apprehension of the offender and related efforts of law enforcement officials.

Crime news has always been popular. It has been said that after 1575, "it hardly seems possible that a really first-rate murder, especially if it was complicated by an illicit love affair, or a hanging went unreported."[49] Historically, treason, murder, and witchcraft were the most popular story lines. Early crime coverage was laden with details of criminal acts intertwined with moral exhortations to the readers about the dangers of sin within reports that are surprisingly similar to the infotainment content of much of today's crime news.[50] Through the eighteenth and into the early nineteenth century, crime-related street literature (broadsides, pamphlets, sermons and speeches) were the main vehicles for news of crime and justice and maintained the idea that crime news was for profit and entertainment.[51] In the mid 1830s, crime reporting became a prominent— though not highly regarded—specialty in the previously mentioned penny press.[52] The emergence of specialized reporters marks the beginning of the aggressive marketing of crime news to the public. The evolution since has been for news to be produced more and more as a salable commodity.[53] By the late 1800s, newspapers came to be produced by modern corporations with large advertising revenues, staffs, and circulations. Crime coverage increased further with the introduction of a new type of mass entertainment newspaper collectively known as **yellow journalism**.[54] This new journalism emphasized the details of individual crimes and with this shift, police officers replaced court personnel and witnesses as the primary source of crime information.[55] A shift that persists to this day.

An examination of the process by which news is created is revealing for understanding the content of crime news. Two models for the process of news creation—the market model and the manipulative model—compete.[56] The key for both models is **newsworthiness**—the criteria by which news producers choose which of all known events are selected to be news. In the **market model**, newsworthiness is determined largely by public interest, and journalists simply and objectively report and reproduce the world in the news. Under this model, reporters are regarded as reactive news collection agents who meet the needs of the public interest. In the **manipulative model**, news is selected not according to general public interest but according to the interests of the news agencies' owners. Under this model, the media purposefully distort reality and proactively use the news as a means of shaping public opinion in support of large social institutions and the status quo.[57]

Both models are inadequate because they ignore the organizational realities of news production, which by its nature, makes rendering an objective, unbiased, mirror image of reality impossible.[58] Crime news displays characteristics that can be interpreted as indicative of both the manipulative and market models but that can best be understood within an **organizational model** of news production.[59] Factors related to the organizational needs of news agencies steer the process.[60] Because of the organizational nature of its birth, crime news is inherently subjective, though not necessarily ideologically biased.[61] What the public receives as news is capsulized, stylized, and commodified information.[62]

The bulk of news, then, is less discovered than formed by journalists working under organizational pressures. One organizational pressure on news agencies is that as organizations they need to routinize their work to plan and schedule the use of resources. But news organizations are in the unique organizational position of dealing with a commodity, news, that by definition is supposed to be unique and unpredictable. Their core organizational task, then, is to routinize the processing of nonroutine events. To do so, news media personnel must become active co-creators of the news. They cannot be totally reactive, nor can they be totally proactive. In practice, they are somewhere in between—reactive to truly unexpected events, proactive and part of the creation process for the rest of the news.

The construction of crime news can be understood as the coupling of two information-processing systems—one being news agencies, the other being the government.[63] The reporter *beat system*—under which reporters cover specific subject areas (for example, state politics or downtown crime)—restricts a journalist's sources and perspectives so that, in general, news journalists report on those at or near the top of the social hierarchy and those who threaten them—particularly those at the bottom—to an audience mostly located in the middle.[64] In addition, as profits have fallen, contemporary traditional journalism has become more the processing of news releases and press conferences than a news gathering endeavor.[65] This means that in news of crime and justice we normally hear criminal justice system and government officials talking about individual criminals and street crimes.[66]

Regarding which crimes get selected to be crime news, unexpected or unusual events will be selected, but they will be presented in terms of previously established stories and explanations.[67] The better an event fits the established themes, the more likely it is to be selected. Other, more specific criteria for news selection include the seriousness of the event, whimsical circumstances, sentimental or dramatic elements, and the involvement of high-status persons.[68] In the case of crime news, seriousness is the primary factor. In that crimes occur in the opposite proportion to their seriousness and that the news criterion for seriousness is harm to individuals rather than overall social harm, the media report those crimes that are least common and thus construct a crime reality at odds with the social reality of crime.[69] The result is that to the extent that reporters are encouraged to report the unique crime, it is more difficult for the public to estimate the typical crime.[70]

Within the news production process, there are checkpoints through which crime news is processed and passed along. Those that are processed to the final checkpoint become crime news. First coined in 1950, the term for a person controlling the processing checkpoints is **gatekeeper**.[71] Shown in Figure 1.2, a key gatekeeper in the crime news process is the crime reporter. To provide a steady stream of crime stories, a crime reporter must develop reliable police sources and maintain their trust.[72] Although sometimes critical of law enforcement, successful crime reporters develop a working relationship with the police that benefits both.[73] Over time, the two sides develop similar work experiences and outlooks. second key gatekeeper has evolved on the law enforcement side—the public information officer (PIO). Prior to the development of PIOs, interaction with the media was an ad hoc, idiosyncratic process. As the marketing of crime news has heightened, the competition among sources of crime and justice information for news media attention has sharpened. While law enforcement agencies still hold the central position in the construction and defining of the crime problem, other public agencies and private lobby and pressure groups have joined the competition. In addition, new media and the Internet have allowed private individuals to enter the crime news gatekeeping process.[74] The public information officer emerged as the criminal justice system's response to this competition.

New media and other participants notwithstanding, crime news still comes largely from information supplied by the police. And crime news, because it is prepackaged and popular, helps news organizations in their routinization task[75],

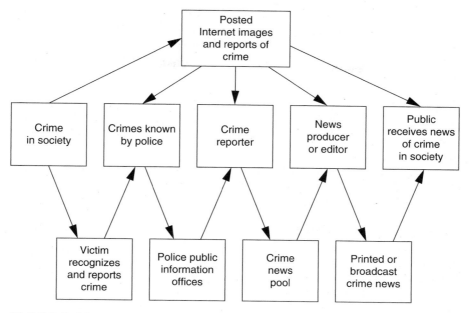

FIGURE 1.2
The Internet Has Altered the Crime News Gatekeeping Process By Allowing News of Crime to Bypass Victims, Police, and Even News Agencies and Flow Directly to the Public.

and can be gathered at little cost[76], makes up a large part of the total news. The gatekeeping process filters out the vast majority of crime from becoming crime news and makes any correspondence between crime news and actual crime unlikely. News, entertainment, and advertising are still what most people think of when they consider the broad categories of mass media content, but a fourth content type, infotainment, which crosses all of the traditional media boundary lines, has emerged as a significant area for contemporary crime and justice.

Infotainment

The most important change in contemporary crime-and-justice media is the explosion of infotainment products. **Infotainment** can be defined as the marketing of edited, highly formatted information about the world in entertainment media vehicles. The feel with infotainment media is that you are learning the real facts about the world; the reality is that you're getting a highly stylized rendition of a narrow, edited slice of the world. In that infotainment combines aspects of news, entertainment, and advertising under a single umbrella, its emergence makes it less sensible to discuss the three traditional media components separately. News, entertainment, and advertising are no longer unique media spheres due to infotainment's influences.[77]

Crime perfectly fits infotainment demands for content about real events that can be delivered in an entertaining fashion, and infotainment content based on

crime and justice has existed for centuries. Crime pamphlets and gallows sermons
are two early examples, but infotainment has always played a minor role in the
media's crime-and-justice content. Why did infotainment explode in the late
twentieth century? The basic answer to this question is that as the media, led
by television, became more visual, intrusive, and technologically capable, the
viewing audience simultaneously became more voyeuristic and entertainment
conscious.[78] The ability of satellites to instantaneously beam information around
the world has allowed the public to watch riots, wars, and other events as they
happen, heightening the dramatic entertainment value of what previously would
have been reported as after-the-fact news events, or not reported at all. For
example, with the use of news helicopters, it is now common for local television
stations to follow high-speed car chases and broadcast them live. Irrespective of its
social importance, a visual event that might not have been mentioned in the news
a decade or two ago can be a contemporary lead news story as a result of simply
having been videotaped. Along the same lines, the growth of surveillance cameras
provide the footage for a bevy of television programs that rely on showing crimes
as they happened. By providing a large inexpensive pool of visual events to market, such technological improvements have allowed for much of the infotainment
programming that exists today. However, while improved technology increased
the potential amount of infotainment, it does not explain its current popularity.

The quantity of infotainment programming is tied to the second reason that
news and entertainment has blurred. With expanded hours and new networks competing for narrowing audience shares, many more hours of programming were
needed and networks had greater difficulty attracting and holding an audience.[79]
The addition of entertainment elements to news content was embraced as a
solution.[80] Beginning in the late 1980s, modern crime-related infotainment programs
began to appear on television, and the line between crime-and-justice news and
entertainment dissolved.[81] Today a clear demarcation between news and entertainment in the media no longer exists, and consumers are hard pressed to differentiate
crime-and-justice news from crime-and-justice entertainment. This blurring is particularly apparent in traditional news content as even the most serious and violent crimes
are often given an entertaining slant. We still look to news to provide a reliable
record of what's real, but today's stew of journalism, entertainment, and infotainment
makes establishing what is real regarding crime and justice a haphazard process.

These programs have never been hugely popular (*Cops* enjoying the highest
ratings), but they continue to have substantial audiences and are extremely profitable. Led by television, print and radio followed suit, and today all media produce substantial amounts of infotainment content across a broad spectrum of
shows such as celebrity sports, lifestyles, interview, game, and pseudoscience
shows. Some of the more successful are found within the host of crime-
and-justice infotainment vehicles and reality programs were the among the first
pseudo–news programming. As a result, the crime-and-justice media landscape is
populated with varied infotainment products that did not exist a decade ago.
Within this media crime-and-justice infotainment world, the crime control
model dominates.[82] Employing real crimes, reenactments, and documentary-
like formatting, the realism in which these shows cloak themselves encourages

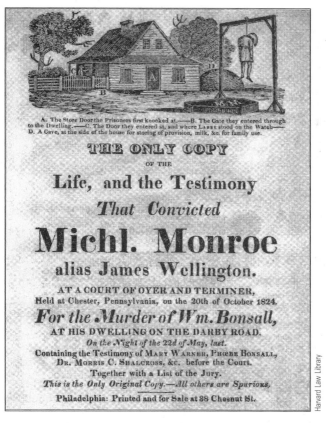

A. The Store Door the Prisoners first knocked at.——B. The Gate they entered through to the Dwelling.——C. The Door they entered at, and where LARE stood on the Watch—— D. A Cave, at the side of the house for storing of provision, milk, &c. for family use.

THE ONLY COPY
OF THE
Life, and the Testimony
That Convicted
Michl. Monroe
alias James Wellington.
AT A COURT OF OYER AND TERMINER,
Held at Chester, Pennsylvania, on the 20th of October 1824.
For the Murder of Wm. Bonsall,
AT HIS DWELLING ON THE DARBY ROAD.
On the Night of the 22d of May, last.
Containing the Testimony of MARY WARNER, PHŒBE BONSALL,
DR. MORRIS C. SHALCROSS, &c. before the Court.
Together with a List of the Jury.
This is the Only Original Copy.—All others are Spurious.

Philadelphia: Printed and for Sale at 38 Chesnut St.

Harvard Law Library

The focus in this nineteenth century crime news pamphlet is on a violent, predatory crime and criminal. The symbolic hanging, and the visual rendition of the crime scene with a promise of one-of-a-kind details are all precursors to elements found in contemporary crime-and-justice media.

their acceptance as accurate pictures of the world.[83] However, contrary to their image of reality, these programs are clearly structured along entertainment lines. They commonly employ the oldest entertainment crime story structure known: "*crime → chase → capture*"[84] in which the commission of a crime is followed by its investigation and the pursuit of offenders, climaxing in their arrest or death. Three types of crime–and–justice infotainment are common: news magazines and Web sites, reality-based crime shows, and media trials. Collectively they dominate the contemporary mass media crime–and–justice infotainment market.

Newsmagazines and Web Sites.   News magazines and Internet news Web sites extend the application of the entertainment values found in lesser degrees in much of the daily news content. Daily newscasts, because of time and format constraints, cannot afford to spend much time on any single story. They therefore cannot fully develop an entertainment context. However, newsmagazines and Internet news sites can devote more content to the most interesting (that is, the most sensational, violent, dramatic, or scandalous) stories. They provide access to large amounts of information, visuals and opportunities to share opinions about crimes. Within these avenues, an event can be fully constructed as an entertainment vehicle with stereotypic story lines, plots, characters, victims, villains, and dramatic endings.[85] At one end within this genre is voyeuristic content. Electronic versions of the supermarket tabloid newspapers, these include trash-TV talk shows emphasizing confrontation and sexual deviance, tabloid news shows emphasizing bizarre, violent crimes, and Web sites advocating bizarre content and theories. At the higher end is informational content exemplified by weekly newsmagazine shows such as *60 Minutes* and Web sites associated with established news agencies.

Other than matters of taste, what makes programs at both ends of the spectrum worrisome is that by presenting expanded, apparently in-depth stories they convey the impression that an issue is being discussed from multiple sides and that a full contextual review of a topic is being provided. However, as in regular news, in newsmagazine programming high-profile, sensationalist crimes and criminals are emphasized, with a focus on individual, random, stranger-on-stranger acts of violence. They continue the broader popular media's painting of crimes and criminals with portraits that are simplistic and individualistic. As within these other media outlets, newsmagazines and Internet crime news sites reflect the process of **commodification**, the packaging and marketing of crime information for popular consumption and commercial profit. The impact that the economic goals of commodification have on media crime and justice content cannot be overemphasized. When a significant source of public knowledge about crime and criminality is steered by what is popular and profitable the public's ability to evaluate criminal justice policies unavoidably suffers.

Reality-Based Crime Shows.   As news drifts more toward entertainment, entertainment programmers looked to traditional news formats to design talk shows and documentaries that would be accepted as credible and realistic by their audiences. In doing so, they have produced some of the more successful television programming thus far in the twenty-first century, and virtually all aspects of life have been presented as a reality program at one time or another. Reality-based crime shows that entertain by sensationalizing real stories about crime and justice are of particular interest. These shows typically employ dramatizations of actual crimes interspersed with police narrative and interviews or actual video footage that features police officers investigating crimes, questioning suspects, and making arrests.[86]

Concerns with these programs arise directly from their claim to be presenting reality—that they are objective purveyors of true stories about crime and justice. Despite their use of the trappings of traditional news and journalism, crime reality shows are thinly disguised entertainment, and the reality that they construct is not pretty. They mix reconstructions, actors, and interviews and employ camera angles, music, lighting, and sets to enhance their dramatic and entertainment elements. Viewers are further encouraged to accept the content as straightforward through the use of self-labeled "correspondents" and "reporters."

B o x 1.2   Michael Jackson Homicide Case

Due to the victim's immense celebrity status, popularity, bizarre aspects of his lifestyle, and prior legal problems, the homicide prosecution of his personal physician, Dr. Conrad Murray, for the death of the "King of Pop" Michael Jackson by acute Propofol intoxication has generated another heavily covered media trial. Media attention began with the discovery of Jackson's body and continued through the coroner's autopsy and report, a police manslaughter investigation, and the Los Angeles District Attorney's filing of charges. Media spin-offs, such as the *This Is It* film, Michael Jackson's brother's reality show, and numerous interviews and stories by people variously connected to the singer began to appear long before the case proceeded to trial.

Gene Blevins/LA DailyNews/Corbis

Law and order, social control, and the point of view of law enforcement officials dominate within stereotyped portraits of crimes, criminals, and victims.[87] The crime-and-justice world found in reality-based crime shows appears as a violent, crime-prone underclass held in check by the police.

Media Trials. Society has long been intrigued by the inner workings of the criminal justice system. Prior to cameras being allowed into America's courtrooms in the late 1970s, the most realistic-looking views of judicial proceedings came from courtroom television dramas and classic films like *To Kill a Mockingbird*. Today the drama is often "real," or at least not based on fictional cases (see Box 1.2). Cameras have moved into courtrooms to cover deliberations, to record the emotional responses of participants, and to conduct interviews with participants. Some made-for-TV courtroom shows are more akin to game shows than to judicial proceedings. The media hijacking and dramatization of actual criminal cases has invigorated the **media trial**—the co-optation of a regional or national crime or justice event by the media, which are developed and marketed along entertainment style storylines as a source of drama, entertainment, and profit.[88]

Media trials are distinguished from typical news coverage by the massive and intensive coverage that begins either with the discovery of the crime or the arrest of the accused. In a media trial, the media cover all aspects of a case, often highlighting extralegal aspects. Judges, lawyers, police, witnesses, jurors, and defendants are interviewed, photographed, and frequently raised to celebrity status. Personalities, personal relationships, physical appearances, and idiosyncrasies are commented on regardless of legal relevance. Coverage is live whenever possible, pictures are preferred over text, and text is characterized by conjecture and sensationalism. A media trial is, in effect, a dramatic miniseries developed around a real criminal case. The history of these media trials reveals that they occur with regularity. In the twentieth century more than two dozen trials were declared the "trial of the century" by the press.[89] Proto media trials can even be found in the late nineteenth century, the best known being the 1893 Lizzie Borden ax murder trial. Over the course of the twentieth century, interest in these trials by the media, the public, and the marketplace grew steadily. Following their period of intense public and media scrutiny, the trials pass into popular folklore and relative obscurity. Recognition of names such as Fatty Arbuckle, Sacco and Vanzetti, Bruno Hauptmann, the Rosenbergs, Patty Hearst, and others have faded after onetime mesmerizing public interest and media attention.

In the coverage and marketing of these trials, the trials become palettes for the social construction of the criminal justice system.[90] They provide simplistic explanations of crime within the authoritative and dramatic vehicle of a "real" trial. In practice, crime in these productions is nearly universally attributed to individual characteristics and failings rather than to social conditions. Media trials represent the final step in a long process of merging news and entertainment—a process that now often results in extensive multimedia and commercial exploitation. That the source of media trials is the judicial system eases the merger, for media trials allow the media industry to attract and entertain a large general audience while maintaining its public image as an objective and neutral reporter of news. The end result is that in media trials the merging of information and entertainment is fully achieved.

CRIME AND JUSTICE AS A MEDIATED EXPERIENCE

Each step in the evolution of types of media and their content brings the **mediated experience**—the comparative experience that an individual has when he or she experiences an event via the media—versus actually personally experiencing an event a bit closer to each other.[91] More than ever before, an individual today can experience crime and criminal justice through the media and come away with the sensation of actual experience. Media presentations are evolving toward a media reality that is ever closer to an actual real-world experience and, thus, is more popular and more profitable. Radio provided sound, live coverage, and home delivery. Films provided continuous action and eventually sound and were therefore closer to actual experience than either print or radio. Television provided a combination of image, sound, live coverage, and home delivery—a mediated experience that was both similar to actual experience and easy to access. Recent media technological developments have evolved to create new media delivery vehicles that increase access and choice in media consumption and move the media-created realities closer to experienced reality. The World Wide Web, Ipods, and other new media have immensely increased the choices people have regarding media content. Lastly, introduction of electronic interactive games and computer-generated images have moved the mediated experience via virtual and augmented reality to be physically competitive to a real-world experience while simultaneously shifting the audience from passive observers of events to electronic participants.

This evolution of the media has had a significant impact on the criminal justice system; today mediated crime-and-justice experience and knowledge dominates real-world crime-and-justice experience and knowledge. Despite media impressions to the contrary, most Americans have limited direct experience with crime and the criminal justice system. Receiving a traffic ticket remains the most common form of contact between citizens and law enforcement. Of those victimized by crime, having something stolen is far more common than violent victimization. Violent victimization also tends to be concentrated in lower class social groups. Thus, for most Americans the mediated experience is the main source of their crime-and-justice experience and knowledge. In addition, for most of us, experiencing crime and justice via the media is preferable to experiencing crime-and-justice events directly. Few seek out the experience of being a crime victim, but many enjoy seeing crimes committed in the media. The mediated experience—where one is warm, dry, safe, and able to see and hear from multiple points of view with the capacity to pause and replay the experience—is also preferable to actual experience for many other criminal justice events such as working a street patrol, attending a criminal trial, or serving a prison sentence.

The cumulative result of this ongoing media evolution is that today we live in a multimedia web where content, particularly images, appear ubiquitously throughout the media landscape in a vast unavoidable morass of mediated information, events, personalities, and products.[92] Caught in the mutations, the nature of contemporary crime and justice has changed. In some instances the mediated event blots out the actual event so that what people believe happened based on widespread media renditions supplants what actually happened. The facts of an event such as the videotaped beating of Rodney King become irrelevant in the face of the mediated rendition of the event. This trend toward media portrayal over reality is particularly powerful in crime and justice where pop news, entertainment, and advertising combine with the pervasive infotainment content found in newsmagazines and Internet sites, reality-based shows, and media trials to construct our mediated crime-and-justice reality. And from this mediated reality we create our crime-and-justice policies.

Today, we live in a multimedia culture with media driven crime-and-justice policies. What we believe about crime and justice and what we think ought to be done about crime and justice is based on a view of reality that has been filtered and refiltered through the electronic, visually dominated, multimedia web. Thus a crime will appear on the news, its reenactment in film and television programming, its 911 dispatch tape in a pop song as background; its participants will be interviewed in print and on radio and television talk shows and their experiences discussed and dissected on the Internet and chronicled in books. In such ways mediated crime-and-justice experiences become more socially significant and influential then actual experiences.

In sum, five realities of twenty-first-century media are important for crime and justice

1. Our mass media is an electronic, visually dominated media. Print and audio are secondary in social impact. Content is fluid and moves quickly from medium to medium. Images have more value than other media content, and multimedia renditions of events are the norm. The evolution of the media has been toward the goal of making mediated experience indistinguishable from actual experience. Within this evolution, new media is altering the manner in which crime-and-justice information is collected, disseminated, and interpreted.

2. The current marketing structure of the media is geared toward narrowcasting, or targeting smaller, more homogenous audiences than were previously the focus. However, content is constantly reformatted, reused, and looped to ultimately reach multiple and varied audiences.

3. The media must be understood as a collection of for-profit businesses. Each media business must make money to survive, and the primary purpose of media is not to entertain or inform an audience but to deliver an audience to an advertiser. From a media business perspective, advertising is the most important content. From the consumer and social impact side, the most important content is often infotainment. New media has begun to drastically change the profitability of older media, especially print-based ones.

4. Media businesses exist within a highly competitive environment. Most new media ventures fail, and the life spans of media outlets and products are brief. Content must be marketable and must quickly attract an audience. Crime content remains a high-profit area.

5. The U.S. media resides in a nonpaterrnalistic relationship with the government. The government is not prone to directly involve itself in determining content (though the government does enjoy holding periodic hearings about content). Generally, except for some broad parameters, the media determines both content and marketing. The government role in the mass media is largely as a hands-off regulator, issuing licenses and controlling access to broadcast frequencies. Profitable content that may have negative social effects will remain common.

What these media realities collectively mean is that the U.S. mass media is driven by market considerations. The media environment is best understood as a multimedia knowledge commodity web existing in a freewheeling marketplace. Within this market, content appears and reappears in varied and dispersed contexts, and images have the greatest value. Crime and criminal justice content has become a particularly valuable media commodity. The real world of criminal justice has reacted to this media commodification process, and the two sides have entered a twenty-first-century ballet in which each leads the other, spinning off criminal justice policies. In this dance, two views of the media's impact on justice coexist. In one popular perspective, the media are criticized as criminogenic and as undermining the values of law and order. In the second perspective, popular among academics, the media are criticized as purveyors of fear, moral panics, factual distortions, and supporters of the status quo.[93] Being many things with diverse content, contemporary media in reality does both.

In that the criminal justice system is a process that runs from criminality through law enforcement, courts, and corrections to criminal justice policies, the balance of this book explores this media—criminal justice relationship within a systems perspective. Media constructions of crime, law enforcement, the judicial system, and corrections as currently portrayed in the mass media are presented first, followed by chapters dedicated to media's relationship to crime control and policy formation. Lastly, the expected impact of new media on crime and justice is discussed.

CHAPTER SUMMARY

- Much of our knowledge about crime and justice come from the media, and media and crime and justice are intertwined.

- The knowledge we gain about crime and justice from the media influence our criminal justice policies.

- New media has accelerated the flow of crime-and-justice knowledge and content.

- Crime-and-justice content has been historically popular in all types of media.

- Print media was the first media to generate a mass market. Print also allowed stricter control of access to information.

- Sound media established the business model of today's media and was the first broad-based home media. Radio also popularized crime infotainment programs and live coverage of criminal justice events.

- Visual media was the first media to blanket society and with the introduction of television brought crime images directly into the home.

- New media has changed the nature of the media-consumer relationship via narrowcasting, on-demand access, and interactivity.

- Crime news remains a profitable commodity, which due to the nature of its creation unavoidably provides an inaccurate picture of crime. Gatekeepers filter the crimes of the day and pass along the most unique newsworthy ones.

- Infotainment is the most important recent media development, with newsmagazines and Web sites, reality-based crime shows, and media trials dominating contemporary crime and justice content.

- As with much of the world, crime and justice is a mediated experienced for most Americans.

WRITING ASSIGNMENTS

1. Write an essay of the changes that you have observed since your childhood in the way crime and justice is portrayed in the media. Discuss which changes you see as positive and which ones you feel are negative and the reasons for your view. As part of your essay discuss whether you feel that the media today more often promote crime control or due process goals.

2. Compile and give a short description of a list of events that have been looped in the media. Note how many are originally real versus fictional events and how the original event has been altered and used in new media contexts.

3. Write up a list of criminal justice memorial policies and note the characteristics of the persons and events they memorialize and the policies they established. Discuss what the characteristics of the crimes and victims say about criminality and crime in America and what the resulting policies suggest as a general philosophy of criminal justice.

4. List some common social experiences, such as attending a concert, a football game, or meeting new people, that you prefer experiencing via new interactive media. Discuss why you prefer the mediated experience over the real-world experience and the advantages and disadvantages of mediated experiences over real ones.

5. Keep a media diary for one week, noting how much and what types of media you consume. Note in your diary your individual preferences for different types of media and why you prefer particular types of media (music over films possibly), certain types of content (action over romance maybe), and different types of programming (reality crime shows over situation comedies perhaps).

SUGGESTED READINGS

Bailey, F. and D. Hale. 1998. *Popular Culture, Crime and Justice.* Belmont, CA: Wadsworth.

Carrabine, E. 2008. *Crime, Culture and the Media.* Cambridge, UK: Polity Press.

Greer, C. 2009. *Crime and Media: A Reader.* London, UK: Routledge.

Jewkes, Y. 2004. *Media and Crime.* London, UK: Sage.

Meyrowitz, J. 1985. *No Sense of Place.* Oxford, UK: Oxford University Press.

2

Social Constructionism

CHAPTER OBJECTIVES

After reading Chapter 2, you will

- Have a theoretical foundation for exploring media, crime, and justice
- Understand the primary concepts of social constructionism
- Know how to use social constructionism to follow developments in criminal justice policy

THE SOCIAL CONSTRUCTION OF CRIME
AND JUSTICE

Malcolm Gladwell in his book, *Blink*, describes the shooting of Amadou Diallo by four New York undercover officers, providing an example of a social construction with tragic consequences. Applying stereotypes and cultural narratives, the late night officer-citizen meeting was rapidly socially constructed by the police officers with Mr. Diallo erroneously constructed as a gun-wielding threat. The unarmed Diallo was shot forty-one times.[1] This capability for social constructions to drive social behavior for good or ill has been long recognized. In his 1922 book, *Public Opinion*, Walter Lippmann remarked: "For the most part we do not first see, and then define. We define first and then see.... We pick out what our culture has already defined for us, and we tend to perceive that which we have picked out in the form stereotyped for us by our culture."[2] By pointing out that society sees reality largely as society has constructed and agreed to see it, Lippmann insightfully described the core idea of social constructionism.[3] By detailing the consequences of the process in one case, Gladwell points out its importance. Under social constructionism, people create reality—the world they believe exists—based on their personal experiences and from knowledge

29

gained through social interactions.[4] Sometimes the process is rapid as was the case in the Diallo shooting, other times it reflects a slow lifetime long construction effort. The process is the same for everyone although the end result, your personal idea of reality, can contain highly individualistic elements. Understanding the social construction of reality process and the concepts of social constructionism helps to understand the impact of the media on crime and justice.[5]

The traditional Western viewpoint is that reality and knowledge of the world are independent of human processes and grounded totally in autonomous, freestanding events. Social constructionism sees reality in a different light. **Social constructionism** views knowledge as something that is socially created by people. Beginning from the premise that accepted knowledge about the world need not mirror an objective reality, social constructionism focuses on human relationships and the way relationships affect how people perceive reality. Social constructionism emphasizes the shared meanings that people hold—the ideas, interpretations, and knowledge that groups of people agree to hold in common.[6] In the social constructionist view, shared meanings are invariably the result of active, cooperative social relationships and may or may not be tethered to objectively measured conditions in the world.[7] In social constructionism people tacitly agree to see the world in a specific way.

It follows that in social constructionism, the degree to which a given constructed reality prevails is not directly dependent on its objective empirical validity but is instead strongly influenced by shifting cultural trends and social forces. The world may be in one state, but people can believe it is in another state and act accordingly. In fact, social conditions may be seen as major social problems at one time and then subside, without the physical situations they concern having undergone any real change. Regarding crime, for example, not only can social behaviors be criminalized or decriminalized independent of changes in victimization or offense rates; in social constructionism such mismatches are expected.

THE SOURCES OF SOCIAL KNOWLEDGE

Social constructionists seek to understand the process through which agreement is constructed and the forces and conditions that influence when an accepted construction changes—that is, when a society's agreement about its reality alters. Within the social construction perspective, perceptions of social conditions change as social knowledge about those conditions change. People acquire social knowledge from four sources: personal experiences, significant others (peers, family, and friends—also called conversational reality), other social groups and institutions (schools, unions, churches, government agencies), and the media. In addition to personal experience, we also learn about and define reality from the experiences of others, and to a considerable extent, from the portrayals found in the media. The social construction of reality theory recognizes three kinds of reality: experienced reality, symbolic reality, and socially constructed reality.

Experienced Reality

The first source of knowledge, **experienced reality**, is one's directly experienced world—all the events that have happened to you. Knowledge gained from experienced reality is relatively limited but has a powerful influence on an individual's constructed reality. For example, in a survey of citizens in Los Angeles, California, researchers found that nearly twice as many citizens credited direct and conversational reality sources of knowledge as more important than media sources in forming their views of the police.[8] Along the same lines, personal victimization is the most powerful source for defining one's view of how serious a particular crime is. However, even in the fixated-with-crime society found in the United States, personal victimization remains comparatively rare. Serious victimization tends to be concentrated in high-risk groups of citizens comprised mostly of lower income and minority persons. Irrespective of the impression one might get in the media, crime-and-justice experienced reality is not widespread. What is widespread is access to symbolic reality.

Symbolic Reality

The next three sources of knowledge—other people, institutions, and the media—share their knowledge symbolically and collectively form one's symbolic reality. All the events you did not witness but believe occurred, all the facts about the world

If the Old West had mass media

you did not personally collect but believe to be true, all the things you believe to exist but have not seen, make up your **symbolic reality**. The difference between experienced and symbolic reality can be illustrated with a few questions: Do you believe the moon exists? Why? Because you can see it directly. You have experienced reality knowledge of its existence. Do you believe the moon has an atmosphere? Why not? Because you have been told it has no air, you've read it has no air, and you have seen pictures of men in space suits on the moon.[9] You have based your belief about the moon's atmosphere on symbolic reality knowledge. Both experienced and symbolic knowledge can shape our view of reality. Now let's apply these ideas to crime. How many serial killers have you personally met? For most of us the answer is none. Yet if asked to list some common characteristics of serial killers, you would likely be able to offer an answer you believe to be correct. Your response would be based totally on symbolic reality knowledge. In fact, most of what we believe about the world comes from symbolic reality. In large, advanced, industrialized societies like the United States, media dominate our formation of symbolic reality, overwhelming our limited experienced reality knowledge and symbolic reality information we receive from other people and institutions. It is because so much of our social knowledge is gained symbolically from the media that there is concern over media's content. Media are centrally situated in the distribution of knowledge, and what we see as crime and justice is largely defined, described, and delimited by media content.

Socially Constructed Reality

The knowledge individuals gain from their experienced and symbolic reality is ultimately mixed together, and from this mix we each construct our own "world." The resulting **socially constructed reality** is perceived as the "real" world by each individual—what we individually believe the world to be like. This subjective reality differs to some degree between individuals because their experienced realities differ and what they incorporate from their symbolic realities varies. However, individuals with access to similar knowledge and who frequently interact with one another tend to negotiate and construct similar social realities. The pun "Reality is a collective hunch" is an apt summary of this social construction process. The end result is a socially constructed subjective reality that directs social behavior. People behave according to how they believe the world is. Significant for crime and justice, the media comprise the most important element in defining crime-and-justice reality for most people.[10]

The Social Construction Process and the Media

The role of the media in the social construction process is diagrammed in Figure 2.1, which presents four stages of social constructionism. In Stage 1, we have the actual physical world we live in. In this stage, events such as crimes or terrorist acts occur and are noted by individuals and organizations. The physical world and its properties and conditions provide the boundaries that the following stages must normally work within. Competing constructions

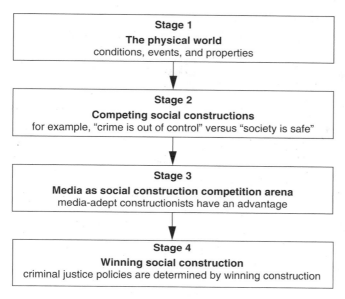

FIGURE 2.1 The Stages of Social Construction

cannot maintain credibility if they obviously run counter to the physical reality of the world. For example, a mayor of a city might wish to forward a social construction of her community as peaceful and safe. However, if there is rioting in the streets, her social construction would not be competitive for long.

In Stage 2, competing constructions first offer differing descriptions of what the physical world is like—what the physical conditions and facts of the world are. Frequently these descriptions are of social conditions that have been identified as social problems, such as drugs or crime. Hence, a social construction of the crime issue might include statistics and stories to support the construction that crime is out of control. Second, constructions usually offer differing explanations of why the physical world is as it is purported to be. The constructions will forward various histories and theories to map out how and why their description of the physical world happened. Therefore, statements like "crime is out of control because the criminal justice system is too lenient" might be part of a construction. Finally, based on their descriptions of the world and their explanations of why it so exists, these competing constructions often argue for a set of public and individual policies that should be supported and pursued. "In order to get crime under control, we must impose longer prison sentences" is an example of one such policy position.

In Stage 3, the media help filter out competing constructions. This is where the media play their most powerful role. Persons forwarding constructions compete for media attention, and the media tend to favor positions that are dramatic, are sponsored by powerful groups, and are related to preestablished cultural themes. In this way, media act as filters, making it difficult for those outside the mainstream to access the media and promote their constructions. By giving some constructions more credibility and coverage than others, the media make it hard for other constructions to gain legitimacy. Construction advocates who are not adept with the media are effectively shut out of the social construction competition. In effect, they never get on the playing field. For example, disorganized, poor, crime-ridden neighborhoods frequently find it difficult to get their other community problems successfully constructed as serious social problems. They are not seen as unimportant; they are not seen at all.

Stage 4 represents the emergence of a dominant social construction of the world. Because most of us have very little direct experience with crime-and-justice reality, the media play an important role in the construction that eventually prevails. The most important result of the social reality construction competition is that the winning dominant construction directs public policy. The social policies supported by the public and the solutions forwarded by the policy makers are tied to the successful construction.[11] For crime and justice, this socially constructed reality will define the conditions, trends, and factors accepted as causes of crime; the behaviors that are seen as criminal; and the criminal justice policies accepted as reasonable and likely to be successful.

THE CONCEPTS OF SOCIAL CONSTRUCTIONISM

The perspective of social constructionism involves a set of concepts that further detail how the social construction competition works. Basic to the social construction process are claims makers, who compete with one another and argue for the social acceptance of their specific constructions of reality.

Claims Makers and Claims

Claims makers are the promoters, activists, experts, spokespersons, and sometimes celebrities (see Box 2.1) involved in forwarding specific claims about a social condition.[12] As long ago as 1916, Ivy L. Lee, a founding member of the American public relations movement, noted:

> It is not the facts alone that strike the public mind, but the way in which they take place and in which they are published that kindle imaginations. The effort to state an absolute fact is simply an attempt to give you my interpretation.[13]

Hence, claims makers do more than just draw attention to particular social conditions; they shape our sense of what the conditions mean and what the social problem is. Every social condition can be constructed in many different ways. For example, crime can be constructed as a social, individual, racial, sexual, economic, criminal justice, or technological problem, and each construction implies different policy courses and solutions. These solutions are imbedded in the claims made by the competing claims makers.

Claims can be thought of as coming in two basic flavors: factual and interpretative (see Figure 2.2).[14] **Factual claims** are statements that purport to describe

---

B o x 2.1   Tiger Woods Accident and Social Construction

The aftermath of Tiger Woods' traffic accident provides an example of how a minor crime can become a major crime story when celebrities are involved as well as examples of claims-making and attempts to promote competing constructions of reality. Excerpts from a statement from Tiger Woods.com on December 2, 2009, reflect a construction of the accident as a result of personal failings and claims of its aftermath as a private family matter. *"I have let my family down and I regret those transgressions with all of my heart. I am dealing with my behavior and personal failings behind closed doors with my family. Those feeling should be shared by us alone.... there is an important and deep principle at stake which is the right to some simple, human measure of privacy.... Personal sins should not require press releases and problems within a family shouldn't have to mean public confessions."*

As the parade of women claiming relationships with Tiger Woods grew and the pre-accident construction of Woods began to erode due to massive media attention, a second statement acknowledging the affairs and an altered constructed reality was shortly posted. TigerWoods.com Posted December 11, 2009: *"I am deeply aware of the disappointment and hurt that my infidelity has caused to so many people.... I am profoundly sorry and ask forgiveness.... After much soul searching, I have decided to take an indefinite break from professional golf."*

Lori Moffett-Pool/Getty Images

---

the world. These are statements about what happened and are promoted as objective "facts" about the world. For example, "crime is out of control" is a claim about the physical condition of crime in society. Factual claims are also made to categorize or type an event. A statement along the lines of "This murder is an example of the rage that is common on our highways" would be a factual claim

---

B o x 2.2   Example of Crime Claims from Politicians

National candidates are expected to have policies on local crime issues as the follow-ing claims about capital punishment reflect. President Obama stated in his book: *"While the evidence tells me that the death penalty does little to deter crime, I believe there are some crimes—mass murder, the rape and murder of a child—so heinous that the community is justified in ... meting out the ultimate punishment."* (Barak Obama, *The Audacity of Hope*, 2006, p. 58). Similarly, Sarah Palin stated: *"If the legislature passed a death penalty law, I would sign it. We have a right to know that someone who rapes and murders a child or kills an innocent person in a drive by shooting will never be able to do that again."* (Sarah Palin, Campaign Web site, www.palinforgovernor.com, "Issues" Nov. 7, 2006). Both politicians combine a factual claim about murder with an interpretative claim about what policy needs to follow.

---

forwarded to categorize a murder as fitting into a specific type of killing—in this case, road rage. Factual claims are the descriptions, typifications, and assertions re-garding the extent and nature of conditions in the physical world.

Interpretative claims are statements that focus on the meanings of events. They do one of two things: either they offer an explanation of why a set of fac-tual claims is as described, or they offer a course of action—a public policy—that needs to be followed to address the conditions or events described in the factual claims (see Box 2.2). Together, factual and interpretative claims target the beliefs and attitudes that people hold about the world: what they think the conditions of the world are, what they feel are the causes of those conditions, and what they think the solutions are.

One strategy involving claims often used to get a social construction accepted by the public is called linkage. **Linkage** involves the association of the subject of the social construction effort with other previously constructed issues (see Box 2.3). For example, drugs are often linked to other social problems such as crime. The strategy of linkage would be to argue that a drug must be criminalized or other

Crime is out of control...	because of the lax sentencing of criminal judges.
Factual claim	*Interpretative claim that offers an explanation of why crime is out of control*

Cocaine is a dangerous drug...	whose use and sale must be criminalized.
Factual claim	*Interpretative claim with associated policy*

F I G U R E 2.2 Examples of Factual and Interpretative Claims

---

B o x 2.3   Linking Satanic Cults to Serial Homicide

Phillip Jenkins provides an example of an attempt to link satanic cults to serial
murder:

> Estimates about the numbers of victims varied greatly, but one commonly cited
> figure suggested that some fifty thousand ritualistic sacrifices occurred each
> year. In 1988, for example, the American Focus on Satanic Crime (a work
> especially targeted at law enforcement professionals) suggested that Satanists
> are connected with "the murders of unbaptized infants, child sexual abuse in
> day-care, rape, ritual abuse of children, drug trafficking, arson, pornography,
> kidnapping, vandalism, church desecration, corpse theft, sexual trafficking of
> children and the heinous mutilation, dismemberment and sacrifices of humans
> and animals. [They are] responsible for the deaths of more than 60,000 Americans
> each year, including missing and runaway youth."

SOURCE: Phillip Jenkins, Using Murder (New York: Aldine de Gruyter, 1994, 197) quoting Alan Peterson, "The
American Focus on Satanic Crime," foreword.

---

types of crime will increase. The linkage of crime to danger and calamity is also
employed in the social construction process, and crime-and-justice issues are often
linked to the endangerment of health, welfare, families, and communities.[15] The
acceptance of a claim of linkage between one social phenomenon and another
issue that is already seen as harmful raises the concern and public importance of
the linked social phenomenon.[16] Hence, the social importance of drug abuse is
heightened when drugs are linked to crime, and the same linkage makes other
correlates of crime, such as poverty, appear less important.

Claims makers hope to have their claims accepted as the dominant social construction of reality. For a construction to be successful, its claims must be accepted.
If the dominant social construction becomes "crime is out of control," then those
who have made that claim have been successful. When forty-first President Bush
stated that the culture of violence in our schools must be addressed, he was forwarding a claim about the world that also suggested a response to the claimed condition of the world. New laws and policies directed against the "culture of school
violence" indicated the success of the president's construction of a new social problem. To further enhance their likelihood of success, claims makers also frequently
make use of preestablished constructions, or frames, to advance their claims.

Frames

In the social construction of the crime-and-justice arena, prepackaged constructions, or **frames**, include factual and interpretative claims and associated
policies. A frame is a fully developed social construction template that allows
its users to categorize, label, and deal with a wide range of world events.
Frames simplify one's dealing with the world by organizing experiences and
events into groups and guiding what are seen as the appropriate policies and
actions. Regarding crime and justice, preexisting frames make the processing,
labeling, and understanding of crimes easier for the person holding that frame's

view of reality. If a crime can be quickly placed into a preestablished frame, it will be seen as another example of a particular type of crime needing a particular type of response. A senseless murder, for example, might become "another predator killing that resulted from a lenient criminal justice system." Such crimes can be cognitively dealt with and quickly tied to a policy position. You do not have to spend a lot of time understanding a crime that has been fitted into a crime-and-justice frame. The cause of the crime, explanations for why it occurred, and what needs to be done are already built into the frame. Certain U.S. crime-and-justice frames have deep historical roots and criminologist Theodore Sasson describes five long-standing crime-and-justice frames that compete today in the United States.[17] All five frames offer explanations of crime, point to specific causes, and come with accompanying policies. These frames are summarized in Table 2.1.

Faulty Criminal Justice System Frame.   The first frame holds that crime results from a lack of "law and order." People commit crimes knowing they can get away with them because the police are handcuffed by liberal judges and the prisons are revolving doors. The only way to ensure public safety is to increase the swiftness, certainty, and severity of punishment. Loopholes and technicalities that impede the apprehension and imprisonment of offenders must be eliminated, and funding for police, courts, and prisons must be increased. The

T A B L E 2.1   Crime-and-Justice Frames

Frame	Cause	Policy	Symbols
Faulty system	Crime stems from criminal justice leniency and inefficiency	The criminal justice system needs to "get tough."	O. J. Simpson "Handcuffed police" "Revolving door justice"
Blocked opportunities	Crime stems from poverty and inequality	The government must address the "root causes" of crime by creating jobs and reducing poverty.	"Flipping burgers" at McDonald's; Dead-end, low-paying jobs
Social breakdown	Crime stems from family and community breakdown	Citizens should band together to re-create traditional communities.	"Take back the streets" "Family values"
Racist system	The criminal justice system operates in a racist fashion	African Americans should band together to demand justice.	Rodney King; O. J. Simpson; "Profiling"
Violent media	Crime stems from violence in the mass media	The government should regulate violent imagery in the media.	"Life imitates art" Copycat crimes

faulty system frame is symbolically represented by the convicted, repeat rapist or by the image of inmates passing through a revolving door on a prison.

Blocked Opportunities Frame.   This frame depicts crime as a consequence of inequality and discrimination, especially in unemployment, poverty, and education. People commit crimes when they discover that the legitimate means for attaining material success are blocked. Unemployment, ignorance, disease, filth, poor housing, congestion, and discrimination all contribute to a crime wave that is seen as sweeping our nation.[18] "If you're going to create a sink-or-swim society, you have to expect people to thrash before they go down" is an example of a claim associated with the blocked opportunity frame.[19] To reduce crime, government must ameliorate the social conditions that cause it. Blocked opportunities are symbolically portrayed through references to dead-end jobs held by inner-city youth, such as flipping burgers at McDonald's.

Social Breakdown Frame.   This frame depicts crime as a consequence of family and community disintegration, skyrocketing rates of divorce, and out-of-wedlock births. Social breakdown has both conservative and liberal versions. The conservative version attributes family and community breakdown to "permissiveness," which is exemplified by the protest movements of the 1960s and 1970s and government-sponsored welfare. The liberal version attributes family and community breakdown to unemployment, racial discrimination, and the loss of jobs and income. An example of a social breakdown claim was made by then President Bill Clinton: "In America's toughest neighborhoods, meanest streets, and poorest rural areas, we have seen a stunning breakdown of community, family and work at the heart and soul of civilized society. This has created a vast vacuum into which violence, drugs and gangs have moved."[20]

Racist System Frame.   The racist system frame focuses on the criminal justice system rather than on crime. This frame depicts the courts and police as racist agents of oppression. In this frame, police resources are seen as dedicated more to the protection of white neighborhoods than to reducing crime in minority communities. Black offenders are more likely than whites who commit comparable offenses to be arrested, convicted, and sentenced to prison, and the death penalty is administered in a racist fashion. In radical versions of this frame, the basic purpose of the criminal justice system is to suppress a potentially rebellious underclass. An example of this claim was offered by then Undersecretary of State Nicholas B. Katzenbach: "We have in these United States lived under a dual system of justice, one for the white, one for the black."[21] The racist system frame is symbolized by the beating of motorist Rodney King and the trial of O. J. Simpson.

Violent Media Frame.   It is not surprising in a culture swamped in media that a frame reflecting concerns about the media exists. The media violence frame depicts crime and social violence as a consequence of violence on television, in the movies, in popular music and in video games. It is argued that violence in the mass media undermines respect for life. To reduce violence in society, this frame directs us to first reduce it in the mass media. It is forwarded by claims such as the following: "By the time the average child reaches age 18, he will have witnessed some 18,000 murders and countless highly detailed incidents of robbery, arson, bombings, shooting, beatings, forgery, smuggling and torture."[22] The media violence frame is symbolically referenced by allusions to violent visual media, videogames, and musical lyrics. Theodore Sasson notes that despite being perceived as the least important general explanation of crime and violence, media violence is seen as at least a partial explanation of violent crime by nearly all Americans. Violent media is not seen as the most important source of our cultural violence, but there is a broad consensus that the media substantially contribute to violent crime.

How Frames Influence Crime-and-Justice Policy.   All five frames are supported by some portion of the public, and the frames are not mutually exclusive. People often simultaneously support more than one frame, applying one frame to one set of crimes and criminals and another frame to other events. Crime-and-justice claims makers can guarantee a level of support if they can fit their social construction within one of these frames. Analogous to a political candidate running as a Republican or a Democrat, and thereby being assured of the votes of loyal party members, these five established frames are resources that can be tapped by criminal justice claims makers to forward individual claims and policies. By fitting their claims and desired policies within one of these preexisting frames, they tap into a pool of public support. Many crime-and-justice events can be differently constructed using different frames. For example, in Table 2.1, O. J. Simpson's murder trial is symbolic for two frames: Those who thought him guilty of murder see his acquittal as evidence that the criminal justice system is faulty and must be tougher; those who saw him as innocent see his arrest and prosecution as an example of a racist criminal justice system. Similarly, the 1999 Columbine High School shootings were used as support for the social breakdown frame, with the shooters portrayed as coming from dysfunctional families; the media violence frame, with the shooters portrayed as under the spell of violent videogames; and the faulty system frame, with the system blamed for not recognizing dangerous youth and preventing their acquisition of weapons.

The five frames jockey with one another for influence over how criminality is understood in society, which criminal justice policies enjoy public support, and how new crimes and criminals are perceived. The process through which crime-and-justice frames fall in and out of favor is closely tied to the social construction competition that is constantly being conducted in the media. In addition to being part of their own frame, by focusing on certain types of crimes or giving access to specific frame promoting claims makers, the media can boost frames ahead of one another.[23] As will be discussed in later chapters, although all five frames get some media play, recent crime-and-justice content and portraits tend to favor the faulty system and social breakdown frames over the other three. In addition to these fully constructed frames, less comprehensive social construction tools, known as narratives, are available to claims makers.

Narratives

Central to entertainment media but also common in news and infotainment, narratives are popular and useful in the social construction of crime-and-justice reality. Not to be confused with genres or standard story lines, and unlike frames, which are fully developed crime-and-justice constructions, **narratives** are less encompassing, preestablished mini-social constructions found throughout crime-and-justice media.[24] Narratives are crime-and-justice portraits that the public already recognizes and has embraced. Narratives are not broad explanations of crime and do not include wide-scale public policy directions like frames; instead narratives outline the recurring crime-and-justice types and situations that regularly appear in the media.[25] The "naive innocent" who stumbles into victimization is one recurring crime narrative. The "masculine, heroic crime-fighter" who cannot be swayed by corruption or hardship is another. The most popular, longest-running criminal narrative is the "innately evil predatory criminal" highlighted in serial killer movies. Table 2.2 describes additional common criminal justice narratives found across the media. Narratives can be utilized to quickly establish the characteristics of a criminal, a victim, or a crime-fighter and as supportive examples for larger crime-and-justice frames. In practice, narratives are frequently linked to the faulty system frame by inferring a simplified single-cause explanation of crime and shared elements of random, predatory violence and innocent victims.[26]

The existing cultural stock of narratives that can be drawn upon also influence what is said and not said about crime. They provide ready-made story lines to apply to current crime-and-justice events and thereby give a sense of predictability and understanding to even the most senseless criminality. As socially shared symbols of crime and justice, their use reduces the need to explain cause and effect, and accompanying crime-and-justice interpretative claims can remain unstated yet implicitly accepted. The evil predatory criminal narrative, for example, offers an explanation

T A B L E 2.2   Examples of Common Crime-and-Justice Narratives

Narrative	Costume	Characteristics
The PI	Cheap suit and car	Loner, cynical, shrewd, shady but dogged
The rogue cop	Plainclothes disguise, often has special hi-tech equipment	Maverick, smart, irreverent, violent but effective
The sadistic guard	Unkempt uniform	Low intelligence, violent, racist, sexist, perverted, enjoys cruelty and inflicting pain and humiliation
The corrupt lawyer	Expensive suit and office	Smart, greedy, manipulative, dishonest, smooth talker and liar, able to twist words, logic, and morality
The greedy businessman	Very expensive office and home, trophy wife	Very smart, decisive, and polished, unquenchable sometimes psychotic need for power and wealth

of the most heinous crimes. In the same way that a wolf by its nature preys on others, a violent crime needs no further explanation than to evoke the descriptor "evil predator." In the same vein that you don't need an explanation for why a wolf attacks sheep, but would need one to explain a wolf that did not, the predatory criminal narrative supplies an explanation for why criminals attack the law-abiding. Without having to expressly spell it out, the predator criminal narrative explains that it is just the innate nature of criminals; it's what they do and what they are. In the crime-and-justice social construction competitive process, narratives are often applied to specific criminal events, which are then attached to larger constructions and forwarded as examples of what is wrong in society.[27] In crime-and-justice social constructionism, these special focus events are called symbolic crimes, and they play an important social construction role.

Symbolic Crimes

Symbolic crimes are crimes and other criminal justice events that are selected and highlighted by claims makers as perfect examples of why their crime-and-justice construction should be accepted.[28] The beating of Rodney King, the kidnapping and murder of Polly Klaas, the murder trial of O. J. Simpson, the Columbine school shootings, and the September 11th World Trade Center bombings (see Box 2.4), are well-known symbolic crimes. Symbolic crimes are trumpeted to convince people of the existence of a pressing crime-and-justice problem and a desperately needed criminal justice policy. They are taken up by claims makers and forwarded as either "the types of crimes we can expect to happen more often because we have allowed a set of conditions to fester" or as "an example of what a new criminal justice policy will correct if we implement it." Frequently, a symbolic crime is used for both—to show what happens because of, in their view, obviously erroneous past practices and conditions, and as evidence to argue for specific policy changes.

To fulfill their persuasive social construction function, symbolic crimes are often the worst, most grievous examples that can be found. The formula for using symbolic crimes in crime-and-justice social construction is simple:

Step 1. Find the worst crime you can—the most innocent victim (child victims are often used) or most heinous criminal (animalistic predatory serial killers are popular).

Step 2. Link your construction to your symbolic crime (for example, to raise the issue of pornography, after a child murder claim that "this child would be alive today if the suspect did not have access to pornography."

Step 3. Success equals an increased importance of your issue and public acceptance of your construction (social acceptance of media with sexual content declines as more people see this sort of media as having serious, sometimes deadly consequences).

Thus, if you wish to forward capital punishment as a necessary social policy, as a claims maker you would seek out a symbolic crime committed by someone who had murdered previously, avoided execution, was released into society, and killed again. If you are opposed to capital punishment, you would look for a case

B o x 2.4   Symbolic 9/11 Terrorist Attacks

Images of the 2001 September 11 attacks on the World Trade Center buildings in New York remain the symbolic crime for the ongoing U.S. war on terror. In these attacks, the Islamic terrorist group al-Qaeda hijacked four commercial aircraft in mid-flight and flew two of them into the World Trade Center Towers in New York City, and one into the Pentagon in Washington, D.C. The fourth crashed in Pennsylvania due to passenger heroics. The Trade Center Towers in New York were selected by al-Qaeda because of their symbolism of the United State's economic power, with the terrorist goal of socially reconstructing them to be a "new symbol of U.S. vulnerability" (Tuman, 2003, p. 65).

AP Photo/Carmen Taylor/FILE

where an innocent individual was wrongly executed as your symbol of the wrong that results from a policy of capital punishment.

As the social construction process is distilled into a single, concrete, emotion-laden dramatic event that can be easily portrayed by the media, quickly interpreted by the public, and difficult for opponents to argue against, an effective symbolic crime can be the difference between winning and losing a social construction competition. When claims makers win a social construction competition, they gain another benefit—they gain ownership of social problems and issues.

Ownership

Ownership is the identification of a particular social condition with a particular set of claims makers who come to dominate the social construction of that issue. Claims makers own an issue when they are sought out by the media and others for

---

B o x 2.5   Ownership, the Media, and Criminal Justice

Phillip Jenkins relates how ownership of "serial murder" by the FBI resulted in sub-stantial tangible benefits for the agency: "The dominance of the FBI's experts can be observed throughout the process of construction. They successfully presented them-selves as the best (or only) authorities on the topic, and they assisted journalists and writers who reciprocated with favorable depictions of the agency. The federal officials stood to gain substantially ... because establishing the reality of a problem provided added justification for their BSU (Behavioral Science Unit), a new and unorthodox unit seeking to validate its skills in areas such as profiling and crime scene analysis. Once it was established that the FBI could and should have jurisdiction over this type of crime, it was not difficult to seek similar involvement in other offenses that could plausibly be mapped together with serial homicide."

Additional implications of ownership are described by Suzanne Hatty: "We live in a knowledge society comprised of 'authorized knowers,' [Certified experts] and individuals not associated with the State or its agencies. Within the system of knowl-edge production, the version of reality of the authorized knower is privileged [and] individuals not certified as experts have limited means by which to challenge the legitimacy of the [claims] issued by the 'authorized knowers.' Within the arena of crime and deviance, the police are the dominant group. By virtue of their proximity to crime, the police are seen to possess first-hand knowledge not available to others. Further, the police define the categories of behavior understood as criminal and through their collection of statistical data and their unique access to acts of disorder; they maintain control over discussions about crime in society. The police are assisted by journalism. The partnership between police and journalists ensures that the police continue to shape the problem of crime, and that the news media continue to pres-ent the public with visual images of deviance. This mutually beneficial arrangement promotes the legitimacy of both the police and the media as credible sources of expert knowledge [about crime] in society."

SOURCE: Phillip Jenkins, *Using Murder* (New York: Aldine de Gruyter, 1994); Suzanne Hatty, "Police, Crime and the Media: An Australian Tale," *International Journal of the Sociology of Law* (vol. 19, 1991), 171–172.

---

information regarding the problem and for opinions regarding the reasonableness of competing social constructions and policies associated with the issue. Some groups by virtue of their superior power, finances, status, organization, technology, or media access have more ability to make their constructions appear legitimate—to make their version of reality stick—and to take effective ownership of an issue. Because of their media access and control of crime data, law enforcement agencies have pro-prietary ownership of crime. When a new type of crime is constructed, law enforce-ment usually has the first call regarding how that crime will be constructed and related policy choices debated. Box 2.5 describes the application of the social con-structionism concept of ownership to the relationship of the media and criminal justice and provides a specific example of the FBI and serial murder.

THE SOCIAL CONSTRUCTION PROCESS IN ACTION

"Victim rights,"[29] "cyber stalking"[30] and "juveniles armed with assault rifles"[31] are a few of the recent crime and justice social construction efforts described in the research. Three additional well-documented criminal justice social construc-tions are reviewed here to demonstrate the social construction process applied to crime and justice.[32]

Social Construction of Road Rage

In this example, a new crime was constructed by the media. The media do not usually take on this role as much as they act as a filter and playing field among various claims makers, but an example of a media-created crime can be seen in the construction of road rage. Joel Best analyzed the imagery concerning highway violence from several major newspapers and television stations. He found that after an initial story dealing with highway violence appeared, the media began linking a number of different types of highway incidents together as a new type of crime today known as "road rage." Best summarizes:

> In short, the media described freeway shootings as a growing problem, characterized by random violence and widespread fear. Without official statistics or public opinion polls bearing on the topic, reporters relied on interviews with their sources to support these claims. Thus, the eleven network news stories used thirty-eight clips from interviews: eleven with law enforcement officials promising to take action or advising caution; thirteen victims describing their experiences; ten person-in the-street inter-views revealing public concern; and four experts offering explanations.[33]

Best found that the media sought not only to describe but to explain and inter-pret the problem. The media would say, for example, that highway congestion cou-pled with the anonymity of the car could trigger these violent outrages in people. The media also offered competing interpretative claims for the problem of highway violence. Some interpreted it as a faulty system frame problem and that more law enforcement was the solution to the problem. Others saw it as a traffic problem. Freeway violence would be lessened if the roads were not so congested. Other claims were that freeway violence was a gun access problem, or a lack of courtesy problem (fitting the social breakdown frame). Best concludes that in this case the media was the primary claims maker in the construction of road rage, taking on this role in part because of a slow news period. Needing crime news and a new crime, the news media went out and constructed one.

Reconstruction of Driving Under the Influence

Media can also influence the crime construction process by raising the perception of a crime's seriousness. An example of this type of influence can be seen in the public's evolving beliefs about drinking and driving. Driving under the influ-ence has been legally defined as a crime for a long time. However, until recently there was not broad, consistent public support for its prosecution. Not surpris-ingly, enforcement was lax and haphazard. Prior to the 1980s, DUI was socially constructed primarily as an individual rehabilitation problem. News accounts told of how lawmakers wanted to lessen the penalties for DUI. During this period,

Sean Murphy/Stone/Sean Murphy

Socially constructed by the news media, today "road rage" is recognized as a new type of crime.

lawmakers rationalized that the current penalties were too harsh and that the imposition of stiff penalties such as license revocation would interfere with the offender's ability to work. The media used nonpejorative words like *errant* to describe the actions of those convicted of DUI.

Beginning in the 1980s, new claims makers such as MADD (Mothers Against Drunk Driving) attacked this dominant social construction of the drunk driver.[34] Whereas drunk drivers had been seen as troubled individuals, when socially reconstructed, they became individuals who cause trouble. MADD could not have done this without waging a successful media-based social construction campaign that, in turn, affected how this crime was seen by the public.

Since the 1980s, DUI has been constructed as a much more serious crime. The drunk driver is now characterized as a "killer drunk" and one of society's pressing problems. There was clearly a shift in the media's construction of drinking and driving and subsequently how society reacted to drinking and driving. No longer viewed as an individual problem needing treatment, DUI offenders were now constructed as a menace to society, and support grew for much stricter DUI laws and their enforcement and prosecution. DUI was successfully reconstructed and is now seen by most people as a serious crime deserving harsh punishment.

Competing Constructions of the Arrest of Rodney King

One infamous example of social constructionism in crime and justice is the arrest and beating of Rodney King, caught on videotape on the night of March 3, 1991. After a high-speed car chase, Mr. King was arrested and violently subdued by

CNN/Handout/3rd Party · Misc/Getty Images

A frame from a citizen video showing Los Angeles police officers subduing Rodney King. Disagreement over the interpretation of the footage resulted in three different social constructions of the Rodney King arrest competing for public acceptance.

members of the Los Angeles Police Department. This event provides an example of the social construction competition process in which different constructed realities strove to become the dominant view. Even though the arrest was videotaped and many factual claims about the event were unquestioned, such as how many times Mr. King was struck, a competition regarding cause and interpretation of the beating—the constructed interpretation of the event—developed.

Three different constructions of the cause and meaning of the event competed, with each construction suggesting widely different policies. In Construction A, King resisted arrest and the beating was justified by King's prior actions. The law enforcement policy implications from this construction are minimal. The police were justified; therefore, the police officers were not acting inappropriately, and no changes are required.

In Construction B, the beating was unjustified but was an isolated incident of unwarranted police violence carried out by a few rogue police officers. The officers were not acting appropriately but were also not typical or representative of L.A. police officers. This version implies the policy response of firing the bad apples and reprimanding the officers involved in misrepresenting the incident. Targeted internal individual discipline is all that is needed.

In Construction C, the beating is unjustified and seen as an example of an endemic problem of unwarranted and consistent police violence toward minorities.

Fitted within the racist system frame, the officers are seen as acting as many L.A. officers would have acted, and the beating reflects an organizational tolerance of excessive violence toward minorities. The policy changes required from this construction involve drastic change in the L.A. police culture. It indicates the need to revamp the administration and training of the department and make extensive organizational changes.

In the end, Construction C and its interpretation won the construction competition. The L.A. police chief eventually resigned, and a new, African-American chief was hired. The Rodney King beating displays how even for events in which factual claims are not disputed, vigorous competition among interpretative claims related to those facts can still occur.

SOCIAL CONSTRUCTIONISM AND CRIME AND JUSTICE

The ultimate social importance of social constructionism is found in its implication for criminal justice public policy. As discussed in Chapter 8, the media and their crime-and-justice content influences the social construction of crime-and-justice reality by supplying the narratives, symbolic crimes, and information needed to create factual and interpretative claims. The media further provide the arena for the crime-and-justice social construction competition to be held, favoring media-savvy claims makers. This in turn encourages a particular set of social attitudes and perceptions about crime and justice and changes how serious some crimes are viewed by the public.[35] Predatory criminality, victim rights, terrorism, white collar crime, and an overly lenient justice system are recent examples of criminal justice social construction efforts.

Media emerge as one of three engines of social construction of reality. As diagrammed in Figure 2.3, our most influential social construction engine is composed of personal experience and information received directly from people close to us, our **conversational reality**. Together these two components provide the foundation of our personal socially constructed reality. When we have applicable experiences or direct access to people we personally know who have had applicable experiences, we trust that knowledge above all other. The media, comprised of news, entertainment, advertising, and increasingly infotainment, create a more pervasive, broadly distributed information engine in the social construction process. The media establish and maintain powerful frames for perceiving the broader, distant world while controlling the distribution of widely shared social knowledge—or knowledge not gained directly or from our conversational reality. The content of this socially shared knowledge at any particular time is largely determined by the gyrations of the media. The third social construction engine is knowledge supplied by the various institutions, organizations, and agencies that collect and disseminate statistics, information, and claims about the world. Annual FBI and Department of Justice reports about crime in America are examples. The institutions of the third engine have a dependent relationship

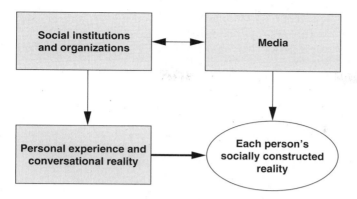

F I G U R E 2.3 The Engines of Social Construction

with the media. Little knowledge can be disseminated directly from these institutions and organizations to individuals, so agencies and institutions of the third engine must utilize the media for effective distribution of their factual and interpretative claims. The media, in turn, tap these organizations for credible, newsworthy, and interesting claims makers, claims, and marketable infotainment.

The single most important insight to be gained from a social constructionism perspective is recognition of the social construction competition that is constantly being waged. Social construction of crime-and-justice reality is constant, and recognizing the claims makers, claims, and strategies involved helps in following the competition. All views of reality are constructed, and being aware of this aids in deciding which of the competing crime-and-justice constructions you embrace. The social construction process is not inherently pernicious or evil, but we must recognize the process to thoughtfully evaluate the criminal justice policies that result.[36] The adage "where policy makers stand is determined by where they sit" (or policy choices are determined by the social, political, or organizational position one holds) directs us to consider the positions of claims makers—who they represent and what they stand to gain or lose by having their claims accepted or rejected. Ultimately, the prize from social construction is not the construction of any particular crime-and-justice issue but influence over the social construction process. Access to the media and the social reality media construct are the grand goal. If you can influence a reality-defining engine in a society, you can create the social reality of that society for many people. Therefore, winning one social construction contest puts you on the inside track for winning future contests in the same manner that successfully constructing a new type of crime in the present makes it easier to construct new ones in the future. If one set of claims makers gain control of the media social construction engine, other claims makers and constructions will no longer be competitive. If punitive criminal justice policy and predatory criminality totally dominate media content, entire frames and alternate ideas about crime and justice will disappear from serious public consideration. With these concepts and concerns in mind, we turn to the social construction of criminals, crime, and justice in the media, beginning in Chapter 3 with crimes and criminals.

CHAPTER SUMMARY

- Social constructionism views knowledge as the result of people interacting and coming to agreement about facts and ideas about the world.
- People socially construct their view of reality from their direct experiences and from information they pick up symbolically via language and images from other people and the media.
- Followed by information received directly from significant others (our conversational reality), personal direct experience is the most influential in the social construction of reality process. The media and other social and government institutions rank next in influence but because fewer people have direct experience or conversational reality access, the media is more important in the construction of crime and justice reality than in other social areas.
- The social construction process involves competing constructions forwarded by claims makers who argue that their claims about of reality be adopted by other people. Claims can be either factual (describing the world) or inter-pretative (explaining the world).
- Five common crime and justice frames exist and allow for the rapid social construction of new crimes. These frames are faulty criminal justice system, blocked opportunity, social breakdown, racist system, and media violence. Each frame encourages different policy approaches to deal with crime.
- In the construction of crime and justice, linking a crime to an already accepted social problem is a common strategy.
- Led by the "evil criminal predator," narratives are small, preestablished, commonly recognized mini-portraits found in crime and justice media.
- Symbolic crimes are high-profile crime and justice events that are used to champion specific crime and justice constructions.
- An important goal in the social construction competition is "ownership" of a crime–and–justice issue. Social construction ownership gives a claims maker greater access to resources, the media, and policy development.
- The ultimate prizes in the crime and justice social construction of reality process are the criminal justice policies society adopts.

WRITING ASSIGNMENTS

1. Write a brief essay about the expectations of college you had when you were in high school and what your sources of information about college life were. Why was the information the media supplied important—or was it?

Discuss whether the constructed reality you had of college in high school differs from the reality you found and what role media supplied information played in your initial perceptions.

2. Deconstruct recent news media coverage of an ongoing criminal case, listing the claims makers, their factual and interpretative claims, and any use of narratives, symbolic crimes, linkage, and ownership. Note which of the five common crime frames the story best supports.

3. Find and summarize a media story that fits each of Sasson's five frames.

4. Research either the Rodney King arrest or the O. J. Simpson murder trial and apply how the social construction process was utilized in both instances to construct the events as symbolic crimes and the social and policy impacts of the social construction of these events.

SUGGESTED READINGS

Barak, G. 1995. *Media, Process, and the Social Construction of Crime*. New York: Garland.

Best, J. 1995. *Images of Issues*. New York: Aldine de Gruyter.

Gergen, K. 1999. *An Invitation to Social Construction*. Thousand Oaks, CA: Sage.

Jenkins, P. 1994. *Using Murder: The Social Construction of Serial Murder*. Hawthorne, NY: Aldine de Gruyter.

Potter, G. and V. Kappeler. 2006. *Constructing Crime*. Prospects Heights, IL: Waveland.

Spector, M. and J. Kitsuse. 1987. *Constructing Social Problems*. New York: Aldine de Gruyter.

3

Crime and Criminality

CHAPTER OBJECTIVES

After reading Chapter 3, you will

- Comprehend the common media portraits of criminality
- Understand why the media gives special attention to predatory criminality
- See the link between media portraits of criminality and criminological theories
- Identify the issues and concepts associated with criminogenic media
- Understand violent media as a cause of social aggression
- Recognize the nature of copycat crime
- Appreciate the relationship between terrorism and the media

CRIMINALS, CRIMES, AND CRIMINALITY

A mainstay since ancient Greek theater, portraits of crime and justice are a media staple. From its classical beginnings, Western literature continued to reflect the interest in crime and justice, with romantic and heroic criminals appearing as common figures in the ballads, plays, and folktales of medieval England. Similarly, crimes and criminals have been ubiquitous elements in American media. With large-scale industrialization, urbanization, and ethnic immigration in the nineteenth century, crime became one of the nation's principal social concerns.[1] Spurred by growing public worry about crime, by the second half of the nineteenth century the dominant image of the criminal in popular culture had shifted from a romantic, heroic portrait to conservative, negative images. The newspapers, dime novels, and magazines of the late 1800s created the stereotypical portraits and themes of crime and justice that would later dominate movies and television—portraits and themes still common in today's media. What does this portrait of criminality look like?

Picture Post/Hulton Archive/Getty Images

A 12-minute "Western" filmed in New Jersey, the 1903 film *The Great Train Robbery* was one of the first "narrative" movies (which aim to tell a story). The film introduced many features still common in today's crime media—gun-wielding criminals, brazen crimes, brutal murders, dramatic chase scenes, and violent fatal apprehension of the criminals.

Criminals

Since the beginning of the twentieth century, in addition to being the central theme of police, detective, heist, and gangster stories, criminals and their crimes have been popular secondary plot elements in love stories, Westerns, comedies, and dramas. In the pretelevision era, media criminals in films, radio, and print enjoyed full lives and were often decisive, intelligent, and attractive individuals. Whether basically good or bad, criminals were shown as active decision makers who went after what they wanted, be it money, sex, or power. They controlled their lives, lived well, and decided their own fates. These early media portraits of criminals allowed audiences to identify with the criminals until the end, at which point the criminal was usually shot and killed.[2] Early media criminals allowed audiences to savor the danger and sin of crime yet still see it ultimately punished.

This portrait began to change with the decline of film and radio as the primary mass media in the late 1940s. The introduction of commercial television, an even more pervasive, direct, and influential medium, began the shift to more one-dimensional heroes and villains. Criminality in the cinema and in radio, however, had provided a fifty-year pool of criminal narratives for television to tap. Not surprisingly, television programming at first constructed images of crime and justice similar to the ones found in film and radio but in much greater quantity, filling as much as 40 percent of prime time programming during the 1970s.

The portrait of criminals found in today's media has almost no correspondence with official statistics of persons arrested for crimes. The typical criminal portrayed in the entertainment media is mature, white, and of high social status, whereas statistically the typical arrestee is young, black, and poor—what they have in common is that both are male.[3] Female offenders are primarily shown linked to male offenders and as white, violent, and deserving of punishment. They are paradoxically portrayed as driven by greed, revenge, and often love.[4] In general, the image of the criminal that the news media propagate is similar to that found in the entertainment media. Criminals tend to be of two types in the news media: violent predators or professional businessmen and bureaucrats. Furthermore, as in entertainment programming, they tend to be slightly older than reflected in official arrest statistics. Overall, the news media underplay criminals' youth and their poverty while overplaying their violence.[5] Although other types of criminals are periodically shown, the violent and predatory street criminal is what the public takes away from the media's constructed image of criminality.[6] If there is a single media crime icon, it is predatory criminality—a construction that frames and dominates the media crime-and-justice world.

Predatory Criminality

In their entertainment, news, and infotainment components, the media construct **predatory criminality**—criminals who are animalistic, irrational, and innately predatory and who commit violent, sensational, and senseless crimes—as the dominant crime problem in the nation. History reveals that the image of the predator criminal has dominated in the media for more than a century. Comparable to the hunting down of witches by the medieval Christian church, modern mass media have given massive and disproportionate attention to pursuing innately predatory criminals as the prime crime-and-justice goal.[7] Dominating the media's content are repeated claims that crime is largely perpetrated by predatory individuals who are basically different from the rest of us and that criminality stems from individual deficiencies. Over the past hundred years, media portraits have shown criminals as more animalistic, irrational, and predatory and their crimes as more violent, senseless, and sensational. The media have successfully raised the violent predator criminal from a rare offender in the real world to a common, ever-present image in the media-constructed one. The public is led by the media to see violence and predation between strangers as an expected fact of life. While terrorists are currently also popular predatory villains, nowhere is the predatory image stronger than in the recent media social construction of the ultimate predator, the serial killer.

The social construction of the serial killer as a significant new type of criminal began in the 1980s and took off in the 1990s.[8] The commodification, public embrace, and effects on criminal justice policy from the media portrait of serial killers demonstrate the media's crucial role in the social construction of criminality. With the construction of serial killers, the prior generic portrait of predators as dangerous but still human was supplanted by the portrait of animalistic killing machines more akin to gothic monsters than human offenders.[9] The media portrait also implied that these serial killers were everywhere and were the perpetrators of most violent crimes. Historian Philip Jenkins, however, reports that although there is evidence of a small increase in the number of active serial killers, in reality serial killers account for no more than 300 to 400 victims each year, or 2 to 3 percent of all U.S. homicides whereas domestic violence accounts for about one-third of all murders.[10] However, media coverage of serial murderers and the success of fictional books and films about serial killers have swamped the picture of criminality the public receives. The result is that serial killers are commonly perceived as the dominant homicide problem in the United States and as symbols of a society overwhelmed by rampant, violent, incorrigible predatory criminality.[11]

The media focus and immense public interest in violent predatory criminality is ironically tied to a socially palatable explanation of crime. While constructing crime as a frightening (and hence entertaining) phenomenon, predator criminality also presents crime as largely caused by individual deficiencies. This individual-level explanation frees mainstream society from any causal responsibility for crime. Such a perspective puts forth part of the crime problem (the individual offender) as the main problem and any social factors given causal credence such as devil worshiping or cult memberships tend to be on the social fringe rather than conventional social conditions. Predatory criminals are portrayed as springing into existence unconnected to any larger social, political, or economic forces. As constructed, the predatory killer is divorced from humanity and society.[12] Created by bizarre circumstances and individual flaws, irreparably separated from society and driven by alien needs, the predator criminal is both enjoyably evil and guiltlessly destroyed. In contrast, while criminals are often portrayed in depth in the media, their victims frequently are not. Counterparts to the criminals—victims of crime—occupy a surprisingly low profile in the media.

Crime Victims

Crime victims, although sometimes important for determining a crime's newsworthiness, are often ignored in the news media. A typical crime victim is not a newsworthy or entertaining one. When described, victims tend to be portrayed as female, very young or old, or a celebrity.[13] News coverage also routinely depicts criminal violence against females differently from that against males and underplays the victimization of minorities.[14] The ideal crime victim from a news perspective is a child or pregnant woman.[15] Some crime victims may be increasing in visibility, however. Since the 1990s, the news' construction of child murder victims has shifted from their killers' stories to emotional soft-news stories about the impact on victims' family and community.[16] Within this new

This 1947 comic book story is an early example of the media portrait of predatory killers.

infotainment-formatted coverage of crime victims, the advocacy of victim rights has also been constructed as a needed reform.[17] In this victim-focused news, the families of crime victims are shown as doubly victimized, once by the offender and again by the justice system.

In the entertainment media, victims normally play one of two extreme roles. Victims are portrayed either as helpless fodder or as wronged heroic avengers. Murder victims in particular are marginalized, and homicide frequently happens to characters who mean little to the other characters or to the audience.[18] The audience is encouraged to react to murders in entertainment not with a "My God how horrible" response but with a "How curious, I wonder how it was done" reaction. Entertainment crime victims are predominantly white and male—but the entertainment media also manages to overrepresent young women in excess of their real victimization rates. Entertainment trends in female victimization are fewer female villains, more female assistant heroes, and many more female victims.[19] Common entertainment victim narratives also abound. One is the "Undeserving Victim," usually one of the first killed to establish the evilness of the villain and justify their violent death at the end. Another is the "Stupid Victim," often a police officer, who is never smarter than the criminal or crime-fighting hero and ends up stumbling into their death. A good example is the off-duty police officer killed while trying to single-handedly capture the criminals. A final victim narrative is the "Lazy Victim." This is one who is killed while doing something wrong or improperly—the security or correctional officer watching television instead of their surroundings, for example.

Overall, the victimization rates of persons in the media correlate more with fear of crime than with the public's actual victimization risk. In addition to media victim portraits being demographically mismatched with official victim statistics on age and gender, greater proportions of both news and entertainment media victims are portrayed as randomly selected, having no prior associations with their assailants. Crime victims in the media are shown as innocent and as non-contributory to their victimization.[20]

Aside from these misleading constructions of victimization, which paint crime as a random unavoidable event, victims are of secondary importance in the media. Only if they transform into crime fighters in the entertainment media or have a preexisting newsworthiness (are already famous or a vulnerable child or pregnant woman) are they focused on by the news media.[21] Unlike the real world of crime, where existing relationships between victims and criminals are the most significant factor in the generation of violence, in the media-constructed world the more important relationship is between the crime fighter and the criminal. This holds true even in police reality programming where the interactions between the police and offenders/suspects dominate the shows. Overall, most victims in the media exist only to be victimized; once that function is fulfilled, if still alive, they are shunted aside to allow the central contest between the heroic crime fighter and the evil criminal to be played out.

Crimes

With predator criminals as the common grist for the media mill, it is not difficult to predict what crimes consumers are likely to find in the media. Not surprisingly, crimes that are most likely to be found are those that are least likely to occur in real life. Property crime is underrepresented, and violent crime is over-represented. Through the twentieth century, Murder, robbery, kidnapping, and aggravated assault made up 90 percent of all prime time television crimes, with murder accounting for nearly one-fourth.[22] In contrast, murders account for only one-sixth of 1 percent of the FBI Crime Index. At the other extreme, thefts account for nearly two-thirds of the FBI Crime Index, but only 6 percent of television crime. Due to the multimedia web and the constant recycling of content, entertainment media content greatly overemphasizes individual acts of violence, even during periods when new content is less violent.[23]

The content of crime news reveals a similarly distorted, inverted image. Violent crime's relative infrequency in the real world heightens its newsworthiness and leads to its frequent appearance in crime news. Thus, crime news focuses on violent personal street crime such as murder, rape, and assault, with more common offenses like burglary and theft often ignored. According to one study, murder and robbery account for approximately 45 percent of newspaper crime news and 80 percent of television crime news.[24] With regularity, the news media take the rare crime event and turn it into the common crime image. Furthermore, trends that do occur over time in the amount of crime reported in the news have little relationship to trends in societal crime. Neither the content nor the total amount of crime news reflects changes in the crime rate. Crime news also focuses heavily on the details of specific individual crimes, whereas only a minuscule percentage of stories deal with the motivations of the criminal or the circumstances of victims. Even in the news, the focus is on entertaining crimes with dramatic recitations of details about individual offenders and crime scenes. By and large, crime is cast in the media within constructions where large differences exist between what the public is likely to experience in reality and what they are likely to gather from the media. An area of crime that has large social impact but small media attention is white-collar crime.

White-Collar Crime

Despite encompassing a broad range of acts that cause significant social harm,[25] **white-collar crime** has not been a media focus[26] and exemplifies the adage that a crime's social impact does not always equal its news value. It is ignored because it is difficult to generate and maintain moral panics about white-collar crimes and criminals.[27] Subsequently, media portraits of economic crimes are rare and when produced are framed in celebrity-focused stories or formatted as infotainment and differentiated from "real" crime.[28] Therefore, while extensive coverage of a specific white-collar crime will occur—provided there is some newsworthy link such as a significant fine, prosecution, or company liquidation[29]—and periodic films dealing with white-collar crime are produced,[30] white-collar crime remains a small part of total news and entertainment media content. Rooted in the traditions of muckraking and yellow journalism,[31] white-collar crimes and their media portraits harken back to the 1800s. Historic symbolic white-collar crimes include Ponzi[32] schemes and the Teapot Dome scandal and more recently by Love Canal, Three Mile Island, Enron, WorldCom, and Martha Stewart

Box 3.1   Martha Stewart White-Collar Crime

The Martha Stewart case is an example of social impact not equaling media impact, the reverse of most white-collar crimes where social impact outweighs comparatively meager news coverage and value. Businesswoman, television host, and magazine publisher, Martha Stewart was indicted on charges of securities fraud and obstruction of justice connected to her sale of about 4,000 shares of ImClone systems stock in 2001. Her 2004 trial resulted in convictions for conspiracy, obstruction, and false statements and a five-month prison sentence and a $30,000 fine. Other lesser known male CEOs who stole millions received far less coverage than Ms. Stewart and often avoided jail time (Self, R. 2007, "Stewart, Martha" p. 271). In comparison to other white-collar crimes such as the collapse of Enron and WorldCom, which cost shareholders, employees, customers and government billions, her crime was inconsequential, yet received extensive news media coverage.

AP Photo/Bebeto Matthews

(see Box 3.1). The amount of coverage did increase following Watergate in the 1970s, but news reports continued to not attribute criminal wrongdoing to corporations, instead focusing on harm, charges, and probes, not on corporate criminal liability.[33] Coverage has continued to shift attention onto specific individuals[34] and has remained sparse and haphazard into the early years of this century.[35] However a cycle of massive accounting scandals and economic crisis resulted in an obvious recent increase in coverage and a parade of dramatized arrests of white-collar executives.[36] Although a current cycle of media interest is apparent, it remains to be seen whether the increase simply reflects a spate of sensational corporate crimes during a period of economic turmoil and a likely return to the low levels of media attention normally found.[37]

Why has media attention to white-collar crime been historically low? With public disinterest a major factor additional reasons include that these crimes involve indirect harm to victims and provide few striking visual images, are highly complex and boring, frequently cover years before resolution, and require specialized knowledge on the part of journalists.[38] In gist, white-collar crime stories are hard to make telegenic and are often killed in the news selection filtering process because they are not "news" in the traditional sense.[39] White-collar crimes typically are punished by a civil penalties, placing them outside of the criminal justice system and outside of traditional crime news that originates in police reports. News media organizations also likely fear litigation and withdrawal of advertising from the negative portrayal of powerful economic entities.[40] Counterbalancing these coverage-reducing factors are recent increases in investigative reporting as a journalism practice, the availability of Internet sources for information, and the efforts of various advocacy groups to serve as spokespersons.

Irrespective of recent trends, similar to other crime news, white collar crime, when currently covered, is more often treated in infotainment renditions of corporate celebrities in trouble, normal people turning to fraud, high-visibility fraud such as identity theft, or long-term concealment of and failure of government entities to discover fraudulent enterprises.[41] Analogous to how corrections are covered, predatory individuals, the failure to detect and punish them, and failure to protect the public dominate the news media construction of white-collar crime. However, dissimilar to how other crime is constructed, corporate offenders are rarely cast as pathological, and white-collar crime is sanitized and "decriminalized" as technical law violations rather than as real crimes.[42] Reflecting this construction, when arrested white collar criminals often attempt to socially reconstruct their crime as noncriminal activity.[43] For example, criminal dumping and chemical pollution cases are often described as accidents.[44] White-collar crimes that are reported are likely to be cast as caused by criminal individuals—a bad apple explanation—rather than as common corporate practices while the harm of such events and the criminogenic nature of certain industries are downplayed.[45]

In the entertainment media, white-collar crime is also infrequently examined despite a long history traceable back to Upton Sinclair's 1906 book *The Jungle*.[46] There have been more films since 1970, but white-collar crime films remain a small percentage of the total number of films with few commercially successful, recent exceptions being *Catch Me If You Can, Wall Street*, and *Erin Brockovich*.[47] In the entertainment story lines, businessmen are often portrayed as criminals but they are shown usually committing crimes of violence such as murder or running businesses as fronts for drug smuggling, terrorism, or violence-based extortions.[48] The white-collar criminals in the entertainment media are more often street criminals dressed up as executives than businesspeople engaged in criminal business practices.[49]

Overall, white-collar crimes are treated by the mass media as infotainment, as individual and corporate celebrities in trouble or as violent predators disguised as executives.[50] Corporate scandals and corporate predators are constructed to fit a predatory criminal icon and thus to better match the wider construction of crime and criminality found in the media. But the social reality of white-collar crime may be undergoing a social reconstruction similar to that of drunk driving in the 1990s. There is evidence that the general public began to see white-collar crime more seriously in the early 2000s and there has been more attention to white-collar criminality of late.[51] If real, a positive side of this shift is that media coverage has been described as more of a deterrent to white-collar crime than formal sanctions. In these cases and for these offenders public shaming in the media can be effective.[52]

Has the portrait of crime, white collar, street, and other, changed over time? The portrait of criminals and crimes in the media does display a number of evolutionary trends. Criminals have become more evil, heroes have become more violent, victims have become more innocent, violence has become more graphic, and crimes have become more irrational.[53] This perhaps would not be a concern if the portraits of crime and justice in the media were balanced in other aspects and presented various competing explanations of crime. That, however, is not the case. As constructed, the most common and popular media crime narratives forward particular explanations of crime. They thereby encourage support for certain criminological theories and the disparagement of others. The **popular criminology** common in the media (see Box 3.2) does not pretend to be empirically accurate or theoretically valid but its audience far exceeds that of academic criminology.[54] Surveying the media, what criminological theories do well in the media constructed world of popular criminology?

Criminological Theories and the Media

Before answering the question just posed, a brief overview of criminological theories is needed. Criminological theories can be grouped along a number of dimensions, one being where a theory locates the primary cause of crime. Applying that criterion, crime theories fall into five groups. The first group includes the **rational choice theories**, which state that there is no cause of crime and no difference between the law-abiding and the criminal. Crime is seen simply as a rational, freewill decision that individuals will make when the gains from committing a crime outweigh the likely punishment from committing it. Criminals are essentially normal people making bad decisions. To control crime, these theories argue that society must deter crime by ensuring that punishments outweigh the rewards of crime and that punishments are known beforehand, are certain to be implemented, and are quickly administered.

The second group is comprised of the **biological theories**, which place the cause of crime in the innate genetic or constitutional nature of criminals. The more primitive theories looked for specific physical traits (or Lombrosian-based atavisms) as signs of criminality; more recent ones look to genetic traits or biological trauma. Criminal justice policies associated with biological theories of crime focus on medical interventions and control of procreation. The appellation "natural-born killers" is often applied by the media as a code phrase for these theories.

Group three are the **psychological theories**, which view crime as caused by defective personality development. Based on the work of various psychoanalytic and personality development theorists, Sigmund Freud being the best known, these theories explain criminality as the result of mental deficiencies or criminal personalities. In these theories, people commit crime because their "personality" is ill formed. Associated policies are based around counseling and therapy. In the

---

B o x   3.2   The D.C. Snipers

Epitomizing the popular criminology predator criminal icon that dominates media content, a real-world example is found in the 2002 killing spree of then forty-one-year-old John Mohammad and seventeen-year-old Lee Malvo. Mohammad and Malvo went on a three-week sniper spree in October, 2002 in the Washington, D.C. area. Ten people of varied ages, gender, and races died. The manhunt for the shooters generated an enormous amount of news media coverage and the release of many false leads and much misinformation. For example, a profile prior to the arrests predicted that a lone older white male would be the sniper when in fact, two nonwhite shooters, one a juvenile, were involved. The interplay between the media and law enforcement during the sniper spree was tense with the authorities reluctant to release details of their efforts and the media commenting on the skill of the snipers in evading arrest (Duffy 2002). Public panic and pressure to capture the killers eventually led to the authorities releasing corrected information about the vehicle being sought and Mohammad's and Malvo's subsequent arrests. John Mohammad was executed in November, 2009. Lee Malvo is serving six consecutive life sentences without the possibility of parole.

Newscom

media, these theories come in "twisted psyche" and "sexual deviant" portraits best shown in Alfred Hitchcock films like *Psycho*.

Group four, **sociological theories**, look at social groups as the loci of the basic causes of crime. Criminals are criminals because of the people they associate with, or share a neighborhood or culture with. Whereas the psychological theories

HBO/The Kobal Collection

The cable television series, the Sopranos, and other media portraits of organized crime, continue the popular view of crime as a violent type of business enterprise and criminal as deviant entrepreneurs.

argue criminal personalities, the sociological ones argue criminal environments. These theories, and media renditions of them, argue that essentially normal people are forced or steered into crime by their social circumstances. Found most often in films that can profitably express society as part of the cause of crime, media portraits supporting sociological theories are found less often in other media. Strain, blocked opportunity, and culture conflict are the sociological theories that receive the most media play. Although there are hints of the need to change the social structure in these theories, their basic orientation is usually conservative. The means of fixing the individual criminals generated by the bad environments is to better fit and adjust the criminals to law–abiding society, changing their socialization and only secondarily changing their social environment.

Finally, there are **political theories**, which emphasize the political and economic structure of a society as the root cause of crime. The distribution of political power; unequal access to influence and material goods; and racism, oppression, sexism, and elitism are all central to these theories. Unlike the other theory groups that tend to focus on the need for individual offenders to change, these explanations are more likely to argue for social changes, restructuring society relationships and revamping the criminal justice system.

Which of these five theoretical perspectives do well in the media and which are disparaged? A historical assessment suggests that different theories have been popular at different times. Nicole Rafter notes:

> The media tend to reflect the criminological theories popular at the
> time. During the 1930s, crime films tended to portray a [sociological]

perspective which painted the urban ethnic inner city as the basic cause of criminality. The 1940 and 1950s films were Freudian based [psychological theories] with deviant personalities the root cause. The 1960s and 70s brought labeling and critical criminology [political theories] to the fore. The 1980s saw films indicting drugs and family violence [a mix of theoretical perspectives].[55]

These criminological theories are usually not explicitly laid out in the media and crime and justice media content searches will not find many criminological theory discussions. Support is more often set inside of portraits of criminals and is transmitted via the portrayed characteristics of offenders and their crimes inferring one theoretical explanation of crime as more credible over another. It is in the media construction of criminality that the hidden support for differing criminological theories of crime is found.

Criminality in Today's Media

Embedded throughout the media, the most common narrative of criminality is the psychopathic criminal, sometimes given super-villain traits to create seemingly indestructible murderous super-criminals popular in slasher and serial killer films.

Psychotic super-male criminals generally possess an evil, cunning intelligence and superior strength, endurance, and stealth. Crime is an act of twisted, lustful revenge or a random act of irrational violence. A historical trend has been to present psychotic criminals as more and more violent and bloodthirsty and to show their crimes more and more graphically. Hence, murderous violence that once typically took place completely off screen came to be represented in scenes that were violent but not graphic (such as the shower murder in Alfred Hitchcock's film *Psycho*). Since the 1980s, violence has been shown in graphic hyperviolent close-ups. As the most popular construction of criminality, the psychopathic criminal clearly supports the individually focused biological and psychological theories to the exclusion of other criminological perspectives. Crime is innate, an act of nature gone bad and not society's fault.

Less common but still popular narratives are those of **business and professional criminals**. Best known through the many media portrayals of organized crime, these portraits are characterized as shrewd, ruthless, often violent, ladies' men. Predators disguised as white-collar executives and more directly dangerous than the typical white-collar offender. If psychopathic criminals are mad dogs, these criminals are cunning wolves. The core message is that crime is simply another form of work or business, essentially similar to other careers but often more exciting and rewarding if, perhaps, more violent. The business and professional criminal portraits also forward individually based psychological theories of criminal personality and psychopathic explanations. However, the classical school of crime garners support in these constructions, and elements of political and economic causes also can be found. Thus these media portraits of criminality tend to be more complex and multitheoretical, spreading the responsibility for crime over both the criminal and

David Appleby/Universal/Everett Collection

Media portrayals of the heroic criminal such as Russell Crowe in the 2010 film *Robin Hood* remain the standard for narratives of the wronged hero forced into criminality to pursue justice against a corrupt establishment.

society. It is likely that this very complexity and society having a share of the blame for crime makes these narratives less popular than the more simplistic and guilt-free for the consumer psychopathic criminal portrait.

A third group of popular criminality narratives are **victims and heroic criminals**. These portraits are the least common and present an alternative perspective that supports sociological and political explanations. Although the criminal as hero and the criminal as victim appeared early and have been presented regularly throughout the history of the media, such narratives have always been less frequent in number than those of the criminal as a psychopath or professional. Depending on how the portrait is structured, this "Robin Hood" criminality narrative supports strain, blocked opportunity, labeling, and critical criminology theories.

If you look closely, you will find that the media have attributed a wide range of factors as plausible causes of criminality and provide some support for every criminological theory.[56] However, the dominant and loudest messages in terms of their frequency and popular appeal point to individually based theories of crime and away from social ones. In addition, while criminological theories come into and go out of fashion with criminologists, the criminological ideas imbedded in the media do not. Criminologists drop discredited theories, but the media recycle them.[57] Therefore, even primitive theories of crime such as demonic possession continue to be presented as credible explanations of crime in the media. "The devil made me do it" still carries weight in the media as a valid cause of crime.

In sum, the criminological theories that focus on individual characteristics as the cause of crime clearly fare the best. Of these, the psychological ones, often combined with political or biological elements, are the most popular. The single most common portrait of a criminal features an upper-middle-class person gone berserk with greed.[58] Indeed, greed, revenge, and mental illness are the basic motivations for criminality in the vast majority of crimes shown in the media. In addition, the psychotic criminals portrayed in the media frequently hold positions of political or economic power. The repeated message is that crime is perpetrated by individuals who are different in substantially basic ways from the law-abiding, that criminality stems from individual problems, and that, when not inborn, criminal conduct is more often than not freely chosen behavior.

The dominant media construction of criminals, crimes, and criminality is thus simultaneously both unsettling and conservative. It is unsettling in its emphasis on violent predatory criminality, which is portrayed as random and largely unavoidable. It is conservative in that the explanations of criminality emphasize individual traits as causes and minimize social and structural ones. Social changes are called for far less frequently in the media world of crime and justice than is elimination of evil individuals. Not surprisingly, such a construction, with its emphasis on predatory criminality, has raised accompanying issues concerning its social effects. Specifically, what is the relationship of the media to crime and violence in society? Do we copy what the media constructs and we consume?

CRIMINOGENIC MEDIA

Criminogenic media refers to media content that is hypothesized as a direct cause of crime. A continually debated issue is the causal position of the media. Does exposure to media precede or parallel aggressive or criminal behavior? In other words, do the media cause changes in subjects or do predisposed individuals selectively seek out and attend to media content that supports their already preordained behaviors? The public long ago came to its conclusion. As early as 1908, worries appeared that the media (then newspapers and books) were creating an atmosphere of tolerance for criminality and causing juvenile delinquency, and ever since public opinion polls have consistently reported the public's belief in the causal role of the media in crime and violence in society.[59] More than two out of three Americans feel that television violence is a critical or very important cause of crime in the United States, and one-fourth feel that movies, television, and the Internet combined are a primary cause of gun violence in the country.[60] The media violence frame, as described in Chapter 2, continues to find substantial public support.[61]

Three criminogenic media issues are discussed here. The first area addressed is whether violent media generates aggressive behavior. There has been a great deal of research and public interest regarding this question and the final answer is still being debated. However, most researchers today conclude that the media is a significant contributor to social aggression and as good a predictor of violence as other social factors. Most crime is nonviolent, though, and one can be aggressive without breaking the law (by being rude for example), so even if the media are an important cause of social aggression, media still may not be an important cause of crime. Therefore, the next, more directly relevant discussion for crime and justice looks at the media as a cause of crime, focusing on the generation of copycat crime. The basic question is this: Does the presentation of crimes in the media result in people copying those crimes? The final discussion looks at the relationship between the mass media and terrorism. Media-oriented terrorist events have emerged as one of the most worrisome problems of the twenty-first century, and the relationship of the media to terrorism and the use of the media by terrorists is a critical contemporary issue.

Violent Media and Aggression

Driven by the folk logic of "monkey see, monkey do," establishing whether "child see, child do" holds true in terms of the media and aggression has proved more difficult than first expected. Research on the link between media depictions of violence and social aggression initially revolved around two competing hypotheses: one conjecturing a cathartic effect and the other a stimulating effect. In brief, the cathartic effect hypothesizes that exposure to media violence acts as a therapeutic release for anger and self-hatred. In contrast, the stimulation effect hypothesizes that a diet of media violence stimulates violent behavior and fosters supportive moral and social values about violence.[62]

Researchers positing a stimulating effect have explored a number of causal mechanisms through which the media could cause aggression. The most commonly advanced mechanism involves imitation, in which viewers learn values and norms supportive of aggression and violence, learn techniques to be aggressive and violent, or learn acceptable social situations and targets for aggression. Advocates of a stimulating effect feel that children, in particular, learn aggression the same way they learn other cognitive and social skills—by watching parents, siblings, peers, teachers, and others. Accordingly, the more violence children see, the more accepting they become of aggressive behavior, and the more likely they are to act aggressively.

Some researchers have argued that the media are not established as a cause of aggression or violence.[63] They assert that to conclude that the media cause negative social behaviors such as violence is unjustified and premature. In their view, exposure to violent content and violent behavior is linked—but not causally. Rather, both stem from the predispositions of some media consumers who seek out violent content and act violently because of their predisposition to aggression. If this position is correct, eliminating portrayals of violence in the media will not reduce the level of violence in society because the number of individuals predisposed to violence will remain the same. Advocates of this model argue that the evidence of a link between violent content and social aggression has not been shown. Although experimental studies confirm that visual media violence can lead to short-term imitation, researchers do not know exactly how and to what extent the media cause long-term changes in aggressive behavior. Despite the general agreement that there is a persistent positive association between violence in the media and viewer aggression, the substantive importance of this relationship remains undetermined and an assessment offered nearly half a century ago remains valid: For some children under some conditions some media is harmful. For other children under the same conditions, or for the same children under other conditions, it may be beneficial. For most children under most conditions, most media is probably neither particularly harmful nor particularly beneficial.[64]

Why can't the media's effect on aggression be definitely measured? It is difficult to separate the effects of media on society or individuals from all the other forces that contribute to violent behavior. Media influences are so intertwined with other social forces that finding strong, direct causal effects should not be expected. However, after one hundred years of concern and seventy years of research, a small to modest but genuine causal role for media violence regarding viewer aggression has been established for most beyond a reasonable doubt.[65] Violent media does cause social aggression; violent media is not the sole cause, or the most important cause, and its causal impact is frequently overstated and overestimated, but it is a cause.[66]

Another undeniable finding is that the cathartic-effect hypothesis has been discredited: People do not become less violent due to media violence. Contrary to what the catharsis theory predicts, when viewing is combined with frustration or arousal, viewers are more rather than less likely to behave aggressively. Current research is exploring the magnitude, mechanism, and significance of a stimulating effect. It is not yet clear whether media portrayals of violence increase the proportion of persons who behave aggressively, encourage already-aggressive persons to use aggression more often, encourage aggression-prone persons to use greater levels of aggression, or some combination of these outcomes.[67] We also do not fully understand who is most likely to respond to media violence, under what conditions a violence-enhancing effect will take place, and in what ways media content influences behavior. There is certainly a connection between violent media and social aggression, but its strength and configuration is simply not known at this time.[68]

We are a more aggressive society because of our media, and violent media help create a more violent social reality. However, although research does show a link,[69] social aggression is not necessarily criminal, nor is most crime violent. In addition to the stated unknowns concerning violent media and social violence, the greatest problem in applying the "violent media causes social aggression" research to the "media causes crime" question is that the validity of extrapolating from this research to a relationship between media and crime is highly question-able.[70] Consequently, even if the media does significantly foster aggressive be-havior, it is a separate question whether media influence extends beyond aggressiveness to cause criminal behavior.

Media and Criminal Behavior

There are inherent difficulties in researching and examining possible relationships between the media and criminal behavior. First, experiments are even more dif-ficult to conduct in this area than in the area of social aggression, so that most of the available evidence consists of anecdotal reports rather than empirical studies. Second, the ways in which media may be affecting crime are numerous. The media could be increasing the number of criminals by turning previously law-abiding persons into criminals. Media portrayals may be helping already active criminals successfully commit more crimes by teaching them better crime tech-niques. Media may be increasing the seriousness or harmfulness of the crimes that are committed by making criminals more selective or violent. They may be fos-tering theft and other property crimes by cultivating desires for unaffordable things. They may be making crime seem more exciting, satisfying, and socially acceptable. Any of these processes would result in more crime, or more crim-inals, or more costly crime. Third, research is also difficult because an aggregate, society-wide media criminogenic effect is likely to be small and intermixed with many other crime-generating factors. In addition, the pool of at-risk individuals who are likely to be criminally influenced by the media is probably small. All of these factors make identifying media criminogenic effects a difficult research question to pursue.

Because of these difficulties, few empirical studies address the criminogenic effects of the media. In the best-designed empirical study of media effects on offi-cially recorded crime, Karen Hennigan and her colleagues examined aggregate crime rates in the United States prior to and following the introduction of television in the 1950s. Hennigan's study examined the idea that television, at least initially, influences property rather than violent crime. They explain their empirical findings thusly:

> Lower classes and modest life-styles were rarely portrayed in a positive
> light on TV, yet the heaviest viewers have been and are poorer, less
> educated people. It is possible that in the 1950s television caused
> younger and poorer persons (the major perpetrators of theft) to compare
> their life-styles and possessions with (a) those of the wealthy television
> characters and (b) those portrayed in advertisements. Many of these
> viewers may have felt resentment and frustration over lacking the goods
> they could not afford, and some may have turned to crime as a way of
> obtaining the coveted goods and reducing any relative deprivation.[71]

Whether this process applies today is unknown because we can no longer separate mass media's influences from other social processes. Hennigan and her colleagues speculate that television still contributes to an increase in property crime rates to some unknown degree, although other research has failed to tie the media to aggregate crime levels. Recent reviews have concluded that any link between exposure to violence media and general levels of violent criminal behavior is weak at best and moderated by consumer predisposition and age, media content and social factors.[72] A significant relationship between swings in media content and general criminality in society has not been shown and if it exists is more likely to influence property crime than violent crime, but what about the influence of media portrayals on individual criminality?

Copycat Crime

Public interest in the relation of mass media to copycat crime emerged with the entertainment media of the nineteenth century.[73] One of the earliest examples of media specifically created to generate crime were the how-to manuals for terrorism published by anarchist Johann Most in 1885. In his book, *Revolutionary War Science*, Most provided instructions on how to make nitroglycerin, dynamite, inflammable liquids, and poisons and advocated their use in antigovernment bombings and attacks. The 1886 Chicago Haymarket Square bombing is thought to have been a direct result.[74]

Growing concern that media messages could influence people to commit crime also sparked investigations and censorship drives against the media in the early 1920s. Partly in response to these concerns, in 1929 the Payne Foundation underwrote the first large-scale studies of the social impact of media—at that time, the consequences of movies. Portions of this research examined the effects of movies on deviant, asocial, and violent behavior by juveniles. Combined with public concerns about the influence of the cinema, these research efforts prodded the film industry to create an internal review panel, the Hays Commission, to oversee the content of films and quell the increasing calls for government intervention.[75] The film industry adopted a self-imposed code that forbade crimes shown in film "to teach methods of crime, inspire potential criminals with a desire for imitation, or make criminals seem heroic and justified." A media-generated criminogenic effect was clearly not in doubt.

Despite these early concerns, research, and industry and government responses, specific knowledge about criminogenic media effects is still sparse. Ironically, despite the long-ago conclusion that media can be criminogenic, there is no lack of information available today on how to commit crimes. Far more than in previous eras, a large body of material detailing how to commit specific crimes is readily available in films, on television, from the Internet, and in printed form. Texts come complete with diagrams and directions on how to commit robberies, murder, and numerous acts of terrorism, and countless visual examples are accessible. Why is the research so limited when the questionable content is so available and the concerns span five generations?

The reason research is limited is because what seems a simple matter—determining when a media-induced copycat crime has occurred—is complicated by the intrinsic nature of copycat crime. For a crime to be a **copycat crime**, it must have been inspired by an earlier, media-publicized or generator crime—that is, there must be a pair of crimes linked through the media. The perpetrator of a copycat crime must have been exposed to the media content of the original crime and must have incorporated major elements of that crime into his or her crime. The choice of victim, the motivation, or the technique in a copycat crime must have been lifted from the earlier, media-detailed crime.

These limits make identifying copycat crimes for study problematic because two independent but similar crimes may be erroneously labeled a copycat pair, and true copycat crimes may easily go unrecognized and unidentified. Too few copycat crimes or criminals have been identified to allow for generalization or for scientifically adequate research; the result is that although the term *copycat crime* has appeared for many years, little empirical research touches upon this phenomenon.[76] Instead, researchers have relied on anecdotal evidence to gauge the extent and nature of copycat crime (see Box 3.3). The slowly growing file of compiled anecdotal reports does indicate that criminal events that are rare in real life are sometimes committed soon after similar events are depicted in the media.[77] There have been enough real-life incidents that have replicated media portrayals in such detail that they invite a commonsense conclusion that copycat crimes occur regularly.[78] Collectively, these anecdotal examples provide a significant and growing body of evidence establishing the reality of copycat crime.

If there is a consensus regarding the nature of copycat crime, it is that a media criminogenic influence will concentrate in preexisting criminal populations. In the anecdotal case histories, most of the individuals who mimic media crimes have prior criminal records or histories of violence,[79] suggesting that the effect of the media is more likely qualitative (affecting criminal behavior) rather than quantitative (affecting the number of criminals). The limited research also indicates a pragmatic use of the media by offenders, with borrowing media crime techniques as the most common practice. Copycat offenders usually have the criminal intent to commit a particular crime before they copy a media-based technique.[80] In a seminal study of copycat crime in the 1960s, media researchers Melvin Heller and Samuel Polsky state:

> A significant number of our subjects, already embarked on a criminal career, consciously recall and relate having imitated techniques of crimes. For such men, detailed portrayals of criminal techniques must be viewed as a learning process.[81]

Available research suggests that copycat crimes occur regularly at an unknown but significant rate. The studies further report that copycat crimes are largely limited to existing offender populations but that they influence a substantial proportion—20 to 40 percent—of offenders, including juveniles.[82] Copycat criminals are also more likely to be career criminals involved in property offenses than first or violent offenders (although a violent copycat episode will usually receive a greater amount of media coverage when identified due to the greater newsworthiness of violent crime). The specific relationship between media coverage and the generation of crime remains unknown, as do the social context factors that are most important. There is no evidence of a strong media criminalizing effect on previously law-abiding individuals. The media influence how people commit a crime to a greater extent

B o x 3.3   Grand Theft Auto and Copycat Crimes

A number of crimes each year are linked to movies, books, music and music videos, television programs, and other media products. Video games have been especially targeted as crime generators and one game, Grand Theft Auto, has undergone great public scrutiny due to its story line and a number of crimes that have been described as caused by playing the game. Released October 2001, the game story of Grand theft Auto III revolves around a player/character "Niko Bellic" who has been betrayed by his girlfriend during a bank robbery and is sent to jail. While he is being transferred to jail an attack on the police convoy sets him free. As Bellic, the game player begins to work his way up in the criminal world. The gamer undertakes various missions, such as bank robberies, assassinations, stabbings, street racing, car-jacking and prostitution (Hourigan 2008). Killing a police officer earns a large number of points in the game.

In the real world, on June 7, 2003, an officer found eighteen-year-old Devin Moore sleeping in a stolen car and Moore was taken to the Fayette, Alabama, police station. During questioning, Moore grabbed the officer's gun and shot him twice, once in the head. Another officer heard the shots and came rushing at which time Moore fired several more shots, hitting him several times, once in the head. Moore then shot the dispatcher several times; once in the head. Moore picked up keys to a police cruiser, which became his getaway car. All of his criminal acts had counterparts in the game. After Moore was captured he was quoted as saying to police, "Life is like a video game. Everybody's got to die sometime." At trial, it was revealed that Moore, who had no prior criminal history, had purchased Grand theft Auto as a minor and had played to game for hours a day over a number of months and had played the Grand Theft Auto for hours before stealing the car he was found and arrested in. Described as a compulsive violent video game player Moore's attorneys argued a "GTA defense"—that he lost touch with reality and was acting out the virtual violence scenarios he had experienced in the video game. Despite his attorney's efforts, the GTA defense was unsuccessful and Moore was sentenced to death in 2005 and is currently on death row. Relatives of the three victims subsequently filed an unresolved multimillion-dollar lawsuit against Sony Computer Entertainment America, Take-Two/Rockstar, GameStop, and Wal-Mart claiming that Moore committed the 2003 murders after continuously playing the video game Grand Theft Auto III.

Two other recent incidents have been attributed as Grand Theft Auto copycats. The first occurred in Thailand in August 2008 when a nineteen-year-old high school student wanted to act out the Grand Theft Auto carjacking scene (www.dailymail.co.uk). He carjacked a taxi and murdered the taxi driver. Upon arrest he stated that: "He wanted to know if it was as easy in real life to rob a taxi as it was in the game." A police spokesman said the youth was an obsessive player of Grand Theft Auto. No sign of mental problems was found during questioning, and he confessed to committing the crime because of the game. Thai authorities banned the game after this incident. The second GTA copycat crime occurred in June 2008 in Long Island, New York (Crowley, K. 2008). Police arrested six teenagers for a crime spree. The kids mugged and beat a man, attempted a carjacking, and vandalized a vehicle before being arrested by Garden City police. They confessed that they were imitating acts seen in Grand Theft Auto and emulating the popular player/character "Niko Bellic" found in the game. (A video of the story can be found on YouTube).

SOURCES: "Can a Video Game Lead to Murder?," CBS News, March 6, 2005; Crowley, K. 2008. "Video Villains Come to Life," *New York Post*, Friday, June 26; "Grand Theft Auto pulled from sale after Bangkok teen murders taxi driver to see if it was as easy as in the game," Daily Mail Online, Aug. 4, 2008. www.dailymail.co.uk/new/ worldnews/; Hourigan, B. 2008. The moral code of Grand theft Auto IV. *IPA Review*, July: 21–22. For a general review of research on violent video games see Anderson, Gentile, and Buckley. 2007. *Violent Video Game Effects on Children: Theory, Research and Public Policy*. Oxford University Press.

than they influence whether people commit a crime, and media content is errone-ously often described in the media as a crime trigger. In reality, the media are most often a crime rudder, molding crime's form rather than being its engine.

By what mechanism do the media generate copycat effects? Here again, knowledge is limited and speculation prevails. In that the concept implies the imitation of an initial crime, the obvious starting point in discussing copycat crime is imitation. Gabriel Tarde was first to offer a theoretical discussion of copycat crime in the late nineteenth century.[83] Focusing on violent crime and observing that sensational violent crime appears to prompt similar incidents, he coined the term *suggesto-imitative assaults* to describe the phenomenon. In a pithy summation, he concluded, "Epidemics of crime follow the line of the telegraph."[84] However, imitation came to have a negative connotation among social scientists who saw it as a simple, less cognitively demanding activity. Subsequently, Tarde's writings were largely ignored in criminology until the 1970s, when a surge of copycat crimes involving airline hijackings and media interest in them led to renewed attention to the role of imitation in the generation of crime.[85] Picking up directly from Tarde's earlier perspective, initial copycat crime researchers attributed copycat crime to a process of simple and direct imitation based on social learning principles.[86]

Imitation came to be criticized as too simplistic a process to fully explain copycat crime; it failed to explain why most children imitate aggression within socially acceptable limits and only a few imitate aggression with a real gun. Critics have also noted that imitation theory focuses on the copycat criminal and tends to downplay other social factors. Today imitation is considered a necessary but insuf-ficient factor in the generation of copycat crime. The primary flaw in imitation theory is that it generally implies that the copycat behavior must physically resem-ble the portrayed behavior and therefore falls short in explaining any generalized effects or innovative applications.

Partly in response, another mechanism, more general than imitation, by which media portrayals activate similar behaviors, has been posited.[87] Through this mechanism, termed **priming**, the portrayals of certain behaviors in the me-dia activate a cluster of associated ideas within the potential copycat offender that increase the likelihood that he or she will behave similarly but not necessarily identically.[88] Priming holds that when people experience an event via the mass media, ideas having a similar meaning to those contained in the media content are activated for a short time, and these thoughts can result in related actions. Thus after viewing violent media, individuals will be primed to have more hostile thoughts, to see aggression as justified, and to behave more aggres-sively.[89] Priming can be understood as providing a set of ideas and beliefs that construct a particular social reality—the perception that the nature of the world is such that a particular type of crime is appropriate, justified, and likely to be successful.

A cognitive theory concept of "**scripts**" from the field of communication also has copycat crime applications. Linked to priming, scripts are seen as preestablished behavioral directions that individuals hold in their memory and scroll up to direct their actions as needed. Such cognitive scripts serve as a guide for behavior by laying out the sequence of events that one believes are likely to happen and the behaviors that one believes are appropriate in particular situations.[90] It is thought that criminal scripts can be acquired by observing criminogenic media during fantasy role-playing, a part of normal child development. Role-playing encourages the generalized acquisition of social role scripts—the role-playing child for example acquires the persona of the social role and subsequently acts like he or she thinks a doctor, athlete, or gangster would in various real-world settings beyond the ones specifically modeled. The more salient the observed criminality, the more the child ruminates upon, fantasizes about, and rehearses it.[91] Cues, such as the presence of a gun, first observed in the media and later encountered in the real world, would activate the acquired criminal scripts.[92]

A study by Allen Mazur offers an example in the area of crime.[93] Mazur reported that bomb threats directed at nuclear energy facilities increased significantly following increases in news coverage of nuclear power issues. Mazur's study is important in that it indicates that the media may initiate crimes even when they don't provide precise models to copy; the bomb threats to nuclear facilities followed news stories that were not bomb-related. In Berkowitz's conceptualization, the news media coverage primed some people to make bomb threats even though the coverage did not provide a specific bomb-threat model to copy. In Huesmann's terms, the coverage activated similar "threatening scripts." John Hinckley's assassination attempt on President Reagan is a well-known example of a crime where media priming and activation of a film-based behavioral script occurred.

At this time, copycat crime appears to be concentrated in predisposed, at-risk individuals primed by media characterizations of crime to activate acquired criminal scripts and social roles.[94] Diagramed in Figure 3.1, there are multiple cognitive paths between the media and criminality that copycat criminals can take. Social cognition theory provides two paths: (1) a systematic central path that requires a copycat offender to evaluate information and is likely related to instrumental planned copycat crimes such as a bank robbery; and (2) a heuristic peripheral path that is quickly traveled with little information evaluation and likely leads to emotional spontaneous copycat crime such as an impulsive assault or hate crime.[95]

A third path is also possible through **narrative persuasion** from entertainment media content.[96] Most media consumed is narrative or story-telling based and consumer interaction with narrative media is qualitatively different from the first two paths. The variously termed concepts of "transportation," "engagement," or "absorption" have been used to describe this type of media interaction. As narrative persuasion describes the most common use of media and provides an opportunity to influence individuals who would ordinarily be resistant to media influence due to the "suspension of belief" that is a hallmark of entertainment narrative involvement, this path is speculated to be the most significant copycat crime path.[97] The narrative persuasion path allows for influence resistant media consumers to be affected by story characters who model both attitude and behavior change.[98] Thus, a consumer who is initially unlikely to copy a particular crime would be persuaded to do so by observing a model who is portrayed as also initially unwilling to commit an offense but who

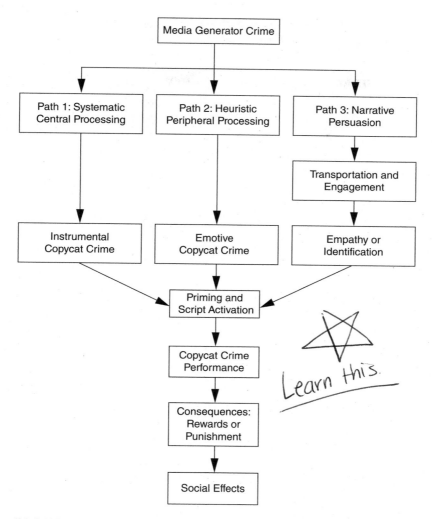

FIGURE 3.1 An Individual Level Copycat Crime Model

undergoes a transformation in the narrative in which the crime comes to be seen in a positive manner.

These individual-level paths and social dynamics lead to the society-level model of copycat crime shown in Figure 3.2. The amount of copycat crime in a society is seen as the result of the interaction of four factors: the initial crime and criminal, subsequent media coverage, the social context, and the characteristics of the copycat criminal. The model denotes a process in which select, usually successful, highly newsworthy crimes shown in popular entertainment narratives or news stories emerge as candidates for copying. The media coverage and portrayals first affect individuals by inviting them to identify with the initial

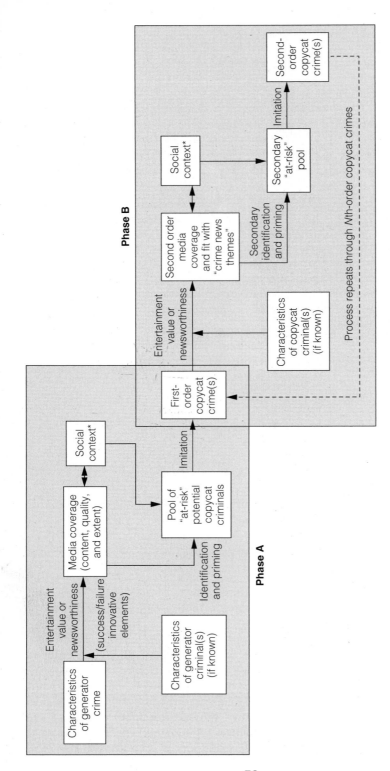

FIGURE 3.2

Aggregate Model

*Social context includes social norms regarding crime; news reporting and entertainment; opportunities to copy; social tensions (racism, economic strife, and so forth); organization of mass media (state, private, profit, nonprofit, accessibility, regulation, audience size, and credibility).

crime and criminal and thereby prime a pool of potential copycat criminals. A susceptible at-risk individual—that is, a person who sees other people and the media as profitable crime information sources—is thought to be at special risk for copycat behavior, but social factors are seen as more significant for copycat crime rates than individual ones.[99] The size of the copycat crime pool is affected both by the level of media distribution of the criminogenic content and by other social context factors such as social norms regarding deviance and violence; the preexistence of social conflicts; the number of opportunities available to the potential offender to copy a crime technique (there are more opportunities to copy a car theft technique, for example, than a bank robbery technique); the nature, credibility, and pervasiveness of the mass media; and the size of the preexisting criminal population. Unfortunately, contemporary U.S. society scores high on all of these criteria; therefore, the generation of copycat crimes should be high in the United States compared to other countries. After the at-risk copycat pool emerges, the first wave of copycat crimes results through a process of generalized primed imitation, limited by and adapted to the copycat criminal's opportunities (Phase A).

Should these first-order copycat crimes receive further media attention, and particularly should they be incorporated into a news media crime theme, the likelihood of additional copycat crime increases (Phase B). This extended reiterative process is regarded as much more likely to occur with violent crime because of the high news value of violence.[100] The aggregate model reveals a paradox. The process is more common for property crime and property offenders through first-order copycat crimes (Phase A). But violent copycat crime and offenders are most likely to generate second and higher-order imitations (Phase B) as they are more likely to become the focus of intensive news media attention. Once more the media is likely to take the rare real-world event, the violent copycat crime, and make it the more significant, better known event in the public's constructed reality. The accepted social construction of a copycat crime is more likely to be of a violent crime such as a bombing even though in actuality copycat property crimes are probably far more common.

It is clear that copycat crimes occur fairly regularly, but the number of such crimes generated by the media is not known. Even before the September 11, 2001, World Trade Center and Pentagon attacks, the copycat crimes that generated the most concern were those related to terrorism. Today, terrorism's relationship to the media is the leading cause of anxiety in the media, crime, and justice area.

Media-Oriented Terrorism

Terrorism's relationship with the media epitomizes the dangers of copycat effects. Carlos Marighella, a Communist insurgent terrorist in the 1960s, described the terrorists' aim in their interactions with media:

> These actions, carried out with specific and determined objectives, inevitably become propaganda material for the mass communication system. ... The war of nerves or psychological war is an aggressive

technique, based on the direct or indirect use of mass means of communication and news in order to demoralize the government. In psychological warfare, the government is always at a disadvantage since it imposes censorship on the mass media and winds up in a defensive position by not allowing anything against it to filter through. At this point it becomes desperate, is involved in great contradictions and loss of prestige, and loses time and energy in an exhausting effort at control which is subject to being broken at any moment.[101]

The strength of the symbiotic media–terrorism relationship is such that in many ways the modern terrorist is the creation of the media. If mass media did not exist, terrorists would have to invent them.[102] Media and terrorists share several needs. Most fundamentally, both are trying to reach the greatest number of people possible. Driven by their mutual goal to maximize audience size, **media-oriented terrorism**, where violence is scripted to earn publicity has significantly increased.[103] Media-oriented terrorism is "propaganda by deed," a purposely symbolic crime, and today a steady stream of terrorist acts can be identified as media-oriented terrorist events characterized by the selection of high-visibility targets, graphic terrorist acts, pre-event contact with media outlets, and post-event videos, interviews, and other media accommodations.[104]

Like politicians, terrorists have learned to manipulate media coverage to bypass editorial gatekeeping and contextual formatting by journalists and go directly to the public with their message.[105] In the process, terrorism has become a form of infotainment and public theater. On the other side, the media can be thought of as "terrorism oriented" in terms of the commercial value of terrorist events. Due to the huge audience it attracts, media-oriented terrorism is highly valuable to media organizations.

> For the media, terrorism is dramatic, often violent, visual, and timely.
> Unlike wars which are usually protracted and highly complex events …
> acts of terrorist violence normally have a beginning and an end, can be
> encompassed in a few minutes of air time, possess a large degree of
> drama, involve participants who are perceived by the viewing public as
> unambiguous, and are not so complex as to be unintelligible to those
> who tune in only briefly.[106]

All of this transformed terrorism into high ratings for the media. And as the media pursued terrorists, terrorists became media wise. They now understand the dynamics of newsworthiness and the benefits of news coverage: increased legitimacy and political status; heightened perception of their strength and threat; and an increased ability to attract resources, support, and recruits.

Contemporary media-oriented terrorists are guided by five principles.[107] First, their acts are not tactical in nature but are aimed at distant external audiences. Second, victims are chosen for symbolic meaning to maximize fear and public impact. Third, the media are eager to cover terrorist violence and will devote significant resources to reporting terrorist events. Fourth, the media can be activated, directed, and manipulated for propaganda effects. Fifth, target governments are at a disadvantage because their choice is usually between censorship and allowing terrorists to use the media. The application of these principles has resulted in the spread of media-oriented terrorism around the world. In the research literature on terrorism, no doubts are expressed that the media motivate copycat terrorist acts or that a substantial number of terrorist events are aimed primarily at garnering publicity.[108]

However, gaining media attention is not guaranteed, particularly for terrorist groups not linked to al-Qaeda. Worldwide, many more acts of terrorism are committed than are reported in the media, and U.S. media give more coverage to terrorism aimed at U.S. citizens or property.[109] Coverage of domestic terrorism, at least prior to the September 11, 2001, attacks, received little coverage and coverage today is focused on events with casualties.[110] The resulting competition for media attention causes terrorists to escalate their violence because more violent and more dramatic acts are necessary to gain news coverage as the shock value of ordinary terrorism diminishes. Occupation of a building, for example, no longer garners world or even national coverage in many instances. As long as news reporting is a commercial product whose content is influenced by sensationalism, violent terrorist acts will garner disproportionate coverage.

In the end, the impact of media coverage on terrorism is twofold. First, coverage of a terrorist act encourages copycats.[111] As with general copycat crime, there is much anecdotal evidence that terrorist events such as kidnappings, bank robberies in which hostages are taken, plane hijackings, parachute hijackings, planting altitude bombs on airplanes, suicide bombings and online beheadings of hostages occur in clusters. These copycat effects are especially strong following a well-publicized successful terrorist act using a novel approach. Second, although their numbers wax and wane, the pattern of these violent performances suggests that media-oriented terrorism has become a persistent element of the total terrorism picture since the 1972 Olympics when Palestine Liberation Organization terrorists killed members of the Israeli Olympic team.[112] The World Wide Web has also provided a new avenue for terrorists to disseminate their messages and has partly supplanted their need to attract news media attention in order to reach their target audiences.[113] Today terrorism is often a twisted public relations "infotainment" effort. Like other types of crime, terrorism would still exist if the media disappeared, but the media–terrorism relationship exacerbates the prevalence of these acts. Terrorism performed for both old and new media is a common feature in the twenty-first century.

CRIMINOGENIC INFOTAINMENT

The public's interest in crime-related media, the large proportion of media that is crime related, and the skewed content of the media have raised alarms. The greatest concerns are associated with the media's predatory portrait of criminality and a media criminogenic effect. The cumulative result of the violent predator image, which favors individually based criminological theories as the best explanations of crime, is a social reality in which broad-based social and structural causes of crime are disparaged. The media create a social reality wherein pernicious effects from criminogenic media are plausible and likely.

Where does the research about violent, criminogenic, and terrorism related media lead? The existing research suggests the following propositions. Most people exposed to pernicious media will show no negative effects. Some small proportion of people—the proportion is not clear—will show slight effects, concentrated more in attitudes than in behaviors. Strong behavioral effects are relatively rare and are most likely to appear in at-risk individuals predisposed to crime, but the reality of long-term effects on a large number of people remains a distinct possibility. In addition, the media's ability to generate greater numbers of predisposed at-risk individuals also appears to be real. Therefore, the media's criminogenic effects will be enhanced as their current criminogenic content in combination with racial and ethnic strife, income disparities, and poor social conditions contribute to future numbers of people at risk for negative media influences. Violence-prone children and adults are especially at risk for emulating media violence. When sex and violence are linked, hypermasculine males are most influenced to be sexually aggressive. When the news media sensationalize crime and make celebrities of criminals, the danger of imitation for notoriety increases. When successful crime is detailed, criminals will emulate it. And when a successful terrorist event is shown or a terrorist group is able to gain the attention of the media, media-oriented terrorism will increase.

Whether criminogenic effects, such as copycat crime, emerge in any particular individual depends on the highly idiosyncratic interactions of the content of a particular media product (its characterizations of crime and criminals), the individual's predispositions (personal criminal history, family, and environmental factors), and the media's social context (preexisting cultural norms, crime opportunities, and pervasiveness of the mass media). A media-generated criminogenic effect ultimately depends on the combined influences of social context, media content, and audience characteristics. The more heavily the consumer relies on the media for information about the world and the greater his or her predisposition to criminal behavior, the greater the likelihood of an effect.

Media effects are real, but it is also apparent that the media alone cannot make someone a criminal. You can get an idea of what it would be like if the media went away by looking at the United States before the mass media existed. What you will find is a violent land with many violent people.[114] That fact is the core reason it does not make sense to blame the media for the bulk of our violence and crime today. Based on our heritage, we would certainly be a violent and crime-burdened society today without the media's influences, but are we more violent and criminal because of them? This is also true. Violent media alone does not make a violent person, but violent media can apparently make a violent person more often violent. Criminogenic media won't make a law-abiding person a criminal, but a preexisting criminal may become a greater threat. The media play their role after the biological, economic, and social factors do. To blame only the media is to ignore a host of more significant factors. But while you can argue that the media is not the main engine in our crime rate, media do facilitate the packaging and delivery of a criminogenic rate boast.

In the end, the media's influence on the behavior of most of us is to cause us *not* to do certain things. The media do not turn law-abiding people into criminals or nonviolent people into assaulters, but they keep people from flying, taking a foreign vacation, going downtown, or opening their door. It makes us wary of each other and in doing so makes us more isolated and subsequently more dependent on the media for our knowledge about crime and other social conditions. Media cannot be painted as the dominant cause of crime in society, but their portraits of criminality cannot be ignored. By painting crime in a particular hue, the media color the actual world as violent, predatory, and dangerous. They supply criminal role models and techniques, create a conducive social atmosphere for the predisposed few to emulate the crimes they see, hear, and read about, and provide the theoretical ideas that explain it all to the public while largely absolving that public of any social responsibility. With this image of criminality in mind, Chapter 4 looks at the relationship between the media and the first line of response to crime, law enforcement.

CHAPTER SUMMARY

- Portraits of crime and justice appear throughout the history of media and have continued to be a staple of all types of media content.

- The portrait of criminals found in the media has almost no correspondence with official statistics. The typical media criminal is mature, white, and of high social status, whereas statistically the typical arrestee is young, black, and poor. The media does get the gender of criminality correct—most criminals are male in both the media and real world.

- Media female offenders are primarily shown as white, violent, and driven by greed, revenge, and often love. When they offend females are usually shown as deserving of punishment.

- The media construct criminals who are animalistic, irrational, and innately predatory and who commit violent, sensational, and senseless crimes as the dominant crime problem in the nation.

- Victimization rates in the media correlate more with fear of crime than with actual victimization risk. Victims are frequently portrayed as randomly selected, having no prior associations with their assailants, as innocent, and as noncontributory to their victimization.

- Crimes that are most likely to be found in the media are least likely to occur in real life. Property crime is underrepresented and violent crime is overrepresented.

- Criminological theories that focus on individual characteristics as the cause of crime fare the best in the media. Greed, revenge, and mental illness are the basic motivations for criminality in the vast majority of crimes shown in the media.

- The repeated media message is that crime is perpetrated by individuals who are substantially different from the law-abiding, that criminality stems from individual problems, and that, when not innate, criminality is freely chosen behavior.

- Criminogenic media refers to media content that is hypothesized as a direct cause of crime. It is not known what the effect of the media is on the overall crime rate. The current consensus regarding copycat crime is that a criminogenic influence concentrates in preexisting criminal populations.

- Terrorism's relationship to the media has resulted in copycat terrorism and media-oriented terrorism being common elements of twenty-first-century acts of terror.

- The cumulative result of the media image of criminality is a social reality in which broad-based social and structural causes of crime are disparaged and where criminogenic media effects are plausible. Criminogenic behavioral effects are most likely to appear in at-risk individuals predisposed to crime.

WRITING ASSIGNMENTS

1. Write a position paper on how much crime and violence in society would disappear if there were no crime-and-justice media. Discuss whether you feel that some types of media (films or books, for example) are more criminogenic than others or whether some content is more dangerous than other content. Conclude your paper with which public policies you would support to reduce media criminogenic influences and which policies you would be adamantly against.

2. Write a critique of the film *The Silence of the Lambs* as a construction of predatory criminality. Discuss why the predator criminal image enjoys lasting popularity.

3. Watch an entertainment film based on a real serial killer and write an essay comparing the media rendition with historical facts about the case. Some examples: Ted Bundy and the film *The Stranger Beside Me*; Charlie Starkweather and the films *Badlands* and *Murder in the Heartland*; Aileen Wuornos and the film *Monster*; Henry Lee Lucas and the film *Henry: Portrait of a Serial Killer*.

SUGGESTED READINGS

Boyle, K. 2005. *Media and Violence: Gendering the Debates*. Thousand Oaks, CA: Sage.

Fisher, J. 1997. *Killer Among Us: Public reactions to Serial Murder*. Westport, CH: Praeger.

Leitch, T. and B. Grant. 2002. *Crime Films*. Cambridge, UK: Cambridge University Press.

Nacos, B. 2007. *Mass-Mediated Terrorism*. Lanham, MD: Rowan and Littlefield.

Rafter, N. 2000. *Shots in the Mirror: Crime Films and Society*. Oxford, UK: Oxford University Press.

Rome, D. 2004. *Black Demons: The Media's Depiction of the African American Male Criminal Stereotype*. Westport, CT: Praeger.

Simpson, P. 2000. *Psycho Paths: Tracking the Serial Killer through Contemporary American Film and Fiction*. Carbondale, IL: Southern Illinois University Press.

Sumser, J. 1996. *Morality and Social Order in Television Crime Drama*. Jefferson, NC: McFarland.

Tuman, J. 2010. *Communicating Terror: The Rhetorical Dimensions of Terrorism*. Thousand Oaks, CA: Sage.

4

Crime Fighters

CHAPTER OBJECTIVES

After completing Chapter 4, you will

- Know the major divisions in the media portrait of law enforcement and crime fighting
- Understand the differences between professional and civilian crime fighters
- Recognize the media portraits of lampooned police, G-men and cops
- Appreciate the differences between media portrayed police work and real-world police work
- Appreciate the differences between the media portraits of private eyes and private citizens with the media portraits of police officers
- Understand the link between media portraits of crime fighting and public support for anticrime policies

LAW ENFORCEMENT: A HOUSE DIVIDED

After criminality, the media pays the most attention to fighting crime. In the United States, law enforcement has high visibility coupled with low public knowledge.[1] That is, the public is exposed to large amounts of crime-fighting content in news, entertainment, and infotainment, most of it terribly distorted if not plain wrong. The first problem with the media construction of law enforcement is that it is schizophrenic, persistently presenting two competing law enforcement frames of "good cop" or "bad cop." In the good cop frame, the criminal justice system, particularly the police, are part of a justice machine with dedicated professionals using the latest technology to repeatedly prove that crime does not pay. In the competing bad cop frame, the criminal justice system and its police are so inefficient and bound by regulations, politics, corruption, and incompetence that only the outsider rogue cop or citizen crime fighter can get anything positive accomplished.

The professional soldiers in the media war on crime usually occupy law enforcement positions, but lawyers, judges, wardens, and corrections officers also sometimes morph into crime fighters. These are the professional, career soldiers in the media's portrait of the war on crime, and they are often matched up with a competent criminal justice system filled with effective crime scene technicians and experts in criminalistics to help solve crimes. When the professionals of the criminal justice system are the main crime fighters in the media, civilians usually have a minor role, frequently serving solely as hapless victims. The war-on-crime professional soldiers either expertly or incompetently (depending on whether they are within a good cop or bad cop frame) wage a war against predatory violent crime. The terms *war* and *soldier* are not used here simply as colorful adjectives; across the media, crime fighting is depicted as a never-ending battle against evil doers.[2] The enemy is everywhere, the battlegrounds can be anywhere, and anyone may be caught in the crossfire at any time. The media portraits of law enforcement reflect two basic divisions of bad and good cops, professionals or citizens existing under an overarching construction of warlike combat as the most effective anticrime policy.

In addition to the good cop/bad cop schizophrenia, another split exists in the media's portrait of law enforcement. In the media, crime is fought by either criminal justice professionals or private citizens. When civilian crime fighters are portrayed as the primary crime fighters, the police and the criminal justice system are downplayed and often disparaged. The effectiveness of civilian crime fighters is enhanced when paired with an incompetent criminal justice system. When civilian crime fighters are on the scene the traditional criminal justice components and personnel—especially the police—become part of the crime problem either through corruption or ineptitude. The "citizen soldiers" in the war on crime are shown to be successful where the bureaucratic, hampered, and often not so bright, career law enforcers are not.

This media house divided subsequently projects two conflicting messages about law enforcement. The first is that the expertise to deal with crime can only be found in the criminal justice system. The need to enhance the criminal justice system and unleash the police is a core message in the media's construction of crime fighting. The second and opposite message is that the incompetence of the criminal justice system and its people requires that individuals protect their own homes and communities and solve crime themselves. In the first social construction, we are told to wait for heroes to save us; in the second we are told we had better save ourselves. What the two messages share is that the solutions will require violence.

Whether a criminal justice or a civilian hero is emphasized is not, for the most part, related to the type of crime being portrayed. Most types of crime stories are comfortable with either official or civilian heroes. Popular mystery and detective tales in which the search for clues is the key story element have employed both private investigators and police as their heroic sleuths. Similarly, crime thrillers that feature endangered victims and heroes; modernized Westerns in which heroic outsiders reluctantly clean up a town; crime, revenge, and vigilante stories in which a victim/hero is injured and retaliates; and action crime stories that feature superhero crime fighters all utilize both criminal justice employees and private citizens as heroes.[3] Within these stories both civilian and professional crime fighters can be either law-abiding role models (good cops) or less straight-and-narrow adventurers, gunfighters, loners, and sometimes criminals themselves (bad cops). The first group represents the incorruptible all–American hero narrative; the more ambiguous individualistic and self-reliant second group represents our cultural admiration of the rebel. The rebels seem to enjoy themselves more and appear to be effective more quickly (not having to wait for search warrants or worry about repercussions from using entrapment or coercion), so it is not surprising that they outnumber the law-abiding crime fighters in the media. As the largely inaccurate legends of Jesse James, Bonnie and Clyde, Wild Bill Hickok, Eliot Ness, and Al Capone exemplify, media reconstructions have habitually made folk heroes out of criminals and heroic crime fighters out of less-than-stellar individuals. By-the-book crime fighters are usually outdistanced by kick-your-butt, recently suspended, or wanted ones. Be it professionals or civilians, good cops or bad cops, it is undeniable that the media supplies a great number of law enforcement depictions. Solving crimes and apprehending criminals is an immensely popular media pastime.

MEDIA CONSTRUCTS OF PROFESSIONAL SOLDIERS IN THE WAR ON CRIME

Culturally, we have long been fascinated with the police and their work. We relish and devour media that is front-end-loaded, which concentrates on the origins of crime and crime's investigation and solution. As discussed in Chapter 3, our first crime-and-justice love is media constructions of crime and criminality. Once crimes have been committed, the people who enforce the laws and pursue the criminals are second in media and public interest. We relish the investigation, pursuit, and capture of criminals by formal agents of the law.[4] Three stereotypes of professional law enforcement are found in the media: lampooned police, G-men, and cops.[5] Like most media constructions, once created they never totally disappear and all three compete for influence today. Each contributes in its own way to the social construction of law enforcement.

Lampooned Police

Lampooned police appeared soon after the birth of the film industry and initially were introduced by the Keystone Kops and Charlie Chaplin films in the 1920s. Lampooned police is a popular media narrative that satirize law enforcement as foolish, slapstick character police officers. These depictions continue to be popular with the public, if not always with real police. Some of these early portrayals of the police so upset the International Association of the Chiefs of Police, for example, that its members passed a 1913 resolution pledging to change the depictions.[6] The Barney Fifes, Inspector Clouseaus, and vaudeville-styled *Police Academy* and *Super Trouper* films all provide escapist entertainment. Like gallows humor, they allow serious issues of police power and crime control to be discussed indirectly and in less threatening portraits. A police force that can be poked fun at is not one that is likely to be perceived as oppressive. Similarly, crime

The lampooning of police officers and formal law enforcement is found in some of the earliest silent movies. Shown are the Keystone Kops, a popular early media lampoon of the police first seen in 1912.

that can be resolved by cartoon violence is less threatening. However, when the satire is felt to reflect a reality of incompetence or when it undermines the public support of police, these images raise an outcry among law enforcement personnel.

G-Men and Police Procedurals

G-men, also historically known as "crime-busters," arose during the Depression and have periodically been invigorated by media attempts to provide more realistic content. G-men represent a media law enforcement frame that focuses on effective, professional crime-busters. Tough federal agents emerged in the 1930s media

---

B o x 4.1   The Hays Code in Hollywood

The Hays Code, adopted by major American movie studios in response to the criticisms voiced by the Hays Commission, imposed severe limitations on celluloid crime and justice:

> *General Principles*: 1. No picture shall be produced that will lower the moral standards of those who see it. Hence the sympathy of the audience should never be thrown to the side of crime, wrongdoing, evil or sin. 2. Correct standards of life, subject only to the requirements of drama and entertainment, shall be presented. 3. Law, natural or human, shall not be ridiculed, nor shall sympathy be created for its violation. . . .

> *Crimes Against the Law*. These shall never be presented in such a way as to throw sympathy with the crime as against law and justice or to inspire others with a desire for imitation. 1. Murder: a. The technique of murder must be presented in a way that will not inspire imitation. b. Brutal killings are not to be presented in detail. c. Revenge in modern times shall not be justified. 2. Methods of Crime should not be explicitly presented:

>> a. Theft, robbery, safe-cracking, and dynamiting of trains, mines, buildings, etc., should not be detailed in method. b. Arson must subject to the same safeguards. c. The use of firearms should be restricted to the essentials. d. Methods of smuggling should not be presented. 3. Illegal drug traffic must never be presented.

SOURCE: Will H. Hays, *President's Report to the Motion Picture Producers and Distributors' Association* (Washington, DC: U.S. Government Printing Office, 1932).

---

as Hollywood responded to the Payne Fund research on the film industry and its social impact.[7] The resulting Hays Commission heavily criticized the movies for glorifying criminals and encouraging copycat crime (see Box 4.1).[8] In response, the movie and radio industry shifted to G-man portrayals, in which federal law enforcement agents rather than criminals were the heroes. Stars such as James Cagney, who had previously played criminals, now found themselves cast as heroic crime fighters. These crime fighters were shown as professional, straight-laced, and, Cagney aside, usually boring. This change in the construction of law enforcers marks the media shift from the local neighborhood "officer friendly" portrait of police officers, who were well meaning but largely incompetent against serious crime, to that of professional federal crime-busters. Previously, if police officers were shown at all, more often than not they were just there, walking a beat, personable but largely irrelevant. In contrast, the new crime fighters were aggressive, smart, and proactive. Because they were clearly not local police officers, the shift to G-men crime-busters also marks the beginning of a long-term denigration of local law enforcement. The G, after all, stood for "government" and that government was the one in Washington, D.C. With the exception of local sheriffs in Westerns, local street police would not commonly be presented as capable of dealing with serious crime again until the 1970s. The tradition of professional, crime-busting portraits successfully made the transfer in the 1950s to television and continued as

WARNER BROS/THE KOBAL COLLECTION/Picture Desk

Based on the investigation of cases by two Los Angeles Police Department detectives, *Dragnet* was one of the first and most successful police proceduralstyle crime programs. Originating on radio in the late 1940s and running on television from 1952 to 1959 and again from 1967 to 1970, *Dragnet* emphasized police jargon and the technical aspects of law enforcement. Episodes began with the promise that "the story you are about to see is true; the names have been changed to protect the innocent."

the dominant crime-fighting narrative. *Dragnet* on radio and then television, and *Dick Tracy* in the comics and later films are well-known early examples.

Beginning a bit after and then paralleling the G-men portraits, the police procedural originated in the United States in the 1940s. Police procedurals attempt to portray the back-stage realities of police investigations in dramatic media portraits. They were, in essence, the first infotainment docudramas produced on working in the criminal justice system. The crime fighters in these portraits normally rely heavily on teamwork and criminalistics to solve crimes. Especially well suited to television's stereotyping, simple story lines, and preference for short-term violent events, the police procedural presents policing in infotainment-based constructions in which a continuous response to an unending series of violent criminal acts is needed. Crime and the fight against it is constructed as the reserve of professional experts (see Box 4.2). Civilians and other law enforcement personal should not get involved, and do so at their peril. Analogous to the manner in which real and fictional crimes and criminals coalesced in the 1980s to socially construct serial killers, the G-men and the police procedurals portraits and the ongoing real-world police reform movement of the first half of the twentieth century collectively constructed criminality as a threat to middle-class lifestyles while encouraging a faith in expert police knowledge as the crime solution. The combined effect of the media portraits and the police professionalism movement was the social construction of aggressive proactive policing as the best policy course to address an apparently burgeoning crime problem.[9]

Cops

The cops frame originated in the 1970s with the return of media portraits of professional, competent, local law enforcement heroes, which had disappeared from the media with the demise of the Western local sheriffs in the 1950s. In a small number of television shows, like *Dragnet*, the professional police hero was kept alive until the 1970s when the cop narrative emerged. With the release of the film *Dirty Harry* in 1971, the premiere of the television show *Police Story* in 1973, and the publication of the novel *The New Centurions* in 1970, local street police as heroes was once again in vogue. The new cops construction portrayed the local police as aggressive, crime-fighting, take-no-prisoners, frontline soldiers in the war on crime. Far from irrelevant, they were now the combat grunts who fought the crime war battles. Community policing, public service, traffic, and order maintenance duties were nowhere to be found in this new construction of the local police. Police became paramilitary units, citizens became civilians and collateral damage, and crime fighting became urban warfare. Local "cops" emerge in this construction as professional, gristled soldiers engaged in preemptive law-and-order battles—combat-hardened street soldiers in an unpopular war. Within the cop construction, criminality was simultaneously portrayed as the result of evil and weak individuals making bad choices. The criminals were clearly enemies, not citizens who had broken a law, and they had to be defeated as opposed to being deterred or rehabilitated.

Within this constructed world of domestic combat, special socialization by a veteran crime fighter was needed to change the naive civilian police recruit into the professional frontline crime-fighting soldier.[10] Police, like the combat veteran, have to be initiated into the police culture and instilled with the special knowledge and skills needed to survive in combat and deal with rampant criminality. Gaining this special knowledge frequently involved a violent unlearning of prior social conceptions picked up in the civilian world and the police academy. To survive, cops adopted the antibureaucracy attitude of the World War II–era private eye. Middle-class status, liberal attitudes, those college criminology

The character Dirty Harry marks the return of effective and aggressive local police to the media portrait of law enforcement in the 1970s.

and criminal justice courses, official police department procedures—all must be forgotten. As Dirty Harry says to his new Mexican American partner, "Don't go letting that sociology degree get you killed."[11]

Highly popular, several different cop narratives are found today.[12] One of the most popular is the "rogues," officers who go off on their own in their pursuit of criminals and justice. Throwing off the restraints of agency approval, due process, and legal procedures, they display single-mindedness in a less than legal but usually moral crusade. Also common are the "corrupt cop" narratives, which have the officers taking the extra step and actually joining the dark-side forces of crime and evil. At the other extreme are "honest cop" narratives, which trace the hardships of cops trying to do the right thing in a corrupt police culture. "Buddy cop" stories work off the conflicts and complications from opposite personalities forced to work together; mismatched racial partners are a standard. A relative to lampooned police "comedy" and "action comedy" cop narratives toss reality to the winds. Comedy portrayals incorporate harmless slapstick violence in which bullets and punches fly but no one gets seriously hurt. Action comedies liberally add in explosions and spectacular stunts in which only the bad guys are seriously injured. Two recent additions to this family are "female cop" stories and "aging cop" stories. Female cop narratives have the positive, if yet unfulfilled, potential to lift women from their stereotypical crime-and-justice portraits as pseudomasculine or hyperfeminine creatures to equal crime-fighting heroes.[13] Aging cop stories are a market response to the aging of the baby boom generation and the need to provide heroes they can identify with. In these stories, a weathered but still virile (mentally, physically, and sexually) police officer manages to be successful on all fronts. Except for the woman cop story lines, hypermasculinity is the common thread throughout the cop narratives. These portraits collectively reduce the crime issue to a contest between individuals. Not only is a social solution not needed, in the cop narratives crime is no longer even an agency problem. To solve crime, you don't need a criminal justice system, or even a police department. You don't even need a few good men, just one good cop will do.

On the journalism print side, the combat cop was accompanied and enhanced with the marketing of true crime books, many written by newspaper crime reporters. These reporter memoirs are traditionally initiation narratives about a reporter's introduction into the cop world.[14] Similar to the necessity for police recruits to discard misleading knowledge acquired in the police academy and college to become effective combat cops, in these true crime narratives journalists have to be socialized into the ways of the street police. In the process they have to leave behind their journalistic sensibilities and social values and learn that fighting the modern predatory criminal is a different world.

In these true crime books the crime is usually homicide, and the reader looks over the cops' shoulders as they pursue criminals and clean up after violent messy events. (Of course, the other popular view in the true crime tradition looks over the shoulders of criminals while they violently create messy events. Not surprisingly, an interest in crime fighters is only exceeded by fascination with predator criminals. Tales of serial killer narratives dominate the true crime genre.) The cop-oriented true crime memoirs contribute to the comforting illusion of police expertise, and that crime, while pervasive, is effectively being handled by dogged, heroic police work.[15]

Turning to the news portrait of professional crime fighters: despite great interest in law enforcement, the news media rarely focus on individual crime fighters except in police brutality cases.[16] Instead, they prefer to focus on crimes and criminals. In the news, law enforcement is normally referred to as generic agencies rather than individual police officers. When individuals are interviewed, they are most often administrators or media-relations specialists. Therefore, most individual crime-fighter portraits come not from traditional news but from either pure entertainment content or infotainment products. Infotainment programming fills in whatever gap exists between the entertainment and news portraits in the public's construction of the modern professional crime fighter. Reality police shows, a subset of infotainment programming, are of special interest because these shows are promoted as delivering a slice of unaltered crime fighting and, unlike the news, focus heavily on individual crime fighters.

Police as Infotainment: "Who you gonna call?"

First appearing in 1989, police reality programs have become a regular part of the crime-and-justice media, with the theme song of one show, COPS, becoming a pop music hit.[17] In these productions, viewers are invited to share a real street cop's point of view as a partner officer. Not surprisingly, the demographic that most future police officers will be recruited from—young, white males—are their largest audience component. The attraction of these shows is clearly voyeuristic, with content running the gamut from dealing with ordinary street crime to the unusual violent predation. The cooperating police departments also have editorial input into the end product and routinely eliminate any scenes of police violence, malfeasance, or ineptitude. In her study of these shows, Pamela Donovan found that the final construction invariably shows the police as sensitive, knowledgeable, and competent, never careless, corrupt, foul-mouthed, or overwhelmed.[18] In a companion study, Aaron Doyle points out the highly selective picture of criminal justice found in these programs, which overrepresents both violent crime and the proportion of crime solved by police.[19] One police infotainment show, *COPS*, was found to grossly overrepresent violent crime. Violent crime such as murder, rape, aggravated assault, and robbery made up 84 percent of all the crimes shown in one season studied.[20] Reflecting the operation of the backwards law—the media presents the opposite of crime-and-justice reality and the distribution of violent and property crimes on these shows are consistently opposite their real-world proportions.

Crime selection aside, how realistically do these reality shows portray police work? In the view of Paul Kooistra and his colleagues, "Crime [fighting] on these shows is a caricature that is shaped more by the organizational demands of television than by carefully documented representations of reality."[21] Unlike the traditional news, where you can see the commentators and reporters and where editing decisions are more apparent, reality programming works from a different process in its format, style, and texture. In these shows, there are no production clues, narrators, actors, scripts, or hosts to suggest editing or formatting. The infotainment audience does not easily realize and are not given hints that they are receiving a heavily reconstructed piece of reality. As shown in Figure 4.1, because the content is presented as if unaltered, the constructed reality found in reality programming is

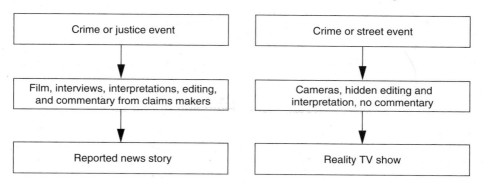

Crime News

With crime news it is clear that you are getting a condensed event, usually described and explained to you by someone clearly in a position of authority.

Infotainment Police Reality Programming

With reality programming the molding of content is hidden and difficult to discern. A live documentary feel is given to the portrait of police work, and you are encouraged to believe you are seeing unedited raw video footage.

| Crime or justice event | Crime or street event |

| Film, interviews, interpretations, editing, and commentary from claims makers | Cameras, hidden editing and interpretation, no commentary |

| Reported news story | Reality TV show |

FIGURE 4.1 Crime News Compared with Police Reality Programming

more misleading than the constructed reality portrayed in the news where the editing and production decisions are clearly visible.

For reality shows, production techniques are borrowed from entertainment shows. These programs are formatted to unobtrusively fill in missing facts and scenes to hide the editing and molding of their content. Time gaps are smoothed over, and holes in knowledge or action are filled. It is through their production techniques that these shows can grossly misrepresent police work and still manage to come across as reality programming. As criminologist Gray Cavender points out, realism is achieved in these efforts by mimicking the early entertainment "police procedural" films of the 1940s and 1950s and applying an entertainment style of "gritty realism."[22] Employing low-cost production values establishes an atmosphere of "being there" for the viewer. Ironically, producing reality programs cheaply results in increasing their believability.

The demographics on these shows constructs crime so that nonwhites account for more than half of all suspects shown, about two-thirds of the police are white, and more than half of the victims shown are white. These shows construct a reality in which the most typical police crime-fighting events are white police battling nonwhite criminals while protecting white victims. In addition, almost 75 percent of the crimes portrayed in these infotainment shows are cleared by arrest, compared with the 18 percent clearance rate for property crime and 44 percent clearance rate for violent crime reported in the Uniform Crime Report statistics. Because of these factors, reality police programs most closely resemble pure entertainment media portrayals of crime fighting. As found in other media, the media crime-and-justice backwards law is equally applicable to police reality shows.

The backwards law results in these infotainment shows promoting two claims about crime fighting.[23] The carefully chosen and edited footage encourages the claims that:

> The police are in a contest with criminals who are unlike law-abiding citizens. Reality police shows further encourage the construction of criminals as predatory deviant others, people who are unlike the rest of us.
>
> The police invariably get it right. The people they stop really are criminals. Viewers never get to see the police battering down doors to the wrong apartment or arresting the wrong person. Legal rules invariably hamper the police needlessly and get in the way of effective law enforcement. There appears to be no reason to place legal checks on how the police do their job, and constitutional safeguards make no sense.

In the end, crime control is applauded, due process is disparaged. Individual causes of crime, assumed guilt of suspects, and an "us versus them" portrait dominates these constructions. The police emerge as our best defense, but they need help—in this constructed world, the audience and the police must work together to fight crime. Analogous to videogames, viewers are prodded to become interactive—to be on the lookout, call in tips, and help catch fugitives—to, in effect, enlist in the war-on-crime.

What is the effect of these shows? Aaron Doyle reports that most viewers see the shows as realistic and think of them as informational rather than entertainment, as more similar to local news than to fictional storytelling.[24] Society is seen to be in decline and in a constant state of crisis because of spiraling crime, particularly violent street crimes committed by lower-class offenders, and aggressive law enforcement is shown as the last hope. Another concern with the portrait of police work found in police reality programming comes from its effect on real police. Doyle reports that, like courtroom cameras influencing trial attorneys, there is anecdotal evidence of police tailoring their behavior for the cameras, behaving not as they actually do but as they believe the audience expects them to. Shows like *COPS* appear as a fantasy come true for police officers raised on the media's fictional police heroics found in entertainment crime dramas.[25] Here is the law enforcement career as they were led to believe it would be, full of crime-busting excitement. Finally, the solution proffered in police infotainment programming is drawn from the faulty system frame: crime is out of control because the criminal justice system is misaligned. Society needs tougher crime control: due process and civil rights are part of the problem, and more unfettered police are needed. The real world must be altered to better match the media-constructed one. Recent media portrayals of forensic science and its capabilities is another area that has been credited with constructing unrealistic expectations in the real world.

Dusting for Saliva: The CSI Effect, Forensic Science, and Juror Expectations

The most recent iteration and a revival of the police procedural is found in the current spate of forensic science based shows led by *CSI* and its spin-offs. The new law enforcement crime fighting hero is a crime scene investigator. These shows are having an unexpected real-world impact where the public thinks every crime can be solved if the proper scientific method is used.

As related in Box 4.2, the difference between crime scene investigations and their media portrait is large. These front-end-loaded "howdunnit" rather than "whodunit" shows depict police agencies with limitless resources, small caseloads, unrealistic scientific testing procedures, impossible forensic test time frames, and inaccurate depictions of what crime scene investigators actually do.[26] They present a prosecutorial view of investigation and give the impression that trials are mere formalities.[27] Based largely on surveys of criminal justice professionals,[28] a CSI effect has been credited with influencing juror expectations and assessment of evidence. Specifically, it is felt that lack of forensic evidence is interpreted by jurors to indicate sloppy police work and cause jurors to discount eyewitness testimony. Police, prosecutors, and judges have reported that they have had to explain the lack of irrelevant forensic evidence or employ unnecessary expert witnesses to accommodate juror media-driven expectations. As a group, they feel compelled to explain the differences between *CSI* shows and trial uses of forensic evidence, in gist, holding trial evidence to television

Box 4.2   The CSI Effect

Robert Voets/CBS Photo Archive/Getty Images

The scene, on TV, is of a dead kid in a high school bathroom. This, in itself, is not funny. What cracks up the senior forensic criminalist at the State Police Crime Laboratory is watching the forensic crew work a case on CBS's drama *CSI: Crime Scene Investigations.*

[Real] crime scene investigators don't tackle murder suspects or pack heat. They don't storm into the lab demanding DNA reports. They don't prance around in leather pants and a halter top. It can take days to fingerprint a scene, months to process a single DNA sample. Most of that used to be inside crime scene stuff—shoptalk for cops and forensic scientists. Then *CSI* and a handful of bloodstained copycats took over prime time.

Real-life investigators are watching this gross new world and bracing for each boob-tube breakthrough. They call it the "CSI effect," a phenomenon in which actual investigations are driven by the expectations of the millions of people who watch fake whodunits on TV. It has contributed to jurors' desires to see more forensic testimony from the stand. Academic programs are springing up to accommodate people who now want to be forensic scientists. And it has spurred a phenomenon that defense lawyers call "junk science," in which high-paid, underqualified consultants are hired to lend a little razzle-dazzle to a case because in prime time we've learned that virtually anything left behind can solve a crime: sofa cushions, a dead insect, lint.

Jurors watch TV shows in which investigators walk onto scenes soaked with forensic evidence. Then they want to know why there's no DNA on the suspect's shirt collar or blood on his hands. Why aren't the hairs at the scene a match for those found inside the accused's cap? Even in the face of eyewitness testimony, juries are starting to say, "If all the possible forensic tests weren't done in a case, maybe somebody else committed the crime."

standards.[29] Anecdotal CSI effects have also been reported for offenders so that car thieves dump ashtrays in stolen cars in hopes of generating a pool of alternative suspects and rapists use condoms and force victims to shower to avoid leaving DNA evidence.[30] At the opposite extreme, there is a concern with these shows reifying forensic evidence when it is presented in a trial to a level where its validity and accuracy is unquestioned by jurors.[31] A dual CSI effect has been hypothesized. If no forensic evidence is presented, an increase in acquittals has been posited. If forensic evidence is available, convictions are expected to increase.

Not all credit these shows with a substantively important CSI effect however.[32] In one study that surveyed jurors, there is evidence of nearly half of them expected scientific evidence in every criminal case. However, in the same study when an effect on verdicts was explored the expectation of forensic evidence did not translate into more acquittals when it was absent, and, significantly, viewers of the *CSI* shows were more likely to convict without scientific evidence than nonviewers except for rape cases.[33] At this time, while many in the criminal justice field believe that a CSI effect operates, there is no empirical study that has shown a CSI effect on jury decisions. In that a number of studies conducted prior to the *CSI* shows established the compelling power that scientific evidence has on juror verdicts,[34] there may be a CSI effect on attorneys and judges who report that they prepare and conduct their cases differently because of anticipated juror expectations. The CSI effects that have been established are the belief by criminal justice professionals that these shows influence jurors and a renewed popularity and interest in the field of criminal forensics.[35]

Police and the Media

In the 1990s, there was a transition to community policing in the real police world and a media fixation on criminal profiling in the media–constructed one. In the resulting mix, the media did not simply lionize police professionalism or technical expertise. Criticisms of the police abound in the media, but as the media drifted into infotainment content, media dependence on police cooperation increased. The police are sought, quoted, and catered to on one hand, marginalized and criticized on the other. In Table 4.1, the basic differences between media cops and real–world street officers are summarized. From an "endless budget" to their actions, media cops hardly compare to their real–world counterparts. And when the real police do not act like their media portraits, the unrealistic public expectations generate real–world public dissatisfaction with law enforcement.[36]

Factual and fictional cop narratives remain popular and, as shown by the development of women and aging cop portraits, are flexible enough to evolve and to respond to changing politics, demographics, and market needs.[37] In addition to female lead crime fighters, the emergence and acceptance of minority actors as lead heroic cops is another healthy trend. The media–constructed world of professional crime-fighting soldiers is secure. Ironically, this world is largely constructed in the entertainment and infotainment segments of the media. The traditional news media do not normally focus on crime fighters except when they suffer a personal fall from grace or are killed. That is, individual crime fighters become newsworthy when they become criminals or victims. This lack of traditional news media attention is also true for their counterparts, the citizen soldiers in the war on crime.

TABLE 4.1   Differences between Media Cops and Real Cops

	Media Cops	Real Cops
Action	Never a dull moment. They are doing something, about to do something, or planning to do something.	Tedium and adrenaline are both experienced. Filling out forms is the norm. Action is unexpected, not predictable.
Crime	Fighting serious crime is foremost. Felonies are most common. Each crime is unique and exceptional. Cops are attuned to these nuances and pay attention.	Felony arrests are rare; officers often spend time preventing crime and defusing social situations. The repetitive scripts of excuses and explanations for breaking the law rapidly dull their impact and the believability of suspects.
Violence	Cops are violent. They menace, fight, and shoot and kill with relative impunity. Physical force, even brutality, is part of their tool kit for solving crimes.	Officers also live in a mean world, but usually one of potential rather than actual violence.
Heroes and villains	Clearly defined good and evil with any ambiguities resolved by program's end.	The good and the bad is mostly gray. Good people do bad things; bad people sometimes perform good acts. Most people have elements of both.
Status	Patrolmen are often dumb background foil; plainsclothes detectives are the brilliant problem solvers.	Officers are gatekeepers of the criminal justice system who make the crucial early decisions.
Insight	With an almost psychic awareness of what people are thinking and where the clues are, they uncover the truth. Omniscient qualities allow them to defy procedures and still triumph.	Officers are given almost no advance data for encounters and are under great pressure to obey procedures and policy.
Closure	There are almost no unsolved cases on at the end of the story.	Events have a middle, but no beginning and no end. Cops arrive when incidents are in progress and rarely see the resolution of cases they confront.
Justicee	Cops rarely deal with law, which is often seen as an obstacle to justice and as legal technicalities used by shyster lawyers. The hero cop directly dispenses justice, makes things right, and avenges wrongs.	Real cops must obey the law. Because of the complexity of the law and the emphasis on due process rights, its glacial pace leaves cops enforcing rules they do not think work.
Back stage	Sanitized back stage. No matter how crude, the hero cop rarely alienates an audience.	Sex, lies, and stupidity are common themes. Cops often make fun of, complain about, or criticize many of the people they encounter, both victims and suspects.

T A B L E 4.1 Differences between Media Cops and Real Cops (Continued)

	Media Cops	Real Cops
Budget and Resources	Uncapped endless budgets with forensics, equipment, and reinforcements readily available.	Hard limitations on the amount of evidence gathering and testing, investigation time, and departmental resources that can be devoted to a case.
Chronology	Time compression. Events are edited to render swifter progress of the narrative and rapid resolution.	The forever war with long periods of stasis. Cops understand how long it can take the system to resolve an issue.
Audience and public awareness	Godlike powers of observation by audience who see clues, verhear conversations, perceive revealing facial close-ups, and receive voiceovers with insider information kept from the cops. The audience ends up knowing more than the cops.	Uniformed police are first on the scene. They see what no one in the public sees except for perpetrators and victims, misery and blood at close quarters.

Source: Adapted from David Perlmutter, *Policing the Media* (Belmont, CA: Sage, 2000), 41–52.

MEDIA CONSTRUCTS OF CITIZEN SOLDIERS IN THE WAR ON CRIME

The second major brigade of media crime solvers comes not from the official world of criminal justice and government agencies but from the ranks of citizens. When portrayed, these "citizen soldiers" in the war on crime often save the day for bungling police officers. Other times they battle the corrupt forces of government and official law enforcement.

Private Investigators

One division of these civilian crime fighters occupies the boundary between civilians and police officers. They are the independent contractors of law enforcement, the private investigators or PIs. Private investigators were popularized in film noir movies in the 1940s. Historically male, sexual, debonair, hard-boiled, and smart, the PI lives on the borderline between criminality and the law-abiding, solving crimes with inside knowledge combined with the freedom to act outside the restraints of agency policies and due process rules. In addition to these semiprofessional private eyes, another group of personally motivated private citizens take on solving crimes as a hobby or due to some personal connection with a crime victim.

Private Citizens

Predating the private eyes, private citizens have been successful media crime fighters for at least 600 years, as can be seen in the tales of Robin Hood and other citizen heroes. Although usually adult white males, citizen crime fighters in the media include a diverse group: elderly female novelists (Angela Lansbury in *Murder She Wrote*), teenagers (the *Bobbsey Twins* and *Hardy Boys*), and even children (*Tom Sawyer*) and cartoon dogs (*Scooby-Doo*).

The citizen crime fighter can be found in a number of entertainment narratives that share the characteristic of being outside of and sometimes in conflict with the traditional criminal justice system. Rooted in the Western, "heroic" outsiders who save the day remain a popular crime-fighting narrative. Unfettered by official red tape and due process considerations, the heroic outsider can cut to the heart of the crime problem and quickly and usually violently deal with it. Riding or driving off into the sunset, as it were, after his work is done. Avengers and vigilantes are related to the victim crime-fighter narrative. In these portrayals, the citizen crime fighter has a personal interest or has been personally wronged by a criminal. At the extreme are tales where the citizen hero has been unjustly criminalized by the official criminal justice system. These criminal Robin Hood heroes are among the oldest Western citizen crime-fighter narratives available. A more recent citizen crime-fighter narrative is the superhero, which originated in Depression-era comic books and today is found in action films. Still cartoonlike and clearly functioning as an escape from reality for their audiences, these crime fighters are the most "outside" of the outsiders. Mutants, aliens, ninjas, or just "regular" people who apparently are impossible to kill or defeat, these superheroes overcome massive odds to prevail and, as Superman states, defend "truth, justice, and the American way."

The success that private citizens and private investigators have enjoyed when solving crime in the media has been impressive. For example, media researchers Robert and Linda Lichter found that private citizens and private investigators solved many of the crimes shown in prime time television programming.[38] Crime fighters of every other type failed to capture the criminal more often than they succeeded. Cops, being rule bound, cannot possibly be as effective as private investigators. By contrast, private eyes and private citizens proved almost incapable of failure. This tradition of citizen success coupled to official police failure has deep roots. Penned in the 1840s by Edgar Allan Poe, the very first detective stories had the French police fumble and fail while citizen-hero, outsider American detective Dupin, solved the crimes.[39]

Combined with the media's proclivity to show professional crime fighters as loners and mavericks, as not fitting comfortably into their agencies, the cumulative media message clearly is that it is outsiders who save the day and that ordinary law enforcers are unequal to the task of fighting crime. Collectively, the citizen soldier crime fighters further reveal the media tendency to present crime not as a social problem but as an individual contest. In these portraits private citizens supplant the entire criminal justice system. Crime fighting becomes a private issue of good versus evil between autonomous individuals. The larger society, and particularly its formal institutions, is little involved if not a direct obstacle to successful crime fighting. The message is that if you have a crime problem the regular police are unlikely to be helpful, and you had best deal with it on your own.

PROFESSIONAL VERSUS CITIZEN
CRIME FIGHTERS

The basic distinction between media crime fighters is whether the crime fighter is a member of the established criminal justice system or a citizen. If one combines the citizen crime fighter with the rogue, special-unit, maverick law enforcers, criminal justice system outsiders and marginalized employees are far more common and more successful in the media-constructed world of crime fighting than traditional mainstream criminal justice system personnel. Successful crime fighters are usually portrayed as antisocial, unattached loners even when they are members of an established law enforcement agency—the icon of Clint Eastwood's *Dirty Harry* is a prime example. The media super-cop is accordingly usually not a regular cop at all but someone from outside the system or a maverick officer within it. Whether an outsider or not, the successful crime fighter is usually a heroic white man of action. Media crime fighters are portrayed as very effective in solving crimes and apprehending criminals but not at all effective in preventing crime. They are better agents of punishment than deterrence. The basic crime-fighting narrative is that early crimes are successful and that a criminal enterprise has been ongoing for years. Only later, after the hero has arrived on the scene, are crimes unsuccessful. Similar to the manner in which crime is covered in the news, media crime fighters are reactive and incident driven rather than proactive and community problem oriented.

The main message these crime-fighter constructions convey about crime is that crime is not a social problem to be solved at the community level. Instead it is an invading social evil that must be confronted and destroyed. The social construction of law enforcement repeatedly points out that a crime "war" is being waged, and society needs crime *fighters*, not peace officers or God-help-us, legal due process protections, social services, or community-based rehabilitation programs—all of which come across as blatantly naive and wrong-headed. Because of crime's insidious nature, the traditional criminal justice system's due process constraints and rehabilitation mandates make it unable to cope with crime. The system needs the assistance of either a rebellious law enforcement insider who is willing to ignore or bend the law or an unencumbered civilian outsider. Justice, which in the media means law enforcement, is achieved by individual stars, not by the criminal justice system. Effective conformist law enforcement officers are rare, and when they are portrayed, they normally have to resort to innovative special tactics, weapons, technology, and support units to successfully deal with crime. More frequently, the crime fighter is portrayed battling serial killers and terrorism in military-like actions (see Box 4.3). The media world of crime and terrorism is not a world for standard operating procedures and community-oriented police officers, or for the unarmed, the hesitant, or the faint-hearted. The media message concerning crime fighting is one of "legitimized corruption"; solving crimes and preventing terrorism requires breaking the rules.[40]

Also significant in media portrayals of law enforcement is the use of violence. Violence has been an element in the depiction of crime and justice

---

B o x 4.3   Crime Fighting and Terrorism

Terrorists as criminals have long been a popular entertainment media story line. Compared with the typical media serial killer who kills victims one at a time for a comparatively low body count, terrorists are particularly evil and dangerous predators who seek to kill thousands in mass murder events. They are especially good foils for the modern media crime fighter. They also allow crime fighting to be expanded to a global conflict that involves secret undercover operatives like Jack Bauer and specialized military units. Special villains seeking world domination justify special tactics such as torture unfettered by due process and operations that cross international boundaries and legal systems.

---

throughout media history, but in the twentieth century the entertainment media came to portray both crime fighters and criminals as more violent and aggressive and to show this violence more graphically. Since the 1960s, a distinct style known as ultra-violence—which entails slow-motion injuries, detonating blood capsules, and multiple camera views—has become common entertainment media content. Indeed, so brutal have media crime fighters become over the course of the last century that they now have more similarities to older gangster portraits than to older crime-fighting heroes. In today's media, the distinction between the crime fighter and the criminal has all but disappeared in regard to who initiates violence and how much force is used.

Finally, the increasing emphasis on graphic violence has resulted in a kind of media weapons cult. Over the years, weapons have become increasingly more technical and sophisticated but less realistic. More important, guns are shown as useful problem solvers and necessary crime-fighting tools in modern America. In the media, the people who get their way, both heroes and villains, are the ones who have the guns. Furthermore, weapons—especially handguns—tend to be portrayed as either ridiculously benign, so that misses are common and wounds minor and painless when the crime fighter is the target, or ridiculously deadly, so that shots from handguns accurately hit moving, distant people, killing them quickly and without extensive suffering when the crime fighter is shooting. People in crime-and-justice media who use guns seldom suffer psychological, social, or legal repercussions. A street gun battle is played out and everyone is back at work the next day. Adding to the unreality, when a gunshot victim is described, rarely is the victim's pain or that of the victim's family or friends shown.[41] In general, the media play up the violence and play down the pain and suffering associated with criminal violence and gunplay.

In conclusion, the construction of law enforcement as a criminal justice endeavor dominates over the courts and corrections and is portrayed as a glamorous, action-filled process of detection and pursuit that glorifies violence. Dealing with crime is a battle of good versus evil. Historically this battle was invariably won by the good guys, but today an increasing number of evil criminals escape; corrupt, brutal police officers are more common; and crime control goals are heavily advanced over due process protections.[42] Civil liberties are ignored and degraded as mushy-headed hindrances that result in a less safe, more violent society. Professional crime fighters compete with citizen crime fighters for attention and effectiveness, but in both groups individual loners tend to be the most successful. Translated to the real world, the need for special undercover police units, vigilantes, and individual armed protection is implied. In the end, the media's social construction of crime fighting shows crime not as a social problem at all but as an individual concern to be solved by force and technology by either a core of beleaguered frontline cops, special tactic federal officers, or individual well-armed civilians.

CHAPTER SUMMARY

- The portrait of crime fighting in the media is split between crime fighters employed by the criminal justice system—police officers and investigators and government agents—and those outside of the system—private investigators and private citizens.

- Dealing with crime is shown as a battle that must be violently fought.

- Criminal justice–employed crime fighters are portrayed as satirized lampooned officers, professional federal agents, or hardened street cops. Rogue police officers willing to break the rules are the most effective. From these portraits, the public draws unrealistic expectations about the capabilities of the police and their activities.

- Private citizens and private investigators are often shown as better at dealing with crime than the police.

- Crime control trumps due process in the media crime fighter world. Due process protections and departmental policies are portrayed as hindrances to effectively dealing with crime.

▪   Crimes in the media are solved by aggressive investigations backed by science and technology. Crime is not presented as a social problem tied to other social problems.

WRITING ASSIGNMENTS

1.   Watch five episodes of a crime show and summarize the portrait of crime fighters shown.
2.   If available, participate in a ride-along with a local police department and compare the experience with your prior media impressions of policing.
3.   Write an essay describing the connection between the portrayal of guns, violence, and victims in the media and the crime-fighting policies that are implied in these portrayals. Include a discussion of the media usually portraying crime fighting as an individual battle between a predatory criminal and a heroic crime fighter rather than as a social problem, and state what criminal justice policies are encouraged and discouraged by this portrait.
4.   Write an essay about possible reasons that civilians are portrayed so often as successful crime fighters and the traditional police are portrayed as unsuccessful in the entertainment media.
5.   Come up with additional differences between media police and real police beyond the ones mentioned by David Perlmutter, or differences between real and media crime scene technicians as described in Box 4.2. Apply the same exercise to other criminal justice positions.
6.   Watch an episode of the show *COPS* and write a paper discussing the use of editing and formatting in the portrayal of police, offenders, and victims.

SUGGESTED READINGS

Doyle, A. 2003. *Arresting Images: Crime and Policing in Front of the Television Camera.* Toronto: University of Toronto Press.

Fishman, M. and G. Cavender, eds. 1998. *Entertaining Crime: Television Reality Programs.* New York: Aldine de Gruyter.

Lawrence, R. 2000. *The Politics of Force: Media and the Construction of Police Brutality.* Berkeley, CA: University of California Press.

Leishman, F. and P. Mason. 2003. *Policing and the Media.* Devon, UK: Willan.

Permutter, D. 2000. *Policing the Media.* Thousand Oaks, CA: Sage.

Wilson, C. 2000. *Cop Knowledge.* Chicago, IL: University of Chicago Press.

5

The Courts

CHAPTER OBJECTIVES

After reading Chapter 5, you will

- Recognize the media portraits of the judicial system, judges, and attorneys
- Comprehend the concept of media trials
- Appreciate the love-hate relationship between television and the courts
- Know the judicial mechanisms available to deal with publicity
- Understand the issues associated with media strategies to maximize access to judicial proceedings and minimize government access to media-held information

MEDIA, INFOTAINMENT, AND THE COURTS

"Law in our time has entered the age of images, legal reality can no longer be properly understood, or assessed, apart from what appears on a screen."[1] For many in today's world, mass media images are their primary source of knowledge about law, lawyers, and the legal system. In addition to being an important source of knowledge about the judicial system, judicial images found in the media are significant in another way. Courtrooms are a society's formal social construction arena where the significance and meaning of a wide range of social behaviors are determined—for example, the courts have recently defined, or at least attempted to define, what is or is not insane behavior, proper or improper childcare, and intrusive or acceptable government law enforcement policies. Judicial proceedings function, therefore, not only as mechanisms for resolving individual disputes but also as mechanisms for legitimizing the broader society's laws, policies, government agencies, and social structure. Accordingly, anything that influences the public image of the courts invariably influences the courts' ability to be a legitimizing mechanism and to fulfill their function as definers of acceptable social boundaries.

If the media's renditions of court proceedings influence how the public sees the courts, in turn, the public's perception of the courts results in expectations of how judicial proceedings should look and play out. Media-induced public expectations cycle back to affect the real courts. How the judicial system conducts procedures, how attorneys and judges try cases, and how participants behave in courtrooms are all influenced. The mass media portrait of the judicial system constructs a reality that the public comes to expect and the courts subsequently strive to fulfill. The judicial portrait found in the media is examined in three realms: the entertainment media's construction of the courtroom; the development of infotainment style media trials; and the concerns associated with pretrial publicity, government access to media-held information, and media access to government-held information. The end result of the collective media portrait of the courts is the modern construction of the judicial system as a source of high drama and infotainment.

COURTS, ATTORNEYS, AND EVIDENCE

Directly and indirectly, the media paint a distorted image of the courts. When portrayed indirectly as in the law enforcement–focused media, the courts are often alluded to as soft on crime, easy on criminals, and due process–laden institutions that repeatedly release the obviously guilty and dangerous.[2] In law enforcement portraits of crime fighting, most of the criminals being fought are recidivists, which implies that criminals go through the court system and return to the streets undeterred and unrehabilitated. The message is clear: the legal system is an obstacle and a frustration to investigators trying to protect the law-abiding and searching for the truth.[3] When shown directly, court officers are often more engaged in fighting crime than in practicing law.[4] When shown practicing law, they are usually immersed in high-stakes dramatic trials. In accordance with the media's myopic concentration on the rare event in reality such as murder, media-rendered court procedures emphasize the rare-in-reality adversarial criminal trial as the most common judicial proceeding.[5] Less often are preliminary procedures or informal plea bargaining shown, and post-trial steps are even less common. In contrast to real court systems, in the media, most defendants go to trial. The courts and the law are constructed in the media as complicated, arcane contests practiced by expert professionals and beyond the understanding of everyday citizens. The confrontations, oratory, and deliberations in the media courtroom are in stark opposition to the criminal justice system's daily reality of plea bargains, compromises, and assembly-line justice. None of the media judicial images you are likely to see represent the reality of the judicial system.

As with most components of the criminal justice system, the dominant popular image of courtrooms was initially constructed within Hollywood films.[6] The construction of the judicial system found in the cinema differs in basic ways from the typical constructions of crime and law enforcement found in the media. For one, courtroom films more often locate the obstacles to justice in society and the legal system rather than within individual offenders. And because they also frequently show the impediments to justice being overcome, trial films do not require an incorrigible criminal who must be destroyed. Courtroom films, however, do reflect the operation of the backwards law; that is, they present the opposite of crime-and-justice reality. Films feature the ever-popular crime narratives of murder, abuse of power, and sex, not the more mundane matters of property and contracts generally before the courts.

Although movies loosely based on actual events are still popular, recent courtroom portraits have evolved from the fictional and highly unrealistic media courtroom stories where attorneys investigate and solve crimes by eliciting confessions during cross-examination to showing more nontrial, backstage aspects of practicing law. This trend can be traced to Hollywood's need since the 1960s to appeal to audiences that have been raised on television. Television programmers, in turn, have applied a soap opera format to TV courtroom dramas. Scriptwriters and television programmers attempted to add more realism to their shows by revealing more of the backstage behavior and private lives of their crime-fighting lawyers.[7]

The next step for television was to develop courtroom docudramas in which real cases are turned into infotainment, reenacted, and adjudicated in realistic-looking courtroom scenes. Lastly, spurred by the immense popularity and profits of the first O. J. Simpson trial in the 1990s, the infotainment format has been incorporated into a number of contemporary court-based media productions.

Currently, the social construction of the courts is rendered through a triumvirate of trial and law films, infotainment-style pseudo judicial programs, and heavily publicized media co-opted live cases. All of these media judicial portraits emphasize rare events (trials), uncommon charges (homicide), improbable evidence (criminalistics and CSI laboratory results), and unlikely interactions (dramatic adversarial confrontations) to collectively present a heavily skewed unrealistic picture of the courts and the rendering of law. How are the attorneys, the practitioners of law, portrayed in these renditions?

Crime-Fighting Attorneys

Although criminal law is only one area of law and in the real world most attorneys practice other specialties, most lawyers in the media are criminal lawyers and specialize in criminal law.[8] Based on the most prominent media images of courtrooms, most law school graduates apparently wanted to attend the police academy. In the media, the protectors of due process are also frequently advocates of crime control. Thus, although shown less frequently than police officers in the entertainment media, attorneys and judges, when they star, are like their law enforcement counterparts, often expending as much effort solving crimes and pursuing criminals as they do interpreting and practicing law.[9]

The crime-fighting lawyer has not always been the dominant image. In earlier generally uncritical portraits of the judicial system such as the film classic *To Kill a Mockingbird*, lawyers were constructed as homespun, simple yet crafty all–American jurists.[10] In contrast, in the contemporary period legal skill and justice are less important and have been replaced by attorneys hunting down predator psychopaths or involved in sundry action scenes. Trial scenes are now more likely to be episodes imbedded within a thriller, and heroic lawyers are as likely to appear in fight and chase scenes as in court proceedings.[11]

When they are not also crime fighters, attorneys can expect to be portrayed negatively. For example, Robert and Linda Lichter found that in prime time television programming attorneys are more likely than police officers to be shown as greedy and nearly as likely to be shown as corrupt. In sum, in another backwards portrait, attorneys in the media are not shown spending much of their time practicing law, and when they do practice law, it is overwhelmingly criminal law. A group that has particularly suffered in its media constructions are female attorneys.

Female Attorneys

Similar to the portrayals of policewomen, female attorneys—while enjoying a longer tradition in the media—are frequently defeminized as career women or projected as creatures dominated by sexual conflicts or repression. The media construction of the female lawyer frequently assumes the incompatibility of the social roles of attorney and woman. Even so, female attorneys appear to fare better than media policewomen in that some aspects of their likely real-world experiences are portrayed.[12] The scarcity of female lawyers, the gender-based attitudes prevalent toward women lawyers, and the social friction generated by

Michael Desmond/© ABC/courtesy Everett Collection

Perhaps representing a shift and serving as a counter example to the common portrait of female attorneys in the entertainment media as young and occupying lower agency positions, Candice Bergen was portrayed as a full partner in her law firm in the television show, Boston Legal.

the clashing of traditional female social roles and their functioning as effective attorneys can all be found in their media constructions. However, like police-women, their sexuality and unresolved sexual tensions are likely to dominate their media portrayals. Female attorneys are more often shown as young, white, single, childless, and in lower-echelon positions in their law firms and criminal justice agencies. They also share with male attorney portrayals an unrealistic level of involvement in dangerous and sensational criminal law cases.

In sum, the courts and attorneys are usually unrealistically constructed in the media. Rare real-world events and activities are common in media judicial portraits; common judicial procedures and attorney duties are rare in the media. Although not as wildly inaccurate as the image of police, the courts and attorneys are still more often shown in crime-fighting narratives than in more realistic story lines. Even when the portrayals are based on real cases, the infotainment criteria that drive the selection of cases culls out the usual and nonviolent case in favor of the abnormal and predatory. Some of these selected cases become multimedia, pop culture bonanzas, generating enormous markets, profits, and spinoffs for news, entertainment, and info-tainment media.[13] Termed "**media trials**," these judicial miniseries have become the most important single contributor to the social construction of the courts in America.[14]

MEDIA TRIALS

Media trials involve the social construction of select criminal justice cases that are taken up by the media, commodified, and mass marketed as massive infotainment products. Learning about the courts from these trials is analogous to learning geology solely from volcano eruptions. You will be impressed and entertained but you will learn little about the common workings of the courts. The first notorious mass-mediated trials in the United States appeared after the establishment of the first mass media, the daily penny press newspapers. One of the first was the 1859 trial of anarchist John Brown, which attracted daily coverage and widespread dissemination via telegraph. A later example is the 1875 trial of nationally known preacher Henry Ward Beecher, a judicial narrative built around an adultery trial. The Lizzie Borden 1893 trial for the ax murders of her parents foreshadowed the lurid murder trials involving celebrities and set the stage for a steady parade of media trials throughout the twentieth century. Media trials have been a consistent presence in the media, crime, and justice world and were constructed every three to five years over the course of the twentieth century. Increasing in frequency as the century ended, they show no evidence of abating in the twenty-first century.

Contemporary media trials are distinguished from typical judicial news by the massive and intensive coverage that begins either with the discovery of the crime or the arrest of the accused.[15] The media cover all aspects of the case, often highlighting extralegal facts. Judges, lawyers, police, witnesses, jurors, and particularly defendants are interviewed, photographed, and frequently raised to celebrity status. Personalities, personal relationships, physical appearances, and idiosyncrasies are commented on regardless of legal relevance. Coverage is live whenever possible, pictures are preferred over text, and text is characterized by conjecture and sensationalism.[16]

In 1927, Charles Lindbergh made the first solo, nonstop New York to Paris flight in the airplane *Spirit of St. Louis*. He returned an international hero and the most famous man in the world, becoming, in effect, the first mass media celebrity. The kidnapping and murder of his infant son in 1932, and the subsequent trial and execution of Bruno Hauptmann for the crime, foreshadowed today's massive coverage of media trials. Shown are the reporters gathered to cover the 1935 trial of Bruno Hauptmann.

In their coverage of these trials, the media offer direct and individualistic explanations of crime: lust, greed, immorality, jealousy, revenge, and insanity.

One factor behind the recent increase in the number of media trials is that twentieth-century news organizations competing for ratings increasingly structured the news along entertainment lines, presenting it within frames, formats, and explanations originally found solely in entertainment programming. Eventually fast-paced, dramatic, superficial presentations and simplistic explanations became the norm. As this trend developed, criminal trials came to be covered more intensely, and news organizations expanded their coverage from hard factual presentations to soft human interest news, emphasizing extralegal human interest elements.[17] The process culminates in the total combining of news and entertainment in the media trial and today it is the sensational, titillating, and dramatic judicial elements which receive media attention.[18]

Media Trial Effects

When media trials began to be televised in the 1960s, heightened concern arose over their effects. In the Estes case in 1965 (which resulted in banning television cameras in courtrooms), Chief Justice Earl Warren stated: "Should the television industry become an integral part of our system of criminal justice, it would not be unnatural for the public to attribute the shortcomings of the industry to the trial process itself."[19] The passage of time has not reduced this concern. The basic issue is whether attorneys, judges, and other participants react to the presence of television cameras by altering their courtroom behavior. The fear is that participants will change the way they testify, argue, and construct their cases to fit the needs of the electronic visual media and that attorneys will audition for massive external television audiences rather than litigate before small courtroom audiences. Media-driven changes have already been documented in religion, sports, and politics; small live audiences are often less important (and sometimes skipped entirely) in preference for large, external media-supplied ones.[20]

The relationship between the media and the justice system is further strained by media trials because different considerations and values govern the means by which each obtains knowledge and evaluates its worth. The criminal justice system is guided by legislative and constitutional mandates, and the courts have the task of separating legally relevant from irrelevant information. Media, however, respond primarily to newsworthiness and entertainment considerations. Each side's considerations dictate what facts are presented as well as when and how they are disclosed. Traditionally, in the courtroom information is imparted in a form and by a process different from that preferred by the media. Courtroom knowledge is extracted point by point in long story lines following legal procedures and rules of evidence. Moreover, the information is specially prepared for a limited audience of a judge or jury.

In contrast, media renditions are outwardly directed and developed in accordance with entertainment values rather than legal relevance. They are brief, time- and space-limited constructions that must make their points quickly, and they are built around whatever film or dramatic elements are available. In sum, the courts have traditionally presented internally controlled, front-stage events to a small, specific audience of judges and jurors, whereas media-produced products tend to present dramatic backstage information to an external, general mass audience. This inherent conflict between media and justice systems crystallizes in the media trial where the courthouse becomes the production stage for the media. With the ascendance of media trials, the traditional courtroom audience became secondary to the external media audience both inside and outside of the courtroom.

For these reasons, despite their relatively small numbers, media trials are crucial in the social construction of crime-and-justice reality.[21] They serve as massive public stages that disseminate crime-and-justice knowledge to vast audiences of ordinary citizens.[22] In a media trial, both the jury and the vicariously attending public can decide between one reality constructed by the state in which the accused is guilty and another constructed by the defense in which the defendant is not guilty. As the dominant delivery medium of these trials, visual media direct the facts that are selected, constructed, and presented to the public. Not surprisingly, media trials involve cases that contain the same elements popular in entertainment programming—human interest laced with mystery, sex, bizarre circumstances, and famous or powerful people (see Box 5.1). In their coverage, the media simplify the task of reporting, interpreting, and explaining a trial. As in the entertainment media,

---

B o x   5.1   The O. J. Simpson Media Trials

An example of the commodification and marketing of a media trial. Books, films, photos, souvenirs, songs, toys, and games are all spinoffs of a high-profile, intensely covered trial.

The first Simpson trial was of the sinful rich genre. The trial's storyline could be found in numerous novels and Hollywood films: handsome, rich, successful ex-athlete is accused of murdering his ex-wife and her friend in a jealous rage amid a sea of rumored drug abuse, sexual deviance, and fascinating characters—racists cops,

---

recurrent themes dominate media trial constructions, and crime is nearly universally attributed to individual failings rather than to social conditions. The three most common types of media trials utilize narratives taken directly from entertainment media: abuse of power, the sinful rich, and evil strangers.[23] These themes provide the news media with powerful preestablished conceptual frameworks to present and mold the various aspects of a trial's coverage.[24]

Media trials that fit the **abuse of power** theme include those cases in which the defendant occupies a position of trust, prestige, or authority. The general rule is the higher the rank, the more media interest in the case. Cases involving police corruption and justice system personnel in general are especially attractive to the media. **Sinful rich media trials** include cases in which socially prominent defendants are involved in bizarre or sexually related crimes. These trials have a voyeuristic appeal, and the media coverage aims to persuade the public that they are being given a rare glimpse into the backstage sordid world of the upper class and powerful. Love triangles, deviant sex, and inheritance-motivated killings

beautiful women, and offbeat acquaintances. Indeed, a large part of the interest and ultimate social impact of this trial stems from the way it became a long-running mass media entertainment vehicle—a drama-in-real-life, covered more along the lines of a sports spectacle than a criminal trial that ran for ten months. In the aftermath of a 1995 criminal trial acquittal, a civil jury found Simpson monetarily liable and awarded $8.5 million to the victim's families. Simpson remained a focus of periodic news stories and in 2008 he was convicted of armed robbery and kidnapping and sentenced to fifteen years in prison. His second criminal trial did not match up with the media trial themes as his first one did and his reduced celebrity status resulted in significantly less media attention.

In terms of legal significance, Simpson's 1995 criminal trial was clearly not the trial of the century as it was christened by the media—it is better described as the signal television event of the twentieth century, demanding thousands of hours of coverage. Regarding the trial's social impact, most commentators focused on race relations, with few reporting any positive effects. Other concerns specific to the judicial system generated from the coverage included the prospect of more criminal defendants refusing to plea bargain, a skepticism about police testimony, more judicial gag orders on trial participants and less camera access, restrictions on attorneys' use of political rhetoric in front of juries, and the general degrading in the public's eye of judges, juries, attorneys, and the judicial system. Coverage of the trial represented American media and culture at one of its lowest voyeuristic ebbs, and the judicial system continues to be exploited regularly in "twenty-first-century media trials."

SOURCES: G. Bains, "The Criminal Trial as a Sports Spectacle." *Mclean's 108* (February 20, 1995): 55; G. Barak, ed., *Media, Process, and the Social Construction of Crime*. New York: Garland, 1995; Fox, Sickel and Steiger, *Tabloid Justice*; S. Gaines, "O. J. Simpson, Mark Fuhrman, and the Moral 'Low Ground' of Ethnic/Race Relations in the United States." *Black Scholar 25* (1995): 46–48; J. Garvey, "Race and the Simpson Verdict." *Commonwealth 122* (1995): 6; D. Gelernter, "The Real Story of Orenthal James." *National Review* (October 9, 1995): 45–47; B. Handy, "Our Mutual Houseguest." *Time 146* (October 16, 1995): 108; S. Pillsbury, "Time, TV, and Criminal Justice: Second Thoughts on the Simpson Trial." *Criminal Law Bulletin 59*(3) 1997: 3–28; R. Rosenblatt, "A Nation of Painted Hearts." *Time* (October 16, 1995): 40–46; F. Schmalleger, *Trial of the Century*. Englewood Cliffs, NJ: Prentice Hall, 1996; J. Walsh, "Special Report: The Simpson Verdict." *Time 146* (October 16, 1995): 62–64; and M. Whitaker, "Whites v. Blacks." *Newsweek 126* (October 16, 1995): 28–34.

among the rich and famous are primary examples.[25] The category of **evil strangers** is composed of two subgroups: non–Americans and psychotic killers. Non-American evil stranger media trials may involve—depending on the time and political climate—immigrants, blacks, Jews, socialists, union and labor leaders, anarchists, the poor, members of counterculture groups, members of minority religions, or political activists and advocates of unpopular causes. Foreign terrorists provide recent examples. Psychotic killer media trials usually focus on bizarre murder cases in which the defendant is portrayed as a maddened, predatory killer—exemplified historically by Lizzie Borden (in spite of her acquittal) and more recently by Jeffery Dahmer, John Wayne Gacy, and other serial killers.

All three media trial types have long histories in popular entertainment narratives, and these preestablished entertainment narratives help determine the content of the coverage in the real cases. Entertainment story lines provide the news media with the frames by which to measure, choose, and mold aspects of real trials that will be reported and highlighted. Media trials reinforce the similarity between news and entertainment, inspiring news personnel to structure their coverage along familiar entertainment narratives and providing the fodder for entertainment personnel to author the distorted fictional constructions that are referenced in the news.[26] Courtroom attorneys rely on both to construct their infotainment-structured evidence narratives for juries. The public receives the responsibility-diverting message that the rich are immoral in their use of sex, drugs, and violence; that people in power are evil, greedy, and should not be trusted; and that strangers and those with different lifestyles or values are inherently dangerous. Table 5.1 lists some well-known examples of media trials and their outcomes.

Merging Judicial News with Entertainment

Media trials represent the final step in a long process of merging judicial news and entertainment—a process that today results in multimedia products and extensive commercial exploitation. The Internet has extended this process and provides detailed information about these cases to a much greater degree than was previously available. The Internet also provides a vehicle for the public to become active trial participants in dedicated trial chat rooms, providing running evidence and testimony assessments complete with votes on guilt or innocence. If prior coverage of media trials resembled a miniseries, today it is more like a game show. Along with extensive interest, the money to be made from a popular long-running media trial is enormous. That the source of media trials is the judicial system eases the merger and heightens the profits, for media trials allow the news media to attract and market to large audiences while maintaining their preferred image as objective and neutral. A trial is also a natural stage for presenting drama and comes supplied with tax-supported sets, lead and secondary characters, extras, and dialogue. Media trials provide the media with ready-made narratives for entertainment vehicles in the form of movie scripts, episodes for weekly crime and law dramas, and content for infotainment talk shows, books, and other commercial spinoffs. They become, in effect, an entire media industry line.

The social impact and importance of media trials is seldom connected to the extent of social harm from their associated crimes. Their significance comes from the attention they receive and the public debate they engender generated from the intense media and public focus on the trial proceedings. These trials are significant because they influence the public's attitudes and views regarding crime, justice, and society for years.[27] A specific concern for a judicial system experiencing a medial trial is the generation of a secondary effect on nonpublicized cases. Following a media trial, a coverage effect influences the processing and disposition of similarly charged but unpublicized cases.[28] This coverage echo has been described a number of times in the literature:

> But while the impact of the press is most direct on specific cases covered, there is good reason to believe that [their] sway extends considerably beyond the cases actually appearing.... From the cases that are covered, officials become conditioned to expect demands for stern treatment from the press, and in the unpublicized cases they probably act accordingly.[29]

T A B L E 5.1   Media Trial Examples

Abuse of Power

Rodney King Beating (1992)	*Trial.* Four Los Angeles police officers were accused of using excessive force in arresting Rodney King following a car chase. The acquittals in the state trial triggered riots in Los Angeles, leaving fifty-three people dead, more than 7,000 people arrested, and more than $1 billion in property damage. *Verdict.* In the first state trial, the jury acquitted three of the officers of all charges and was unable to reach a verdict on one charge against the forth. In a subsequent 1993 Federal trial on charges of violation of civil rights, a federal jury convicts two of the officers and finds the other two not guilty. No disturbances follow the verdict.
Clinton Impeachment (1999)	*Trial.* President Clinton is accused of obstruction of justice and perjury while attempting to conceal an affair with a White House intern. *Verdict.* The president is found innocent of the charges as U.S. Senate's votes on both articles of impeachment fall short of the two-thirds majority required by the Constitution to convict.
Bernard Madoff Ponzi Scheme (2009)	*Trial.* A former chairman of the NASDAQ stock exchange, he was accused of securities, wire, and mail fraud; money laundering; theft; false SEC statement filings; and perjury. His massive Ponzi scheme investment operation was estimated to have cost his clients billions. *Verdict.* He pled guilty to eleven felonies and was sentenced to 150 years in prison.

Sinful Rich

Leopold and Loeb (1924)	*Trial.* Nineteen-year old Richard Loeb, the privileged son of a Sears Roebuck vice president, and nineteen-year-old Nathan Leopold, the son of a millionaire box manufacturer, were accused of kidnapping and murdering a fourteen-year old boy from one of Chicago's most prominent families. *Verdict.* Both were convicted and sentenced to life in prison. In 1936, Loeb was slashed and killed with a razor while in Joliet penitentiary. In 1958, after thirty-four years of confinement, Leopold was released from prison. He died peacefully in August, 1971.
Sam Sheppard (1954)	*Trial.* An Ohio doctor who was tried for the murder of his wife. *Verdict.* Found guilty by a jury of murder in the second degree and sentenced to life in prison. Sheppard won a retrial in 1966 after a successful U.S. Supreme Court appeal arguing prejudicial impact from news coverage surrounding his first trial. He was acquitted by jury in the second trial and died in 1970 at the age of forty-six of liver failure.
Patty Hearst (1976)	*Trial.* The granddaughter of newspaper publicist William Hearst, she was kidnapped by a left-wing radical group (the Symbionese Liberation Army) and held for ransom. After months in captivity she appeared in bank robbery surveillance video carrying a weapon. *Verdict.* She was convicted of bank robbery and served nearly two years in prison. She was pardoned by President Clinton.

(continued)

	Trial	Verdict
Kobe Bryant (2004)	Professional basketball player, he was charged with sexual assault of a nineteen-year-old female employee of a Colorado hotel.	Criminal charges were dropped and a civil lawsuit against Bryant was settled out of court.
Evil Strangers		
Non-Americans		
Bruno Hauptmann (1935)	A German immigrant, Hauptmann was accused of the 1932 kidnapping and murder of the infant son of aviator Charles Lindbergh.	He was found guilty and electrocuted in 1936.
Timothy McVeigh (1997)	A right-wing terrorist and former U.S. military member he was accused of bombing the Oklahoma City Federal building, which killed 167 people.	He was convicted and executed in June 2001.
Ramzi Yousef (1997)	An al-Qaeda–linked terrorist accused of the 1993 bombing of the World Trade Center which killed six people.	He was found guilty and sentenced to life plus 240 years.
Khalid Shaikh Mohammed (2010)	A member of al-Qaeda, he is described in the 9/11 Commission report as masterminding the September 11, 2001 attacks. He is accused of war crimes and mass murder.	Trial in civilian court pending. If convicted, he faces the death penalty.
Psychotic Killers		
Lizzie Borden (1893)	She was accused of the 1892 ax murder of her father and stepmother.	She was acquitted by a jury and died in 1927 at the age of sixty-seven.
Ted Bundy (1979)	He confessed to more than twenty murders committed across the country from 1973 to 1978.	He was executed in Florida in 1989 for the 1978 murder of twelve-year-old Kimberly Leach.
Jeffery Dahmer (1992)	A cannibalistic serial killer who preyed on Milwaukee young men from 1987 to 1991, he was accused of killing seventeen men.	Sentenced to fifteen consecutive life terms, he was killed in prison by another inmate in 1994.
Scott Peterson (2004)	He was tried for the murder of his pregnant wife, Lacy Peterson, and his unborn son.	He was convicted and sentenced to death.
Dennis Rader BTK Killer (2005)	Known as the BTK (bind, torture, kill) serial murderer, he was accused of killing ten people in the Wichita, Kansas area from 1974 to 1991.	Pled guilty and received ten consecutive life terms.

This unwillingness [to plea bargain] appears to occur relatively infrequently. It is most likely to occur when there is strong pressure upon the prosecution to obtain maximum sentences for a particular class of crime: for example, after a notorious case of child rape, the prosecutor may refuse to bargain, for a time, with those charged with sex offenses involving children; after a series of highly publicized drug arrests, for a time, to engage in reduction of charges from sales to possession.[30]

Additionally empirical evidence of a punitive echo is found in a study of a decade of felony case processing in Dade County, Florida. Following a heavily covered case involving child abuse at a daycare center a significant jump in similarly charged cases occurred.[31] The implication of a publicity spill-over effect is that media attention influences the processing and disposition of a large number of cases, the majority of which receive no coverage. Such effects are, of course, heightened when live television is part of the media trial package.

Live Television in Courtrooms

Often a component in the construction of media trials, live television coverage of judicial proceedings represents the most intrusive media interaction with the judicial system. The schizophrenic judicial posture toward televised proceedings is shown by its embracement in the first O. J. Simpson criminal trial and its banishment from his civil trial. The judiciary has long been skeptical about visual coverage of trials. Recognition of photography's unique potential for disruption originated with Bruno Hauptmann's trial for the kidnapping and murder of Charles Lindbergh's baby son in the 1930s.[32] In response to problems that arose during this trial, the American Bar Association in 1937 issued a new rule (or canon) regarding the use of photographic equipment at trials:

> Proceedings in court should be conducted with fitting dignity and decorum. The taking of photographs in the courtroom, during sessions of the court or recesses between sessions, and the broadcasting of court proceedings are calculated to detract from the essential dignity of the proceedings, degrade the court and create misconceptions in the mind of the public and should not be permitted.[33]

This recommended ban on photography in the courtroom was widely adopted and was extended in 1952 to include television cameras as well. Despite the extension of the ABA rules (which are unenforced recommended standards of expected conduct), the first trial to receive television coverage took place in 1953 in Oklahoma City, and the first to receive live coverage in 1955 was in Waco, Texas. These cases stand as exceptions to the more broadly upheld aversion to television in the courts that existed into the 1980s.

The Supreme Court first reviewed the question of television access to courtrooms in *Estes v. Texas* in 1965.[34] The Estes trial received intense regional television coverage with nightly news reports broadcast from the courthouse. The Court reversed Estes's conviction, ruling that television was unavoidably disruptive and should have been banned: "Television in its present state and by its very nature, reaches into a variety of areas in which it may cause prejudice to an accused.... The televising of criminal trials is inherently a denial of due process."[35] In the Estes aftermath, most states severely limited television's access to their courts, and many simply banned all television coverage.

However, encouraged by the development of less obtrusive television equipment, various states continued to experiment with televising proceedings. In 1979 the Florida Supreme Court allowed television reporting from trial courts without requiring the permission of defendants. Florida's procedures were reviewed by the U.S. Supreme Court in 1981 in *Chandler v. Florida*.[36] At that time, the Court rejected many of the assumptions about television it had forwarded sixteen years earlier. The most significant assumption it rejected was that televising a criminal trial without the defendant's consent is an inherent denial of due process. Emphasizing the modernization of the medium, the lack of evidence of a psychological impact from televised coverage on trial participants, and an increase in the public acceptance of television as a fact of everyday life, the Court upheld the *Chandler* conviction.

Unstated by the Supreme Court, additional reasons for this reversal also developed in the years between *Estes* and *Chandler*. Backed by surveys of the public, during this period there was growing concern among the judiciary that the public lacked confidence in the courts' ability to confront crime and criminals.[37] The courts were viewed as part of the cause of a steadily increasing crime rate. In this negative atmosphere, televising trials began to look like a possible counterweight to negative public perceptions. As front-stage events constructed for public consumption, trials show the justice system at its best. It was increasingly felt that the cameras would show impartial justice, fair procedure, conviction of the guilty, and imposition of fair sentences. By contrast, the seamy backstage of the criminal justice process—the plea bargaining, the procedural inefficiency, the arbitrary decision making inherent in police and prosecutor discretion—would go unseen. Televising trials, in other words, was seen as unlikely to hurt and likely to be potentially helpful in shoring up the judicial system's poor public image. By the 1980s, the courts saw televised trials as a means of presenting controlled, formal front-stage events to the public while protecting their backstage assembly-line processes from exposure.

The basic question of whether or not to allow television cameras in the courtroom was never whether the media had the freedom to report courtroom matters—broadcast journalists could attend and report trials on the same basis as other reporters, that is, without their cameras—but concerned the effect of expanding the trial audience to include persons not in the courtroom. In the 1960s—at the time of the *Estes* ruling—the court feared the effects of this expansion on both the trial participants and the expanded electronic audience. By the 1980s, the courts felt that a broadly expanded audience of external spectators was a good thing that would have an uplifting impact on the negative image of the courts. In addition, judges came to accept the news media and became more comfortable with the measures necessary to control media behavior during trials.

In addition, as predatory criminality became the dominant social construction of crime and began to influence criminal justice policy, the constitutional importance given to defendants' rights diminished in favor of general social interests and increased support for electronic media access. As a result, opposition to courtroom television evaporated. The *Chandler* decision marks a remarkable shift in the attitude of the judicial system toward the presence of television in courtrooms. In 1976, all but two states prohibited cameras in courtrooms. As of 2005 all fifty states allow some type of coverage at either the appellate or trial level or both. The *Chandler* decision emerged as a broad victory for the electronic media and the assumption of media access to judicial proceedings.

The effects of cameras on actual courtroom proceedings are no longer seen as a prime concern, but the effects of those cameras on those outside the courtroom is still worrisome. Most worrisome is that public disturbances and full-scale riots have been triggered by court decisions in highly publicized cases.[38] Other unresolved issues include a chilling effect on victims reporting crimes, particularly victims of rape, witnesses seeking to avoid embarrassing coverage being reluctant to testify, heightening the public's fear of crime, distorting the public's beliefs about the workings of the judicial system, encouraging copycat crimes, and publicly pillorying defendants who are eventually found innocent. However, the infotainment value of media trials is too great, public interest too high, and none of the negative effects or speculated concerns severe enough to curtail coverage. In fact, the social and economic pressures to grant media access are so great that even in trials that are obviously flooded with massive coverage, the cameras and intense media scrutiny are usually allowed.

So it is that today intensive, and sometimes intrusive, news coverage is accepted as a fact of life in the judiciary. Future clashes between the two are to be expected as the media seek access to previously backstage judicial proceedings and as media technology makes recording and marketing them easier. The media are aided in this process by the society wide effects of the electronic visual mass media over the last fifty years, which has undermined public support for closing off social institutions. Country clubs, golf courses, prisons, bars, fraternal organizations, and a host of other institutions, as well as the courts, are less successful in claiming a traditional right to insulate themselves from broad public and media access. Currently the evolution of the media and the judiciary's unsteady relationship has three areas of concern and unresolved conflict—the effect of pretrial publicity, the appropriate judicial mechanisms to be used by the courts when they are faced with intense media attention, and access by both sides to information held by the other.

PRETRIAL PUBLICITY, JUDICIAL CONTROLS, AND ACCESS

Pretrial Publicity

In 1807, Aaron Burr's attorney claimed that jurors could not properly decide his client's case because of prejudicial newspaper articles.[39] From this initial point of contention, the media and courts have continued to joust over pretrial publicity. Ironically, despite their adversarial history and contentious interactions, the media and the judicial system react to criminal events in much the same manner. Both concentrate on constructing a particular version of reality to be presented to a specific audience—jurors, viewers, or readers. The relationship between the media and the judicial system is sometimes cooperative, but more often each jealously guards its information while attempting to discover what the other knows. This is particularly true during the investigative and pretrial period of a case. Publicity before and during a trial may so affect a community and its courts that a fair trial becomes impossible and due process protections such as the presumption of innocence are destroyed. The media especially create problems when they publish information that is inadmissible in the courtroom and construct a community atmosphere in which finding and impaneling impartial jurors is not possible.

Unfortunately it is not always clear when particular media content is prejudicial. **Prejudicial publicity** can take two forms: factual information that bears on the guilt of a defendant and emotional information without evidentiary relevance. Factual information includes allusions to confessions, performances on polygraph or other inadmissible tests, and past criminal records and convictions. Emotional information includes stories that question the credibility of witnesses or present the personal feelings, stories about the defendant's character (he hates children and dogs), associates (she hangs around with known syndicate gunmen), or personality (he's a mean-spirited, bad-tempered degenerate), and stories that inflame the general public (someone has to be punished for this!).

Despite the concerns about prejudicial coverage, the U.S. Supreme Court has not operationally defined prejudicial coverage for the lower courts. Faced with ambiguity and forced to render largely subjective determinations, both trial and appellate courts have focused on jurors as the key to determining the fairness of a trial. In practice, the operational definition of an impartial juror is derived from the 1807 Aaron Burr case: "An impartial juror is one free from the dominant influence of knowledge acquired outside the courtroom, free from strong and deep impressions which close the mind."[40] Though not a precise rule, this definition does eliminate ignorance of a case or a total lack of exposure to media coverage as a requirement for impartiality. Jurors can be exposed to extensive media content regarding a case and still be considered impartial. If a jury is deemed impartial and uninfluenced by media coverage, then the proceedings are usually considered fair.

Paralleling this issue is the concern that trial publicity will result in unwarranted harm to a defendant. Appeals courts have thus far not recognized media coverage as a mitigating factor in sentencing decisions. Left unaddressed are cases in which a defendant is found innocent of criminal charges but has his or her reputation permanently ruined by publicity. The consequence of publicity has been described in this way in relation to government officials who have been investigated:

> Once again the tendency to portray public officials accused of criminal or unethical activities as guilty [is displayed].... We find it appalling that long after many of these individuals have been found innocent of the accusations against them, the disproved accusations continue to be repeated as almost a permanent addendum to their name in news stories.[41]

The concern is that live television coverage incites such negative feelings against defendants that, even if they are later acquitted, the feelings are irreversible. The modern media have constructed a new verdict: legally innocent but socially guilty. In the process, media coverage confounds the concepts of legal guilt (is the defendant legally responsible for a crime?) and factual guilt (did the defendant actually commit the criminal behavior?). Factual guilt is not always equivalent to legal guilt, and the general public little understands and is poorly instructed by the media in the differences between the two. If defendants who have been found innocent are subsequently still punished by losing their career or reputation because of publicity, then the criminal justice system loses legitimacy with those who identify with these defendants.

Judicial Mechanisms to Deal with Pretrial Publicity

Faced with a case that will generate significant pretrial publicity, the courts have two strategies they can pursue. One is proactive and seeks to limit the availability of potentially prejudicial material to the media. The second is reactive and seeks to limit the effects of the material on the proceeding after it has been disseminated to the public by the media. Under the first strategy, if a court deems information to be prejudicial, it acts to restrict either media access to the information or, if the material is already in the media's possession, restricts the publication of the information. **Proactive mechanisms** include closure and restrictive and protective orders (see Box 5.2). This approach directly clashes with the First Amendment protection of freedom of the press and has been vigorously resisted by the media. It has also not been a favored strategy of the appellate courts, as shown in test cases in which the Supreme Court has been more likely to uphold appeals by the media where a proactive strategy has been used.

Appeals by the media have been less successful when the courts employ a reactive strategy, allowing the news media access and publication but attempting to compensate for negative effects from the resulting publicity. In this approach, trial court judges can invoke a number of reactive steps to limit the negative effects. These **reactive mechanisms** are generally preferred over closure, restrictive orders, and protective orders because they do not directly limit the activities of the media and thus do not directly undermine the First Amendment freedom of the press.[42] They rest on the premise that even if most of the public may be influenced and biased by media information, an unbiased jury can still be assembled and an unbiased trial conducted. Applying a reactive strategy, judges can expand jury selection (the voir dire), grant trial continuances, grant changes of venue, sequester jurors, and give special instructions to the jury to counteract the effects of publicity (see Box 5.3).

Current case law and legislation provide little direction concerning the appropriate use of these reactive mechanisms, and little empirical research is available regarding their relative effectiveness. Therefore, although each mechanism has recognized strengths and weaknesses, its application is based on unproved but commonly accepted assumptions concerning its effectiveness and appropriate use. Given the pervasiveness and intrusiveness of the media, these after-the-fact

---

B o x 5.2	Proactive Judicial Mechanisms to Control Prejudicial Publicity

Mechanism	Description of Procedure
Closure	Closure involves isolating judicial proceedings from outside (public and press) attendance. Closure is felt to be a very effective means of preventing prejudicial coverage once a proceeding has begun because there can be no prejudice if there is no coverage. In opposing closure, the media argue that they are proxies for the general public and therefore have a right of access to the court proceedings under the open trial provision of the Sixth Amendment.
Restrictive orders	The next most effective step available to control prejudicial materials is the use of restrictive orders (also termed prior restraint or gag orders). Restrictive orders prevent the media from printing or broadcasting information. If information is not published, it cannot cause bias. Not surprisingly, the media have argued vigorously for the right to publish what they have already discovered, and this right has generally been upheld.
Protective orders	The third judicial mechanism used to limit the availability of prejudicial materials is the protective order. Trial participants are a common source of prejudicial information. By issuing a protective order, the trial judge prohibits attorneys and others from making statements outside of the courtroom. These orders are most effective in the early stages of a case. The legal rationale behind protective orders allowing speech to be restricted is that trial participants possess privileged information regarding a criminal case and no longer have the same First Amendment right to freely speak as a member of the general public. As it now stands, it is currently easier for a trial judge to restrict the speech of a trial's participants, excluding the defendant, than to close a proceeding or to restrain the media from publicizing information and statements they have obtained.

---

attempts to compensate are often costly and disruptive, and, most important, of questionable effectiveness in massively covered media trials.[43] Evidence suggests that media influences may persist even when the legal system makes efforts to limit that influence.[44] Proactive mechanisms are more effective, but they tend to close off the judicial system and therefore run counter to the society-wide, media–driven trend to open social institutions. They also preclude any positive social effects that might be generated from media coverage. Although sometimes employed, proactive mechanisms continue to lag in popularity, reserved for the rare and unusual case and challenged whenever used.

Regardless of which strategy judges employ, to enforce their decisions trial judges rely on contempt-of-court rulings to deter and punish those ignoring their orders regarding media publicity. In practice, the threat of a contempt finding works better with local criminal justice system personnel, as they have to consider future

B o x 5.3	**Reactive Judicial Mechanisms to Control Prejudicial Publicity**

Mechanism	Description of Procedure
Voir dire	Voir dire, "to speak the truth," is a process in which prospective jurors are queried regarding prejudice. Attorneys can prevent jurors from serving either through challenges for cause, where they must state a valid reason for eliminating a juror, or through peremptory challenges (normally limited in number) that do not have to be supported by a reason. Voir dire will only identify those jurors who admit knowledge and prejudice about a case, and it is based on the premise that jurors will recognize themselves as biased and truthfully admit it.
Continuance	Continuance is simply a delay in the start of a trial until media coverage and its effects are thought to have subsided enough to allow an unbiased trial. The practice is based on the premise that media interest in the case will wane and that jurors will forget details of past media reports. Disadvantages include that it is inconsistence with the defendant's right to a speedy trial and the possibility that witnesses and evidence may not be available at a later time.
Change of venue	A trial may be moved from a location in which the case has received heavy media coverage to one in which it has received less coverage and is of less interest, and where residents are assumed to be less biased. Although costly and questionable in effectiveness, venue changes are deemed necessary in certain cases—for example, in rural areas where the jury pool is limited and a major crime is likely to be the dominant news story for a long time.
Sequestration	Isolating a jury to control the information that reaches it can be very effective if the jury has not been exposed to prejudicial information prior to being impaneled. However, it is costly and disruptive to jurors and is felt to generate animosity toward the accused.
Jury instructions	The simplest and least expensive judicial mechanism that can be invoked, jury instructions comprise the directions the trial judge gives to the jury. They fundamentally consist of telling jurors to ignore media coverage. Empirical studies that have examined this mechanism suggest, however, that for the most part standard jury warnings do not eliminate publicity generated bias and that juries commonly discuss prejudicial information despite instructions not to.

dealings with the court, and less well with jurors, witnesses, reporters (especially those from other jurisdictions), and other temporary participants. As a last resort, a mistrial can be declared and a retrial ordered if jurors are exposed to or admit to being influenced by prejudicial news once a trial has begun (see Box 5.4). A retrial can be thought of as the ultimate reactive judicial remedy for media publicity—but

---

Box 5.4   Amanda Knox's Italian Media Trial

© AP Photo/Antonio Calanni

A media trial that generated international media attention was the 2009 trial of American college student Amanda Knox in Italy for the murder of her British roommate, Meredith Kercher. Ms. Knox and her Italian boyfriend were accused of killing Ms. Kercher during a violent sex game. The pretrial publicity surrounding the trial of Ms. Knox became an issue as a posting from a "Friends of Amanda" Web site states:

"The mission of the Friends of Amanda was to achieve some measure of balance in the pre-trial publicity. Prejudicial and erroneous public accounts resulted from leaks and false information from the closed-door year-long pre-charging proceedings. As we have stated, turning around the "super tanker" of negative publicity against Amanda Knox has been a slow, difficult, and laborious process. We believe we have now had a significant impact in achieving some balance in what has been reported and have achieved our purpose. Now that a public trial is underway, we will stand back and let the international public see what there is to be seen in the public trial proceedings. We hope only for fairness and justice in the proceedings for all, including for Amanda Knox." (downloaded 1/11/2010 from http://www.annebremner.com/Amanda_Knox.htm)

Ms. Knox was found guilty and sentenced to twenty-six years in prison. At press, she is currently in prison in Italy and appealing her conviction.

---

it also represents an expensive failure of the judicial system and does not prevent the recurrence of renewed massive coverage.

In addition to pretrial publicity and strategies to deal with the media, access to files, records, notes, photos, and databases have raised concerns. Issues here take two forms: those related to the media desiring access to government controlled and collected information and those related to government agencies gaining access to media collected and controlled information.

Media Access to Government Information

In a significant number of instances, a government agency has possession of information that the media deems newsworthy. Oftentimes the government is reluctant to release such information, and in response the press has worked to increase its access to government-held data and files. The first national response to obtaining information held by the government was the federal Freedom of Information Act, adopted in 1966. This act opened up numerous government files to the media and the public. A later associated law was the Government in Sunshine Act, passed in 1976, which prohibits closed government meetings that concern public policy. Both of these efforts have been duplicated in numerous states but have had mixed results in easing the news media's access to government files and information.

Part of the cause of the mixed impact of the laws targeted at access stems from the federal Privacy Act in 1974. Concerns over privacy and misuse of information collected by government regarding individuals led to support for a counterbalance. The goal was to control the misuse of government information and to restrict access to certain information in criminal files and judicial records. Information required to be disclosed under the Freedom of Information Act cannot be withheld under the auspices of the Privacy Act, but the boundary between the two acts has always been blurred. Further muddying the water, while expanding government access to privately held information, the effects of the Patriot Act of 2001 and the Homeland Security Act of 2002 on media access to government-held information are not yet clear. As in other areas regarding the media, the lower courts, agency personnel, and the media operate without clear rules in determining when privacy supersedes public interests, and decisions are rendered on a case-by-case basis. To date the overall effect of this legislation has been more symbolic than significant, and today the media's access to government-held files and information varies significantly by jurisdiction.

Reporters' Privilege and Shield Laws

On the opposite side of the knowledge-control issue, the media sometimes possess information that the courts or law enforcement officials want but that reporters do not want to provide. Controversy generally revolves around journalists' claims to the right of a **privileged conversation**. Journalists argue that they should be protected from having to divulge information or identify their sources to the same extent that communications between husbands and wives, attorneys and clients, priests and penitents, and psychiatrists and patients are protected. In each of the latter relationships, the courts cannot compel disclosure. Journalists argue that to fulfill their constitutional function as watchdogs of government activities and to guarantee their access to information, their news sources must be similarly protected.

Opponents to the extension of privileged protection to media sources have argued that the media should have no more protections or privileges than the average citizen, whose duty to provide testimony in criminal matters has been regularly affirmed.

Paralleling media efforts for recognition of a constitutional right to privileged conversation protection, the media has also lobbied for shield laws, or legislative protection from forced divulgence. The first reporters' shield law was passed in Baltimore, Maryland, in 1896. Since then, the media have continued to lobby successfully for shield laws, and currently thirty-five states and the District of Columbia offer shield law protections.[45] Most qualify the protection afforded reporters and provide a judicial test to be applied to assess whether the media's information is relevant and whether it can be obtained from other sources.[46] The effectiveness of shield laws is questionable, though, as the protection they afford the media is subject to state court interpretations and judicial rulings.[47] Often the degree to which reporters are shielded depends not on what a state's laws say but on a judge's attitude toward the press.[48] A second serious deficiency with state shield laws is that they operate only within each state, and contemporary news organizations are national and international in scope. Because of these deficiencies, few journalists believe their state's shield laws provide substantial help in protecting confidential files or preventing forced testimony.

Currently, the media are seldom asked to provide information. But due to the absence of new Supreme Court decisions, a narrow interpretation of shield statutes at the state level has occurred. When judges and law enforcement personnel do request information, reporters can usually be forced to divulge it—especially if the information can be shown to be central to a case and is unavailable from other sources. The media's efforts have made obtaining their information more costly, time consuming, and difficult, and in that sense they have successfully increased control of their knowledge. But like the courts themselves, the media are now also more open to inspection and more often pressed for access and information from nongovernmental sources such as citizen and lobby groups. Ironically, the very process of access that the media initiated has cycled back to affect their own social reality.

THE COURTS AS TWENTY-FIRST-CENTURY ENTERTAINMENT

Today phrases such as "government in the sunshine" and "freedom of information" reflect a larger, media-driven social trend toward greater openness of public institutions. The two social institutions involved in this trend, the media and the criminal justice system, play critical roles (see Box 5.5). It was inevitable that the courts, as central players in these struggles, would be pressured by the media, especially the electronic media, to open their institutions to scrutiny. Simultaneously, the media have also felt the pressure to open their institutions, processes, and files and have suffered through their own exposés of backstage activities. For better or worse, the courts and media are tightly coupled in the twenty-first century, and both internal courthouse and external media audiences dance to an infotainment tune.

The place where the change in the dance is most readily observed is in the courtroom. In the process of defending or prosecuting, lawyers construct reality. In the courtroom, they reach into the popular culture for images and symbols. The popular characters and plot lines serve as the building blocks for courtroom social reality construction by evoking what "everybody knows" about the world. Prosecuting attorneys invoked the mystery narrative to deliver an evidence-based story to jurors; defense attorneys counter with a beleaguered hero narrative to construct their client as the innocent victim of state power.[49] As the dominant media in the United States have moved from print to visuals, so has the style of legal story construction. Today, one is much more likely to see visual representations in courtrooms: videos, computer-based animations, and reenactments that reflect the influence of the visual electronic mass media.[50] The end result is that infotainment has worked its way into court proceedings.

Commenting on this process regarding a case that involved a baby-sitter's sexual affair with her charge's father and her shooting of his wife, Richard Sherwin states:

> The role of the litigator, unlike that of journalist, is to come up with a narrative truth [or social construction] that can successfully compete against a counter-narrative [a competing social construction] offered by the other side. Consider the case of Amy Fisher. In the sense of the prosecution Amy Fisher represented threats to the established moral order. As a consequence, [she] would have to pay the penalty for her transgression. On the side of the defense, Fisher would be framed within a counter-narrative. The image of Lolita gives way to "the poor unfortunate," the victim.... In Fisher's case, it is a story of psychological disturbance and parental complacency in the face of her increasingly desperate, and futile, cries for help … [established social] myths and archetypes contribute to this process. When a crime occurs, the media, and in time the lawyers for the parties involved, struggle to come up with the most compelling means [to present their construction] conveying what occurred and what it means. In this way, Amy Fisher comes to be known as "the Long Island Lolita."[51]

In their utilization of narratives, the courts provide a perfect small-scale model of the social construction process. For the internal judicial audience, two constructions of reality are created by competing claims makers who use factual and interpretative claims (evidence and explanations) and submit them to an audience (judges and jurors) that chooses and validates one or the other (guilty or not guilty verdicts). The media have tapped into this internal judicial social construction process and transformed the judicial system into a massive public infotainment machine. Attorneys, judges, defendants, witnesses, and victims sometimes protest, but more often they embrace their celebrity status and the chance to play a leading role. The courts have found their place in the twenty-first-century world of media, crime, and justice, and it is as a combination studio and production company where the most popular and gripping crime-and-justice dramas are cast and marketed.[52]

B o x 5.5   The Legacy of CourtTV

CourtTV (today called truTV) was created in 1991 with two goals: it would not only entertain viewers with real-life legal dramas, but would teach them something about the judicial system. CourtTV featured continuous live trial coverage as its programming core and built on prior success of pay-per-view cable networks like HBO. Its philosophy regarding content distinguished CourtTV from other then available crime and justice media content. Trial selection employed an infotainment screen and CourtTV producers looked for melodrama, popular issues, and charismatic lawyers. Over its history CourtTV has broadcast the majority of its cases along the lines of abuse of power, sinful rich, and evil strangers (see pages 112–116). CourtTV's style of trial coverage created the now common news media use of on-screen crawl lines and subtitles, the use of attorneys as anchorpersons and reporters, and the use of subject area experts to explain scientific tests and to provide background information. It was the date-rape trial of William Kennedy Smith, a member of the Massachusetts Kennedy family, in 1991 that first brought CourtTV national prominence. Ratings continued to increase with the trial of Lorena Bobbitt in 1994, a wife who had severed her husband's penis and argued a defense of spousal rape. After the O. J. Simpson trial in 1995 ratings declined however, and CourtTV began to expand to non court related content.

Both positive and negative effects of CourtTV's style of coverage have been argued. Proponents argued that gavel-to-gavel coverage resulted in an improved public view of justice by examining significant social issues, providing understanding of criminal trial procedures, teaching the public the importance of legal technicalities such as rules of procedure and evidence, and enhancing public monitoring of elected officials. Supporters saw CourtTV as painless legal education and noted that not a single overturned decision resulted from its coverage. It is unarguable that CourtTV provided a more complete picture, at least of one judicial trial, over then existing news, entertainment, and infotainment content. CourtTV effectively exposed the judiciary and criminal procedures to public scrutiny.

On the other hand, opponents of the network argued that, as it was a commercial venture, an unavoidable profit motive would drive sex and drama cases to be overly selected for broadcast. It was argued that in many ways, CourtTV was as misleading as any prime time legal drama because their cameras broadcast more than the jury ever heard, confusing the viewing public when verdicts differed from the infotainment-formed public consensus. Because juries had access to only legally relevant evidence while the viewing public had access to both legally relevant and infotainment knowledge, the concern was that coverage increased public mistrust of the system when jury verdicts clashed with public perceptions of guilt such as in the O. J. Simpson trial. This concern is related to the larger phenomenon of public injection into trials as pseudo-arbiters. CourtTV content bias included portraying trials as common (continuing the backwards law) and the glamorization of litigation by making murder and other violent crime trials the center of the legal universe (ignoring that most cases in the criminal justice system are plea bargained and involve theft). This

All these developments can be understood as a broad social reconstruction of the courts by the media simultaneously carried on within entertainment, news, and infotainment media. The notable transformation of attorneys from lawyers to crime fighters in the entertainment media is one indicator of the wider social ideological transition from left to right and the shift of the courts from a judicial system

portrayal created a "snippet effect" of justice by providing a full picture of a small but very entertaining part of the entire system.

The impact of CourtTV is difficult to determine. Notwithstanding the concerns, CourtTV represented an improvement over prior trial coverage. CourtTV also laid the foundation for a popular set of entertainment television programs such as *Oz*, *Law and Order*, and *The Practice* based on inside backstage views of the criminal justice system. The main social effect was that America changed into a nation of vicarious jurors. The foundation for today's Internet-based viewer participation in criminal cases was put down by CourtTV. Studies of a direct relationship between watching CourtTV and perceptions however show that viewers thought they had learned something from watching a CourtTV trial but had not learned anything substantial. A large portion of it viewing audience did not learn criminal or civil law fundamentals for example. However, CourtTV viewers did understand that CourtTV trials were the exception, not the norm.

In sum, as a result of CourtTV the criminal justice system as a whole is covered today in greater detail by all media. Following its premiere in 1991, all other networks and news stations have come to follow the CourtTV pattern. In a now accepted infotainment style, today's media generally focus on the stories about the trial participants as they are outside the courtroom and work to have viewers emotionally invest in trial outcomes. The final legacy of CourtTV is gavel-to-gavel judicial infotainment. Currently, the descendant of CourtTV, TruTV, has branched out into more infotainment "caught on video" reality programs, or as TruTV calls it, "actuality" television. TruTV also maintains TruTV video, a streaming video player, where viewers "can watch footage of car chases, dumb criminals, gun fights, drunk drivers, drug busts, naughty girls, police, things that blow up, taser attacks, naked thieves and more!" Courts as infotainment marches on.

SOURCES: Bennack, F., May 1999. The National Conference on Public Trust and Confidence in the Justice System, Washington, D.C. Brill, S. July, 1994. Letters: Personal Grudge? *ABA Journal* 80, p. 10; Courtroom Television Network, 1992. *Viewer's Guide* 24 cited by Nasheri, 2002, p. 31 in *Crime and Justice in the Age of Court TV*; Cox, D. and G. Jan. 29, 1996. "Lights, Camera. Justice?" *The National law Journal*, p. A12; Cripe, K. L. 1999. "Empowering the Audience: Television's Role in the Diminishing Respect for the American Judicial System." *UCLA Entertainment Law Review* 6 pp. 235–281; Dershowitz, A. May 1994. At Issue: Court TV. *ABA Journal* 80, p. 46; Doug J. 2002. Executive Vice President and General Counsel of Court TV, N.Y, interview cited by Hasheri 2002, p. 50 in *Crime and Justice in the Age of Court TV*; Harris, D. 1993. "The Appearance of Justice: Court TV, Conventional Television, and Public Understanding of the Criminal Justice System." *Arizona Law Review*, 35, p. 785; Keygier, M. K. 1995. "The Thirteenth Juror: Electronic Media's Struggle to Enter State and Federal Courtrooms." *The Catholic University of America CommLaw Conspectus* 3, p. 785; Nasheri, H. 2002. *Crime and Justice in the Age of Court TV*. New York: LFB Scholarly Publishing, LLC. Paul, A. 1997. "Turning the Camera on CourtTV: Does Televising Trials Teach Us Anything About Real Law?" *Ohio State Law Journal* 58 p. 655. Podlas, K. 2001. "Please Adjust Your Signal: How Television's Syndicated Courtrooms Bias Our Juror Citizenry." *American Businesses Law Journal* 39, p. 1; Rapping, E. 2003. *Law and Justice as Seen on TV*. New York: New York University Press; Sullivan, T. 1999. Sullivan Special Project Producer, CourtTV, interview cited by Nasheri 2002, p. 32 in *Crime and Justice in the Age of Court TV*. Takata, S. 2006. "Review: Crime and Justice in the Age of Court TV." *Criminal Justice Review* 31, pp. 389–391. www.trutv.com downloaded May 12, 2009.

to a source of public entertainment.[53] Today, the courts struggle to construct public images that better align with their traditional social reality—that of the courts as fair, impartial institutions that determine truth and dispense justice by the rule of law. To what extent the media will degrade this historical construction remains to be determined, but the current public expectations and media content are clearly steered by infotainment values and tabloid-style content has been credited with increasing public doubt of the fairness of the judicial system.[54] For the near future, it appears that the judicial system will be seen more as a source of entertainment than a source of justice. Another set of criminal justice institutions would also like to reconstruct its media portrait. Corrections have fared even worse than the courts and Chapter 6 explores the historically poor media–corrections relationship.

CHAPTER SUMMARY

- The media portrait of the courts is as a source of drama and infotainment and is unrealistically constructed. Rare real-world events and activities are common; common judicial procedures and attorney activities are rare.

- The courts are alluded to as soft on crime, easy on criminals, due process–laden institutions that repeatedly release the obviously guilty and dangerous.

- When they are not crime fighters, attorneys can expect to be portrayed negatively in the media.

- Female attorneys are frequently defeminized as career women or shown as sexual creatures forwarding the incompatibility of the social roles of attorney and woman.

- Media trials which regularly appear every three to five years involve commodified and mass marketed cases displayed as massive infotainment products. The three most common types utilize narratives taken from entertainment media: abuse of power, sinful rich, and evil strangers.

- New media provide a means for the public to be active media trial participants rather than just trial followers.

- The U.S. Supreme court reversed its view of courtroom television from the Estes to the Chandler cases and after being banned for much of the last century, television cameras have become a common element in newsworthy trials.

- Prejudicial publicity has been the greatest concern of the courts regarding the news media.

- There are two strategies for dealing with pretrial publicity. Proactive mechanisms include closure and restrictive and protective orders; reactive steps include expanded jury selection, granting trial continuances, granting changes of venue, sequestering jurors, and jury instructions.

- Journalists argue that they should be protected from having to divulge information or identify their sources in order to fulfill their constitutional function as watchdogs of government activities and to guarantee their access to information. The news media has also lobbied for shield laws, or legislative protection from having to provide information.

- The courts' place in the twenty-first century is as a combination studio and production company where the most popular and gripping crime-and-justice dramas are cast and marketed.

WRITING ASSIGNMENTS

1. Write an essay discussing how a trial by jury is a small-scale example of social constructionism.

2. View and critique the portrait of the judicial system found in a commercial courtroom film, noting if the criminal law is shown in a positive or a negative light.

3. Attend a session of first appearances at the local courthouse and compare the processing of cases there with judicial processing shown in the media.

4. Watch a week's worth of crime shows and note violations of and adherence to due process protections. Also note and summarize pro and con comments on civil liberties, judges, attorneys, and the judicial system.

5. Write a paper discussing why, even though the courts determine what happens to offenders, media portraits of the courts are fewer in number than those of law enforcement.

SUGGESTED READINGS

Bailey, F., and S. Chermak. 2004. *Famous American Crimes and Trials*. Westport, CT: Praeger.

Bergman, P., and M. Asimow. 1996. *Reel Justice: The Courtroom Goes to the Movies*. Kansas City, MO: Andrews and McMeel.

Bruschke, J., and W. Loges. 2004. Free Press vs. Fair Trials: Examining Publicity's Roles in Trial Outcomes. Mahwah, NJ: Lawrence Erlbaum.

Lenz, T. 2003. Changing Images of Law in Film and Television Crime Stories. New York: Peter Lang.

Nasheri, H. 2002. *Crime and Justice in the Age of Court TV*. New York: LFB Scholarly Publishing LLC.

Sherwin, R. 2000. *When Law Goes Pop*. Chicago: University of Chicago Press.

6

Corrections

CHAPTER OBJECTIVES

After reading Chapter 6, you will

- Comprehend the common entertainment media portrait of corrections
- Appreciate the news media portrait of corrections
- Know correctional personnel concerns regarding negative news coverage
- Understand why television and infotainment programming give corrections scant attention
- Understand how media portraits of prisoners, correctional officers, and correctional institutions are connected to public support for correctional policies

HISTORICAL PERSPECTIVE

"What we've got here is a failure to communicate" (*Cool Hand Luke*, 1967).

These words of the warden in the film *Cool Hand Luke* apply as much to the social construction of corrections as they did to Paul Newman's film character. The last step in the criminal justice system, the field of corrections, is also the last thought. Society has always been more interested in catching criminals and holding media trials than in what happens to convicted offenders in our correctional institutions.

In colonial America, jails and prisons were places to hold offenders until they could be otherwise punished, usually by a corporal method such as branding, flogging, or hanging. Corrections were of little interest as institutions or as symbols of criminal justice policy. Following the enlightenment, when loss of freedom became the punishment rather than just the precursor to punishment, societal interest in prisons, prison programs, and prison conditions increased, but never to the level of interest held by policing or courtroom proceedings. Although incarceration rates have steadily increased since the beginning of

B o x 6.1   Incarceration Rates and the Media

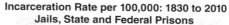

Incarceration Rate per 100,000: 1830 to 2010
Jails, State and Federal Prisons

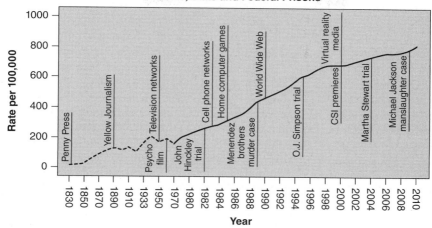

Note: 1830, 1840, 2009, 2010 rates are estimated.

Noting that the far left side covers the 140 years from 1830 to 1970 and the right side the 40 years from 1970 to 2010, Box 6.1 displays the growth in the incarceration rate in the United States along with major developments in media technology and noteworthy crime and justice media events. As shown, the incarceration rate in the United States has greatly increased since 1830, the dawn of mass media. The incarceration rate grew slowly for more than a century covering the print and early visual media eras until beginning a rapid increase during the electronic visual media era in the 1970s. Incarceration rates then hovered below or near 200 per 100,000 residents until the 1980s before more than doubling in the 10 years from 1980 to 1990. The rate continues to climb rapidly into the twenty-first century, currently exceeding 750 incarcerated persons per 100,000 residents, one of the world's highest. A causal connection between media evolution and correctional incarceration rates, of course, is not proven but the simultaneous emergence of harsh punitive correctional policies, pervasive infotainment content and various types of new media in the 1970s is apparent.

SOURCES:
Beck, A. and D. Gilliard. 1995. *Prisoners in 1994.* Bureau of Justice Statistics Bulletin, NCJ-151654. Washington, D.C.: U.S. Department of Justice.
Beck, A. and J. Karberg. 2001. *Prison and Jail Inmates at Midyear 2000.* Bureau of Justice Statistics Bulletin, NCJ-185989. Washington, D.C.: U.S. Department of Justice.
"Bureau of Justice Statistics—Table on number of persons in custody" downloaded April 24, 2009 from http://www.ojp.usdoj.gov/bjs/glance/tables/corr2tab.htm.
Cahalan, M. 1986. Historical Corrections Statistics in the United States, 1850–1984. Rockville, MD: Westat, Inc.
Harrison, P. and A. A. Beck. 2006. *Prisoners in 2005.* Bureau of Justice Statistics Bulletin, NCJ-215092. Washington, D.C.: U.S. Department of Justice.
Sabol, W. and H. Couture. 2008. *Prison Inmates at Midyear 2007.* Bureau of Justice Statistics Bulletin, NCJ-221944. Washington, D.C.: U.S. Department of Justice.

a mass media as discussed in Box 6.1, corrections has always been the stepchild of the criminal justice system. The police get the glory and the courts get the public spectacles, but corrections—both monetarily in the real world and symbolically in the media-constructed one—get the shaft.

Like a plain child who puts his worst face forward for the camera, correctional institutions have contributed to their poor image. Historically, corrections suffers from its own lack of media sophistication. Correctional personnel have been notorious for poor media and public relations, frequently blocking access to inmates and staff, withholding information, and stonewalling in times of crisis. Fortress corrections has been both a mentality and a philosophy in the field.[1]

Despite the correctional field's historic adversarial relationship with the media, the media have played a strong role in correction's public image. It is a tenet of social constructionism that the more remote the subject, the more the public perception of it will be shaped by media content. Unlike experiences with the police, who are seen in public daily, and the courts, whose institutions are prominently displayed in our cities and can be easily visited, few people have direct knowledge about corrections. Most of the general public has neither experience knowledge (from having visited a jail or served a correctional sentence) nor conversational knowledge (from talking with people who work or have been in prison). Most of the public is severely limited, therefore, in the amount of non-media-rendered information it has about prisons, jails, prisoners, probation and parole, and other correctional programs. Access to direct nonmediated knowledge of corrections is concentrated in the poor. The affluent, who influence correctional policy more, construct their corrections reality largely from media renditions.[2]

Adding to the significance of this lack of direct experienced or conversational knowledge about corrections is the historical distrust between corrections personnel and the news media. The information flow from corrections to the media can be kindly described as a trickle.[3] The scarcity of information about corrections from correctional personnel compounds the public's lack of experienced and conversational knowledge. Combined, the public's lack of direct information about corrections and the correctional field's inability to successfully get realistic correctional information into play in the news and infotainment media makes the public dependent on the unrealistic correctional images and stereotypes found in the entertainment media. Driven by profit motives, the entertainment media have not been overly concerned with projecting an accurate image of corrections. Instead, the entertainment media use the institutions as backdrops to construct stories of social power and personal morality that have little connection to correctional issues.

Lacking other sources of knowledge, the public constructs its perception of corrections from the source most easily and consistently available. The limited visual images of corrections found in television programming, news, and infotainment shows and the print-based descriptions of corrections contribute to the public perception, but prison films are by far the most influential sources for determining the social construction of corrections.[4] The importance of the prison film is due to the fact that books and magazines are less widely distributed and lack the visual impact of film. For its part, television has produced only a handful of programs based on corrections that have lasted beyond one season.[5] News stories and

Cameron Davidson/Alamy

Literally an island and thus a perfect icon for the near but isolated realm of corrections, Alcatraz has served as a popular setting for a number of films.

documentaries about corrections tend to be few in number and negative in content. Infotainment media that touch upon corrections are also rare and usually divorced from reality, dominated by violent "escape from prison" videogames. This leaves commercial films as the primary medium that creates and supports the dominant social construction of corrections.

SOURCES OF CORRECTIONAL KNOWLEDGE

Prison Films

Unlike most of the media, the film industry has extensively portrayed corrections and, as stated previously, motion pictures are the primary source of knowledge about correctional issues.[6] The attraction of prison movies lies in their ability to combine escapist fantasies that purport to reveal the backstage brutal realities of incarceration with tales of adventure and heroism. Although one of the longest-running genres (movies have been made about corrections since the early 1900s), prison films make up only about 1 percent of all films. Unfortunately, the image of corrections found in this small percentage is largely negative. Correctional movies commonly show either harsh, brutal places of legalized torture or uncontrolled human zoos that barely contain their animalistic criminals.[7] And unlike crime films, which also focus on crime fighters and even occasionally on victims as well as on the criminals, correctional films nearly universally focus on the inmates.

Within this fixation a particularly twisted construction of U.S. corrections dominates. Narrative staples of the genre include convict buddies, evil wardens, cruel guards,
craven snitches, bloodthirsty convicts, and inmate heroes. Nearly all prison films dwell
on stories of injustice and the effect of harsh treatment on individuals, and the focus is
usually on an inmate's reaction, adjustment, and triumph over the correctional system.
The movie world of corrections is a place where long-suffering virtue is rewarded and
where, ironically, one has to look to the prisoners to find moral, honest men.

These correctional archetypes exist within fantasies about sex, violence, and
salvation built around cinematic constructions marketed as "insider views" of the
realities of prison life. Unique to correctional films are pervasive promotional
claims of "based on a true story or actual event." Lacking other information
sources, claims of being true and accurate are stressed more with prison films
than with films about any other part of the criminal justice system. As criminologist Nicole Rafter observes, "No other genre so loudly proclaims its
truthfulness."[8] But despite their claims of verisimilitude, prison films distort their subject more than other criminal justice movies. Except perhaps for the media portrait
of superhero crime fighters, the construction of reality found in prison films is more
distant from the real world than the entertainment realities constructed for criminality, law enforcement, and the courts. However, due to their validity claims and the
lack of other information sources to counter them, prison movies remain the most
influential correctional social construction source for the general public.

In an extensive content analysis study, Derral Cheatwood named four different prison film narratives: the nature of confinement, the pursuit of justice, authority and control, and freedom and release.[9] These narratives dominate and guide the
stories of correctional life found in the media. Although the themes take differing
tacks in portraying prison life, all four invariably focus on inmates and take an inmate's perspective. These narratives are found across the history of prison films, but
Cheatwood identifies four eras in which each specific perspective dominates.

Nature of confinement correctional films (1929 to 1942) dominate the
first era and are exemplified by classic films such as *The Big House, I Am a Fugitive
from a Chain Gang*, and *20,000 Years in Sing Sing*. In this perspective, inmates appear
as victims of injustice, either as good men framed or imprisoned by a chance accident or pushed into crime by powerful societal forces. A recurrent message in these
films is the corrupt values of the correctional system and its administrators. This first
era established and cemented the unique correctional backwards law common to
prison films. In prison films the corrections backwards law works through a role
reversal derived from the dynamic of the underdog, wrongly jailed inmates pitted
against oppressive correctional employees. The inmate-hero was born in this era
and has since dominated the portrait of corrections.

Pursuit of justice correctional films (1943 to 1962) dominated the second
era, and *The Birdman of Alcatraz* and *Riot in Cell Block 11* are typical examples. A
more hopeful narrative, these films retained a focus on violence in prison, which
they share with the nature of confinement films. In this era, however, offenders
were portrayed as personally responsible for their actions, less often as victims and
more often as criminals. Confinement is therefore justified, and the focus shifted to
the flaws of the criminal and away from flaws in the criminal justice system.

Although many of this era's films revolve around violence—riots, escapes, and inmate and guard hostility—individual offender rehabilitation is seen as a possibility.

The third era, **authority and control correctional films** (1963 to 1980), is exemplified by films such as *Cool Hand Luke* and *Escape from Alcatraz*. This era reintroduced a pessimistic view of corrections against a continuing backdrop of riot and escape stories. Offender confinement is still justified, but it occurs for less serious offenses. This era is most significant for immortalizing the "smug hack" portrait of correctional officers as the evil foil of the inmate heroes. In these films, correctional officers are borderline crazy, insensitive, and ineffective. Officer corruption is portrayed as universal. The world of corrections is constructed as a freestanding social ecosystem with corrupt correctional officers as just one of the system's species. Like the Galapagos Islands, correctional institutions are painted as strange primitive islands, long separated from mainland society, where bizarre species have evolved to fill unique local niches. Within this isolated ecosystem, all facets of prison life became subject to exploitation, producing the first, if unrealistic media portrayals of real prison problems—rape, racism, and drugs.

The fourth and current prison film era, **freedom and release correctional films**, is represented by futuristic science fiction films about prison colonies and prisoner transportation systems, exemplified by the films *Escape from New York, The Fortress*, and *Aliens 3* or by throwback renditions of early-era portraits represented by films like *Holes* and *The Shawshank Redemption*. Extreme violence appears for the first time in prison movies, and the "prison action film" appears. The ambiguity and

Buena Vista Pictures/Courtesy: Everett Collection

The film, The Rock, is a prison action film set in Alcatraz in which Sean Connerly as an aged, unjustly imprisoned "James Bond" helps Nicolar Cage save San Francisco from a renegade military unit. Imprisonment issues have been replaced by gun battles, intrigue, and biological weapons.

confusion about the function and role of prisons in society is reflected in these films, which finalize the process of humanizing the inmates and dehumanizing the guards. In this era, the keepers are certifiably insane and are sometimes inhuman part-machine creatures or simply holographic projections. Images of prison violence, rape, and death remain common.[10] The correctional world as constructed in these films reflects the fantasy world of comics more than any recognizable social reality.

With this sometimes bizarre, always myopic, long-running cinematic base of information, the public is more disadvantaged in constructing an alternate worldview of corrections than it is in constructing other components of the criminal justice system. The true issues and needs of corrections are absent or perversely distorted in these constructions. Prison films remain silent on the fundamental issues of imprisonment, reveling in violence and cruelty instead.[11] In these movies, the kept are the heroes and the keepers are the villains. In film, correctional institutions are as removed from their real-world counterparts as most science fiction films are from the NASA space program. Unfortunately, when the other limited sources of correctional information available to the public are examined and added, their contribution does little to correct the dominant prison film constructions of a world sprinkled with a few good men among a population of violent, crazed, sex-driven individuals. True to form in getting it backwards, in the media, more often than not, the best men are wearing inmate jumpsuits; some of the most crazed, violent, evil ones are wearing correctional officer uniforms.

Correctional Television and Infotainment

In television entertainment programming, corrections is the least-shown component of the criminal justice system—and therefore by extension the least important. Television has had fewer shows focused on corrections and they have been shorter lived than any other aspect of the criminal justice system.[12] The few television programs that have featured jails or prisons have either been slapstick comedy or featured inmates rather than staff. More often, television information about corrections is communicated through indirect negative allusions to correctional alumni, the recidivist offenders found in law enforcement shows. With habitual criminals outnumbering first offenders by more than four to one on television, media indirectly constructs corrections as ill equipped and unable to rehabilitate offenders. Instead, media imply that the corrections system is for criminals simply a stepping-stone from which they frequently return to society as worse criminals than when they were sentenced. With the scarcity of programming that looks directly at corrections, perhaps the greatest impact of television on the social construction of corrections is as a means of extending the life and reach of commercial prison films. Television's recycling of the more than one hundred corrections movies made since the 1920s provides a continuous, negative media loop in which corrections is constructed negatively anew for each succeeding generation.

The infotainment genre has slowly discovered corrections (see Box 6.2). There are now television programs with titles like "Inside American Jail," "Intervention," "Street Time," and "Parole Board" that mirror popular court and police counterparts. The delay in correctional infotainment programming is partly due to the fact that, as noted, prison entertainment films already market

B o x 6.2   Paris Goes to Jail—Corrections and Infotainment

AP Photo/Kevork Djansezian

Paris Hilton leaving Los Angeles County jail.

Corrections receives an infotainment treatment when a celebrity receives a jail sentence, even a short one. When Paris Hilton was sentence to jail the event received international coverage. An example of the coverage and social construction of her corrections encounter from the ABC Good Morning America Web site shows a typical portrayal of U.S. jails.

For Paris Hilton, Jail Will Be an 'Awful, Hellish Place'

Paris Hilton's Stint in Jail Will Be No Four-Star Retreat
America's favorite party girl has been ordered to jail, and her stay there will be no trip to the Hilton. A judge sentenced Paris Hilton to 45 days in a Los Angeles county jail Friday for violating her probation. Come June 5, Hilton will be confined to a seg-regated 8-by-12-foot cell in a Lynwood, California, detention center for women. Her designer duds won't be welcome. "She will be in an orange jumpsuit, and everything else, the accoutrement, the makeup, is an absolute minimum," said Sgt. Steve Whitmore of the L.A. County Sheriff's Department.

Hilton's cell phone, her crystal-encrusted trademark, will be banned as well. But not being able to text and talk with her celebrity friends will be the least of Hilton's worries. "Forty-five days in L.A. County Jail is really rough. That's an awful, hellish place," said criminal defense attorney Dana Cole. "Conditions are miserable, people take showers under cold dripping water, the food is completely inedible."

Publicity-Hungry Celeb Goes Silent
The scene outside the courthouse Friday looked like a red carpet event, with paparazzi and an entourage struggling to catch a glimpse of the star inside. But Hilton couldn't act her way out of the alcohol-related reckless driving conviction against her. "I'm very sorry, I did not do it on purpose at all," she pleaded to judge Michael Sauer. Sauer threw the book at her.

(continued)

B o x   6.2   Paris Goes to Jail—Corrections and Infotainment (Continued)

Despite her penchant for publicity, after hearing her sentence, the 26-year-old celebutante left the courthouse and said nothing. Howard Weitzman, Hilton's attorney, said he'd appeal. "She's been selectively targeted in my opinion to be prosecuted because of who she is," he said. Prosecutors denied they targeted Hilton, who pleaded no contest in January to reckless driving and driving under the influence. She was stopped twice after that and charged for violating her parole. "No one in Los Angeles is above the law," said Los Angeles city attorney Rocky Delgadillo (downloaded January 24, 2010 from http://abcnews.go.com/GMA/story?id=3143374&page=1).

Ms. Hilton served 23 days in a Los Angeles jail followed by 40 days of home confinement. Following her release she appeared on the Larry King show and noted that "Letters from fans and supporters from around the world, including U.S. soldiers in Iraq and people as far away as India, helped her get through the 23 days in lockup" (downloaded from MSNBC site January 24, 2010 from http://www.msnbc.msn.com/id/19467267/).

---

themselves as accurate portraits of correctional life. The public was told that it was already getting correctional reality programming in movie theaters. Even when greater media interest to create correctional infotainment products exists, correctional administrators have little incentive to cooperate. Coupled with the historical distrust of the media on the part of correctional officials and their reluctance to provide access, correctional content continues to lag in infotainment media. And due to the entertainment criteria that drive infotainment programming, correctional infotainment that *is* created is not likely to result in greater public support for corrections. The historical impact of film documentaries that have focused on corrections substantiates this expectation. Correctional documentaries that have received widespread public play have ultimately resulted in negative attention and criticism for their subject institutions. For example, the documentary film *Titticut Follies*, which shows life in an institution for the criminally insane, and *Scared Straight*, which describes a popular shock incarceration program for juveniles, both resulted in criticisms of the correctional administrators and personnel and lawsuits against the institutions. Whether the current spate of correctional infotainment programs will improve the image of corrections, correctional officers, or correctional programs remains to be determined.

Corrections in the News

Contrary to common impressions, there is not a lack of attention about corrections in the news.[13] In a study of television and newspaper news, Steven Chermak found that 17 percent of crime-and-justice stories involved correctional institutions in some manner.[14] This is still substantively less than the level of attention given to law enforcement or courts, but corrections is not as off-the-radar in the news as it is in television entertainment programming.[15] Most references to corrections, however, are found inside stories focused on a different component of the criminal justice system or are found within stories that trace an individual offender or case as it progresses through the system. Still about one-fifth of the crime–and–justice news at least acknowledges the existence of corrections.

Concerning the mainstay of news coverage, the coverage of individual cases, Table 6.1 reports Chermak's findings and shows how corrections fares compared

TABLE 6.1   Newspaper and Television Crime Stories by Criminal Justice Stage

Stage	Percent of stories
Discovery of crime	18.7%
Investigation	4.2
Arrest	15.4
Arraignment	13.3
Law Enforcement (subtotal 51.6%)	
Courts	
Pre-trial motions	3.7
Plea agreement	2.7
Trial	9.1
Jury deliberation	0.4
Verdict	3.9
Sentence	7.3
Appeal	2.3
Supreme Court decision	0.8
Courts (subtotal 30.2%)	
Corrections	
Probation behavior	0.1
Commitment to prison	0.4
Parole behavior	1.8
Pardon request	0.3
Release from Prison	1.1
Execution	0.5
Corrections (subtotal 4.2%)	
Other Story Types	
Follow-ups[*]	12.7
Other[†]	1.4

Note: N = 1,979 stories.

[*]Follow-ups include either victim, defendant, or crime follow-ups (for example, a story about the impact that a crime had on a victim's family).

[†]Other stories include other court settlements.

Source: Steve Chermak. 1998. "Police, Courts, and Corrections in the Media" page 92 in *Popular Culture, Crime and Justice*, Frankie Bailey and Donna Hale (eds.), Belmont, CA: Wadsworth.

with law enforcement and the courts in terms of news coverage. Individually based correctional stories are usually presented through a reference to an offender's commitment to prison, behavior on parole, or execution.[16] The operation of the front-end focus of the news media on law enforcement is clearly shown. News reports that concentrate on law enforcement activities (discovery of crimes through the formal charging of suspects) comprise more than 50 percent of news stories, court proceedings (pre-trial motions through Supreme Court decisions) about 30 percent, and corrections (probation to execution) less than 5 percent.

As far as individual cases and offenders are concerned, what happens in corrections is not the typical news story focus. Once they leave the courtroom, offenders usually disappear from the news unless they violate parole or probation, are released from prison, or are executed. News stories that discuss correctional institutions are found either inside stories about other criminal justice topics or within lengthy special reports, usually produced by the print media. In television news coverage of corrections, extraordinary events dominate. The more mundane aspects of prison management, legislation, and litigation are unlikely to appear on national televised news.[17] More developed and contextualized issue-focused news stories that discuss the daily operation of prisons, how inmates adapt to the conditions of incarceration, and institutional programs do exist. Unfortunately, they are rare and can distort correctional policies and practices.[18] In contrast, many news stories incorporate day-to-day police and court operations such as arrests, charging, verdicts, and sentencing. Nonincarceration aspects of corrections, such as probation or community corrections, receive even less media attention.[19]

Why do corrections fare so poorly in the news? A number of factors determine the quantity of correctional news coverage. First, compared to other crime-and-justice stories, corrections has a relative low newsworthiness value. News personnel do not think a defendant's correctional behavior is interesting to the public. Once a newsworthy individual enters a correctional institution and settles into the routines of correctional life, unless he or she does something noteworthy in prison, such as dying, the individual is not often seen as particularly newsworthy. Second, corrections stories are difficult to produce because news media traditionally have only limited access to corrections sources. There is no corrections newsbeat that matches the police and court beats in journalism, so corrections stories are time consuming to produce because a preexisting journalism–corrections link does not exist. The information channels and public information officers commonly found in police stations and courthouses, while increasing, remain absent in many correctional institutions. Third, reporters usually have limited prior knowledge of corrections and likely need to be introduced to the discipline during a breaking news story—almost always a negative one involving an escape, assault, or riot. Reporters do not maintain relationships with correctional officials as they often do with police or court officials. The weak news media–correctional personnel relationship is reflected by the fact that correctional personnel are the least likely of all sources to be quoted in news stories, accounting for less than 1 percent of the total.[20]

On the corrections side of the news creation process, the closed environment of correctional programs helps to shield officials from external scrutiny. Correctional officials are more able to control information because media access to inmates is limited by law to a much greater extent than in the other components of the criminal justice system.[21] For corrections administrators, controlling information frequently translates into releasing no information. Prison administrators have a large number of justifications and mechanisms available to limit media access. Claims of institutional security needs; ongoing investigations; prisoner confidentiality, privacy, and rehabilitation considerations; and bureaucratic red tape (especially in arranging interviews) are common justifications to deny access. Delaying mechanisms include using uninformed personnel to slow the release of information to the media (corrections are the least likely criminal justice agencies to employ trained public information officers and to seek positive coverage so that the large majority of prison news stories remain media initiated), directing staff to present themselves as apolitical and inappropriate to comment on political decisions such as punishment policies, and simply being geographically isolated.[22] Ironically, the net result of these information blocks and delaying tactics is that newsworthy offenders are often pilloried by the media before trial, when they are still presumed innocent, and shielded from the media afterwards, when they have been declared guilty.[23]

But while they can limit media access using the above-mentioned blocks and delays, prison officials are not able to significantly control the content of news coverage that does occur because alternate sources of information about correctional conditions are available. These include inside leaked information provided by correctional officers (this source is limited, however, by the historic media portrait of correctional officers as "hacks" and the resultant officer distrust of the media, job loss if their identity is revealed, and confidentiality agreements many institutions require correctional officers to sign); inmates (also limited because inmate interview access is often severe); and inmate families, elected officials, defense attorneys, researchers and academics, and prison support and prisoner rights groups. In addition, because administrators are less likely to have the media competing for access, they cannot use a need for access to influence the content of coverage. Aaron Doyle and Richard Ericson describe this relationship:

> Prison officials are less able to offer "exclusives" or "scoops." Unlike the situations with police, the routine operations of prisons seldom offer news items for which media outlets will compete. As interviews with correctional officials responsible for public relations show, the chief messages they are trying to mobilize consist of "good news" about the system, such as stories about Christmas in prison or prisoners doing woodwork or growing flowers. These represent puny coin in the currency of crime news, compared to accounts featuring more dramatic fare such as official deviance and mayhem within the walls.[24]

Because the media do not have a daily corrections news need, which would give a correctional administrator more influence over correctional news creation and more leverage to influence content, negative coverage of corrections can be produced without much concern. In that there is no media need to maintain ongoing regular access to correctional authorities, the news media need not worry about burning their bridges to corrections; there is no continuous bridge traffic. Negative correctional news can be produced without media concern about subsequent repercussions or access restrictions.

The cumulative effect of these factors is that access to the criminal justice system as well as the resulting media content remains front-end loaded. Compared with the police, who are sometimes eager to interact with the media and who work on the public streets, and the courts, whose main events are usually open to the public and press, the daily lives of prisons are far more shrouded. The pressrooms and available documents such as police blotters and court dockets have no equivalents in corrections. Therefore, most of the news of corrections that is produced is dominated by riots, escapes, and the release or death of newsworthy individuals—just like in the movies. In the end, three types of negative stories typify correctional news. The first are stories about correctional failures to protect the public. These include prison escapes, staff negligence in supervising inmates, and failure to control prisoners. Second are stories of corrections pursuing inappropriate goals in which punishment is absent while amenities are highlighted. The description of prison partying by inmates, plush recreation rooms with color television, and air-conditioned cells are the stock of these stories. Third are stories of **correctional horrors**, which are exemplified by corruption and misconduct exposés. These can be either individual bad-apple stories (the sadistic guard) or systemic corruption stories (the corrupt warden and administration), and they often employ the death of an inmate as the symbolic crime of the correctional system's failure. As Box 6.3 highlights, when presented with a story that fills one of these niches, the media are willing to expend considerable effort and resources, at least for a short time, to explore and construct another correctional system gone bad.

In sum, the news construction of corrections is scanty, and when covered, corrections are marketed in a manner that emphasizes predators and criminogenic institutions. The day-to-day administration of punishment as a loss of freedom and attempts to rehabilitate do not fit common media narratives.[25] The prison sentence as a long tedious block of time where nothing changes is absolute anathema to the dramatic event that is typical of a "hard news" item. There are few dramatic rituals or events involved in prison life, and those that do occur are negative and involve death and violence.

Finally, just as in the entertainment media, news of corrections focuses on the inmates and ignores the staff. After a content study of 1,546 newspaper articles, criminologist Robert Freeman reports that negative stories about corrections significantly outnumber positive ones, and the positive ones tend to focus on inmates, not staff.[26] Thus, as also found in news of crime, law enforcement, and the courts, corrections is covered more often as an act connected to an individual than as an issue connected to a system. Even so, corrections news does focus on policy questions more often than do police and court news. Release policies, institutional conditions (usually as follow-up to riot, death, and escape stories), execution coverage (which sometimes incorporates the debate over the death penalty and the issue of the racial composition of death row), terrorism and corrections (see Box 6.4), and the

B o x 6.3   Media Resources and Correctional Bad News

Bettmann/CORBIS

An Atlanta police source called a veteran police reporter of the *Journal and Constitution* with a blockbuster: The Atlanta Federal Penitentiary was under siege. "He said the [Cuban] detainees had taken over part of the prison and they might have hostages." The tip was passed to the day city editor. Within minutes, amid the normal pressure of an early deadline, the newsroom kicked into high gear. During the eleven-day crisis, the assistant managing editor would assign more than a hundred staffers to the story:

We had constant updates for all seven editions. The Staff produced 9 to 12 new stories daily. In 48 hours we did mini-profiles on 65 of the hostages plus nine others who had been released. And a 5,000 word history of the Marielitos and a 2,500 word piece about what life is like inside the prison.

Four extra open pages provided prison news each day. Photographers were stationed in helicopters, in cherry pickers, in trees, and on rooftops around the clock. Reporters worked shifts at the prison, and each shift included one person who was fluent in Spanish. A Spanish-speaking copyeditor was sent with a news team to Oakdale, Louisiana, to cover events at the federal detention center there, where rioting had begun two days before the Atlanta uprising. A Hispanic copy clerk monitored radio transmissions in the newsroom. Suburban reporters maintained a twenty-four-hour vigil at Dobbins Air Force Base near Atlanta to alert editors if federal troops arrived. (They didn't.) The Washington bureau covered angles at the Immigration and Naturalization service and the Justice Department.

B o x 6.4   Terrorism, Corrections, and the Media

AP Photo

The ongoing war on terror has resulted in additional negative media attention on corrections. First off, terrorists as prisoners create new concerns for correctional personnel. Even a small number of ideologically dedicated terrorists in a prison population will generate a unique and significant challenge and raise fears of personnel, public, and institutional safety and security. Inmate terrorists increase the possibility of the radicalization of other inmates, the targeting of correctional institutions and personnel for terror attacks, and the operating of terror cells from within prisons. Correctional personnel need to be aware that they are viewed as soldiers in an opposing army and as legitimate targets by terrorists. Secondly, following the 2001 September 11th attacks and the Iraq war the number and dangerousness of imprisoned terrorists increased rapidly. Subsequent drives to prevent future terror attacks in the United States resulted in extraordinary correctional practices by the U.S. throughout the world and brought the previously separate realms of military prisons, intelligence gathering, the media, and civilian corrections together.

Driven to deter future attacks in the United States and facing pressing counter-intelligence needs generated by an insurgency in Iraq, a subculture tolerant of the torture of prisoners held in U.S. custody developed. The world media eventually focused on three related story lines. The first and the most dominant concerned the abuse of Iraqi prisoners held in the U.S. military prison Abu Ghraib. Triggered by the

2004 release of graphic photos of prisoners being abused by U.S. military personnel as shown above and therefore a picture-driven and more newsworthy story, prisoner torture at Abu Ghraib quickly become an international news focus. Adding to concerns about the use of torture in Abu Ghraib was the emergence of the second news story line about secret prisons established and run by the U.S. Central Intelligence Agency in various countries around the globe. As with Abu Ghraib, torture of prisoners under U.S. control was alleged. The third story line followed the creation and operation of the military prison in Guantanamo, Cuba, administered by the U.S. military and set up to house terrorist and Taliban combatants. The status of the inmates generated legal challenges and, in turn, more negative news coverage.

Driven by these parallel streams, through the 2000s a steady flow of news stories demonizing the CIA, military prisons, and their personnel added to the preexisting tradition of negative news construction of civilian correctional institutions and personnel. Today, the interplay of media, corrections, and terrorism continues with the trial in civilian court of former Guantanamo prison inmates. The trial of the most infamous defendant, Khalid Sheikh Mohhammed, accused mastermind of the 2001 September 11th attacks, is sure to be constructed as a major media trial in the evil stranger "non-American" ilk. Even before the trials began they generated criticism for creating an unnecessary security risk for New York City and for extending unwarranted due process protections to the defendants. The story line of the secret CIA prisons has also been resurrected and linked to the terror trial proceedings by defense attorneys. They have requested visits to the overseas sites of the secret CIA prisons to gather information that might have relevance regarding the level of coercion involved in obtaining their client statements (and hence their legal admissibility) and the appropriateness of a death penalty sentence should evidence of prior cruel and unusual punishment exist.

Collectively, the social construction of these twenty-first-century correctional "symbolic crimes" has significantly extended the general preexisting negative public perception of corrections. Here are media examples of "smug hack" corrections brought to new heights.

SOURCES:

Berger, J. 2009. "Giuliani Criticizes Terror Trials in New York." *The New York Times*, November 16. Downloaded January 26, 2010 from http://www.nytimes.com/.

Gerstein, J. 2009. "New York Terrorist Trial Raises Stakes" November 13, Downloaded January 23, 2010 from http://www.politico.com/new/stories/1109/29486.html.

Grey, S. and D. Carvajal. 2007. "Secret Prisons in 2 Countries Held Qaeda Suspects, Report Says." *The New York Times*. June 8: A12. Downloaded January 19, 2010 from http://proquest.umi.com/.

Hamm, M. 2008. "Prisoner Radicalization: Assessing the Threat in U.S. Correctional institutions." *NIJ Journal 261*. Washington, D.C.: National Institute of Justice.

Hersh, S. 2004. *Chain of Command: The Road from 9/11 to Abu Ghraib*. New York: Harper Collins.

Hunter, S. 1988. "Terrorists in Prison: Security Concerns and Management Strategies." *Corrections Today* 50(4): 30, 32, 34.

Latanya, A. C. and N. Abeles. 2009. "Ethics, Prisoner Interrogation, National Security, and the Media." *Psychological Services*, 6(1): 11–21.

Priest, D. 2005. "CIA Holds Terror Suspects in Secret Prisons." *The Washington Post*, November 2. Downloaded January 20, 2010 from http://www.Washingtonpost.com/.

Useem, B. and O. Clayton. 2009. "Radicalization of U.S. Prisoners." *Criminology and Public Policy*. 8(3): 561–592.

Vogt, E. 2007. *Terrorists in Prison: The Challenge Facing Corrections*. Inside Homeland Security. Downloaded January 26, 2010 from http://www.nicic.org/Library/022793

Weiser, G. 2009. "Secret C.I.A. Jails an Issue in Terror Case." *The New York Times*, July 2: A20. Downloaded January 25, 2010 from http://proquest.umi.com/.

incarceration of juveniles and mentally retarded offenders all receive periodic coverage. In addition, news stories periodically appear concerning innovative correctional projects such as intermediate sanctions, shock incarceration, or electronic home monitoring. A final irony of correctional news coverage emerges. Although corrections is the least covered component of the criminal justice system, it is the most likely to have its policies, missions, and basic functions discussed in the news. Corrections is comparatively ignored by the media, but at least it is ignored in depth.

CORRECTIONS PORTRAITS AND STEREOTYPES

What are the portraits of corrections that are constructed from these information sources? The three most important ones involve the social construction of prisoners, correctional institutions, and correctional officers. The construction of incarcerated prisoners together with the construction of freed offenders discussed in Chapter 3 provide the public with its cumulative picture of criminality, its nature, and, most important, its amenability to rehabilitation. If inmates are constructed as incorrigible and innately evil, this logically leads toward correctional policies of incapacitation and capital punishment. On the other hand, if inmates are shown as victimized— basically good but misled—then policies of rehabilitation and resocialization make more sense. In essence, the more inmates are constructed as similar to the rest of us, the more it makes sense to offer more help and less punishment. The more they are constructed as different, as predatory and inhuman, the more sensible it is to permanently remove, punish, and execute them.

In the same vein, the manner in which correctional institutions are constructed is important for the correctional policies and programs that make sense to society. If the institutions are violent madhouses filled with irrational predators (inmates or staff), money for work, education, or counseling programs will appear to be wasteful. However, if the institutions are constructed as understaffed, underfunded places where humane correctional officers are trying to supervise large numbers of offenders, some of whom are redeemable, then public monies for these institutions and their programs will make more sense. Again, the more inmates are seen as like the rest of us—if there is a "there but for the grace of God" reaction to the way they are portrayed—the more palatable improvements to conditions and programs in these institutions will be viewed.

Finally, the social construction of correctional officers is important, particularly if they are vilified. The more violent and predatory the staff is shown to be, the less attractive these positions appear to recruits as possible careers and the more the public is led away from putting money into corrections. Why give money to innately corrupt vile administrations or raise the salary of brutal guards? In contrast, a social construction of a humane staff striving to help salvageable inmates brings an opposite reaction. In that frame of mind, steering public resources into corrections would be sensible. With these implications in mind, the portraits and stereotypes of prisoners, correctional institutions, and correctional officers are described.

Prisoners

Two popular constructions of inmates are found in the mass media. One is for male prisoners and the other is for females. The dominant construction of male prisoners derives from the role reversal of a heroic offender caught up in a violent correctional system run by predatory criminal justice system workers. Those in authority are portrayed as predators and those caught up in the system are shown as victims. A minor part in the total media picture of law enforcement and court personnel, in the social construction of corrections such role reversals are common and result in a portrait that frequently sides with the kept rather than the keepers. Tapping into the American cultural tendency to root for underdogs, the irony of the media construction of male prisoners is that most of the predator criminals who terrorized society in the crime-fighting media are reconstructed in the correctional media as victims. The predatory offenders who remain and appear in corrections media constructions are there to threaten the **heroic inmates** and to create an atmosphere of a constant threat of violence within the institutions. In total number, prisoners are constructed as inhuman, dangerous, and deserving of harsh punishment.[27] A small number, however, are heroic victims.

If the male prisoners appear within narrow stereotypes, female inmates fare even worse. With remarkably few exceptions, female inmates are found in constructions containing high levels of gratuitous sex (primarily lesbianism and rape) and correctional officer dominance and sadism.[28] The most common portrait of female prisoners is found in bad-girl, low-budget B movies that have been described as squalid mixtures of sex and violence.[29] The films reinforce stereotypes about female prisoners as violent, worthless, sex-crazed monsters.[30] Not limited to commercial films, this focus on violence and sex in female prisons has also been found in recent reality-infotainment newsmagazines, talk shows, and documentary programs which frame women's imprisonment in a similar fashion and focus on violence, sex, and failed motherhood.[31] Other issues such as drug, sexual, and physical abuse histories are downplayed and it is argued that these images provide unchallenged images of female corrections, especially for young males.[32] Overall, media portraits of female prisoners adhere to the backwards law and focus on atypical female inmates while ignoring the reality facing incarcerated women.[33] The construction of women offenders and female correctional institutions is so juvenile and ridiculous that it could be dismissed if there were alternate information sources to counter them. Unfortunately there are not.

Collectively then, male and female prisoners are often portrayed as victims rather than as offenders. The more normal and similar to law abiding people they appear, the more they are constructed as victims of corrupt correctional systems. Victimization of offenders can come from other predatory, violent, psychotic inmates or predatory, violent, psychotic correctional officers. Both clearly are more dangerous than the struggling inmate heroes. The message is that both need to be removed from the correctional institutions they are terrorizing. The constructed portrait of these institutions reflects the paradoxical construction of their populations—that reform must begin not with the prisoners but with the institutions and staff. Prisoners are either incorrigible and beyond rehabilitation and need to be separated from the redeemable or are the moral superiors to staff and administration and must not be brought down to their level.

Correctional Institutions

The media-constructed universe of corrections contains a galaxy of institutions in which the most sensational and dramatic correctional stereotypes are emphasized. The complex political, social, and economic realities of correctional facilities are ignored, and a corrections template that is stark and bleak is presented instead. **Smug hack corrections**, described as several interwoven portraits of negative correctional imagery, make up the media-constructed correctional world.[34]

Physical brutality in the name of inmate discipline is common. Control is maintained with corporal punishment and severe infliction of pain, often for trivial rule violations. This physical brutality is often linked with the exploitation of inmates as a cheap source of labor and profit. Staff incompetence, corruption, and cruelty are common, ingrained, and unchallenged. Under the thumb of a despotic staff, the prisoners suffer systemic racial prejudice, homosexual rape, and institutionalized violence. If female, the inmates suffer further degradation, sexual assaults, and harassments. Ironically, although the inmates are often shown sympathetically, the overall construction of corrections does not result in public support for correctional programs. The largely negative portraits of correctional officers and staff and the violent institutions they inhabit promotes a nonsupportive public image of corrections. Not only is this negative media image of correctional institutions the historical portrait found in film, but recent media depictions on cable television and in popular literature show little progress.

Correctional Officers

As pointed out, correctional media usually focus on the inmates, frequently ignoring the staff and administration totally, or, when they are portrayed, showing them negatively. The **smug hack** portrayal of correctional officers—caricatures of brutality, incompetence, low intelligence, and indifference to human suffering—dominates. This negative correctional officer construction creates a perception of modern corrections that remains locked in a pre-1960s frame of punitive human warehousing. The media-promulgated imagery provides the baseline for the public's construction of corrections and correctional officers. Whereas the police are heroic rescuers and the attorneys (at least sometimes) are the preservers of truth and justice, media-constructed correctional officers are, more often than not, oppressive villains. If not oppressive, they are irrelevant. In the media, incarceration turns criminal predators into imprisoned prey and villainous criminals into inmate heroes. These inmate heroes need villains to defeat, and the correctional staff members are enlisted to fill that role. The result is that the hero inmates end up as more sympathetic characters than the correctional officers who, along with stereotypic predator prisoners, appear as cardboard cut-out clichés.[35] The accompanying role reversal makes good theater and escapism, but it paints a particularly onerous portrait of correctional officers.

THE PRIMITIVE "LOST WORLD" OF CORRECTIONS

The prison is present in our lives and, at the same time, it is absent from our lives.[36] In the novel *The Lost World*, by Arthur Doyle, an isolated primitive environment filled with prehistoric beasts is found to secretly exist. The media-constructed portrait of corrections shares similarities with Doyle's fictional lost world: primitive predators, bizarre rituals and tribes, a society ruled by the law of the jungle, hidden but existing near our own—there but invisible. The impact of the media on the public's constructed portrait of corrections is due to its primacy effect. That is, like the adage about "making your first impressions count," the first set of information about a person, group, or organization that one receives has greater weight than later information because it creates an initial resilient perception. In constructionist terms, once a construction takes root, it is resistant to change. If the first information is negative, the unflattering initial impression created by that information will tend to dominate and persist even if later information is positive. For corrections, the first impressions are usually picked up from prison films and other infotainment media (see Box 6.5) and are likely to be negative. They also are likely to be reinforced rather than challenged by information provided in the news and infotainment media. The impact of the initial negative messages is compounded for the public through its repeated exposure to the continually rerun prison films and recycled news footage of past prison riots and escapes. It is highly unlikely for the typical media consumer to have positive perceptions of corrections or to have his or her negative perceptions of corrections challenged in the current media environment.

Prison films, tabloid-style crime reporting, television programming, the focus on prison riots and brutal attacks by paroled assailants, and the less-than-flattering portrait of correctional staff and administrators comprise the foundation for the social construction of corrections. This construction has been blamed for helping to heighten the public's fear of crime; for eroding public confidence in the ability of corrections to deter, rehabilitate, or even retain criminals; and for increasing the public's desire to make the system more punitive for all offenders regardless of their offense history or forecast dangerousness.[37] Although there is no conclusive evidence of how viewers are affected by these works[38] and although there exist examples of prison reforms triggered by media,[39] their media images are felt to translate into a lack of public support for real-life correctional institutions while ironically constructing prison as the sole solution to violent crime—in which rising criminality is viewed as proof of their necessity.[40] Like the police who gain public support when crime goes up, corrections, at least in term of more cells, gain public support in times of increasing crime rates, a tendency countered only when economic downturns force institution closures and early prisoner release.

To this point, the tour of the media-constructed world of criminal justice has made its way from the crimes and criminals, to the crime fighters, through the courts, and into the correctional system. In general, neither the criminal justice system nor its employees are positively presented in the media, and the further one moves into the system, the less information is available and the worse the constructed image is. How does this portrait of criminality and criminal justice translate

B o x 6.5   New Media and Corrections—The Facebook Fugitive

Newscom

New media has made slow inroads into corrections in the form of GPS systems to monitor home confinement inmates and the use of live video camera links to conduct family and attorney visits. For good or ill, Internet applications have also begun to appear. Thus, a number of live Web cams sited in correctional institutions can be found in a Google search. And carrying on the tradition of bad news dominating news about corrections, one jail escapee pictured above used Facebook postings to taunt police and merge "being on the run" with the communication capabilities of new media.

An escaped prisoner has been telling the world via Facebook about his life as a fugitive—describing everything from his meals to who his next girlfriend will be ... posting "is thinking, which lucky girl will be my first of 2010!!" Police are trying to use clues left on his Facebook to track down where the convicted burglar may be hiding. (Han, 2009).

To avoid capture, the fugitive had "constructed a web of personal profiles and fan pages, each with varying degrees of privacy. At last count, he had 7,300 fans and 1,300 friends ("Facebook Fugitive Taunts Cops"). In January 2010, after four months on the run his Facebook page was shut down and the 'Facebook fugitive' was reported captured (www.allfacebook.com/2010/01/facebook-fugitive-craig-lynch-caught/).

into criminal justice policy? What public attitudes about crime and justice are associated with these constructions? Which steps to deal with crime are encouraged and which ones are discouraged? The next two chapters answer these questions. Chapter 7 examines crime control efforts based on media communication campaigns and media technologies. Chapter 8 looks at the media's influence on the public's support for various criminal justice policies.

CHAPTER SUMMARY

- The public is most dependent on the media for information about corrections but compared to criminals, crime fighters and criminal trials, corrections is usually ignored in the media.

- The most prevalent portrait of corrections is found in commercial prison films, which construct prison life as violent and dehumanizing while promoting heroic inmates as protagonists. Correctional officers are often villains.

- Prisoners are often portrayed as victims rather than as offenders.

- Female prisoners are portrayed in sexually charged sadistic institutions.

- Correctional institutions are portrayed as stark, bleak violent places staffed by brutal incompetent guards.

- The field of corrections has historically had an adversarial relationship with the news media and the news covers corrections usually after a negative event such as an escape, death, or riot.

- Media access to correctional institutions and inmates has been poor and often blocked by correctional administrations.

- Due to the historical adversarial relationship between media and corrections, infotainment media has been slow to exploit corrections for programming.

- Corrections as an issue is seldom addressed in the media and corrections is constructed as a separate primitive world divorced from mainstream society.

WRITING ASSIGNMENTS

1. Write an essay about why bad news about corrections is more newsworthy than good news and what, if anything, correctional personnel can do to significantly change the public image of corrections. Discuss who is most responsible for the content and nature of news about corrections—correctional administrators, journalists, news agency administrators, or the public?

2. Similar to the differences pointed out in Chapter 4 between media and street police, list differences between media correction officers and real correctional officers.

3. Watch the film *The Shawshank Redemption*, and critique its use of correctional stereotypes and what correctional policies are supported or opposed by the film's portrait.

4. Watch crime shows for a week and note how many criminals are also ex-prisoners. Also note how deterrence and rehabilitation are portrayed as likely outcomes of incarceration.

SUGGESTED READINGS

Bailey, F. and D. Hale. 1998. *Popular Culture, Crime, and Justice*. Belmont, CA: West/Wadsworth.

Freeman, R. 2000. *Popular Culture and Corrections*. Lanham, MD: American Correctional Association.

Mason, P. 2006. *Captured by the Media: Prison Discourse in Popular Culture*. Cullompton, UK: Willan Publishing

Wilson, D. and S. O'Sullivan. 2004. *Images of Incarceration: Representations of Prison in Film and Television Drama*. Winchester, UK: Waterside Press.

7

Crime Control

CHAPTER OBJECTIVES

After reading Chapter 7, you will

- Understand the use of the three types of Madison Avenue–style anticrime ads
- Comprehend the increased use of media technology to process criminal cases
- Appreciate the growth of surveillance of public spaces and associated issues and controversies

MEDIA AND CRIME CONTROL

It's rude to stare. We all have heard this common admonition. Violation of this and other taken-for-granted clauses of the social contract underlie the concerns discussed in this chapter. Much has been written concerning the media as a cause of crime. This chapter examines the increasing use of media and media technology to control crime and to administer justice. These efforts are historically rooted in the success of prosocial entertainment programs and public information campaigns. More recently media technological advances, which allow easy recording, transmittal, storage, and review of moving images, further spurred criminal justice interest. Beginning in the 1970s these factors resulted in a number of media-based anticrime programs and the widespread adoption of media technology in the criminal justice field. Now common, these programs and applications can be divided into three areas: anticrime advertising, case processing using media technology, and public surveillance systems. This chapter examines how the application of media technology within these three areas has changed the reality of criminal justice.

Public Service Announcements Join the War on Crime

Media-based anticrime efforts are targeted at three audiences: criminals, victims and witnesses. Programs targeting criminals are mass media communication campaigns geared to deter offenders from future offending. Programs targeting citizens include media-based campaigns aimed at reducing victimization and solving crimes. All three types of programming are designed to reduce crime and so are usually driven by crime control values. Conversely, critiques of these programs usually raise due process and civil liberty concerns.

Efforts to use the media to reduce and solve crimes are not new. The "Wanted: Dead or Alive" posters on the Western frontier and the FBI's "Most Wanted" list are two long-standing examples of fugitive searches that used available media. What is new is the rapid increase in the number of media-based anticrime efforts since the 1980s. With broad-based support, these efforts use the media to attempt to construct a social reality with less crime. With the ability of propaganda to negatively affect social attitudes established during World War I, projects to positively influence public attitudes using media information campaigns took hold in the 1930s.[1] Social planners and politicians set out to employ the media to generate planned positive changes in public attitudes and perceptions.

In the 1950s, media-based campaigns aimed at changing social practices in health and other areas began to appear. For a time during the 1960s, negative research findings led to widespread pessimism about the media's ability to influence audiences. In the late 1960s, however, bolstered by evaluations of **prosocial television** programming such as *Sesame Street* that found that children display positive social behaviors after watching prosocial television episodes, attempts were again made to use the media to purposely influence the public. Research revealed that programs of various types (animated, adventure, comedy, and fantasy) all have the ability to elicit socially valued behaviors from children and adolescent viewers. In contrast to the bulk of negative assessments of commercial television programming, it was concluded that properly designed television programs can have beneficial effects.[2] Encouraged by these findings, newfound enthusiasm for mass media developed in the 1970s with the expectation that media-generated positive social effects could be gained in a number of social areas—including crime reduction.

From this foundation, media-based anticrime programs proliferated. The current renditions all utilize advertisement-like media messages and collectively separate into three groups. The first group—aimed at offenders—employs ads designed to deter people from committing crimes. These anticrime messages are deployed in existing mass media advertising avenues as **public service announcements** (or **PSAs**). A second group of PSAs—these aimed at citizens— are victimization-reduction messages. Similar in form to the deterrence messages, victim-targeted PSAs use existing mass media outlets to distribute crime-reducing information and work to reduce opportunities for crime by inducing citizens to better protect themselves. The third set of anticrime ads is designed to increase crime clearance and arrest rates by encouraging witness cooperation with law

"...A MAJOR INFLUENCE IN FORMING THE ATTITUDES THAT LED TO THE PRESENT LEGAL SITUATION REGARDING MARIJUANA ... HILARIOUS WHEN VIEWED FROM THE OTHER SIDE OF THE GENERATION GAP, A GAP THIS FILM DID SO MUCH TO CREATE..."
KEVIN SAUNDERS, ABC-TV

THE NATIONAL ORGANIZATION FOR THE REFORM OF MARIJUANA LAWS
presents

MARIJUANA
WEED FROM THE DEVIL'S GARDEN!

One MOMENT of BLISS – A LIFETIME of REGRET!

HUNTING A THRILL, THEY INHALED A DRAG OF CONCENTRATED SIN!

A NORML FILM

"Reefer" MADNESS
A 1936 CLASSIC

poster by bob price

WAKE UP AMERICA! HERE'S A ROADSIDE WEED THAT'S FAST BECOMING A NATIONAL HIGH-WAY!

© Bettmann/Corbis

Media-based anticrime efforts have a long history as shown by the 1930s U.S. government-produced film *Reefer Madness*.

enforcement investigations. Table 7.1 summarizes these three approaches and their basic designs.

Both the earliest and some of the most recent mass media efforts to reduce crime involve media campaigns aimed at drug abusers. Antidrug media campaigns have a historical tie to *Reefer Madness* and similar films produced by the Federal Bureau of Narcotics in the 1930s. Laughable, cumbersome, and today's

TABLE 7.1   Three Basic Types of Media Anticrime Ad Programs

Program Type	Behavior Change Sought	Mechanism	Example
Targeting Offenders			
Deterrence	Voluntary reduction of criminal behavior by criminals	Deterrence	Antidrug public ad campaigns
Targeting Citizens			
Victimization reduction programs	Adoption of self-protective, crime preventive behavior by citizens	Target hardening	The McGruff "Take a Bite Out of Crime" campaign
Citizen participation programs	Increased public cooperation and involvement with law enforcement efforts	Monetary rewards and anonymity	Crime Stoppers

college campus cult movies, these films and the associated media campaign nevertheless facilitated the criminalization of marijuana in the United States.[3]

These early campaigns never generated the hoped-for deterrent effect, however. Although they seemed able to influence public opinion, they did not influence offender behavior. Evaluations of media-based antidrug projects during the 1970s first offered an explanation for the difficulties in using media to induce deterrence. The failure to deter was blamed on the inability to make drug abuse a salient issue for individual drug abusers and the irrelevance of the media campaign messages to the target audience. To be effective, it was found that a media campaign must tailor its content to a specific population, and that population cannot be simultaneously receiving competing conflicting information. The target audience cannot be simultaneously told in PSAs that "this is your brain on drugs" results in your brain being smashed like an egg and that drugs are funny and harmless in movies like *Half-Baked*.[4]

In that the early antidrug campaigns were diffuse efforts and the general mass media content was rife with prodrug images, they were fatally flawed and doomed to failure. In reaction, subsequent successful lobbying efforts have reduced the levels of prodrug information in the media, and more recent media antidrug campaigns are better designed and marketed. Their evaluations indicate that well-designed media campaigns can significantly affect attitudes toward drugs among preteens, teenagers, and adults. Whether behavioral changes and reduced drug use follow as a result has not been substantiated.[5] As in other areas where the media are seen to influence perceptions more easily than they do behaviors, antidrug media messages are more likely to affect the attitudes of non–drug users than the behaviors of drug abusers. Currently available research indicates that the media appear best able to deter offenders involved in victimless crimes such as drug abuse by increasing their fear of health and social consequences rather than through increasing their fear of punishment.[6]

Another problem in using the media to deter crime is that offenders sometimes display a type of anticipatory reaction, termed an **announcement effect**, to the media campaign. Evoked in offender populations, this effect occurs when media publicity causes offender behavior changes in anticipation of a new criminal justice policy or program that has been heavily publicized. This media-induced behavior effect will occur with or without an actual criminal justice change. For example, a jurisdiction can reduce DUIs for a short time just by publicizing that they are instituting an aggressive, special anti-DUI enforcement effort. They do not have to actually have an anti-DUI unit to gain the reduction; publicity about a phantom unit will suffice. Such announcement effects decline and dissipate over time, however.

Announcement effects generated from the publicity surrounding the implementation of new criminal justice policies and programs also interweave with any effects from actual criminal justice changes. This makes separating the media announcement effects from those of the criminal justice programs difficult. New criminal justice policies have been acclaimed as successful by too quickly ascribing the media-induced change in offender behavior to a new criminal justice policy when it is only the announcement effect that has reduced offenses.[7] The entrenchment of an ineffective criminal justice program or policy can result. Because offenders think that enforcement has significantly changed, they are more cautious for a while, and the new policy gets credit and is termed a success. Eventually offenders realize that the new policy or program is not meaningful and resume their offending.

Victimization-reduction Ads

Programs aimed at reducing victimization, usually by teaching and encouraging crime prevention techniques, obviously differ from offender-deterrence programs. Victimization-reduction campaigns strive to increase the use of personal crime prevention techniques by citizens. Crime prevention falls under the umbrella of self-protective behaviors, which include avoiding health risks and other hazards. Identified as key for triggering self-protective behaviors are people's beliefs about their likelihood of being harmed (What are my chances of being robbed?), the likely severity of an injury or illness (Will a robbery be fatal?), the efficacy of recommended precautions (Will doing this prevent a robbery?), and the costs of taking action when compared with inaction (How much time and money is involved?). Persuading people to adopt more self-protective behaviors is difficult because of the complex interactions among these four factors.

Programs advocating the adoption of behaviors to prevent possible unpleasant future events, such as crime, tend to be less successful than those that encourage actions with an immediate recognizable reward, such as an increase in health from exercising or dieting.[8] In general, unless individuals are recent victims of crime, they do not see crime as a likely event, do not feel that they will be injured, see precautions as not particularly useful, and see better uses for their time and money. In addition, perceptions of the importance of crime and the effectiveness of preventive behavior vary considerably among groups. Like campaigns aimed at offenders, messages must be carefully matched to target populations to have any impact. Adding to the difficulty of determining which campaigns actually work, victimization reduction programs have rarely been adequately evaluated. The McGruff "Crime Dog" campaigns in the United States have received the most extensive study.[9]

Victimization-reduction campaigns are considered useful means of disseminating anticrime information to the public and sometimes influencing related attitudes, but they appear to affect behavior only marginally. More significant effects may be beyond their reach. That is, people will change how they feel about crime prevention and more will see it as a good thing, but few will actually begin to take additional precautions. To be effective, programs should tailor their message to their audience; focus their efforts on visual media, which seems to have the greatest impact; present simple messages; and directly and clearly instruct audiences on crime prevention behavior. Most important, additional local community follow-up and the creation of community support organizations such as citizen crime watch groups are necessary to achieve lasting effects. However, similar to the media's deterrent effect on offenders, based on the available data, media-based victimization-reduction campaigns appear able to affect people's attitudes toward crime prevention more easily than their actual behavior.

Citizen-cooperation Ads

Citizen-cooperation ads aim to increase the level of crime-related information made available to law enforcement by the public. These programs (commonly known by the name Crime Stoppers) use reenactments of crimes to obtain information (tips) through anonymous phone calls and reward money.[10] The logic is the same as the "Most Wanted" reward posters of the nineteenth century and the FBI's "Ten Most Wanted" posters traditionally displayed in post offices, now also digitally distributed via the Internet. Getting images and descriptions of wanted suspects and unsolved crimes out to as many people as possible and enticing reluctant citizens with monetary rewards increases the prospects for solving crimes and apprehending suspects. The innovation is using contemporary media to distribute electronic wanted posters, thereby enormously increasing the audience.

Development of these efforts raises a number of questions. The first and most obvious is what is their effectiveness? Do they result in more arrests and solutions of crimes, and are they an efficient means of generating information? Second is the question of the image of criminality that such programs project. Do they perpetuate stereotypes of criminals, victims, and crimes? Third, what is the proper role of the media in law enforcement efforts?

First, no one knows if citizen-cooperation programs affect the crime rate. The number of cases cleared is not great enough to expect an effect on the overall crime rate in a community unless one assumes a general deterrent effect from the mass media coverage. No effect has been reported. But anecdotal evidence does suggest that the programs solve felony cases that are unlikely to be solved

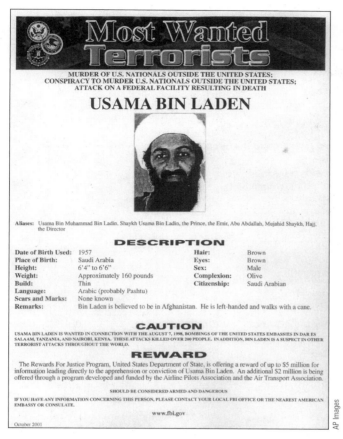

The digital Most Wanted poster for Usama Bin Laden, symbolic leader of the terrorist group al-Qaeda.

otherwise.[11] They appear especially effective in solving cases involving fugitives, bank robberies, and narcotics and may be useful in antiterrorist efforts. The visibility of these programs also increases their effectiveness by attracting secondary tips for unadvertised crimes. Indeed, given the large amount of unsolicited information received regarding unadvertised crimes, crime reenactments shown in the media appear to be more important as vehicles for obtaining tips regarding other crimes than as a means of solving the crimes actually publicized. Bolstered by supportive court rulings and by low operational costs, these programs are generally viewed as cost-effective and their continuance currently assured. Despite their support and successes, critics argue that their gains against crime are outweighed by other negative social effects. Paying for information from anonymous sources is the crux of the uneasiness felt toward these programs. The fear is that paying rewards and providing anonymity for informants will reduce voluntary citizen cooperation and encourage malicious retributive snitching by citizens on their neighbors, family, and friends.

Box 7.1   Anticrime Web Sites

Crime prevention has gone digital and a large number of crime prevention Web sites exist. They run the gamut from non-profit governmental sites to private profit-driven ones and include law enforcement sites, consultants, lobby and special interest groups, and private security firms. The target audiences are citizens, particularly victims of crime, potential customers of security equipment and crime prevention services, and voters. A representative sample list is provided.

> http://www.sandiego.gov/police/prevention/
> http://www.mcgruff.org/
> http://www.crimedoctor.com/crime.htm
> http://www.usscouts.org/mb/mb131.asp
> http://www.personalarms.com/
> http://www.oaaoregon.com/
> http://www.crimereduction.homeoffice.gov.uk/yp/ypgcp05.htm

Second, because citizen-cooperation ads are presented as representative of real crime in a community, the image they portray has great potential to influence the social construction of criminality. Presented in news-like segments akin to reality programming, these anticrime ads focus on unsolved cases in the community committed by dangerous-looking suspects. The image of criminality shown in these ads is similar to that portrayed in the general entertainment media—that of a dangerous, crime-ridden world where violent attacks are common.[12] In addition, these ads are often produced in infotainment programming styles, with mood music, voice-overs, and heightened dramatic elements.[13] Furthermore, by emphasizing predatory violent crimes that appear to be due to greed or irrationality, individual explanations for crime and crime control–based punitive crime-and-justice policies are emphasized while broader structural, social, and economic factors are downplayed.

Finally, what is the proper role of the mass media in law enforcement efforts? Should the media restrict themselves to basic reporting of events or become involved in their resolution? Citizen-cooperation ads shift the media from their traditional roles as watchdog observers and reporters to active infotainment participants in investigating crimes and hunting fugitives. Some argue that the media should cooperate because it is their civic duty. Many news media agencies do not cooperate, however, apparently because they perceive involvement as contrary to the philosophy of separation of press and government.[14] How these concerns are to be resolved is unclear. Unfortunately, we have little independent data to support or lay to rest the expressed fears. We simply do not know at this time if the hypothesized negative consequences of citizen-cooperation programs counteract their positive anticrime effects. For one thing, we don't know how much of an anticrime effect they actually have.

Collectively, PSAs, victimization ads, and citizen-cooperation ads are popular, have demonstrated some positive effects, but have also encountered unanticipated problems. Success has not been as direct or as simple to achieve as first envisioned.[15] Despite their current popularity and transition to the Internet (see Box 7.1), their actual impact on crime levels is ambiguous. All of these efforts aim for behavioral changes in the audience to reduce crime, but most are actually designed to influence attitudes and perceptions about the reality of crime under the belief that attitude changes will subsequently lead to changes in behavior. All three of these media campaign types accordingly rest on a questionable premise, and they have not been able to produce the hoped-for crime reductions. Regardless of these issues, their successes have encouraged the migration of media technology into the criminal justice system as a tool for case processing in law enforcement and judicial efforts. This is the subject of the next section.

CASE PROCESSING USING MEDIA TECHNOLOGY

In general, the ultimate goal in using media technology in criminal justice case processing is to simulate a traditional, live, face-to-face proceeding. Unlike face-to-face encounters, however, participants in media technology–rendered proceedings must interact through the equipment, often testifying directly into a camera or participating by watching a television screen. In contrast to the use of media equipment in news coverage, here the technology has changed from a tangential, temporary visitor to an unavoidable, permanent judicial tool. Media technology has been embraced as a means to efficiently process cases, and cost and speed are the usual factors considered in these applications.

Though the use of media technology has come to be widely accepted in the presentation of physical evidence and testimony, using the technology to create permanent records and conduct live proceedings currently enjoys only limited support. Expanded applications such as prerecording entire trials have been experimented with but generally have been rejected. The acceptability of media technology in the courtroom seems to rest on how much the media-constructed judicial reality is seen as different from the traditional judicial reality. For preliminary and short procedural steps, most participants, including defendants, appear to feel that the integrity of the process is unaffected. With regard to longer, more significant, and more symbolic steps such as trials, concerns and resistance rise.

Judicial System Use

In the judicial system, visual records of arraignments, first appearances, bond hearings, and pleas have proven inexpensive and useful.[16] A single memory device can hold thousands of cases and provide a permanent record that can be consulted should the state of mind of a defendant, his or her comprehension of rights or instructions, or the voluntary nature of a plea later be questioned. Once instituted these systems gain support from both crime control and due process advocates. Crime control proponents like the savings of time and money. Due process adherents feel the knowledge that a permanent record is being created makes law enforcement and judicial personnel more conscientious in following due process rules. Visual records of these procedural steps also provide a means not previously available of resolving any subsequent due process concerns. Furthermore, the same technology used in creating visual records and testimony also allows, if desired, the physical separation of the participants, thus allowing a judicial proceeding to be conducted in a new way—in live media-linked sessions. Judges and attorneys can now be in a courtroom, defendants in a jail, and witnesses in another state, all simultaneously participating in a live hearing.

Recent computer technology advances have brought new issues to the table, however, including the **digital manipulation of visual images**. The same tools that can be used to crop, retouch, and edit images can be used just as easily to distort, alter, and fabricate them. This ability undermines the previously unquestioned validity that pictures enjoyed as evidence. The use of obviously faked but realistic-looking photos in advertising and entertainment—the creation of alien worlds, for example—repeatedly demonstrates the sophistication of visual deception. The uncertain validity of visual images has implications for the evaluation of visual evidence in the criminal justice system. The public is constantly reminded by entertainment media content that it should not automatically believe what it is shown.[17] A potential future problem is that jurors will begin to reject photographic evidence as innately untrustworthy in a manner similar to how jurors now sometimes reject scientific evidence if it does not meet entertainment media standards. Ironically, technological advances may ultimately result in questioning all technologically processed information so that eyewitness and human testimony may again dominate the criminal justice process.

In addition, when the traditional, familiar reality of the judicial system is drastically changed by the use of media technology, resistance to the new reality rises. Even for the now common applications of media technology, the alteration of the reality of the judicial system is connected to three concerns: the effect of media technology on working relationships among courtroom personnel, concerns about depersonalization of the criminal justice system, and the impact of media technology on the legitimacy of the judicial system.

Comments from attorneys (especially public defenders) and judges indicate that the relationships among courtroom personnel can be upset by the introduction of media equipment.[18] It is significant that in a number of pilot projects public defenders remain largely skeptical of the advantages of media technology. Do attorneys deliver equivalent representation if they feel legally and organizationally disadvantaged in media constructed proceedings? If their morale suffers, does their subsequent effort on behalf of clients also suffer? These questions remain unanswered.

A second concern is that expanded use of media technology within the judiciary will almost certainly lead to further depersonalization of criminal justice proceedings. Adjudication within the criminal justice system is based on face-to-face interaction, particularly that the accused are entitled to face their accusers. Extended use of media technology, however, will reduce live, face-to-face encounters between witnesses and defendants, police and the public, attorneys and clients, judges and defendants, and jurors and all the previous groups. These media-mediated interactions will seriously alter the nature of the personal relationships within the criminal justice system. Technological advances that make this equipment more economical, less obtrusive, and more like a live meeting are likely to further this depersonalization.

A third unresolved concern is what is lost in legitimacy and the public image of justice when media technology is employed. In addition to being a means of adjudicating guilt and administering punishment, the judicial system is also a means of legitimizing the whole social system—its rules, laws, and government. Accordingly, the judicial system and its personnel have a symbolic value. Loss of these symbolic qualities may diminish the aura of legitimacy sustaining the entire criminal justice system. From the social construction perspective, how the system is seen as treating individuals is crucial. If people become alienated from the system or if they feel intimidated or dehumanized by it, the benefits from using media technologies in the courtroom will cancel out. If these technologies ultimately result in the further isolation and separation of the police from the policed and the courts from the public, the social costs of such losses would outweigh any administrative benefits that accrue from their use. As crime control values become more popular, there is considerable desire, especially on the part of criminal justice administrators, to make the system more efficient. Nevertheless, the criminal justice system must remain legitimate in the public eye if it is to remain a viable system of justice.

In addition, the visuals created by this technology are frequently used in news reports, contributing directly to the social construction of the public's image of justice. The criminal justice system will become, for good or ill, a less arcane, more open system as its procedures become more visible. The myriad applications of media technology have changed the reality of justice on many levels and have opened previous backstage judicial activities to public scrutiny. Ironically, although the courts are still wary of the news media, the criminal justice system's adoption of media technology has had many of the same effects that were feared from news coverage. The main concern remains whether this new reality of justice comes to be seen as impersonal, unfair, and unacceptable.

The greatest concerns with the use of media technology are not associated with its use in case processing, however. The greatest concerns revolve around the law enforcement use of media technology and the enhancement of law enforcement surveillance capabilities.

Law Enforcement Use

After the development and widespread acceptance of videotaped evidence and testimony in the 1970s, **videotaped interrogations** were one of the first expanded uses of video technology into law enforcement practices. A videotape record is felt to provide more objective, fuller accounts of interactions between police, witnesses, and suspects, as well as evidence regarding the voluntariness of statements, suspects' understanding of their rights, police coercion and interrogation practices, and the physical and mental condition of suspects. Following pilot projects, most have embraced this law enforcement use of media technology. For example, a two-year evaluation of a Canadian experiment in videotaping police interrogations showed that the expected advantages of protection against unwarranted allegations of misconduct, the introduction of accountability in interrogation procedures, and the reduction in challenges to the admissibility of suspect statements were all realized.[19]

The evaluation further reported that suspects did not appear inhibited by the cameras and that the suspect confession rate remained the same. In fact, police, prosecutors, and defense counsel all came to support continuation and expansion of the project—police because it relieves them of the need to take written notes during interrogations and reduces their court appearances, prosecutors because it usually disposes of all legal questions surrounding the police–suspect interview, and defense counsel because it ensures that police more strictly follow legal procedures and because the defense often can use the tapes to demonstrate their client's intent and remorse for sentencing purposes. The interrogation video tapes provide a record of the frame of mind and emotional state of a suspect much nearer in time to the commission of a crime than was previously available.

An increasing number of police departments also use media technology to record the booking of their arrests. These video mug shots provide a pictorial record of arrestees that includes voice, accent, and continuous front-to-profile views. These video records have also allowed changes in two other common law enforcement practices—identification of a suspect from a traditional lineup and identification of a suspect from a set of photographs (a mug book) of known offenders. In a **video lineup**, a crime witness is shown a series of video bookings selected for their similarity. The witness chooses from this video lineup the individual he or she feels is the offender. This process is felt to be fairer than the old practices in that the individuals in video lineups more closely resemble one another than the groups usually assembled for a live lineup, and it provides a permanent record of the lineup for later review should questions arise. In **video mug books**, a computer program searches a pictorial data file for specific characteristics (for example, tattoo, bald, heavy, white, and male) and displays matching images.

SURVEILLANCE

"You watched TV. Now it watches you"[20] neatly summarizes the expected future and concerns regarding modern surveillance systems. The police surveillance stakeout has a long history and has traditionally been an accepted part of police investigations. Surveillance applications based on media technology have been in use for a number of years—for example, surveillance cameras in banks, subways, and department stores—and have recently been expanded to include public schools, airports, highway toll booths, and other locales. The police have also traditionally used temporary camera surveillance of specific locations after obtaining a court order. While not a mass media in that there is no public audience that receives the images,[21] the increase in surveillance is considered a media effect because the current pervasiveness of surveillance is due to advances in media technology, especially in visual communication. Enhanced visual media and communication capabilities and reduced equipment costs, coupled with concerns about terrorism, have created a strong impetus for surveillance systems. Contemporary media technology has also changed the nature of surveillance from on-scene, limited human observers and whatever notes they might produce to the automated technological interception, recording, and transmittal of immense amounts of information.

In the United States, surveillance camera systems have increased exponentially since the 2001 terrorist attacks.[22] Taking advantage of the **surveillance effect**— the psychological effect of fearing that you might be under observation— surveillance programs have expanded the traditional police use of the stakeout and hidden camera to encompass general public space applications. Media technology has made constant surveillance of broad public areas possible, and surveillance cameras permanently mounted on street corners, in patrol cars, and within and without various public and private buildings are common features of communities. The traditional uses of surveillance in stake-outs and banks differ from newer applications in that the areas surveyed were small, and public domain areas were not usually involved. In contrast, the new surveillance programs use media technology in large public areas such as outdoor malls, downtown centers, parks, and residential streets.[23] Traditional surveillance was also aimed at gathering evidence for a specific case or deterring crime at a specific place such as a ticket booth, but today the prime justifications for public surveillance systems are couched in broad-scale public safety and antiterrorism goals. The reality of surveillance has shifted from a rare, narrow, activity determined by a need related to a specific criminal case to a common, pervasive, constant presence. The historical idea that you have to be under suspicion of having done something to be brought under surveillance is no longer the case with broadly targeted, automatic, continuous surveillance systems. This potential surveillance of everyone whenever they appear in public places is the prime cause of unease. Not surprisingly, the use of this powerful and intrusive technology has raised fears concerning its impact on society.

Contemporary surveillance projects aim to provide either retrospective scene analysis following crimes, deterrence of future crimes, facilitation of real-time intervention, or some combination of these goals.[24] Figure 7.1 outlines the two influence paths through which surveillance systems can theoretically effect crime. As shown, both formal effects through law enforcement actions and informal channel effects on citizens and offenders are possible. When, how, and if these systems work in specific applications is still under debate.[25] It is not clear, for example, to what extent offenders take the presence of cameras into account when deciding whether or not to commit an offense.[26] Irrespective of this and other unanswered research questions, adoption of camera surveillance has continued unabated around the world.[27]

History and Issues

The use of telephone wiretaps in the 1900s first raised the specter of surveillance abuse. Writing before the era of electronic eavesdropping and visual technology,

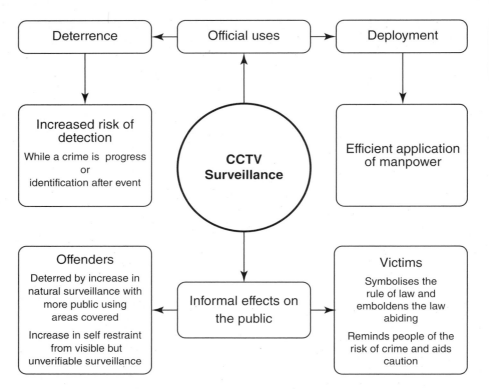

FIGURE 7.1 An Illustrated Model of How CCTV May Affect Crime
Source: Adapted from Williams, (2007, p. 99) "Effective CCTV"

Justices Earl Warren and William Brandeis predicted that "mechanical devices threaten to make good the prediction that 'what is whispered in the closet shall be proclaimed from the housetops.'"[28] Today, the updated quote would be "whatever is done in the dark will be shown on the news." To understand the social impetus for these new surveillance systems and the likely future of police surveillance in the United States, one must look to England. No Western democracy has embraced police surveillance systems more than Britain (see Box 7.2 for a narrative of life under pervasive daily surveillance). The electronic recording of images and pervasive, broad-scale, permanent surveillance systems in use in Britain have resulted in the English population being described as the most surveilled population on the planet.[29]

The rise of surveillance capabilities increased dramatically with the development of modern camera-based systems in the 1960s.[30] **CCTV, or closed circuit television,** was initially used both in the United States and Britain sparingly as an in-store means of apprehending and deterring shoplifters. Although the technology became less expensive and increased in its capabilities throughout the 1970s, the Western political environment remained hostile to expanded use. The Cold War discouraged the use of police surveillance systems that smacked of Communist-style secret police tactics. Western politicians and police chiefs did not want to be viewed as advocates of systems that could be described as "Big Brother" spying.

B o x   7.2   A United Kingdom Story of Everyday Surveillance

[The numbers in parentheses tally surveillance systems.] Thomas Kearns's day starts as usual. At 7:15 a.m. the sounds from his clock radio penetrate his consciousness. At 8:15 he kisses his wife goodbye and shuts the front door of his apartment, children in tow. They head towards the elevator and are captured on a covert video surveillance operation, set up by the local authority, aimed at identifying residents who are dealing in drugs from their premises. (1) As they wait for the elevator their presence is monitored on the concierge's video system twelve floors below, as is their descent for there is also a camera in the elevator. Their routine is preserved and stored for twenty-eight days, or longer if necessary. (2) As they walk to the car, it is not only the concierge who monitors the Kearnses' departure, but Mr. Adams on the fifteenth floor, who has tuned his television to receive output from the Housing Estate's cameras. (3)

Thomas drives to the roadway and, although vaguely aware of the sign that declares "reduce your speed now—video camera in operation" still drives at 10 miles an hour over the speed limit and trips the automatic speed cameras. (4) By 8:30, he has dropped his daughter off at the CCTV-monitored nursery (5) and is heading towards his son's school. He stops at a red light. Had he jumped it, another picture would have been taken to be used as evidence in his prosecution. (6) As they wait in the playground for the start of school, they are filmed by a covert camera secreted in the building opposite to monitor the playground for signs of drug dealing (7) and their goodbye kiss is also captured on the school's internal CCTV system which monitors every entrance and exit. (8) Noticing a nearly empty fuel tank, he drives to the gas station. He knows that he is being filmed as a large sign declares: "These premises are under 24-hour video surveillance." (9) At a railroad crossing, his location is caught on cameras monitoring the crossing to ensure that the intersection of road and track is clear when the train crosses. (10) A few minutes later, he is in the parking garage under the watchful eye of another set of cameras. (11)

As usual, Thomas buys a newspaper and is filmed by in-store security cameras. No one is monitoring the images from the two cameras but they are taped on a multiplex video recorder that records the images on one tape. (12) Before buying his train ticket he makes a telephone call to remind his wife that he will be home late. Unbeknownst to him he is filmed by a covert camera installed to catch vandals and hoax callers. (13) His call made, he buys his ticket, walks to the platform and waits for his train, all of which has been recorded and monitored by the thirty-two cameras operating at the station. (14) On arrival, he walks to his office and smiles for the camera monitoring the reception area. (15) He is, however, unaware that his movements are being recorded by a number of covert cameras hidden in the smoke detector housings as he walks towards his office. (16)

At lunchtime, he is going to visit his sister, who has just given birth. Three monitors in the town hall's CCTV control room (17) watch his movements along the streets. His first stop is an ATM where his face is captured by a camera hidden inside the cash machine. (18) He crosses the road to buy his sister some flowers. Should the CCTV monitor wish, his every turn could be tracked on the 35-camera in-store security system. At the check-out he writes a check but doesn't notice a camera zooming in to ensure that the store has good pictures of his face should he be passing a bad check. (19)

Outside, he hails a taxi for the two-mile journey and, as they cross a major road, the taxi's number plate is photographed by the Metropolitan Police's new CCTV-based automatic license plate recognition system. (20) On arrival at the hospital he is photographed by two cameras covering the main entrance and again as he enters the maternity unit. (21) Having carried out his family duties, he walks to the nearest

(continued)

> **B o x 7.2   A United Kingdom Story of Everyday Surveillance (Continued)**
>
> underground station; here his progress will be recorded on video from the moment he enters the station to the point he boards his train. (22) He alights at the airport to meet some prospective clients and, of course, dozens of security cameras (23) monitor his movements. He escorts his guests to the parking garage where a rental car awaits. They drive out and the license number is photographed automatically. It is then checked against the computerized database of all cars using the airport garages. (24)
>
> They head to a football game in South London where Thomas is treating. In route, they are fleetingly caught by three town's CCTV systems. (25) After arrival, they are photographed as they enter the stadium and while they are seated their faces are scanned and checked against a pictorial database of known hooligans. (26) After the match, they drive to a bistro. As they are unfamiliar with the area they drive slowly looking for the correct turn-off. They are filmed on a mobile camcorder, deployed by the local vice squad in an effort to prevent "curb crawling" in this "red light district." (27) The monitoring officer loses interest when they turn off.
>
> When dinner is over Thomas awaits the 11:14 train where his presence is recorded on the station's cameras. (28) He returns home just before midnight and sits down to check the mail. An official-looking letter informs him that the local police have photographed his son associating with a teenage gang, and wish Mr. Kearns to come to the police station to view the video. (29) Thomas heads to bed, wondering what on earth his son can have done wrong to warrant being photographed by the police.
>
> At the end of his day, Thomas had been filmed by over three hundred cameras on over thirty separate CCTV systems.

In the mid-1980s, as the Cold War dissipated, municipal police CCTV surveillance systems appeared across England. By the mid-1990s, a rapid increase in the number of systems was well under way, and today it is the rule rather than the exception for any reasonably sized British community to have police camera surveillance of its public spaces.[31] By the turn of the century, there were more than 500 operating CCTV systems in England, exploding to an estimated 4.2 million today or about one camera for every fourteen people.[32] Beyond the defusing of the Cold War, rising local crime rates and a declining faith in the traditional criminal justice system's ability to deal with crime has been credited for increased public support for surveillance systems.[33]

Capping the social construction of police surveillance systems as positive and necessary in England was a symbolic crime, the 1993 murder of a two-year-old boy who was recorded on a mall security camera being taken away by his two teenage killers. The use of the security camera video resulted in demands for more camera systems following its widespread broadcast on news programs.[34] The images gave an irresistible push for the adoption of CCTV systems, and the British media shifted from questioning whether surveillance is a good thing to asking why are cameras not everywhere. Similarly in the United States, symbolic crimes, usually murders, have periodically supercharged the slow but sure surveillance creep through society to periods of surveillance surges.[35] Once installed, logic inevitably calls for coverage of larger areas, and every murder or terrorist act intensifies the demand for expanded surveillance.[36]

The result in England has been the normalization of police surveillance systems to the level that CCTV surveillance has been described as a public "fifth utility," along the lines of water, electricity, and telephones.[37] Driven as much by politics as by empirical evidence, United Kingdom CCTV surveillance is today perceived as an affordable and efficient technical fix for crime.[38] One British Chief Constable describes his system as equal to full-time police officers on the beat twenty-four hours all taking notes without meal breaks, holidays, or sick leave.[39] In the aftermath of the September 11, 2001, terrorist attacks and passage of the Patriot Act and related legislation the United States is on track to joining England as a massively camera-surveilled society.[40]

In the United States and elsewhere, camera surveillance programs today take one of two basic forms: completely hidden systems that give potential offenders no indication that they are being observed, and clearly marked, open systems. Although the first form functions more as a means of gathering evidence and aiding in apprehensions, both forms take advantage of the surveillance effect, using the psychological impact of the belief that one might be under surveillance.[41]

How effective are surveillance systems in reducing crime? Evidence based largely on interviews with offenders does suggest that offenders take into account the perceived level of surveillance and the likelihood of intervention when deciding whether to commit some types of crimes, especially instrumental street crimes such as car break-ins.[42] Emotional spontaneous crimes such as assaults are less affected. Evaluations further suggest that the systems are most effective in reducing crime when combined with other interventions,[43] and evidence of crime reduction from public CCTV systems has been reported.[44] However, if the threat of police intervention is absent, the impact of surveillance fades.[45] That is, unless surveillance results in someone showing up to address the observed problem, a surveillance-generated deterrent effect will eventually wane.

Benefits and Concerns of Increased Surveillance

The benefits usually cited for police camera surveillance systems also incorporate the concerns raised about these systems.[46] Thus, a CCTV benefit is to be able to observe and react to previously unnoticed acts; the concern is that net-widening from police arresting more people, particularly juveniles, for minor offenses will result in more people with formal arrest records.[47] A benefit is to be able to expel actual and potential deviants from specific locations; the concern is that profiling, polarization, and radicalization will result as certain groups are targeted for exclusion from public spaces, especially commercial shopping districts (see Box 7.3).[48] A benefit is to provide evidence against offenders; the concern is the development of databases to track and identify specific members of the population based on their prior labeling as individuals that "need to be watched" rather than being surveilled because of their current behavior. A benefit is the creation of quiet, disturbance-free streets; the concern is overpolicing and the suppression of public exuberance and uninhibited but lawful social or political protest and the loss of

---

B o x 7.3   Profiling and Camera Surveillance

Surveillance camera monitors are sometimes accused of profiling when deciding which people to watch. Thus, people at a mall might be watched because of who they

---

informal citizen guardianship of neighborhoods.[49] Lastly, a benefit is the creation of crime-free surveillance zones; the concern is that displacement effects will push crime into adjacent communities without the money or political clout to obtain their own surveillance systems; surveillance would be a privilege and mark communities as "worth watching" while simultaneously making crime invisible without reducing it.[50]

Of the concerns, **displacement of crime** to adjacent areas has been empirically examined along with the additional potential benefit of a diffusion of crime reduction impact. **Diffusion of benefits** is seen as a possible effect from surveillance systems because offenders might not be aware of the boundaries of the surveillance coverage and therefore reduce their offenses in adjacent nonsurveilled areas. In the reported evaluations, evidence of both displacement and diffusion effects have been reported.[51] For example, in the United Kingdom evidence of the local diffusion of benefits in reduced car theft and break-ins has been reported as well as evidence of significant crime displacement to outlying distant

are (teenagers or minorities) rather than because of what they are doing. Norris and Armstrong (1998, p. 8) summarize this issue:

> [Camera surveillance] is more than just crime prevention. It enables a vast amount of visual data, in the form of images on the screen, to be processed and interpreted. What interpretive schemes guide operator judgments? What forms of behavior or people trigger suspicion and at what point does this result in a deployment? Is this deployment confined to explicitly criminal concerns or is intervention directed at regulating matters of decorum and demeanor in public space and aimed at excluding certain types of people?

Research has indicated that demographic profiling does occur. Williams and Johnstone (2000, p. 193) report that CCTV operators selectively target those social groups they believe are most likely to be deviant, singling out certain people and behaviors as inappropriate and therefore warranting surveillance. They found that young males, especially young black males, were regularly targeted for surveillance as much for their race, posture, and dress as for their behavior. In their study, Norris and Armstrong (1999, p. 110) found that in one British community black people were two and a half times more likely to be the object of surveillance, over one and a half times more likely in another U.K. community. The concept of "otherness" comes into play with the social construction of suspicion resulting in blacks and teenagers being more likely to be watched without cause and ascribed criminal intent on the basis of appearance (Morris and Armstrong 1999 p. 118). Of the 900 surveilled events Morris and Armstrong reviewed, forty-five resulted in police deployments, and twelve re-sulted in arrests. One-third of surveillance targets were selected based on categorical criteria such as dress, race, or subculture group membership, whereas surveillance based on suspicious behavioral represents only one out of four uses (Norris and Armstrong 1999 p. 112; see also Goold 2004, chapter 6). Due to these concerns, racial and class based profiling is a persistent criticism levied against the utilization of public space camera surveillance.

English towns from a single system.[52] This suggests that diffusion of benefits may accrue near to these systems while crime displacement can be occurring simultaneously farther away.

The recent appearance of video cameras mounted on patrol car windshields in the United States represents another expanded, mobile use of video technology for surveillance. The mobility of the patrol car extends the practice of general law enforcement surveillance to virtually the entire society without the need for perma-nent fixed systems. Challenges to this practice based on privacy concerns have been rejected by the U.S. Supreme Court, which has stated that an invasion of privacy cannot result unless there is a reasonable expectation of privacy. Because there is no expectation of privacy in a traffic stop or on a public street, the use of in-car video cameras by police on patrol or on fixed streetlight mountings monitoring public streets is allowed under almost all circumstances.[53]

Resistance to even greater adoption within law enforcement agencies appears to arise when law enforcement officers perceive the cameras as an administrative tool, installed to watch them, more than as a law enforcement tool. In reality the cameras are both: the police on the surveilled street or in front of their patrol cars during a videotaped traffic stop are also under surveillance.

Surveillance video transforms the relationships between line police officers, their administration, and the public by providing a reviewable record of officers' street interactions. The benefits of having a visual record are many; administrators and the courts can later review officers' and suspects' actions, and thereby decide liability, voluntary search consent, misconduct claims, and have more credible, objective evidence of behavior and statements for DUI and drug intoxication cases. In addition, the cameras are credited with deterring suspects from resisting arrest and deterring officers from mistreating suspects and engaging in other unprofessional acts.[54] In effect, in a democratic society the technology appears to protect police officers from frivolous charges of abuse and misconduct while protecting the public from actual abuse and misconduct by officers. In addition, the ubiquitous video cameras in citizens' hands means that a surveillance effect may have an impact on the police at least as much as on the public. Research has indicated that citizen-videotaped arrests have a significant negative impact on the public's perception of police use of force.[55] In response, the police are advised to operate under the premise that cameras are everywhere and that any of their actions might be taped.[56] A final ironic consequence of more surveillance cameras in society is their use by offenders to provide early warnings of police raids on premises being used for illegal practices. This turns the acquisition of surveillance technology into an offender/police arms race that law enforcement is not necessarily favored to win.[57]

Balancing Police Surveillance and Public Safety

All surveillance systems raise issues related to the use of media technology in the daily policing of our society. Surprisingly, concerns over Big Brother are usually raised by the news media, law enforcement officers, and external observers, not by the citizens under surveillance, who appear quite ready to trade off a measure of personal privacy for a potential reduction in victimization and fear. The public acceptance of surveillance is high and is linked to the increased exposure of private, backstage behaviors in the news, entertainment, and infotainment media—if privacy is already rare, then surveillance is less offensive. Since the terrorist attacks of September 11, 2001, public support in the United States for surveillance systems has been strong, with close to 80 percent in one poll supporting the installation of surveillance cameras in public places to prevent terrorist attacks.[58]

Unresolved questions concern effects on the legitimacy, symbolic impact, and the public image of justice when surveillance technology is employed. Law enforcement also legitimizes the entire criminal justice system. Accordingly, the police have a symbolic value. On the street, both the presence of a live police officer and the assurance of knowing when one is being observed by the police affirm the values of voluntary consent and public control of law enforcement. Loss of these symbols may diminish the aura of legitimacy sustaining the entire criminal justice system. Misuse or overuse of this technology will construct a social reality of mistrust and cynicism, where fear of crime is replaced by fear of authority. In addition, police surveillance systems may actually be ineffective over the long term, and their use could result in the neglect of broader approaches to crime control. It is feared that reliance on technological fixes for crime can have negative community effects, working against positive community participation, creating a siege mentality, and undermining natural community surveillance by residents. For example, the presence of a police surveillance system might result in fewer phone calls to the police if residents assume that the local police surveillance camera will observe incidents and alert the authorities. Police surveillance by means of technology may thereby undermine natural surveillance by encouraging people to have faith in the disembodied electronic eye and encourage a "why get involved" attitude. Instead of worrying about Big Brother watching them, the public may expect that "Big Father" will sort everything out.

The basic problem these programs present is how to balance police surveillance and public safety—how much safety is gained at what cost? The equation seems clearly to be that increased fear of crime and terror results in increased tolerance for surveillance. Citizens fearful of crime and terrorism are willing to open more social areas to observation, even when the observers are hidden. Orwell's *1984* society of total surveillance is less frightening than a local mugger or homicidal terrorist. The danger is that fear will drive citizens to glibly surrender personal privacy for an unknown measure of personal security. Whether these programs actually reduce crime or protect against terrorist attacks enough to warrant the loss in privacy is an open question.[59] They are capable of producing positive near-term effects for certain types of crime, with vehicle-related offenses appearing to be most effectively deterred. Whether the systems can maintain effects over the long term is not known. How surveillance power is held to account and what limits are placed on its operation are also unresolved issues. The impact of new computing and database technologies will increase the power of surveillance—with the coupling of surveillance cameras to fast, inexpensive computers, facial recognition, vehicle and person tracking, and behavior recognition software are realities. Widespread police access to a real-time, computer-analyzed, media-augmented surveillance data will soon be common-place.[60]

Cameras unavoidably change the nature of the relationship between those being watched and those doing the watching. Most of the time, the negative social consequences of increased surveillance dominate the debate. However, the latest applications have positive potentials also. When the actions of the law enforcers and the public are both monitored, stored, and subject to later review, surveillance cameras can restrain the actions of authorities as much as offenders. It remains to be seen whether the impact of these projects in democratic societies will be greater on the police than on the public. A significant effect on employees has already been reported in correctional settings where the behavior of both correctional officers and prisoners is monitored.[61] Like other two-edged swords, the dual nature of police camera surveillance is apparent. "In the wrong hands it can invade privacy and make Orwell's *1984* a reality. But it can also, in a different political context, be liberating and protective."[62] Which reality will emerge is yet to be determined.

1984: AN ICON BEFORE ITS TIME

Today, the media can be used to influence people's attitudes about crime and make more crime-related information available to the police. Other uses can speed the processing of criminal cases. The technology of the media can be used to videotape police patrols, vehicle stops, and interrogations. And the technology is useful in the investigation, surveillance, and deterrence of crime. The administrative—mostly crime control—benefits associated with these uses follow quickly, and projects have consistently been evaluated as efficient and cost-effective. Increased social fears as well as technological advances that make the equipment more economical, more flexible, more capable, and less obtrusive are hastening wide use of media surveillance. However, there are concerns about potential social costs. If evidence of negative effects is found in future studies, the technological genie will be out of the bottle, and it will be difficult to curtail established practices.

Efforts that do not include surveillance show no behavioral effects, and it appears doubtful that the media can by themselves deter criminal behavior—much as they alone cannot criminalize individuals. Surveillance programs do show deterrence effects, but their ability to deter crime without displacement and other worrisome social effects remains unproven. Media efforts to reduce victimization by teaching crime preventive behaviors have high recognition levels among the general public and have increased public knowledge and changed public attitudes about crime prevention, but they have not yet shown an ability to significantly change crime prevention behavior. Finally, programs designed to increase public cooperation by advertising crimes are effective in gathering information and in solving specific types of crimes. Their effect on the overall crime rate is not known, but it is likely negligible.

With all of these caveats in mind, media technology is still an extremely useful tool, but social costs invariably accompany technological benefits. Costs include increased depersonalization of the criminal justice system; isolation of the police from the policed; increased citizen suspicion of surveillance; polarization of society due to the creation of affluent, technologically secured garrison communities; and possible decreased citizen support and legitimization of the criminal justice system. Finally, when news media convey the message that these efforts are the answer for reducing crime rates and when this is coupled with the entertainment message of crime being generated through individually based causes, crime as a technological rather than a social problem becomes the logical conclusion. The belief that we can engineer our way out of the crime problem through more equipment and manpower is bolstered. The collective lesson is that media-based programs are indeed panaceas for the general crime problem. To the extent that the public believes this and policy makers act on it, resources for other approaches will be drained.

AP Photo/Mumbai Mirror, Sebastian D'souza

The cell phone video image of a terrorist in action in 2008 in the India city of Mumbai shows how new media have increased the informal reactive surveillance of previously low visibility crime and justice events. Outside of totalitarian countries, few events of any social significance or news value today go unrecorded by either security camera systems or personal video-capable devices.

To solve crimes and deter criminals, the government must intervene in its citizens' lives. The media and media technology provide a means to do so in new ways that are felt to be both more efficient and less obviously intrusive. In practice such applications cannot avoid opening up for view new areas of public life, of the criminal justice system, and of police–citizen interactions. In certain instances, such as in the use of patrol car cameras, which record police actions as much as citizen actions, this is clearly seen as a positive course. In other instances, such as in the use of hidden police surveillance systems, the desirability of widely doing so is not so clear. Still, with proper oversight the media and media technology can have both due process and crime control benefits. Media and their technology are a potentially positive but, it must be remembered, ultimately limited resource for criminal justice. The media should be an aspect of our total criminal justice policy, but media cannot be the mainstay of crime and justice policies. Connected to the question of how much of our criminal justice policy should be media based is the question of how many criminal justice policies are media generated. Chapter 8 looks at the broader relationship between the media and criminal justice policy.

CHAPTER SUMMARY

- The roots of media-based anticrime efforts are found in public service announcements, public communication campaigns, and pro-social media that established the possibility of using targeted content to influence people's knowledge, attitudes, and behaviors.

- Using the media to reduce crime and victimization has proved difficult due to unanticipated and counterproductive effects. The primary difficulty is the need to raise concern about crime and its consequences in the target audience without triggering negative effects from raising fear levels.

- Media efforts aimed at offenders are based on deterrence and aim to get offenders to voluntarily reduce their offending.

- Media efforts aimed at victims are based on self-protective behaviors and aim to get potential crime victims to reduce their likelihood of being selected by an offender.

- Media efforts aimed at citizens are based on encouraging cooperation with law enforcement and aim to increase information and tips regarding crimes.

- Media technology, especially visual communications, has been increasingly adopted in the criminal justice system in video interrogations and lineups and visual presentation and records of arraignments, evidence, pleas, and trials.

- The capacity for digital manipulation of visual images has worked to undermine the credibility of pictures as evidence.

- Police surveillance of public spaces has expanded and CCTV systems are common in many U.S. communities. Concerns with these systems involve privacy, displacement of crime, and the impact of a surveillance effect on society.

- Media-based anticrime efforts do not appear to be able to reduce crime on their own. Camera surveillance projects show the greatest impact on actual offender behavior.

WRITING ASSIGNMENTS

1. Write an essay about why media technology has been embraced as a solution for various criminal justice system tasks while some police unions have opposed the installation of video cameras in patrol cars.

2. Write an essay about who should have access to the video records and images produced by a public agency surveillance system and whether

surveillance video should be released to news agencies, used in civil cases, or employed in infotainment programming.

3. Write a paper about where and when surveillance cameras are acceptable and if it should matter if they are hidden or openly displayed. Discuss the phenomenon of a surveillance effect and whether people should be informed that they are within the view of a surveillance system.

4. Research computer-monitored surveillance systems and write an essay about the pros and cons of computer versus human monitors.

5. Count and note the location of the surveillance cameras you notice over a seven-day period. Record what entity (government, business, or private) is operating each camera system, whether you can determine the boundary of the surveilled area, whether there are signs announcing the presence of the surveillance cameras, and whether the cameras are difficult or easy to spot. Relate how you feel about the level of surveillance you discovered.

6. Find five anticrime PSAs and note their target audiences, the crime problems they are addressing, their use of fear, and the behaviors they are trying to encourage or discourage.

SUGGESTED READINGS

Goold, B. 2004. *CCTV and Policing*. Oxford, UK: Oxford University Press.

Norris, C., and G. Armstrong. 1999. *The Maximum Surveillance Society: The Rise of CCTV*. Oxford, UK: Berg.

Norris, C., J. Moran, and G. Armstrong, eds. 1998. *Surveillance, Closed Circuit Television and Social Control*. London, UK: Ashgate.

O'Keefe, G., D. Rosenbaum, P. Lavrakas, K. Reid, and R. Botta. 1996. *Taking a Bite Out of Crime*. Thousand Oaks, CA: Sage.

8

The Media and Criminal Justice Policy

CHAPTER OBJECTIVES

After reading Chapter 8, you will

- Understand the link between media content and criminal justice policy
- Comprehend the policy effects of the backwards law
- Know about the media's crime-and-justice ecology
- Appreciate how immanent justice underlies media crime and justice portrayals
- Learn how technology is advanced as a crime-fighting tool
- See that the assessment of criminal justice policy is based on faulty information
- Recognize how the public crime-and-justice agenda, beliefs about criminality, and attitudes toward policy are influenced by the media

SLAYING MAKE-BELIEVE MONSTERS

The cumulative result of the media's construction of crime, crime fighters, courts, corrections, and crime control are punitive criminal justice policies. When the dominant media portrait is of predatory offenders committing violent crimes in continuous battle with the criminal justice system, nonpunitive policies come across as naive. You don't need crime-fighting heroes to battle wayward citizens who have made mistakes they regret. Nor do you rehabilitate innate predators. In that you very rarely find the regretful offender and usually find the innate predator, the ultimate policy push from the overall media social construction of crime and justice is an obvious conclusion. What remains to be clarified are the pathways through which media content influences criminal justice policy.

Herbert Packer's well-known due process and crime-control models serve as conceptual frames for understanding the criminal justice system, its goals, and the mass media's effects on the system.[1] Both models describe organizational case flows. Under the *due process* model, the criminal justice system is seen as an obstacle course in which the government must prove an accused person's guilt while conforming to strict procedural rules. The system's most important goal under this model is the protection of citizen rights and the prevention of arbitrary and capricious government action. The key determination in this model is legal guilt, which is decided at the end of a long and exacting process. In contrast, in the *crime control* model, the criminal justice system is perceived as an assembly line along which defendants should be processed as quickly and efficiently as possible. The primary goal of the system is to punish criminals and to deter crime. The key determination in this model is factual guilt, which is decided early in the process in accordance with the perceived strength of evidence and police judgment.

Beyond aiding in understanding the criminal justice system, these models are also useful for understanding the conflicting perceptions that exist within the criminal justice system regarding the mass media and their impact on crime and justice policy.[2] Conflicts arise because some view the media as mainly promoting a due process reality by ensuring that the courts do not exercise power capriciously, while others view them as retarding due process protections by increasing the difficulty of finding impartial juries and conducting fair trials. Paradoxically, some also see the media as promoting crime control by educating the public about the functions of the justice system and by enhancing deterrence by publicizing punishment of criminals. Others see them as hindering crime control efforts by interfering with the efforts of law enforcement to investigate and prosecute crimes, by negatively reporting unethical but effective law enforcement practices, and by withholding information and evidence from the courts. Hence even if people agree on the effects of the mass media on the criminal justice system, they may disagree as to whether these effects are good or bad. The same media effect—such as making it more difficult for the police to conduct evidence searches—can be seen by some observers as promoting due process and therefore good, while other observers see it as hindering crime control and therefore bad. Given these competing interpretations, the media can be seen as either enhancing or hindering the criminal justice system. The media do what they do, and their effects are seen as promoting (or interfering with) due process or crime control policies depending on the observer's point of view. Despite the fact that their effects can be variously interpreted, in general, media content forwards the crime control model and disparages the due process model. This imbalance is tied to two crime and justice tenets.

MEDIA CRIME-AND-JUSTICE TENETS

Two crime-and-justice tenets provide insight into the way criminal justice as a social issue is constructed. The first tenet is the "backwards law," which is associated with a particular crime-and-justice "ecology." The second tenet is the "rule of immanent justice," which paradoxically is associated with an enhanced view of technological solutions to crime. The media-constructed reality has the police imbedded in a randomly violent environment where they battle predators more than keep the peace; the courts deal with psychotic offenders and conduct investigations more than dispense justice; corrections exist as a bizarre, primitive lost world of frequent brutality; constant surveillance of the public is the most prudent course, and the entire criminal justice system points unwaveringly toward the need for swift, sure, and increased punishment.[3] In this media-generated Darwinian crime-and-justice reality, survival of the violent emerges as the operative selection rule.

The Backwards Law

In nearly every subject category—crimes, criminals, crime fighters, attorneys, correctional officers, and inmates; the investigation of crimes and making of arrests; the processing and disposition of cases; and the experience of incarceration—the media construct and present a crime-and-justice world that is not found in reality. Whatever the truth about crime and the criminal justice system in America, the entertainment, news, and infotainment media seem determined to project the opposite. The wildly inaccurate and inevitably fragmentary images and facts found in the entertainment and infotainment media reflect this law most clearly. They provide a distorted reflection of crime within society and an equally distorted reflection of the criminal justice system's response to crime. Basic to this process is a front-end-loaded portrait that concentrates on the activities of law enforcement and crime fighters. The further past law enforcement and into the criminal justice system one looks, the fewer criminal justice activities are shown. The lack of system-wide information and the unreality of the narrow information that is available demonize criminality while mystifying the criminal justice system. The result is the exacerbation of the public's lack of understanding of crime and justice while constructing a perverse topsy-turvy portrait of criminal justice reality.[4]

The backwards law also applies to crime-and-justice news content. First, the criminal justice system and its component parts are seldom the subject of news reports. The criminal justice system serves as a background setting for a news story more often than it appears as the subject. When the justice system is explicitly referred to, it is usually the courts that are portrayed, not as institutions but as backdrops to present information about individual cases. Seldom are broader system issues covered. For example, the broader policy issue of sentencing as a range of options incorporating fines, community supervision, and incarceration is not often discussed. Instead, references to sentencing are reported within stories about an individual receiving a sentence, most often prison. Nonincarceration sentencing options such as fines appear in less than 10 percent of news stories.[5] Alternate sentences, such as restitution or community service, almost never appear. Similarly, crime prevention stories are rare when compared to the number of stories about individual violent crimes—and when crime prevention does get covered, the coverage is usually negative. The end result is news that approaches criminal justice policy from the bottom up—that is, as the piecemeal, cumulative result of a focus on individual crimes and individuals rather than as a coherent, system of justice.

The "Virginia Tech massacre" shooter killed 32 in a 2007 rampage. Episodic style coverage of such events drives media influence on criminal justice policy formation.

HO/UPPA/Photoshot

   This bottom-up perspective can be found in the way news stories are formatted, either as episodic or thematic.[6] The more common **episodic format** treats stories as discrete events: a crime is described and a resulting case is followed. The rarer **thematic format** highlights trends, persistent problems, or other systemic phenomena: a crime-and-justice issue or a category of crimes is explored. Episodic formatted stories encourage viewers to place responsibility for social problems totally on individuals and to ignore possible societal forces—an individual committed a crime, why did he do it? Stories told in the thematic format take the opposite approach and effect—a set of problems have developed, what changed in society? The entertainment media reflects the same dichotomy, concentrating on events more than issues—the big heist, the murders, the investigation, the trial, the riot, and so on. By being episodic rather than thematic, the media reinforce the popular view that says crime is caused solely by individual choices and that punitive, harsh deterrent-based policies are the only effective response.
   The media therefore supply a large amount of information about specific crimes and convey the impression that criminals threaten the social order and its institutions with imminent collapse. Media provide less information to help the public comprehend the larger society-wide forces that underlie individual crimes and cases. Rare is the thematic interpretive analysis that places criminal justice information in historical, sociological, or political context. In the absence of system-wide information, the public is left to build its own picture of the effectiveness of current criminal justice policies and the desirability of newly offered ones.

consistent message is that crime is caused by predatory individuals who are inherently different from the rest of us—more ruthless, greedy, violent, or psychotic. Combating these predators requires a special person, an equally tough, predatory, and most important, unfettered crime fighter. Criminality is an individual choice and other social, economic, or structural explanations are irrelevant and can be ignored. Limited to this simplistic, incomplete picture of crime as mostly individual, socially isolated acts, the public is shown that counterviolence is the most effective means of combating crime, that due process considerations hamper the police, and that, in most cases, the law works in the criminal's favor. The public is further instructed to fear others because criminals are not always easily recognized and often are rich, powerful, and in positions of trust.

This constructed social environment, combined with the emphasis on investigations and arrests—the front end of the criminal justice system—ultimately promotes pro–law enforcement and crime control policies. When the public relies on infotainment-formatted media and avoids media that present criminality as a complex social problem, punitive "quick fixes" are supported over preventive long-term approaches to crime.[12] Paradoxically, although the media frequently portray the criminal justice system unfavorably, the solutions they depict as being the most effective—harsher punishments and more law enforcement—entail expansion of the existing criminal justice system. Underlying this construction is a persistent, if often unstated, explanation of crime. The media consistently point to individual personality traits as the cause of crime and to violent interdiction as its solution. If one accepts the media's explanation of crime as being caused by predatory personality traits—by innate greed and violence—then the only valid approach to stopping crime is to hold individual offenders responsible for their past crimes and forcibly deter them from committing future ones. In the media's simplistic notion of crime, the most effective solution is dramatic, individual action that emphasizes violence and aggression, with a preference for weapons and sophisticated technology. By portraying criminality as innate and crime as an act of nature, the logical response is found in revenge, punishment, and immanent justice.

Immanent Justice Rules the Media

Immanent justice is the belief that a divine higher power will intervene, and reveal and punish the guilty while protecting the innocent. The operation of divine intervention in the media becomes most clear in entertainment gunplay. Weapon accuracy and killing power are unequally held by the evil criminals and the good crime fighters, their aim apparently guided by the moral imperatives of right and wrong. Sinful, evil criminals miss or inflict benign flesh wounds while blessed, good crime fighters hit and kill. Similar to the medieval socially constructed reality that made trial by ordeal and combat logical, the modern media reality relies on the moral superiority of the crime fighter to ultimately defeat criminality. Lessened as a social problem, criminality is further reduced to an individual moral battle. The idea that criminals personify evil, which is exemplified in the phase "dangerous criminal underclass," has deep historical roots.[13] A dangerous, immoral underclass, in turn justifies the wide use of violence and punishment. Sin must be resisted and sinners punished.

An evil Nazi who is ultimately destroyed by the ark in the film *Raiders of the Lost Ark*. Evil criminals and their ordained defeat are inherent in the portrayals of immanent justice found in crime-and-justice media.

This good versus evil perspective on crime and justice is also reflected in the common media crime fighter who is motivated by personal injury and revenge; upholding the law is secondary to individual retribution. This media portrait ties into the overall media emphasis on individualism and personal action as the appropriate solution to crime and victimization. The associated media-constructed crime-and-justice policies gain support from our basic cultural values of free will, individualism, and personal responsibility. The result is that an individualized, revenge-oriented justice dominates where, God willing, the good guys win despite heavy odds. This pursuit of individualized immanent justice in the media tends to crowd out other competing constructions of crime and justice and their associated policies. In this fashion, crime is further diminished as a social problem. Instead, it becomes a theological one, albeit not without a role for technology.

TECHNOLOGY ENHANCES CRIME FIGHTING

In contrast to their focus on individual factors as the cause of crime, the media do portray some collective responses to crime as effective, but only if they are technology based. Immanent justice is often helped along by technology and gadgets. If God is not handy, then a good engineer or scientist (not a social scientist, though) will do. Crime-and-justice issues are seen as a technological engineering problem analogous to traffic control. Within this portrait, it makes sense to ignore social and structural sources of conflict such as racism, sexism, and economic inequality and focus on solutions requiring more equipment, manpower, and resources. Suggesting

---

B o x 8.2   Minor Celebrity Crime = Major Media Attention

Tatum O'Neal (cocaine possession), Wesley Snipes (tax evasion), George Michael (lewd act), Lil' Kim (perjury), Hugh Grant (solicitation of prostitute), Winnona Ryder (shoplifting), Britney Spears, Paris Hilton, Lindsay Lohan (her mugshot is below), and Mel Gibson (DUI and various traffic violations) are all celebrities arrested in recent years for nonviolent or victimless crimes. These crimes would be considered comparatively minor and not newsworthy if committed by ordinary people. The large amount of coverage these arrests generated displays how socially unimportant crimes (crimes that have little effect in terms of social harm to society and would have little social impact except for being linked to someone famous) can be newsworthy and have significant media value.

AP Photo/Santa Monica Police, file

---

that we can engineer our way out of crime, such an approach works well for true technological problems like reaching the moon. Unfortunately, for true social problems like crime and poverty, technology-based moon-shot solutions do not work.

Real-World Crime and Justice Problems

In the real world, social problems come bundled together—crime is found with poverty, unemployment, poor health, poor schools, high divorce rates, high out-of-wedlock pregnancy rates, community decay and deterioration, drug use, illiteracy, high school dropout rates, and so on. Communities and societies that experience one of these problems tend to experience most if not all of them together. Unfortunately, the media present crime as largely autonomous from other social problems and not as linked to them in any serious way. With its individually rooted causes and celebrity linkages (see Box 8.2), crime is constructed as an autonomous plague on society, its genesis not associated with other historical, social, or structural conditions. It follows that criminological theories that are individually focused gain more support from the media's construction of crime and justice than do group or culturally focused theories. Retribution and deterrence are trumpeted; rehabilitation and social reform are belittled.

The end product from a constructed backwards world of immanent justice, where policy is steered by divine intervention and derived from contests between good and evil individuals is, ironically, a preference for high-tech policies. Crime in the media is ultimately painted as a technological problem imbedded in a randomly violent, socially impersonal landscape that can only be tamed by more manpower and equipment. But does the public make the connection between the content they see and the policies they support? Do they even pay attention to the implicit policy messages?

CRIMINAL JUSTICE POLICY AND MEDIA RESEARCH

While the content of the media certainly leads toward some policies and away from others, it is worthwhile to examine the research evidence of the media's ability to influence crime-and-justice policy. This section looks at the relationship between media and criminal justice policy, examining the pathways that connect them: the effects on crime's rank on the list of social problems, attitudes about the world as mean and dangerous, fear of crime, and counterproductive and anticipatory effects.

Crime on the Public Agenda

Can the media, by emphasizing or ignoring topics, influence the ranking of issues that are important to the public—that is, what the public thinks about rather than what the public thinks? The hypothesis is that people will tend to judge a social issue such as crime as significant to the extent that the media emphasize it. If true, in time the media will construct the **public agenda**.[14] When a correlation is looked for between media attention and public concern, a weak to moderate relationship is found.[15] Encouraged by this association, the agenda-setting research has concentrated on the media's effects on the public's ranking of issues with the idea that the issues that receive government attention are chosen from the public's list. An early assumption in agenda setting was that the media influence public policy through a linear process. Crime stories appear, crime as an issue increases in public importance, the public becomes alarmed, neighborhood and other public interest groups mobilize and rally for action, and crime-and-justice policy makers respond. Consistent evidence of such a linear process has not emerged from the research, however. The media's influence is seldom direct and is more often modified through multiple steps and social networks.

As the research now stands, a media effect on the public's agenda is generally acknowledged, but unless the effect also appears among policy makers, it is usually regarded as unimportant. The research indicates that media effects are variable; appear to increase with exposure (those who are exposed to the media content mirror the media ranking of issues more closely); are more significant the less direct experience people have with an issue; are more significant for newer, concrete issues than for older abstract ones; diminish quickly; and are nonlinear, sometimes reciprocal, and highly interactive with other social and individual processes.[16] Specifically regarding crime and justice, the media emphasis on crime and associated claims about the nature of crime have been credited with raising the public's fear of being victimized and giving crime an inappropriately high ranking on the public agenda. It is felt that crime's high ranking also encourages moral crusades against specific crime issues, heightens public anxiety about crime, and pushes or blocks other serious social problems such as hunger or health care down or off the public agenda.

Beliefs and Attitudes about Crime

The second question is whether exposure to crime-and-justice claims in the media affect a person's beliefs and attitudes about crime—the claims about crime a person accepts as true, and the feelings about crime a person believes to be justified. George Gerbner and his colleagues investigated the association between watching large amounts of television and general perceptions about the world, with the idea that television creates a particularly pernicious social reality for its audience.[17] This process, first described as **worldview cultivation,** was felt to be directly related to the number of hours of television viewed. The researchers hypothesized that through exposure to television's content most everyone comes to have a similar media-constructed view of the world. Over time the repetitive themes and content of the mass media homogenize viewpoints and perspectives. People would come to think like the media and, consequently, to think alike. Prodded by critiques of their initial research,[18] Gerbner and his colleagues amended their initial hypothesis from one of "worldview cultivation," which stated that all media viewers would be affected, to the current one termed "mainstreaming." **Mainstreaming** posits that the media affect some viewers more than others regardless of exposure level. They now argue that the media are homogenizing society, influencing those heavy television consumers who are currently not in the mainstream to move toward it, while not affecting those already in the mainstream. The significance and extent of a media mainstreaming effect has yet to be determined. Effects on viewer beliefs about the world such as their estimates of the number of crimes in society are acknowledged; effects on the development of mean-world views and mainstreaming are weak and inconsistent and therefore still debated.[19]

One factor that has emerged as important in determining the impact of the media is the local environment of the media consumer. Local conditions and family context in which media information is obtained influence the acceptance or rejection of media-based claims about crime and justice.[20] For example, the relationship between exposure to media content and one's attitudes is expected to diminish when actual neighborhood crime levels are taken into account or if one lives in a violent household. If one's world truly is mean, the media will have less effect on one's view of the world. This conclusion is consistent with the general social construction proposition that media effects are most powerful for issues that are outside of your personal experiences or experienced reality. Media-based claims are expected to have less impact on beliefs about crime among those who have had direct neighborhood experience with crime and thereby have a powerful alternative source of information.

The most relevant crime-and-justice attitude that has been linked to the media is fear of criminal victimization. Fear-of-crime levels are socially important because they encourage support for punitive criminal justice policies and increased personal social isolation. Viewing television crime shows, for example, has been found to be related to fear of crime, perceived police effectiveness, and opposition to gun control.[21] As the most accessible and pervasive potential source of fear, the role of the media is therefore important—but that role is not clear.[22] Currently, research suggests that media exposure to crime content is more strongly related to fear about distant seldom visited places than to fear about local personal victimization. Not surprisingly, the public is more likely to accept fear-generating claims about places known only via the media than about directly experienced communities.[23] It also follows that media consumption is more strongly related to fear of general social violence than to fear of personal risk[24] and fear of urban areas more than fear of nonurban areas.[25]

What does this research say about people's beliefs and attitudes about crime? At the least, heavy media consumers do share certain beliefs about high societal crime and victimization levels and live in a socially constructed world that is seen as more violent and dangerous—and feared—than the socially constructed world of those who consume less media. The most common effects are increased belief in the prevalence of crime, victimization, and violence, and increasingly cynical, distrustful social attitudes. The media provide the individual social construction "bricks" in the form of individual criminal events and associated crime-and-justice claims to build a crime-and-justice reality foundation. With attitudes about crime and justice as mortar, the public blends all of its media knowledge together with personal experiences into a final crime-and-justice social reality. The media's portrayal of crime and justice thus defines a broad public reality of crime. In that the media tend to construct a particular crime-and-justice reality for their consumers, the logical next question is whether the resulting beliefs and attitudes translate into support for specific crime and- justice policies.

Crime-and-Justice Policies

Understanding the relationship between the media and the formation of criminal justice policies is important because media effects translate into how tax monies are spent and what actually happens to offenders and victims. Influence on

---

**B o x 8.3   Three Strikes and You're Out: A Mediated Criminal
Justice Policy**

In the Three Strikes and You're Out legislation, serious crime was redefined and part
of the faulty criminal justice system was "fixed." In 1988, Diane Ballasiotes was
abducted and stabbed to death in Washington state by a convicted rapist who had
been released from prison. In reaction to this crime, a group called Friends of Diane
formed to seek harsher penalties for sex crimes. This group eventually joined forces
with another Washington state policy lobby group that was advocating for Three
Strikes legislation. Despite their combined efforts, however, through 1992 there was
little legislative or criminal justice professional interest in Three Strikes legislation in
Washington. The proposed legislation was perceived as similar to a habitual offender
law already on the books, and a petition drive to get three strikes on a statewide
ballot failed. Although there was some media coverage, up to that time the Friends
of Diane and the Three Strikes groups did not find a receptive social and media
environment. As a result, they were unable to be successful claims makers and
forward a new dominant construction of criminal justice policy.

In 1993, the Three Strikes group (renamed the Washington Citizens for Justice)
allied with the National Rifle Association and succeeded in getting the proposition on
the November ballot. This time, despite some opposition from elements of the
criminal justice professional community, 77 percent of Washingtonians approved
the Three Strikes law. The catalyst for this shift was a tragic "symbolic crime" in
California. As the Washington vote approached, a young California girl, Polly Klaas,
was abducted and murdered. Coupled to this crime, media coverage of Three
Strikes was extensive, and politicians and citizens across the nation and the political
spectrum embraced the new policy as a crime panacea.

A number of social construction concepts clearly come into play in the Three
Strikes saga. With the alliance of the NRA, Friends of Diane was able to become a
much more powerful claims maker—the NRA was a preestablished group that the
media would readily contact. Also, with the kidnapping and murder of Polly Klaas,
the Three Strikes and You're Out claims makers had a tragic and powerful symbolic
crime that they were able to use to reconstruct the crime problem. Symbolic crimes
are crucial as they ensure media access for claims makers while providing dramatic
stories, visuals, and evidence of policies that must be implemented. In Three Strikes,
the Polly Klaas murder became the symbolic event that focused the media's attention
and lifted the new crime-defining legislation to become a new social reality.

---

crime-and-justice policy is the ultimate prize in the competition over the construction of crime-and-justice reality. Victorious, policy-influencing claims makers gain power, resources, and ownership of a core social issue (see Box 8.3).
Recognizing this, they work diligently to garner media attention and favor. It
is also important to distinguish the effect of the media on criminal justice policy
formation from their effect on preexisting popular crime and justice attitudes. To
the extent that the media accurately reflects already established public attitudes,
the media amplify public policy tendencies by simply reinforcing preexisting
punitive attitudes.[26] In this way, the media have a second route of influence on
criminal justice policy, one by legitimizing and amplifying nascent punitive public attitudes, the other by helping to create those attitudes.

B o x 8.4   Media–Criminal Justice Policy Relationship Models

A. Direct Media Influence

Media Coverage → Criminal Justice Policy Change

An investigative news report of ticket fixing leads to a new department policy regarding tickets.

B. No Media Influence External Event

External Event ⟶ ┌→ Criminal Justice Policy Change
　　　　　　　　　 └→ Media Coverage

An external evaluation reveals that low-income defendants are less likely to be offered alternatives to jail sentences. The review and selection process is adjusted as part of a preplanned program refinement cycle at the same time as local media report on the existence of program bias.

C. Simultaneous Media Influence External Event

A prisoner on a furlough program commits a violent rape. As a result, the corrections department reviews and alters the furlough program. Due to media publicity of the rape, the program is also suspended for a number of months and more severe restrictions than otherwise considered are instituted.

　　Researchers continue to explore the nature of the media–criminal justice policy relationship, and they have been able to report clear connections between the two. The results of the research have established that the media can directly affect what actors in the criminal justice system do without having to first change the public's attitudes or agenda. The idiosyncratic nature of the media–justice policy relationship, however, makes predicting the direction and magnitude of media influence in specific situations difficult. The difficulty arises because the media may themselves be claims makers or serve as the voice of nonmedia claims makers, and because the media are as likely to affect criminal justice decision making indirectly as they are to directly influence the formation of crime-and-justice policy. As the models in Box 8.4 show, the media may actually be the cause of a criminal justice policy change (model A). Conversely, an external event may be the cause, while the media simply covers the event prior to the policy change, which would have occurred without media attention (model B). Or the media's coverage of an external event and the event may both be influencing criminal justice policy (model C).

　　The available research indicates that among criminal justice officials, even more than among the public, the media significantly influence both policy development and support. Effects are multidirectional, and media content, the timing and presentation of the claims, and the characteristics and concerns of the general public, claims makers, and the criminal justice policy makers interact to determine the media's influence on criminal justice policies.[27] Misinformation pervades the interplay between crime, politics, and public opinion, however, so as to create a comedy of errors in the formation of criminal justice policy.[28] In what has been called crime control theater, claimsmakers exploit misinformed public opinion with results that range from broad, far-reaching policy crusades and criminal legislation to specific narrow influences on decisions in individual cases.[29] The research difficulty is not in the media's lack of significant policy effects but in determining the form effects will take, and the task of sorting out the effects of the media from the effects of external events is obviously difficult. Compounding the difficulties, another set of unexpected effects arise from the novel manner in which the media relate to criminal justice policy. Three types appear: echo effects, counterproductive results, and anticipatory reactions.

A media coverage **echo effect** (discussed also in Chapter 5, pages 114 and 117) refers to a tendency for officials to treat defendants in unpublicized cases harshly if the press has been demanding such treatment for defendants in publicized cases. For example, a study of the processing of criminal cases prior to, during, and following a highly publicized case involving the sexual abuse of toddlers at a private day care center demonstrated that an echo effect was in operation.[30] Initial analysis showed marked increases in the number of filings of cases involving child victimization following the publicized case and an increase in the sentences of defendants adjudicated guilty. The existence of echo effects portends an influence spillover from the coverage of newsworthy criminal cases onto nonpublicized ones. Diffused but pervasive systemic media effects on a large number of unpublicized cases are likely.

The second unexpected result, **counterproductive effects,** occurs in situations where media attention results in unanticipated consequences, usually involving a crime reduction program. In this effect, some media-based anticrime campaigns have been found to have effects opposite to the campaign goals. For example, a massive multimedia Canadian anticrime campaign was found to actually result in fewer people taking personal anticrime measures.[31] This negative effect was credited to the campaign raising concern about crime to a fatalistic level among the target population, so that they stopped taking any precautions against crime.

A final unique effect is rare for other social research areas, but not uncommon for the media. **Anticipatory effects** seem to reverse the causal order of media attention and criminal justice policy change. It has been discovered that among criminal justice system officials, responses to the media can be either reactive or proactive—that is, they may react to what they have seen and heard in the media or act in anticipation of what they expect to find in the media. In the latter situations, the effect on policy occurs before any observable change in media content. The policy changes occur because criminal justice system officials respond in a proactive manner to anticipated media coverage, perhaps due to seeing negative media coverage of a criminal justice practice in a distant jurisdiction.[32] In these cases, even if the media pay no attention to an issue, an official still acts on the idea that attention might be forthcoming and initiates a new policy or fails to implement a requested policy, to avoid expected negative media attention. In the first instance, a successful policy change cancels the potential coverage, and in the second, the proactive non-policy change is in anticipation of coverage that might never have occurred. In either case, because the media influence policy without any tangible coverage, the task of determining and studying a media policy effect is daunting. The problem is similar to determining how many crimes were not committed as a result of the deterrent effect of a new punishment-based program. Not impossible, but more difficult than counting events that do occur.

Together, anticipatory, echo, and counterproductive effects underscore the idiosyncratic nature of the media–criminal justice policy construction relationship. The unpredictability makes it difficult to determine the direction and magnitude of influence or to specify the mechanism through which the media's influence is being exerted. They add a unique level of difficulty to deciphering the relationship of the media and the criminal justice system. These media–related effects interweave with any criminal justice policy effects. Observed changes can be in anticipation of the media attention (as when prosecutors decide to increase DUI prosecutions to head off potential negative publicity), in anticipation of a policy being changed (as when prosecutors decide to pursue harsher sentences for drunk drivers due to the echo effect from a highly publicized DUI case), or due to a criminal justice policy change directly lobbied for by the media (as when DUI prosecutions increase due to an investigatory media series suggesting that lenient treatment for DUI offenders is common).

There is the real possibility of one effect occurring to prevent a second effect. In such a case, a preemptive decision to not change an established policy in favor of a new policy might occur so as to avoid the anticipated negative media coverage generated by the appearance and subsequent waning of an announcement effect of the (now rejected) new criminal justice policy. For example, a prosecutor sensitive to media dynamics may decide against launching a tougher but expensive new DUI policy to avoid the problem of future negative coverage of the apparent loss of initial prosecutorial effectiveness that will occur when the media-generated announcement effect wanes. At that point, the new DUI policy, cast as suddenly failing to maintain its initial successful deterrent impact, results in the prosecutor being called to task. Sensing this pitfall, the prosecutor might well decide to forgo this or other new policies. The recognition and delineation of the media's role in such a scenario would be Herculean. Indeed, based on the discussion thus far, confidently comprehending any policy effect of the media appears daunting, and it is perhaps surprising that knowledge has progressed as far as it has.

THE SOCIAL CONSTRUCTION OF CRIME-AND-JUSTICE POLICY

As stated earlier, the ultimate impact of social constructionism on criminal justice is found in its implication for criminal justice policy. For it is with our crime-and-justice policy decisions that we decide how we are going to collectively respond to crime, deal with offenders, and spend our taxes. The media's role is not praised. "We have a public dialogue that is segmented and reduced to sound bites, content that dulls an increasingly inattentive populace, and media that provides feedback via call-ins, Internet polls, and narrow constituencies."[33] Figure 8.1 lays out the relationship between the media, social constructionism, and criminal justice policy. As shown, the relationship between the media and their crime-and-justice content influences the social construction of crime-and-justice reality by supplying the narratives, symbolic crimes, and basic information needed to create factual and interpretative claims.[34] The media further provide the arena for the crime-and-justice social construction competition to be held, thereby favoring media-savvy claims makers. This in turn encourages a particular set of social attitudes and perceptions about crime and justice; predatory criminality and an overly lenient justice system are popular. The final and most important influence in this relationship chain is on criminal justice policies. How policies are presented and perceived determines whether they are supported or opposed.

The media are not the most important factor in the construction of crime and justice policy, but their influence cannot be ignored.[35] They remain influential because their content regarding social problems resonates strongly with the emotional framework of the public.[36] Perceptions of crime and justice appear to be intertwined with other social perceptions, and crime-related attitudes are not determined solely by one's perception of the crime problem. Instead, perceptions of crime and justice are part of a larger construction of the nature and health of society. And if perceptions of crime are intricately related to broader perceptions of the world, it is unrealistic to expect that they would change solely in accordance with media presentations of crime. That being said, if there is a

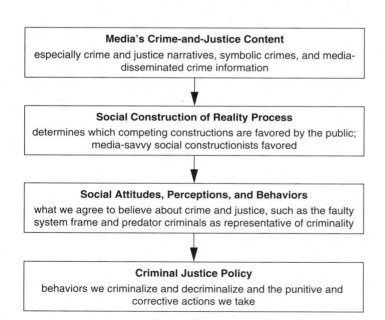

FIGURE 8.1 Media, Social Constructionism, and Criminal Justice Policy

general media effect on criminal justice policy, it is to increase punitiveness and surveillance as the first and sometimes only policy choices.[37] A punitive policy effect, however, need not be the default impact of the media; there is evidence that when media framing of capital punishment shifted from supportive to portraying capital punishment as flawed an associated downward shift in public support for executions followed.[38]

For the most part though, the image of justice that most people find the most palatable and popular is the image that the media have historically projected. This is true for the entertainment, news, and infotainment elements of the media, as similar crimes and criminals appear in each. The repeated message in the media is that crime is largely perpetrated by predatory individuals who are basically different from the rest of us; that criminality is predominantly the result of individual problems; and that crimes are acts freely committed by individuals who have a wide range of alternate choices.[39] This image locates the causes of crime solely in the individual criminal and supports existing social arrangements and approaches to crime control. The media–constructed reality of crime also allows crime to be more easily divorced from other social problems and highlighted as society's greatest threat. In the end, crime-and-justice media advances system-enhancing crime control policies. The media do not provide the public with enough knowledge to directly evaluate the criminal justice system's performance, but media content steers people toward particular policies and assessments. Crime control does consistently better in the media than due process.

Not surprisingly, the overriding concern involves the image of the criminal justice system that the media constructs and the public receives. Learning about the criminal justice system from the media is analogous to learning geology from volcanic eruptions. You will surely be impressed and entertained, but the information you receive will not accurately reflect the real world, whether you're looking at volcanoes or at the criminal justice system. The media-constructed reality of predatory crimes, high-stakes trials, and violent riots contrasts starkly with the criminal justice system's daily reality of property crime, plea bargains, and order maintenance. Ironically, the public is shown that the traditional criminal justice system is not effective and is simultaneously told that its improvement remains the best solution to crime. While critical pieces on criminal justice have increased in frequency and media exposés have led to the exoneration of some wrongly convicted persons, the tendency is to portray misconduct within a ""bad apple"" framework and to preserve the overall portrait of the police and the criminal justice system as the sole solution to crime.[40] These messages translate into support for order over law, punishment over rehabilitation and criminal justice based over non-criminal-justice-based policies.[41] This portrait has naturally led to concern. Criminologist David Altheide observed that: "The only response we seem to have is to wait and to prepare (get armed, lock doors, build walls, and avoid strangers and public places). This may be a good formula for cinema thrillers, but it is lousy for everyday life."[42] Fear and fatalistic acceptance of crime, mystification of the criminal justice system, myopic support for punitive criminal justice policies, and increased tolerance for illegal law enforcement practices all result.

How could the media portray crime and justice better? The news media have the experience and a coverage model to adopt if they wanted to improve. The media are able to provide comprehensive, contextual coverage for sporting events on a daily basis. Sports coverage stands as a model for reporting on individual events, supplemented by statistics, trend analysis, forecasts, commentary, and discussion. Sporting events are consistently placed by the media in their larger social context (the world of sports in this case) and constructed in a way that provides historical understanding and current comprehension. Covering justice like sports would provide the public with a counterbalance to the distorted and currently unchallenged entertainment and infotainment constructions. In that manner, crime could be removed from the realm of the bizarre, grotesque, and sinister and placed in the social world of poverty, loss of community, alienation, group conflict, and psychological disorders.[43]

Sports, however, are covered in breadth and depth because there is a strong public demand and interest. Lacking a similar incentive regarding criminal justice, there is no reason to expect the commercial media to direct their limited resources to delivering an expanded justice portrait. It's not that they cannot do it, but lacking a large enough market they cannot afford to do it. In the social construction of crime and justice we won't get what too few of us are willing to pay for. The crime-and-justice media that will be delivered will be that which can be produced profitably. The most profitable content follows entertainment narratives, formatting, and frames. Whether in news, infotainment, or entertainment, this profitable content carries imbedded messages about criminal justice polices and encourages public support for policies that will fix and enhance what some view as the "faulty" criminal justice system while discouraging support for other approaches.

CHAPTER SUMMARY

- The backwards law says that in many respects the media portrait of crime and justice will be the opposite of what is true. This backwards portrait leads to a crime-and-justice ecology made up of wolf-like predatory offenders, heroic protective crime fighters, and sheep-like victims. Crime control policies are advanced at the expense of due process model policies.

- The solution to crime constructed in the media is often aided by events that reflect a type of "immanent justice" in which fortuitous seemingly divine intervention prevents criminals from prevailing and ensures that crime ultimately does not pay.

- Technology plays a central role in the media–constructed solution to crime. Equipment and surveillance are offered as core crime solution elements.

- Research on the relationship between media and criminal justice policy has focused on agenda setting, beliefs and attitudes about crime, and direct media effects on criminal justice policy formation. Relationships between media and policy have been reported in all three areas but consistent media effects are not reported.

- The relationship between the media and criminal justice policy is complex, hard to predict, and prone to unanticipated effects including news coverage echoes, anticipatory actions on the part of policy makers, and counterproductive consequences from media attention.
- Criminal justice policy development and debate would be better served if crime and justice was covered as thoroughly as sports. The snapshot episodic coverage of crime overwhelms media content that discusses criminal justice policy issues.

WRITING ASSIGNMENTS

1. Detail a recent local crime or criminal justice event that resulted in heavy media coverage and in calls for a change in a criminal justice policy. Discuss how the competing constructions of the issue were framed, whether the event became a symbolic crime, and whether a policy change appeared likely. Note which features of the event make it more or less likely to generate a memorial criminal justice policy.

2. For each component of the criminal justice system list how its media portrait reflects the backwards law and note which component is portrayed in the media least like its actual reality.

3. Write an essay about the use of immanent justice ideas in the social construction of terrorism by both terrorists and governments.

4. Critique the film *Natural Born Killers* (1994) and its depiction of the news media's role in crime and justice.

5. Research the media content regarding a recent local criminal justice policy debate. Note the references to crime-and-justice events by politicians and other policy makers and how the policy alternatives are socially constructed and framed by the media and by claims makers.

SUGGESTED READINGS

Altheide, D. 2002. *Creating Fear: News and the Construction of Crisis.* Hawthorne, N.Y.: Aldine de Gruyter.

Beckett, K., and T. Sasson. 2000. *The Politics of Injustice.* Thousand Oaks, CA: Pine Forge Press.

Callanan, V. 2005. *Feeding the Fear of Crime: Crime-related Media and Support for Three Strikes.* New York: LFB Scholarly Publishing LLC.

Gest, T. 2001. *Crime and Politics.* London, UK: Oxford University Press.

Shichor, D., and D. Sechrest, eds. 1996. *Three Strikes and You're Out: Vengeance as Public Policy.* Thousand Oaks, CA: Sage.

9

Media and Crime and Justice in the Twenty-First Century

CHAPTER OBJECTIVES

Chapter 9 provides

- A summary of what the reader has learned about crime, justice and the media
- An overview of the relationship between media and crime and justice.
- Two postulates that encapsulate the media crime-and-justice relationship
- A description and discussion of two alternative scenarios of the future of the media's role between the public and the criminal justice system
- A discussion of the likely impact of new media on crime and justice

CRIME-AND-JUSTICE MEDIA MESSAGES

By the late nineteenth century, early print-based media contained the same criminal stereotypes and causal explanations of crime found in today's media. Narratives of individually focused crime and retributive justice have been common story lines for more than a hundred years. Composed of ever-multiplying outlets and new media technologies, today a pervasive social reality web constructs a distorted, erroneous crime-and-justice portrait. The merging of news and entertainment media and the constant looping of crime-and-justice content means that the portraits of crime and justice in each will continue to be more alike than different. Infotainment media presentations will continue unabated and new media will speed the distribution of this content and broaden its reach.

Crime-and-justice media messages conform to a backward's law, and the media consistently reverse the real world of crime and justice in their media-constructed world. As a basic rule of thumb, news, entertainment, and infotainment media take the least common crime or justice event and make it the most common crime or justice image. Crime constitutes a constant, significant portion of the total media content; criminals are normally constructed as either predatory street criminals or dishonest businesspeople and professionals; and the criminal justice system is shown as an ineffective, often counterproductive means of dealing with crime. In this media-made reality, traditional criminal justice system personnel and standard practices suffer, but alternatives to the criminal justice system fare even worse.

The lack of realistic information in the media further mystifies and obscures criminality and the criminal justice system.[1] The media emphasize individual personality traits as the cause of crime and violent interdiction as its solution, showing a preference for crimes involving weapons and solutions involving violence and sophisticated technology. Media present criminality as an individual choice and imply that other social, economic, or structural explanations are irrelevant. The "crime fighter" and "war-on-crime" icons suggest to the public that crime must be fought rather than solved or prevented.[2] Media portraits further instruct the public to fear others, for the criminal is not easily recognizable and is often found among the rich, powerful, and seemingly trustworthy. These images tilt public perceptions toward law enforcement and crime control policies. The result is that although the criminal justice system is not shown favorably, the solutions to crime suggested by the media involve expansion of the existing criminal justice system through harsher punishments and more law enforcement. Increasing the punitiveness of the real criminal justice system appears to be the only reasonable policy course. And in a looping cycle, the actions of the real criminal justice system are evaluated by the public against the expectations and desires raised by the media-constructed criminal justice system.

Cumulatively, the media's crime-and-justice content forwards the following claims:

1. Crime fighters must use any means to catch criminals.

2. Corruption runs rampant throughout criminal justice agencies.

3. Bureaucratic red tape and due process protections hinder the honest crime fighters and make it difficult to successfully conclude investigations.

4. Crime fighters need more training and resources because they are not capable of solving crimes legally.

5. Crime is a result of individual characteristics and is not related to social structure, racism, or poverty.

6. Criminals cannot be rehabilitated and, if given a chance, will recidivate.

7. Specific deterrence combined with incapacitation is the only policy approach that will stop criminals from recidivating.

8. The courts allow dangerous offenders to avoid guilt.

9.   Probation and parole allow dangerous offenders to go free.

10.   Prisons make dangerous offenders more dangerous while brutalizing and criminalizing wrongfully incarcerated ones.

The dominant crime-and-justice portrait shows people outside of the criminal justice system and unburdened by due process considerations to be the most effective crime fighters. At the same time, media bolster the existing criminal justice system as being the best policy course. This media–constructed, ineffective, last resort criminal justice system sits within a portrait of a stark social ecology filled with predatory criminals, violent crime fighters, and helpless victims.

The media's influence on criminality, independent of its effect on criminal justice, has not been adequately explored, and the specter of media-oriented terrorism is an issue of immediate concern.[3] The available evidence suggests, and most researchers agree, that the media do affect crime rates and motivate terrorists. Aggregate crime rate studies further suggest that the media affect crime independently of their violent content. In addition, the media likely have a copycat effect more on property crime than on violent crime. The more heavily the potential copycat criminal relies on the media for information about the world and the more predisposed the individual is to commit crime, the more likely a copycat effect is. Violence-prone children and individuals who have difficulty distinguishing fact from fantasy are particularly at risk for aping media violence. When sexual and violent content are yoked, hypermasculine males are most influenced. When the news media sensationalize crimes and make celebrities of criminals, people seeking notoriety imitate those crimes. And when successful innovative crimes, in particular property crimes, are detailed, criminals emulate them.

Media Anticrime Efforts

On the other side of the media social construction equation are media-based anticrime efforts. These efforts appear to be an effective means of disseminating information and influencing attitudes, but their ability to significantly affect behavior has not been established. Although useful in specific areas, media-based anticrime programs are not likely to significantly reduce the overall crime rate. No program has empirically demonstrated a significant long-term and displacement-free effect on crime. Single-handedly, the media and media technology are as unable to deter criminal behavior as they are to criminalize previously law-abiding individuals, and the media should not be looked to as crime panaceas. Even so, media-based anticrime programs can have significant immediate effects, and their careful utilization is warranted.

By constructing crime-and-justice reality, the media also subtly but significantly affect crime-and-justice policies. To varying degrees, media influence the agenda, perceptions, and policies of consumers with regard to crime and justice. These media effects interact with other factors, are not easy to discern, and are difficult to counteract. Perceptions of crime and justice are intertwined with

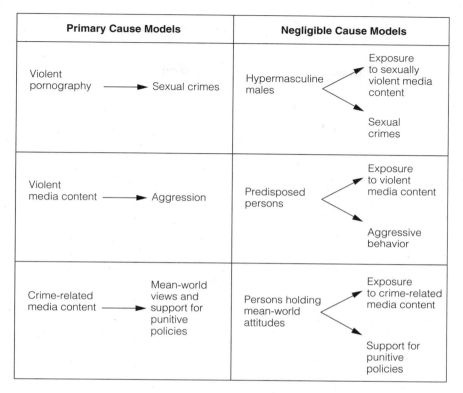

FIGURE 9.1 Competing Models of the Media's Relationship to Sex Crimes, Aggression, and Support for Punitive Criminal Justice Policies

other, broader perceptions of social conditions. Therefore, it is not surprising that consistent relationships have not been found between the media and public attitudes or policies on crime and justice.

As reflected in Figure 9.1, the conflicting arguments of the media as a primary cause versus a negligible cause of crime, aggression, terrorism, and other unwanted behaviors not only posit differing causal relations between the media and behavior but imply vastly different public policies as well. The *primary cause models* argue that a significant, direct linear relationship exists between media content and consumer behavior. In these models, the media, independent of other factors, directly cause undesired social behaviors. If valid, these models indicate that strong intervention is necessary in the creation, content, and distribution of media.

The *negligible cause models* concede a statistical association between the media and some negative behaviors but argue that the connection is due not to a causal relationship but to persons predisposed to certain behaviors seeking out particular types of media and concurrently behaving in ways similar to the behavior displayed in the media. As the relationship is associative and not causal, if these

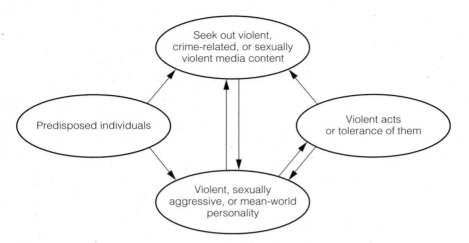

FIGURE 9.2   A Reciprocal Feedback Model of the Media, Crime, and Justice Relationship

models are correct, policies targeted at the media will have no effect on social behavior and the media can safely be ignored.

Neither of these models is felt to accurately describe the media–social behavior relationship. As shown in Figure 9.2, the actual relationship is believed to be bidirectional and cyclical. In addition to people acting out their predispositions while seeking out supportive media and to media causing behavior to be modeled, the media play a role in the generation of people predisposed to crime. As the made-for-TV movie industry exemplifies, real-world crime sometimes results in the creation of criminogenic media. Providing live models and creating community and home environments that are more inured to and tolerant of crime results in more criminally predisposed individuals in society. Therefore, although the direct effect of media content on social behavior may not be large, its influence loops, recycles, and accumulates.[4]

Two Postulates of Media and Crime and Justice

Overall, the media are constant, subtle, and unpredictable crime-and-justice agents—beneficial if carefully used—but they are neither the magic cure nor the powerful demon they are sometimes cast as. Media cannot be ignored but should not be seen as omnipotent. Where do we stand in terms of a broad understanding of media and the social construction of a crime-and justice reality? This question is addressed using two postulates of media, crime, and justice distilled from prior chapters. These postulates will drive expectations about future media, crime, and justice interactions.

Postulate 1: The media more often than not construct the criminal justice system and its people negatively and as ineffective. Yet the cumulative effect is support for more police, more prisons, and more money for the criminal justice system.

The media-constructed reality argues that the criminal justice system does not work well but remains the best hope against crime.

> *Postulate 2:* Media organizations have increasingly blurred the line between news and entertainment, and between fact and fiction. In the process, crime stories have become a mainstay of hybrid infotainment programs and new media content.

Led by the electronic visual media, the media have become more able and willing to portray events previously considered private and to expose and distribute new information previously considered private. Spurred by competition, media present these events and information in an entertainment context to maximize revenues. The result is that all information that goes into and comes out of the media is processed through an entertainment lens and is digitized for maximum dissemination.[5]

Together these postulates result in the continuing disparity between the media-constructed reality of crime and justice and the real world reality of crime and justice. This disparity has developed because the media converge on a single image of crime and justice—an image of rampant, predatory criminality ineffectively checked by traditional criminal justice system methods. Commercial, organizational, and cultural forces drive the media to construct and perpetuate this predatory crime-centered image. As commercial enterprises that must show a profit, media businesses must compete for consumers while keeping their production costs low. This makes them socially aggressive and fiscally conservative. They are not particularly sensitive about their content's social effects and will copy any successful content ideas from their competitors. The result is media that are both redundant and boundary pushing. The media are redundant in that a successful type of content will rapidly spawn imitations and spinoffs.[6] They are boundary pushing in that they are constantly trying to lure new audiences through provocative, titillating content.

This dual process of similar types of media vehicles trying to outcompete each other for consumers is emphasized in crime-and-justice news, entertainment, and infotainment programming. And though the media have increased their capability to discover and deliver information about the world, they have also moved toward greater reliance on prepackaged information, stereotypes, and entertainment-style content. As a result, the public receives an image of crime and justice that is not only distorted but that basically supports only one anticrime policy. Enhanced crime control mechanisms are advanced at the expense of due process protections and social policies that do not rely on the criminal justice system. Guarding against the violent predator criminal becomes the main message and policy focus.

Long-established cultural forces come into play in the wide-scale social acceptance of the media-generated predator criminal icon. As a culture, depictions of predatory criminals both entertain and comfort us. They entertain because they frighten and provide glimpses of realities we are not likely to encounter. They comfort because they relieve our conscience of personal responsibility for crime and violence by constructing crime as not connected to social inequities, racism,

AP Photo

As the smuggled cell phone photos from the hanging of ex-Iraq dictator Saddam Hussein show, new media have made it nearly impossible to have criminal justice proceedings that do not become part of the mass media web and the social construction of crime and justice reality.

or poverty—things society could be held responsible for and might address. The media's maddened, greedy predators are criminals by their own will, or maybe God's will, but certainly not society's will. Such criminals can, therefore, be guilt-lessly battled and eliminated. Together, the commercial, organizational, and cultural forces create a constructed reality that is resistant to alternative broader constructions of crime and justice. The media resist because they cannot commercially afford to seriously challenge the popular construction, and we resist as consumers because we are more comfortable with the narrower, entertaining, and guilt-free picture.

Expanded Public Access to Criminal Justice Procedures

Running counter to the narrow construction of crime is the modern media's ability to expand our access to previously hidden criminal justice realms and thus to expand our crime-and-justice reality. Phrases such as "government in the sunshine" and "freedom of information" reflect responses to a media-driven social trend toward more open public institutions and enhanced scrutiny of public officials. Two dominant social institutions, the media and the criminal justice system, play critical roles in this process, which can be understood as part of the general process of exposing more of the previously private backstage areas of society to the public.[7] In our hypermedia society, closed institutions and proceedings and secret information and sources are automatically viewed with suspicion and challenged. Ironically, the criminal justice system and the mass media are among a handful of social institutions that resist full, open access and struggle to keep their realities closed. New media has made that goal nearly impossible and previously low-visibility criminal justice events are now revealed, more graphic news and entertainment programs are presented, the public's tolerance for surveillance has increased, judicial steps and interactions between the police and citizens are more often recorded, media trials proliferate, and there is increased acceptance of media technology and entertainment formatting in crime and justice.

Mediated Reality

With regard to crime and justice, the critical issue is ultimately the media's role in the social construction of reality. Evidence is building that the media alter reality by affecting the ways in which the audience perceives, interprets, and behaves toward it. The question is no longer whether the media have a substantial impact but how their impact will be felt. These effects cycle through the media in loops where content is extracted from one context or medium, is reframed, and reused, often resulting in new, ambiguous media realities. These looping effects are observed in both real events that are massively mediated, such as the 2009 car accident of Tiger Woods and the 2001 World Trade Center attacks, and in the created-for-media pseudoevents found in crime-and-justice reality shows. The ultimate effect these media-reality loops will have on crime and justice is unknown but already affecting trials (see Box 9.1). Media are evolving rapidly and the distinctions between media types are disappearing.[8] The availability of video and new media technologies has expanded the genre of reality programming, which relies heavily on images of real crimes, criminal investigations, and criminal justice agency activities for fodder. What effect the common use of new media will have on the reporting of citizen crime, authority malfeasance, and other types of crime and justice information is unclear. Pictures invariably increase the newsworthiness of events and new media thrives on images, so perhaps the public debate will move from arguments about factual claims to interpretive ones as there more often will be images available to establish basic facts. Fewer will argue about what crime happened, more will argue about why crime happens. In that way there possibly will be the positive benefit of moving the criminal justice debate to discussions about alternate policies and beyond the current focus on how to best implement a single policy.

The development of interactive media further changes the relationship between media and users and has steadily moved the media experience closer to

---

B o x 9.1   Twitter and Trials

Twittering and access to the Internet via iPhones and BlackBerrys during court proceedings has resulted in mistrials. The presumption of innocence and the underlying logic of criminal trials rely on jurors reaching verdicts based only on legally admissible information that has passed long-established "rules of evidence" tests. However, today jurors sometimes supplement courtroom testimony with Web searches and posttrial updates on the Internet. For example, one jury had sat through an eight-week trial and was already in deliberations when knowledge of Internet searches by a particular juror came to the judge's attention. When the judge investigated, he found that an additional eight other jurors had also conducted Web searches about the trial. These extra-trial information-gathering efforts included looking up news articles, checking Wikipedia, and searching for information on excluded evidence (Schwartz, 2009, A18). Information transmitted from jurors to the outside world also causes concerns when jurors tweet or blog about ongoing trials, thereby releasing information from a trial that might later be sealed, influencing the public perception and reception of still-to-be-rendered verdicts, and opening themselves to influence from return tweets and blog posted replies.

---

direct personal experience. It has also changed the way people interact with each other, with less direct, face-to-face conversation but more face-to-face-like communication via media technology. Individuals are more often physically in one place, psychologically in another. Today people interact less with those physically near them such as neighbors and more with distant people via videophones, digital cameras, home computers, and other "being there" technology. The full effects of interactive media, both in games that emulate the experiences of crime and violence and as a means to carry on personal relationships on the social construction of crime-and-justice reality, will be significant. New media also provide new ways of committing old crimes such as consumer fraud and ways to commit new crimes such as murdering a virtual person (see Box 9.2).

A hybrid reality is in the making in which media-generated reality loops and interweaves with nonmediated reality. Many children today already spend more time in a media-constructed reality than in a directly experienced reality.[9] Across the United States a web of media-linked technology and products gives media reality enormous reach and impact. Unfortunately, we cannot have some of the media forces for social change without having other unwanted forces.[10] We cannot use the media for fighting crime and processing criminal cases or providing media access to criminal justice proceedings without also changing the reality of the criminal justice system. Mixing and remixing media-constructed and real-world events harbingers a future where media constructions of other media constructions will dominate the social construction of reality. Directly experienced reality will lose its social preeminence to mediated knowledge. Crime and justice will be understood and experienced through the mass media reality mixing bowl.

B o x 9.2   Virtual Reality and Crime

The link between the virtual reality worlds created in video and online games and real-world crime will be an increasingly significant media and criminal justice issue in the coming century. Anecdotal reports of video game–linked copycat crimes such as the Grand Theft Auto shootings by Devon Brown (see Box 3.3, page 72) are reported from around the planet. A short list include a fourteen-year-old British boy who was murdered by a seventeen-year-old allegedly influenced by the video game "Manhunt" ("Video Game Sparked hammer murder"). In the game, players gain points with more vicious killings and the killer was described as obsessed with the game. In the United States, the beating death of a seven-year-old by two teenager babysitters was attributed to the video game "Mortal Kombat." In China, a teenager burned a classmate after dousing him with gasoline. The offender is quoted that he had "lost himself" in "World of Warcraft" and committed the crime to transform himself into a "Fire Magician" (Cavalli, 2007). In a new twist, a forty-three-year-old woman in Japan has been arrested for killing her virtual-reality husband. Divorced in the virtual game, "Maple Story," the woman killed the online avatar of her ex-virtual-reality husband by hacking his computer. When he discovered that he was virtually deceased, the victim complained to the police who arrested the woman on suspicion of illegally accessing a computer and manipulating electronic data. The Woman did not apparently plan any real-world revenge ("Woman arrested for killing virtual reality husband"). Drawing general conclusions from anecdotal reports is premature, however, and to what extent virtual reality and video games translate into real-world crime is not known. As virtual realities become more realistic and immersive, concerns about criminogenic effects can be expected to increase.

THE FUTURE OF CRIME-AND-JUSTICE REALITY

What might the future media crime-and-justice reality look like? Let's look at two possible scenarios for the future. Both are driven by crime-and-justice media currently available and both are dominated by the image. One emphasizes crime-and-justice spectacle, the other emphasizes surveillance. While recent academic concern has tended to focus on surveillance, the spectacle of crime and justice is felt to be just as important. Crime-related spectacles have evolved for the audience from an onlooker event to a participatory one, and spectacles are continuously generated in images of crimes and crime victims, investigations of crimes, searches for wanted fugitives, media trials, and final punishments.[11] New media venues and technologies enhance the plausibility of both of the following scenarios.

Spectacles

In the first scenario, a free-wheeling infotainment media dominates the culture in a technologically resplendent journalism driven by an intrusive, near sadistic voyeurism. In this world, the media push the boundaries of taste and decency without constraints. In such an environment, a host of crime-and-justice programs are possible. Live executions would be a natural, with the modern version

Violence would be a mainstay in unrestrained infotainment crime and justice media spectacles.

of the gallows speech again prominent. Following the last meal and hours of life, imbedded retrospective segments of the condemned prisoner's life and crimes, behind-the-scenes interviews with the executioner and other participants, close-ups of the family of the condemned and the victim's relatives at the moment of death, and of course the execution itself would all be compiled into dramatic, entertaining productions. A "Death Row Talk Show" with inmates, attorneys, victim families, and other commentators also has marketing possibilities. Numerous other reality TV programs would also be explored. "The Halfway House," a show based on the activities of various offenders in an urban community corrections home that has been fitted throughout with cameras, would show the lives of drug abusers, prostitutes, and other offenders on probation and living in a court-ordered group home. Driven by the drama of "caught-on-camera" rule-breaking resulting in probation revocation and imprisonment, the show would allow audience input into who should be revoked and who given additional chances. "Hostage," a show where a traveling media production crew is alerted beforehand by a hostage taker or cohort, and provides camera coverage of hostage situations, could be another venue. Each episode would be edited and formatted into an hour-long production containing interviews with hostages and hostage takers, film of law enforcement efforts and conditions inside the hostage site, and entertaining background information on participants. The show would also provide telegenic negotiators to move the incident along to its conclusion. The list of possible infotainment shows based on the entertainmentized stories of persons caught up in crime and justice is endless. Graphic shocking media constructions and shows with titles like "Rape Victim," "Drug Dealer," "Pedophile," and so on would compete for audience shares.

Aggressive, proactive news will take off with news agencies staging their own sting operations aimed at offenders, politicians, police officers, and citizens. Catching people committing illegal acts will be a primary journalistic aim. Journalists will ride along not just with the police but with offenders, filming crimes as they happen and editing the material into entertaining news stories. In the criminal justice system, policy changes will be fast tracked and enacted without public debate due to massive media attention and the emotional impact of widely publicized symbolic tragic crimes. For the general public, expectations of privacy will be all but eliminated. Images taken through a bedroom window, for example, would be legally publishable as the courts rule that if couples don't want their sexual encounters filmed they should not have relations near open windows. Similarly, conversations, files, and information obtained by any means can be utilized by the media as the courts advance the position that media possession of information in whatever form and however obtained is usable under the First Amendment. Prior arrests, personal activities, past marriages, romances, illnesses, and indiscretions great and small all become open to media scrutiny. A new television reality show, "What's Your Neighbor Hiding?," that randomly picks families with solid reputations and investigates and broadcasts embarrassing details of their lives is a big hit.

Surveillance

In the second scenario, the commercial media operates under heavy restrictions, and their ability to cover, comment on, and portray crime-and-justice issues and cases is tightly restrained. At the same time, media technology is applied to its full capabilities in crime control efforts. Combined, these two trends create a society where the watchdog function of the media is disabled while the surveillance and control capabilities of the media and media technology are maximized.

Regarding the elimination of the media's constitutionally mandated government watchdog function, criminal cases would be processed absent media coverage, and verdicts would be announced only after trials are concluded and any sentences imposed. Filming and coverage of police operations, courtroom proceedings, and correctional facilities would not be allowed. Police chiefs, court officers, and correctional administrators could deny without explanation or appeal media access to their agency personnel, records, and meetings. Access to suspects and prisoners would never be granted.

Concerning the commercial media, all televisions will be equipped with sensors that identify viewers so that all "inappropriate" content can be automatically blocked. Other recording devices would be blocked from making copies of all but approved, prepaid materials. All print, visual, and audio entertainment media must be processed, reviewed, and approved by the new Federal Bureau of Media before marketing. Media programmers must prove "no harm" and provide evidence that content will not result in negative social effects on consumers before marketing approval is granted. Media liability is assumed by the courts for any copying by consumers of stunts, crimes, and other injury-causing behaviors contained in the media. Successful damage suits against the media need only show a similarity in the behavior shown in a media product to subsequent consumer

Jefferson County Sheriff's Department/Getty Images

A security camera image of the two shooters from the 1999 Columbine High massacre which killed 13 exemplifies the surveillance scenario.

behaviors resulting in harm or injury. To avoid paying compensation, media companies would have to prove that there is no significant relationship between their media content and consumer actions.

What we watch is no less important than who watches us and media-based anticrime efforts utilizing the full capabilities of the mass media and media technologies proliferate. Information about wanted suspects is continually run as crawl lines across the bottom of all TV programs. All print, visual, and audio media products are required to carry crime prevention public service announcements, reenactments of unsolved crimes, and Most Wanted fugitive descriptions as 25 percent of their advertising allotment and to give these messages prominent times and placement to promote increased citizen surveillance. Most dramatic, all streets and public spaces in communities and the transportation links between them are under the continuous gaze of a national camera surveillance system. In addition, commercial and corporate camera security systems are tied into the overarching government camera matrix. Each of the millions of separate cameras analyzes its video output, automatically recognizing and flagging behaviors such as assaults, break-ins, fires, injuries, vandalism, speeding, reckless driving, loitering in shopping malls, and unauthorized work breaks in corporate areas. The video streams are linked to allow tracking of individual vehicles and persons from one location to another within a single city or from one city to another across the nation. Face recognition programs notify authorities when people are deemed "out-of-place" and when fugitives or terrorist suspects appear. They also allow retroactive searches for specific individuals and reconstruction of any individual's movements and actions that have occurred in a camera's field of view. Alibis and adherence to probation conditions are frequently checked using the video data files generated by the camera matrix. Augmenting the camera surveillance systems are Web and communication tracking software programs accessible by government agencies and private corporations. Although everyone is not watched all the time, it is now possible to determine where the majority of Americans are at any particular time and date.

Obviously, neither future scenario, spectacles or surveillance, is attractive. Fortunately neither is likely to come to full fruition, but both are composed of elements and capabilities already available.[12] Neither scenario contains outcomes that cannot be achieved today. The point they make is that it is vital that we understand how the media and crime and justice interact and plan for the type of media crime-and-justice relationship we desire.

MEDIATED CRIMINAL JUSTICE

Half a century ago W. I. Thomas stated that "if actors define situations as real they are real in their consequences."[13] What it is like to live in a society; how its citizens feel about their government, authorities, and neighbors; and the daily social expectations of people are all strongly influenced by what people see, hear, and read about crime and justice. The social construction of crime and justice loops back to influence the entire social reality of a nation.

Therefore, despite being only one of many social factors, the media cannot be ignored. Exactly how and to what extent the media cause long-term changes in social behavior remains unknown. As reflected in the varied YouTube interactions with crime described in Box 9.3, it is clear that the media play an important and evolving, but not autonomous role. The media are one engine in the crime-production process, working in combination with other more significant engines, increasing and exacerbating the crime problem. Ethnic violence, racial strife, oppressive living conditions, violent cultural history, economic disparities, family destruction, and interpersonal violence are all more important for crime levels and all are subject to enhancement by the media. As with individuals, the media alone cannot criminalize a country—but once a country criminalizes its media through an emphasis on predatory and unrealistic portraits, a slow spiral of increased crime and tolerance for crime begins.[14] For modern societies, the media set the expectations and moral boundaries for crime, guide the public policies, and steer the social construction of crime-and-justice reality.

It must be emphasized that the single most significant social effect of media crime-and-justice content is not its direct generation of crime or other behavioral effects but its effect on criminal justice policies. The fear and loathing we feel toward criminals is tied to our media-generated image of criminality. We see numerous portraits about atypical occurrences near and far, and we see them day after day. The media portray criminals as typically animalistic, vicious predators. The public debate is flooded with dire warnings and sensational crime stories imbedded in a burlesque media, which is predominantly characterized by the demands of the marketplace. This image translates into a more criminal society by influencing the way

---

B o x 9.3   Crime, Justice, and YouTube

In addition to making available innumerable videos of news, trials, crimes, and criminal justice-related sites, the popular Internet site YouTube, where people can post personal videos and view from among thousands of videos posted by others, has resulted in some unique crime-related phenomenon. In a number of instances, offenders have posted video of themselves committing a crime, generating in some cases the arrest and conviction of the offenders and in others a series of copycat crimes. An example of the first instance is provided by the actions of a Texas teenager, a member of an Internet group called "Pranknet," who called a Wendy's restaurant and convinced the employees to inflict $20,000 worth of damages on the business. Posing as a corporate office representative, the teen convinced the employees to activate the fire-suppression system, resulting in foam being sprayed all over the restaurant, to break all of the windows, and to evacuate the restaurant. He then posted an audio recording of the prank call on YouTube (Powell, 2009). An example of YouTube-linked copycat crime is provided by the rise and fall of the activity of "Ghost-riding," in which drivers film themselves sitting atop the roof or hood of a driverless moving car. The copycat wave took off with the release of a rap music video on YouTube by "Mistah FAB," describing the act in "Ghost Ride It" (the official video) at (http://www.youtube.com/watch?v=hJDLRCXR2ZM). A third example involves both the posting of initial offenses and the generation of copycats and spin-off crimes. Called "Bumfights," the videos entail the filming of homeless people forced or bribed to engage in fistfights which are then posted on YouTube. A subsequent wave of "bum-hunting," in which teenage boys attacked the homeless was attributed to the popularity of the bumfights videos. A similar series was generated by "fire in the hole" videos in which offenders would throw drinks or food at fast food workers manning drive-thru windows while yelling "fire in the hole." Viewing of the associated YouTube videos can be seen at www.YouTube.com by entering the above crimes as search terms.

---

we react to all crime in America. We imprison at a much greater rate and make reentry into law-abiding society, even for our nonviolent offenders, more difficult than other advanced but less crime-focused nations. The predator criminal image results in crime-and-justice policy being based on our worst-case criminals with a constant ratcheting up of punishments for all offenders. In its cumulative effect, media constructions provide both violent models to emulate and justification for a myopic, harshly punitive public reaction to all offenders.

The most important lesson running through this book is that a social construction competition is ongoing. The media are both reflections of reality and engines in the reality-production process. If media prominence and a society imbedded in a multimedia web is a description of the present, we expect new media to become an important social construction engine in the future. Although not the sole or even the most powerful cause of crime, the media will be more tightly tied into the other crime-generating engines and their influence recycled, enhanced, and compounded. The result has been a national character and crime-and-justice reality that is individualistic, materialistic, and often violent. American's popular media sets the stage for how we understand crime. It constructs the images that have become

John Stillwell/PA Wire/AP Photo

New media devices have provided new means of gathering people together resulting in a phenomena called a "flashmob". As the dancing flashmob shown demonstrates, most flashmobs are not dangerous. Some youth gangs, however, have tapped into the potential for flashmobs to organize gang fights. Fight locations can be finalized at the last moment and communicated simultaneously to all fight participants, thereby drastically reducing the ability of the police to become aware of a planned fight or to intervene.

the taken-for-granted stories we associate with crime. The images are part of a social construction—assembled together to tell us the nature of crime. But it is a social construction with a paradox: with new and old media providing a 24/7 window, there is now so much attention on crime that the end result has not been an advance in the level of understanding, but an obfuscation of debate. Hysteria reigns and a sensible, rational discussion of how crime might be dealt with seems almost impossible, even as we see more images and more messages, and spend more money trying to deal with the problem.[15] An obscuring flood of media information about crime and justice flows in unabated content looping circles. Perhaps wider recognition of the media, crime, and justice relationship will lessen its policy impact. As it now stands, by encouraging the public to ignore the actual sources of crime-and-justice reality and to unquestionably accept the media-constructed crime-and-justice reality, the media function as a means of avoiding more realistic crime and justice reality.

WHAT YOU HAVE LEARNED

As the reader of this book, you have learned to appreciate the role that the media plays in contemporary crime and justice, especially in the formation of crime-and-justice policy. You have learned about the history and evolution of the media from print to visual to digital and interactive-based outlets and how this evolution shapes the information that the public receives about crime and criminal justice. You know that in the contemporary mediated world of crime and justice, images, speed, and flexible access are key and you understand that infotainment media values steer the selection, formatting, and delivery of crime-and-justice media content. In the new media crime-and-justice world, audiences pick from a vast store of media outlets and control what content they expose themselves to and when they consume it. You have also learned about social constructionism as a perspective to understand the various interactions between the media and crime and justice and can dissect competing social construction efforts, recognizing claims makers and their strategies to promote crime and justice constructions. You now know about symbolic crimes, frames, narratives, and ownership in social construction and can see the process play out as you use media.

Specifically regarding crime and justice, you have learned that the most common media portrait of criminality is that of a violent predator criminal who hunts innocent victims. You have learned that the most common explanation of crime found in the media relies on individual level characteristics—particularly defective personality traits such as greed or innate evilness. You have also learned that the media has the capacity to influence criminal behavior in some people but that there is no evidence of widespread criminalizing effects. You understand that the media more likely provides criminal models and techniques to individuals already engaged in criminal behavior or already decided to commit an offense. You now know that the media works on copycat crime as a rudder more than as a trigger. Along the same lines, you know that the media's role in terrorism is evolving in reaction to the Internet and other new media and that media-oriented terrorism is expected to increase.

Concerning crime fighters, you know that armed civilians and elite rogue law enforcement officers are portrayed in the media as the most successful crime fighters. You understand how forensics and criminalistics have merged with infotainment to produce a "crime fighting scientist" hero that currently reigns in popularity. You further comprehend that the judicial system is shown in a backwards manner with rare events like trials and homicide cases dominating and common events like plea bargains and property cases rare. You know that trials selected for massive coverage parallel entertainment media story lines and sinful rich, power-abusing, or evil predatory defendants. You have a grasp of the historical tension between the courts and the media and the ongoing attempts to balance due process protections and media access to the courts. Concerning the portrait of the criminal justice system, you now perceive how corrections is constructed in a manner that focuses on negative events and images. You recognize the media "smug hack" icon that paints corrections as a set of failed institutions staffed by defective personnel. You know that the media image of these institutions has them filled with violent dangerous individuals who prey on heroic victimized inmates.

Most importantly, you understand that the media's greatest impact on crime and justice is in the area of public policy. You know that the use of the media in anticrime efforts has been increasing in both public service "ads" aimed at reducing crime and in enhanced surveillance based on improved media technology.

© 2003 Ann Telnaes/The Cartoonist Group

Balancing the reality of crime-and-justice media and traditional values is a twenty-first century dilemma.

You comprehend that the effect of these efforts on crime and society is yet to be determined but that public support ensures their increased use. Lastly, you know that media content lends support to punitive over preventive or rehabilitative criminal justice policies but that the exact relationship between media and criminal justice policy is convoluted, shifting, and not fully understood.

From this collective base of knowledge, you can proceed to observe and interact with crime-and-justice media from an informed position, recognizing when your personal social construction of reality is being influenced. You have learned to enjoy crime and justice media in a manner that will allow you to use what it offers in a more insightful and perceptive way. You are now prepared to move from an unconscious consumer of mediated crime-and-justice knowledge to an interactive author of your own socially constructed crime-and-justice reality.

CHAPTER SUMMARY

- Collectively, the media's crime-and-justice content construct a violent, predatory world with an effective criminal justice system. Enhancement of the system and aggressive personal security measures are seen as the best choices for dealing with crime.

- The line between fact and fiction, entertainment and news is increasingly blurred, and infotainment media currently dominates the social construction of crime and justice.

- New media has expanded the access and speed with which crime-and-justice information circulates in society, and a mediated crime-and-justice reality is today the most important source of crime-and-justice knowledge for large numbers of people.

- Media and social forces are currently simultaneously forwarding two scenarios: Spectacles of unrestrained infotainment in which the media will expose and dramatize everything connected with crime and justice and extensive surveillance based anticrime efforts in which media technology and commercial media are used to solve and prevent crime.

- Enhanced by the social effects and communication capabilities of new media, the social construction of crime and justice in the media will continue to obscure the social reality of crime and justice.

WRITING ASSIGNMENTS

1. Write an essay that discusses each of the two scenarios and the social forces and trends that encourage and discourage development of the two. Note how new media might affect each scenario's likelihood of becoming reality and which scenario is most disturbing and what steps you would support (increased censorship, for example) or what social conditions you might tolerate (more minor crime, for example) to prevent either scenario from becoming reality.

2. Write a proposal for a new reality crime-and-justice program or an anticrime PSA you would like to see produced. For the reality crime-and-justice program discuss needed criminal justice agency cooperation, ratings potential, procedural steps and actions to be focused on, target audience, and social impact. For the PSA, rate your script, potential to reach a target offender or victim audience, potential to reduce targeted behaviors, possible unplanned consequences (such as increased audience fear), and likelihood of obtaining funding and sponsorship. Include a marketing plan and suggestions for a campaign mascot and celebrity spokespersons.

SUGGESTED READINGS

Croteau, D., and W. Hoynes. 2001. *The Business of Media*. Thousand Oaks, CA: Pine Forge Press.

Sacco, V. 2005. *When Crime Waves*. Thousand Oaks, CA: Sage.

Weimann, G. 2000. *Communicating Unreality: Modern Media and the Reconstruction of Reality*. Thousand Oaks, CA: Sage.

Wolf, M. 1999. *The Entertainment Economy*. New York: Random House.

Glossary

abuse of power media trials A trial in which the defendant occupies a position of trust, prestige, or authority. The general rule is the higher the rank, the more media interest in the case.

announcement effect Media audience behavior changes in anticipation of a new criminal justice policy that has been heavily publicized in the media.

anticipatory effects Policy changes made when criminal justice officials respond in a proactive manner to anticipated local media, reversing the usual order wherein media attention to an issue causes criminal justice policy changes.

authority and control correctional films A pessimistic cinematic view of corrections against a backdrop of riots and escapes by offenders confined for less serious offenses; this genre is most significant for immortalizing the "smug hack" portrait of correctional officers.

backwards law The idea that media will present an image of criminality opposite that of crime-and-justice reality. In every subject category—crimes, criminals, crime fighters, attorneys, correctional officers, and inmates; the investigation of crimes and making of arrests; the processing and disposition of cases; and the experience of incarceration—the media construct and present a crime-and-justice world that is the opposite of the real world.

biological theories of crime Crime is the result of innate genetic differences or the constitutional nature of criminals.

business and professional criminals A media criminality frame in which criminals are characterized as shrewd, ruthless, often violent, ladies' men for whom crime is another form of work or business, similar to other careers but more exciting and rewarding.

CCTV (closed circuit television) A limited access video system and the most common media technology used in surveillance systems. The term CCTV has become a common acronym for public safety surveillance systems regardless of the underlying technology employed.

CSI effect The impact of criminalistics and forensic science media on expectations regarding evidence-gathering and the use and presentation of evidence in court proceedings. A CSI effect is hypothesized to unduly raise doubts about the strength of a case when forensic evidence and tests are absent and to unduly reduce doubts about case strength when such evidence is present.

citizen crime fighters Two groups of crime fighters popular in the media: private investigators (PIs), who occupy the boundary between civilians and police officers as independent law enforcement contractors, and personally motivated private citizens who take on solving crimes as a hobby or due to some personal connection with a victim.

claims makers The promoters, activists, professional experts, and spokespersons with a particular point of view who make specific claims about a social problem or condition.

commodification The for-profit packaging and marketing of crime information for popular consumption.

conversational reality Information people receive directly from people close to and similar to them, which is combined with personal experiences to make up the most influential social construction engine.

cops A media law enforcement frame that constructs the local police as aggressive, crime fighting, take-no-prisoners, frontline soldiers in the war on crime.

copycat crime A crime inspired by an earlier, news media covered or entertainment media portrayed crime.

correctional horrors Negative correctional news stories often employing the death of an inmate as a symbol of the correctional system's failure and that are exemplified by corruption and misconduct exposés.

corrections backwards law The backwards law applied to the media construction of corrections in which a role-reversal derived from the media portrait of underdog, wrongly jailed inmate heroes are pitted against oppressive, smug hack correctional employees.

counterproductive effects Media-based anticrime campaigns that have effects opposite to the campaign goal of crime reduction.

criminogenic media Media content that is hypothesized as a direct cause of crime.

diffusion of benefits Associated with surveillance systems, diffusion is a bonus benefit from the use of surveillance technology. Offenders are not aware of the boundaries of surveillance coverage and therefore reduce their offenses in adjacent nonsurveilled areas. See also *displacement of crime.*

digital manipulation of visual images Doctoring images through mixing real and nonexistent elements to distort, alter, or fabricate images of the world to produce realistic final images. Public knowledge of this capability undermines the previously unquestioned validity given to photographs as evidence and proof.

displacement of crime Associated with the use of surveillance systems, displacement pushes crime into adjacent communities without surveillance systems. See also *diffusion of benefits.*

echo effect A spillover effect from media news coverage of a high-profile criminal case onto similarly charged but low-newsworthy nonpublicized cases affecting their processing and dispositions.

episodic format The most common crime news format, in which a particular crime is described and a resulting case is followed. Episodic formatted stories encourage viewers to place responsibility on the individual and to ignore societal forces by focusing on the question: Why did this individual commit this crime? See *thematic format.*

evil strangers media trials Trials composed of two subgroups: non-American suspects or psychotic killers. Non-American evil stranger media trials involve ethnic and minority advocates of various unpopular causes. Psychotic killer media trials focus on bizarre murder cases in which the defendant is portrayed as a maddened, predatory killer.

experienced reality Knowledge gained from one's directly experienced world; all of the events that have happened to you.

factual and legal guilt The difference between having committed a criminal act (factual guilt) versus being legally responsible (legal guilt) and thus appropriate for punishment.

factual claims Statements that purport to describe the world and "what" happened; they are put forth as objective, true "facts" about the world.

frames Prepackaged constructions that include factual and interpretative claims and associated recommended policies. A frame is a fully developed social construction that allows the categorization, labeling, and conceptualization of new real-world events that fit into a preexisting frame.

freedom and release correctional films A cinematic view of corrections that emphasizes extreme violence, such as prison action films. The ambiguity and confusion about the function and role of prisons in society is reflected in these films. The keepers are certifiably crazy or dehumanized, and the constructed correctional world reflects the comics more than any recognizable social reality.

Freedom of Information Act Legislation that states that information held by federal agencies must be available to the public unless the information falls within nine specific exempt categories.

front-end loaded The media portrait of crime and justice that concentrates on crimes and their investigation and solution. The activities of criminals and law enforcement or citizen crime fighters are of primary interest, and criminal justice procedures are largely ignored.

G-men A media law enforcement frame that originated in the 1930s and focuses on effective, professional, federal "crime-busters."

gatekeeper An individual occupying a checkpoint in the crime news creation process where crimes are selected, molded, and passed on as candidate news stories about crime. Key gatekeepers in the crime news process are crime reporters and law enforcement public information officers.

Government in Sunshine Act A federal law requiring that meetings of government agencies and departments be open to the public.

heroic inmates The dominant media construction of male prisoners, which employs the role-reversal of offenders being caught up in a corrupt criminal justice system and shown as victims and heroes.

ideal heroes Ideal heroes display the admirable qualities of sacrifice, nobleness, and strength. Sometimes they are traditional by-the-book police officers, but frequently they are rogue officers or civilians.

ideal offenders The outsiders, strangers, foreigners, aliens, and intruders who lack essential humanity and rehabilitative potential.

ideal victims The innocent, naive, trusting, and protection-needing humans; children are the most ideal of the ideal victims in the media.

immanent justice Belief that a divine power will intervene and reveal the guilty while protecting the innocent. Similar to the medieval socially constructed reality that made trial by combat logical, the modern media reality relies on the moral superiority of the crime fighter to ultimately defeat criminality. Criminality is reduced to an individual moral battle of good versus evil.

infotainment Media content that delivers information about the world in an entertainment format.

interactivity The ability of consumer actions and decisions to influence media story lines and content as the story lines and content are being created.

interpretative claims Statements that focus on the meanings of events and either offer an explanation of why the world is as described in associated factual claims or offer a course of action and public policy that needs to be followed.

lampooned police A popular media frame that satirizes law enforcement as foolish, slapstick police work.

legal guilt See *factual and legal guilt.*

linkage Association of one social construction effort with another previously accepted construction so that the significance of the first construction is connected to the latter.

looping Reuse of media content in new contexts and media products.

mainstreaming The idea that the media affect some viewers more than others regardless of exposure level, influencing heavy television consumers who are currently not in the mainstream to move toward it, while not affecting those already in the mainstream. In total effect, the media are hypothesized to be homogenizing society.

manipulative model A model of news creation that has crime news selected not according to general public interest but according to the interests of news agencies' owners. The news media are argued to purposefully distort reality and use the news to shape public opinion to support the status quo.

market model A model of news creation that sees crime news as selected largely by public interest and journalists as objective reporters who accurately reproduce the world.

media–oriented terrorism A terrorist strategy where the primary goal of a terror campaign is to attract media attention. Terrorist acts are frequently carried out in a manner that maximizes media attention and are characterized by the selection of high-visibility targets and locations, graphic dramatic acts, pre-event contact with media outlets, and post-event videos, interviews, and other media accommodations.

media trials A regional or national crime or justice event in which the media co-opt the criminal justice system as a source of drama, entertainment, and profit. They involve the social construction of selected trials as infotainment products that are commodified and mass marketed. Coverage is live whenever possible, pictures are preferred over text, and content is characterized by conjecture and sensationalism. See *abuse of power media trials, evil strangers media trials*, and *sinful rich media trials*.

media weapons cult The media portrait of weapons, especially handguns, that downplays their negative aspects (rarely is the pain of a gunshot realistically shown) and enhances their usefulness as problem solvers and crime-fighting tools. In the media, the people who get their way, both heroes and villains, are the ones who have the guns.

mediated experience The comparative experience an individual has when he or she experiences an event via the media versus actually physically being at an event.

memorial criminal justice policy Linking a criminal justice policy and legislation to an individual by name (such as the Brady law and Amber Alerts); the person is usually the victim of a violent, deadly crime.

modeling personality An individual who looks to and sees other people and the media as profitable crime information sources; these individuals are hypothesized to be particularly susceptible to media copycat effects.

multimedia web The interconnected and pervasive mix of contemporary media exemplified by the constant looping of media content.

narratives Recurring preestablished social roles, characters, and story lines found throughout crime-and-justice media. Narratives are usually associated with a single individual or crime rather than with general criminality or a criminal justice issue.

narrowcasting Marketing media content to small special interest self-selecting groups rather than to large, heterogeneous mass markets. Originally applied to television marketing with the introduction of cable networks, today the principle is applicable to all media.

nature of confinement correctional films A cinematic view of corrections in which inmates are victims of injustice; a good man is either framed or accidentally imprisoned or pushed into crime by powerful societal forces. A recurrent message in this genre is the pervasive corruption of the correctional system and its administrators.

newsworthiness The value of an event or crime to a news agency and the criteria by which news producers choose which crimes are presented to the public as news about crime.

organizational model A model of news creation that has crime news filtered and presented to the public following an assembly-line process within law enforcement and news organizations. Crime news is argued to be stylized information that fits the organizational and production needs of news agencies.

on-demand Time and place access to media content is determined by the consumer rather than by the producer of the content.

ownership Identification of a social condition with a particular set of claims makers who come to dominate the social construction of that issue. Claims makers own an issue when they are sought out by the media and others for information regarding its nature and policy solutions.

personal digital assistant devices (PDAs) Usually small mobile hand-held devices that provide computing and information storage and retrieval. Most PDAs have small keyboards and recent multifunction devices bundle cell phone, video, handwritten notes, Internet, and data capabilities.

pixel policy The fast-paced, media-driven development of contemporary public policy, especially noticeable in crime-and-justice policy formation.

police procedurals A media law enforcement frame that concentrates on the dramatic backstage realities of police investigations. The crime fighters in these portraits normally rely heavily on teamwork and criminalistics to solve crimes.

police reality programs Highly edited television productions in which viewers are invited to share a cop's point-of-view as a partner officer in voyeuristic ride-alongs.

political theories of crime The idea that the political and economic structure of a society are the root causes of crime.

popular criminology The criminological ideas and explanation of crime that are popular with the general public and often have indirectly inferred counterparts in mass media content.

predatory criminality The most common portrait of criminality found in the media, which is characterized by criminals who are animalistic, irrational, innate predators committing violent and senseless crimes.

prejudicial publicity Dissemination by the media of either factual information that bears on the guilt of a defendant or emotional information without evidentiary relevance that simply arouses emotions against a defendant.

priming When people read, hear about, or witness a criminal event via the mass media, priming influences them to hold similar ideas and results in related copycat acts.

Privacy Act A federal or state statute that prohibits the invasion of a person's right to be left alone, restricts access to personal information, and prohibits interception of private communications. The federal Privacy Act permits an individual to access records containing personal information and to control the transfer of that information to other agencies.

private investigator (PI) Nongovernmental independent contractors of law enforcement.

privileged conversation A constitutionally based argument to protect journalists from having to divulge unpublished story information or to identify their sources. It is argued that a privileged conversation protection is needed so that journalists can fulfill their constitutional function as watchdogs of government activities and guarantee future access to story information and sources.

proactive mechanisms Judicial measures such as closure, restrictive orders, and protective orders that are employed to counteract the production of news media publicity. The proactive approach to dealing with publicity directly clashes with the First Amendment protection of freedom of the press and has been vigorously resisted by the media.

prosocial television Programs of various types (animated, adventure, comedy, fantasy) that have the ability to elicit socially valued behaviors and attitudes from viewers. *Sesame Street* is a well-known example.

psychological theories of crime The idea that crime is caused by defective personality development.

psychotic super-male criminals A popular media frame of criminality in which criminals possess an evil, cunning intelligence and superior strength, endurance, and stealth. Crimes committed by media psychotic super-males are generally acts of twisted, lustful revenge or random acts of irrational violence.

public agenda The ranked list of social problems the public see as important and needing to be addressed.

public service announcements (PSAs) Information disseminated in the media in ad-style messages. Anticrime PSAs are a common means of getting crime prevention information to the public.

pursuit of justice correctional films A cinematic view of corrections where offenders are personally responsible for their actions and confinement is therefore justified. Although many of these films revolve around violence—riots, escapes, and assaults—individual offender rehabilitation is seen as possible.

rational choice theories of crime The idea that crime is a rational, free-will decision the individuals will make when the gains from committing a crime outweigh the likelihood of punishment.

reactive mechanisms Judicial procedures used to counteract the effects of news media publicity, which include expanding the jury selection (the voir dire), granting trial continuances, granting changes of venue, sequestering jurors, and giving special instructions to the jury.

scripts Sets of well-rehearsed, highly associated concepts held in memory, often involving causes, goals, and actions that generate a set of cognitive directions that define situations and guide behavior. Once learned, a media-provided behavior script is hypothesized to be able to create behaviors similar to that observed in the media content.

shield laws Legislation to prevent the forced divulgence of sources and testimony from journalists.

sinful rich media trials Cases in which socially prominent defendants are involved in bizarre or sexually related crimes.

smug hack The dominant media portrayal of correctional officers as caricatures of brutality, incompetence, low intelligence, and indifference to human suffering.

smug hack corrections The dominant media construction of corrections that emphasizes physically brutal inmate discipline, corporal punishment and the infliction of pain, and the exploitation of inmates as a cheap source of labor and profit. Staff incompetence, corruption, and cruelty are common, ingrained, and unchallenged. Prisoners suffer systemic racial prejudice, homosexual rape, and between-prisoner assaults.

social constructionism A theoretical view that knowledge is socially created. Social constructionism focuses on human relationships and the way relationships affect how people perceive reality. Social constructionism studies the shared ideas, interpretations, and knowledge that groups of people agree to hold in common.

socially constructed reality The reality perceived as the "real" world by each individual. It is constructed from knowledge each individual gains from his or her experienced and symbolic realities mixed together. The resulting constructed reality is what we individually believe the world to be like.

sociological theories of crime The idea that criminal environments cause crime, and that people are criminals because of the people they associate with or share a neighborhood or culture with.

surveillance effect The psychological effect of believing that you might be under observation.

symbolic crimes Crimes and other criminal justice events that are selected and highlighted by claims makers as perfect examples to support a particular crime-and-justice construction.

symbolic reality Knowledge of the world gained from other people, institutions, and the media that is shared via symbols, language being the most common symbolic system to share knowledge. Art, music, and mathematics are others.

thematic format A crime news format that highlights criminal justice trends and persistent problems. Stories told in the thematic format explore crime and justice issues in terms of their causes and effects and focus on the question: A set of problems has developed, what changed in society? See *episodic format*.

true crime A media law enforcement infotainment frame wherein the audience looks over the criminal's (frequently a killer) or cop's shoulder as they either commit crime or pursue criminals and solve murders.

ultraviolence A media style popular since the 1960s that portrays violence using slow motion, detonating blood capsules, multiple camera views, and graphic visuals and special effects.

victims and heroic criminals The least common media criminality frame, it presents criminals as either victims of injustice or unrecognized good guys. This frame often supports sociological and political explanations of crime.

video lineups A crime witness is shown a series of videotaped images selected for their similarity.

video mug books A computer searches a pictorial data file for specific characteristics (for example, tattoo, bald, heavy, white, and male) and displays matching pictures.

videotaped interrogations Videotaped interactions between police and suspects that provide visual evidence regarding the physical and mental condition of suspects, the voluntariness of their statements, their understanding of their rights, and the use of coercion and adherence to standard interrogation practices by the police.

white-collar crime A crime committed by a respectable person of high social status in the course of his or her occupation. White-collar crime overlaps with corporate and business crime and usually includes fraud, bribery, insider trading, embezzlement, computer crime, identity theft, and forgery.

worldview cultivation A media effect that hypothesizes that watching many hours of television will result in viewers holding general perceptions about the world as being a pernicious and dangerous place.

yellow journalism A term for a style of newspaper coverage first associated with U.S. newspapers in the 1890s that emphasized exaggeration, scandals, and sensationalism regarding crime and other topics.

Notes

Chapter 1

1. Except for discussions of media technology applications in criminal justice, media is considered herein in the narrow sense of popular culture which includes all commercial media in all their forms that are marketed for popular consumption (Asimow and Mader, *Law and Popular Culture*, 4).

2. Rafter, *Crime, Film and Criminology*, 417.

3. Altheide, *Creating Fear*, 128; Dowler, Fleming, and Muzzatti, *Constructing Crime*, 837–850.

4. Leishman and Mason, *Policing and the Media*, 144. Don Oberdorfer historically places the transition to a media driven policy within the coverage of the Vietnam War: "The electronics revolution, which took the battlefield into the American living room via satellite, increased the power and velocity of fragments of experience, with no increase in the power or velocity of reasoned judgment. Instant analysis was often faulty analysis" (Oberdorfer, TET!, 322).

5. Griffin and Miller, *Child Abduction*, 159–176.

6. Although not identical, the policy influencing "symbolic crimes" referred to in this work are analogous to the "signal crimes" described by Innes (2003).

7. Shichor and Sechrest, *Three Strikes and You're Out*.

8. Mathiesen, "Television, Public Space and Prison Population;" Curran, "Communications, Power and Social Order."

9. Surette, "Some Unpopular Thoughts about Popular Culture."

10. Adoni and Mane, "Media and the Social Construction of Reality."

11. This focus on violent predatory crime is tied to a historical interest in crime and justice as theater. Crime and justice has been a source for story lines since antiquity, and the media construct crime as predatory and as a frightening (and hence entertaining) phenomenon caused by individually based deficiencies (Ball, *The Promise of American Law*).

12. Manning, "Media Loops." This concept is related to the idea of intertextuality as decribed by Asimow and Mader, *Law and Popular Culture*, 15.

13. Asimow and Mader, *Law and Popular Culture*, 15.

14. Langer, "Legacy of Suspicion."

15. Dowler, Fleming and Muzzatti, *Constructing Crime*, 837–850.

16. Grodal, "Stories for Eye, Ear and Muscles," 129–155.

17. Gordon and Heath, "The News Business, Crime, and Fear," 227.

18. Papke, *Framing the Criminal*, 35.

19. Gorn, "The Wicked World."

20. Stark, *Glued to the Set*, 237.

21. For an overview see Nyberg, "Comic Books and Juvenile Delinquency."

22. Nyberg, *Comic Books and Juvenile Delinquency*, 61.

23. DeFleur and Ball-Rokeach, *Theories of Mass Communication*, 84; Cheatwood, "Early Images of Crime and Criminal Justice."

24. Cheatwood, "Early Images of Crime and Criminal Justice."

25. Armour, *Film*, xxi.

26. See Leitch and Grant, *Crime Films for a general discussion,* chapter 2, 18–52.

27. Allen, Livingstone and Reiner, "True Lies;" Broe, "Class, Crime, and Film Noir."

28. See Leishman and Mason, *Policing and the Media*, Chapter 4 for a history of police shows on British television.

29. The social impact of television has been compared to the medieval Christian church's influence on European culture (Curran, "Communications, Power and Social Order," 210).

30. Stevens and Garcia, *Communication History*, 143.

31. If you are a typical American, for every ten years of your life you will spend one solid year (8,760 hours) looking at a television screen. In 1990, a Congressional Subcommittee on the Constitution stated: "The typical American child is exposed to an average of 27 hours of TV each week—as much as eleven hours for some children. That child will watch 8,000 murders and more than 100,000 acts of violence before finishing elementary school. By the age of 18, that same teenage will have witnessed 200,000 acts of violence on TV including 40,000 murders" (cited in Perlmutter, *Policing the Media*, 33).

32. Commenting in *The New York Times Magazine* (November 28, 1954, 56) television producer Gilbert Seldes states: "Television finds itself on the defensive, facing investigations and threats. Most of these arise from the part of the program schedule usually held as the industry's worst—its endless stream of crime shows, many of them available to children."

33. Dominick, "Crime and Law Enforcement in the Mass Media."

34. Lichter, Lichter, and Rothman describe early crime-and-justice television content as seeming to require "two shootouts with police, a beating, and a cold-blooded murder" (*Prime Time*, 282).

35. Cole, *The UCLA Television Violence Monitoring Report*; Gunter, Harrison, and Wykes, *Violence on Television*.

36. Flew, *New Media: An Introduction*, 11; Lister, Dovey, Giddings, Grant and Kelly, *New Media: A Critical Introduction*. The 1991 trial of William Kennedy Smith was the first trial to be covered gavel-to-gavel on cable television (CourtTV now truTV channel) (Fox, Van Sickel and Steiger, *Tabloid Justice*.

37. Ling and Campbell, *The Reconstruction of Space and Time: Mobile Communication Practices*.

38. Kiousis, *Interactivity*, 355–383.

39. Grodal, *Video Games and the Pleasures of Control*, 197–212.

40. Grochowski, *Running in Cyberspace*, 361–382.

41. Anderson, "An Update on the Effects of Playing Violent Video Games," 113–122; Anderson, Gentile and Buckley, *Violent Video Game Effects on Children and Adolescents: Theory, Research, and Public Policy*; Sherry, "The Effects of Violent Video Games on Aggression," 409–432; Whitaker and Bushman, "A Review of the Effects of Violent Video Games on Children and Adolescents," 1033-1051.

42. Rogers, *The Diffusion of Innovations*, 215–216.

43. Parks and Robers, *Making MOOsic*, 517–537; Rogers, *The Diffusion of Innovations*, 207.

44. Grodal, *Stories for Eye, Ear and Muscles*, 129–155.

45. Fox, Sickel and Steiger, *Tabloid Justice*, 100; Valier, *Crime and Punishment in Contemporary Culture*, 91–110.

46. Reiner, "Media Made Criminality," 389.

47. Thompson, Young, and Burns, "Representing Gangs in the News," 427; see also Dowler, "Comparing American and Canadian Local Television Crime Stories," 589–590.

48. Gilliam and Iyengar, "Prime Suspects," 561. Yvonne Jewkes discusses twelve news values operating in the twenty-first century that result in crime news focusing on violent rare crimes (*Media and Crime,* 40–60). Robert Reiner summarizes the differences between crime news and crime as the overreporting of serious crime, especially murder and other violent crimes; the concentration on crimes that are solved; and coverage of offenders and victims who are disproportionately older and from a higher social class than their counterparts in reality (*The Politics of the Police,* 141).

49. Drechsel, *News Making in the Trial Courts,* 35 citing Shaaber, *Some Forerunners of the Newspaper in England*.

50. Chibnall, *Chronicles of the Gallows,* 179–217.

51. *Ibid.*, 190.

52. See Chibnall, *The Production of Knowledge by Crime Reporters*, 75–97; Isaacs, *The Crime of Crime Reporting*, 312–320; and Sherizen, *Social Creation of Crime News*.

53. Hughes, *News and the Human Interest Story*, 23.

54. Drechsel, *News Making in the Trial Courts*, 53–54.

55. Drechsel, *News Making in the Trial Courts*, 68; Papke, *Framing the Criminal*, 54.

56. Cohen and Young, *The Manufacture of News*.

57. Ibid., 17–18.

58. Cohen and Young, *The Manufacture of News*; Ericson, Baranek and Chan, *Negotiating Control*.

59. Wisehart ("Newspapers and Criminal Justice") makes a similar point in 1922.

60. Ericson, Baranek, and Chan, *Representing Law and Order*.

61. Ericson, Baranek, and Chan, *Representing Law and Order*; Hall, Chritcher, Jefferson, Clarke, and Roberts, *The Social Production of News*, 335–367.

62. Martens and Cunningham-Niederer, *Media Magic, Mafia Mania*, 62; see also Pritchard, Race, *Homicide and Newspapers*, 500–507.

63. Drechsel, *News Making in the Trial Courts*, 12, 49, citing Sigal, *Reporters and Officials*, 4–5.

64. Gans, *Deciding What's News*, 284.

65. Mason, *Misinformation, Myth and Distortion*, 498; Franklin, *Local Journalism and Local Media*.

66. Lipschultz and Hilt, *Crime and Local Television News*.

67. Cohen and Young, *The Manufacture of News*, 22–23.

68. Lipschultz and Hilt, 2002; Roshier, *The Selection of Crime News in the Press*, 40–51.

69. Warr, *America's Perceptions of Crime and Punishment*, 14.

70. Jones, *The Press as Metropolitan Monitor*, 244.

71. Shoemaker, *Gatekeeping*.

72. Sherizen, *Social Creation of Crime News*, 203–224.

73. Ericson, Baranak and Chan, *Negotiating Control*; Chermak, *Police, Courts, and Corrections in the Media*.

74. Schlesinger, Tumber and Murdock, *The Media Politics of Crime and Criminal Justice*, 399.

75. Chibnall, *The Production of Knowledge by Crime Reporters*; Tuchman, *Making News by Doing Work*, 110–131; Tuchman, *Making News: A Study in the Construction of Reality*.

76. Ericson, Baranek, and Chan, *Visualizing Deviance*; Ericson, Baranek, and Chan, *Negotiating Control*; Ericson, Baranek, and Chan, *Representing Law and Order*; Gordon and Heath 1981; Roshier, *The Selection of Crime News in the Press*; Sherizen, *Social Creation of Crime News*, 212.

77. Although its extensive impact is recent, infotainment has existed in some form since at least the seventeenth century. In the mid-1600s, for example, newspaper weeklies carried details of the more interesting crimes along with moral exhortations to their readers to avoid crime, sin, and evil. Early folk music in the form of crime ballads also established crimes and criminals as accepted sources of social entertainment and narrative. Hanging, public floggings, branding, and other punishments of the time were as much popular entertainment as criminal justice events.

78. Surette and Otto, "A Test of a Crime and Justice Infotainment Measure."

79. The growth of infotainment in television news has been traced to the year 1963 when network television news expanded from 15 to 30 minutes.

Doris Graber quotes a memo from Reuven Frank, executive producer for NBC nightly news: "Every news story should, without any sacrifice of probity or responsibility, display the attributes of fiction, of drama. It should have structure and conflict, problem and denouncement, rising action and falling action, a beginning, a middle, and an end. These are not only the essentials of drama; they are the essentials of narrative" ("The Infotainment Quotient," 483).

80. Brants and Neijens, "The Infotainment of Politics," 150; Graber, "The Infotainment Quotient,"

81. Cavender and Fishman, "Television Reality Crime Programs."

82. Goidal, Freeman and Procopio, "The Impact of Television Viewing on Perceptions of Juvenile Crime," 119.

83. Fishman and Cavender, Entertaining Crime.

84. Cavender, "In the Shadow of Shadows."

85. Tunnel, "Reflections on Crime, Criminals, and Control."

86. Cavender, "In Search of Community on Reality TV;" Oliver, "Portrayals of Crime, Race, and Aggression."

87. Goidal, Freeman and Procopio, The impact of television viewing on perceptions of juvenile crime, 134.

88. Surette, "Media Trials."

89. Wasserman, "No Big Deal."

90. Valier, Crime and Punishment in Contemporary Culture.

91. Grodal, Stories for Eye, Ear and Muscles, 129–155.

92. Manning, "Media Loops."

93. Reiner, "Media Made Criminality," labels the two competing views as subversive and hegemonic.

Chapter 2

1. Gladwell, *Blink*, 194–197.

2. Lippmann, *Public Opinion*, 54.

3. The ideas included within a social construction of reality fall under the broad umbrella of the sociology of knowledge tradition. See also Foucault, *The Archaeology of Knowledge*.

4. Gergen, "Social Constructionist Inquiry."

5. An introduction to social constructionism applied to crime and other social issues can be found in Spector and Kitsuse, *Constructing Social Problems*.

6. Lindlof, "Media Audiences as Interpretive Communities."

7. Spector and Kitsuse, *Constructing Social Problems*, 6.

8. Maxson, Hennigan, and Sloane, *Factors That Influence Public Opinion of the Police*, 10.

9. It is assumed that you are not one of the few astronauts who have been to the moon and have experienced reality to draw upon for these questions.

10. Adoni and Mane, "Media and the Social Construction of Reality;" Sparks, *Television and the Drama of Crime*.

11. Rentschler, "Victims' Rights and the Struggle over Crime," 219–239.

12. Best, *Images of Issues*, 327.

13. As quoted in Sherwin, *When Law Goes Pop*, 142.

14. Joel Best describes a claim as an argument with four elements: that some condition exists; that it is troubling and ought to be addressed; that it has specific characteristics such as being common or increasing, has known causes or serious consequences, or is a particular type of problem; and that a particular action should be taken to deal with it ("The Diffusion of Social Problems").

15. Thompson, Young, and Burns, "Representing Gangs in the News," 427–428.

16. Ferrel, "Criminalizing Popular Culture."

17. Sasson, *Crime Talk*, 13–17. See also Reiner, *The Politics of the Police*, 139.

18. Sasson, *Crime Talk*, 14.

19. David Bruck as cited in Sasson, *Crime Talk*, 15.

20. As cited in Sasson, *Crime Talk*, 15.

21. Ibid., 16.

22. Sasson, *Crime Talk*, 16, quoting Thomas Elmendorf's testimony before the House Subcommittee on Communication.

23. Dardis, Baumgartner, Boydstun, De Boef and Shen, "Media Framing of Capital Punishment," 16–17.

24. In the broader research world, media narratives share many characteristics with "scripts" as developed by cognitive psychologists (see Schank and Abelson, *Scripts, Plans, Goals, and Understanding*). They also are related to the concepts of "motif" and "rhetorical idioms," both of which refer to recurring rhetorical elements and speech used to describe and culturally anchor social problems. Unlike narratives, these are brief common catch-phrases and metaphors used to describe crime. Examples include these phrases: *epidemic, menace, scourge, crisis, blight, casualties, tip of the iceberg, war on drugs, crime, gangs*, or *terrorism* (Ibarra and Kitsuse, "Vernacular Constituents of Moral Discourse," 47). See also Best and Hutchinson, "The Gang Initiation Rite as a Motif in Contemporary Crime Discourse," 384.

25. Examples of popular crime-and-justice narratives are offered by Rafter (*Shots in the Mirror*, 141–146):
(1) Mystery and detective narratives: basic pattern is of the search, most P.I. and cop films fall into this category;
(2) Thrillers: unexpected violence, nail-biters, regular episodic scares;
(3) Capers: complicated audacious heist, planning, organization and member recruitment, and execution;

(4) Justice violated/justice restored: many prison films, false accusations and unjust punishments; (5) Disguised westerns: heroic outsider reluctantly consents to clean up the town; (6) Revenge and vigilantes: lead figure is violated and retaliates; (7) Chronicles of criminal careers: biographies and fictional characters; (8) Action films: lacking developed plots, series of episode transitions with fights and explosions, violent spectacles, epic heroes.

26. Best and Hutchinson, "The Gang Initiation Rite as a Motif in Contemporary Crime Discourse," 388–389; and Sumser, *Morality and Social Order in Television Crime Drama*, 46.

27. Wardle, "It Could happen to You," 515–533.

28. A similar concept is "signal crime" described by Innes ("Signal Crimes," 15–16); Innes, "Signal Crimes and Signal Disorders," 335–355.

29. Rentschler, *"Victims' Rights and the Struggle over Crime,"* 219–239.

30. Wykes, "Constructing Crime," 158–174.

31. Ruddell and Decker, "Kids and Assault Weapons," 45–63.

32. Quinney in his 1970 book, *The Social Reality of Crime*, provides the first effort in applying social constructionism to crime. Jenkins in *Using Murder* in 1994 and Potter and Kappeler in *Constructing Crime* in 2006 provide updated examples.

33. Best, *Images of Issues*, 332.

34. Reinarman, "The Social Construction of an Alcohol Problem."

35. Kupchik and Bracy, "News Media on School Crime and Violence."

36. Rentschler, "Victims' Rights and the Struggle over Crime," 219–239.

Chapter 3

1. Stark, "Perry Mason Meets Sonny Crockett," 236.

2. Rafter, *Shots in the Mirror*; see also Leitch, *Crime Films*.

3. Escholz, Mallard, and Flynn, "Images of Prime Time Justice," 161–180. While not historically reported as the most common image of criminality, media portraits of minorities as offenders do raise concerns that racist and ethnic stereotypes are reinforced. See Bing, *Race, Crime, and the Media*; Mann and Zatz, *Images of Color Images of Crime*; Rome, *Black Demons*; and Shaheen, *Reel Bad Arabs* for discussions of media portraits of minority offenders.

4. Bailey and Hale, *Blood on Her Hands*; Bond-Maupin, "That wasn't' even me they showed," 30–44; Cecil, "Dramatic Portrayals of Violent Women," 243.

5. Lynch, Stretesky, and Hammond found, for example, that regarding chemical crimes, a very small percentage of events are reported as news; those that are reported are likely to be cast as caused by an individual and the harm of the event downplayed ("Media Coverage of Chemical Crimes," 121–122).

6. Graber, *Crime News and the Public*. Travis Dixon and others further report that minorities are represented in news and entertainment in such a way as to encourage the perception of minorities as violent and criminal. See Dixon, "Crime News and Radicalized Beliefs," 106–125; Dixon, Azocar and Casas, "The Portrayal of Race and Crime on Television Network News," 495–520; Dixon and Linz, "Overrepresentation and Underrepresentation of Victimization on Local Television News," 547–573; Dixon and Maddox, "Skin Tone, Crime News, and Social Reality Judgments," 1555–1570.

7. Curran, "Communications, Power and Social Order," 227.

8. Valverde, *Law and Order*. For example, Eric Hickey (*Serial Murderers and Their Victims*, 3) tracks the number of serial murder themed films: 2 (1920s), 3 (1930s), 3 (1940s), 4 (1950s), 12 (1960s), 20 (1970s), 23 (1980s), and 117 (1990s). Yvonne Jewkes (*Media and Crime*, 94–105) describes an analogous process in Britain concerning pedophiles.

9. Simpson, *Psycho Paths*.

10. Jenkins, *Moral Panic*. Rennison, *Intimate Partner Violence*, 1993–2001

11. For discussions of the culture that has developed around serial killers, see Ian Conrich, "Mass Media/Mass Murder;" Jarvis, *Monsters Inc.*, and Schechter, *The Serial Killer Files*, 369–402. For a discussion of the interplay of community and local media when both are faced with an active serial killer see Fisher, *Killer Among US*.

12. The popularity of violent predatory crime is also likely associated with a downward comparison effect. Downward comparison is a psychological process in which people feel better about their own situation when they see someone in a worse one. Therefore, a media image of violent urban crime would have a soothing effect on middle-class suburban Americans by holding up to them a crime-and-justice construction of reality that is more violent and dangerous than what they are experiencing. And, as this violent crime is shown as due to individual deficiencies like greed and innate evil, the apparently better-off-by-comparison rest of America can enjoy a guilt-free boost regarding their crime situation while being encouraged to purchase security products.

13. Chermak, *Victims in the News*; Mawby and Brown, "Newspaper Images of the Victim: A British Study;" Meyers, *News Coverage of Violence Against Women*; Pritchard and Hughes, "Patterns of Deviance in Crime News;" Reiner, Livingstone, and Allen, "From Law and Order to Lynch Mobs: Crime News since the Second World War;" Sorenson, Peterson-Manz, and Berk, "News Media Coverage and the Epidemiology of Homicide."

14. Boyle, *Media and Violence: Gendering the Debates*; Greer, *Crime and Media: A Reader*; Johnston, Hawkins, and Michner, "Homicide Reporting in Chicago Dailies;" Meyers, "News of Battering;" Meyers, *News Coverage of Violence Against Women*; Wilbanks, *Murder in Miami*.

15. Altheide, *Creating Fear*, 146. In a new research direction that explores the effect of media content on victims rather than their media depiction, a recent study reported a relationship between real world victims of crime, their psychological distress from victimization and their amount of television exposure and gratifications sought from television. Minnebo, "The Relation between Psychological Distress, Television Exposure, and Television-viewing," 65–93.

16. Wardle, "It Could Happen to You," 515.

17. Rentschler, "Victims' Rights and the Struggle over Crime," 219–239.

18. Sumser, *Morality and Social Order*, 78.

19. Escholz, Mallard and Flynn, "Images of Prime Time Justice," 161–180; Cecil, "Dramatic Portrayals of Violent Women," 243–258; Sumser, *Morality and Social Order*, 141.

20. Chermak, *Victims in the News*; Meyers, *News Coverage of Violence against Women*.

21. Chermak, *Victims in the News*, 107. Reiner, Livingstone, and Allen ("No More Happy Endings?," 118)

found, however, that since World War II crime films have become more likely to show victims in a central role.

22. Lichter and Lichter, *Prime Time Crime*. Robert Reiner points out that, ironically, in relation to property crime risk, television has become safer than the real world ("Media Made Criminality," 391).

23. Wilson, Kunkel, Linz, Potter, Donnerstein, Smith, Blumenthal and Gray, "Violence in Television Programming Overall."

24. Shelly and Ashkins, "Crime, Crime News, and Crime Views;" see also Dowler, "Comparing American and Canadian Local Television Crime Shows," 583; Duwe, "Body-Count Journalism;" Reiner, Livingstone, and Allen, "No More Happy Endings?," 114–115.

25. For a recent typology see Levi and Burrows, "Measuring the Impact of Fraud," 292–318.

26. Coleman, *The Criminal Elite*, 182.

27. Burns, "Media Portrayal of White-Collar Crime;" Levi, "*Suite Revenge*."

28. Ericson, Baranek and Chan, *Representing Law and Order*; Levi, "Inside Information;" Levi, "The Media Construction of Financial White-Collar Crimes;" Stephenson-Burton, "Through the Looking-Glass;" and Tombs and Whyte, "Reporting Corporate Crime Out of Existence."

29. Levi, "The Media Construction of Financial White-collar Crimes," 1052. Levi (1055) points out that commercial films such as *Wall Street* and *Catch Me If You Can* periodically construct white-collar criminality.

30. Lackey, "Visualizing White-Collar Crime."

31. Coleman, *The Criminal Elite*, 123–124.

32. Ponzi, Charles (1882–1949) namesake and inventor of Ponzi fraud scheme in which investors are lured into providing funds in the belief that they are buying into a high profit venture based on early investors profits which are created simply from the recycled money of later investors minus the money skimmed off for the runner of the Ponzi.

33. Gans, "*Deciding What's News;*" Goff, "*The Westray Mine Disaster;*" Wright, Cullen, and Blankenship, "*The Social Construction of Corporate Violence.*"

34. Cavender and Mulcahy, "Trial by Fire: Media Constructions of Corporate Deviance."

35. Friedrichs, *Trusted Criminals*, 18.

36. Geis, *White-Collar and Corporate Crime*, 77.

37. Friedrichs, *Trusted Criminals*.

38. Friedrichs, *Trusted Criminals*, 18–19; Levi, "Measuring the Impact of Fraud in the UK," 295.

39. Levi, "*White-Collar Crime in the News*," 25.

40. Friedrichs, *Trusted Criminals*, 18–19.

41. Levi, "The Media Construction of Financial White-collar Crimes," 1037. See also Levi and Pithouse, *White Collar Crime and Its Victims*.

42. Tombs, "Corporations and Health and Safety," 23.

43. Levi, "*White-Collar Crime in the News*," 25.

44. Lynch, Stretesky and Hammond, "Media Coverage of Chemical Crimes."

45. Ibid., 121–122.

46. Coleman, *The Criminal Elite*, 123.

47. Friedrichs, *Trusted Criminals*, 19.

48. Lackey, "Visualizing White-Collar Crime Generic Imagery in Popular Film;" Nichols, "White Collar Cinema;" Rafter, *Shots in the Mirror*.

49. Friedrichs, *Trusted Criminals*, 19.

50. Levi, "The Media Construction of Financial White-collar Crimes," 1037.

51. Rebovich and Kane, "An Eye for an Eye in the Electronic Age."

52. Fleming and Zyglidopoulos, *Charting Corporate Corruption*, 140.

53. Shipley and Cavender, "Murder and Mayhem at the Movies."

54. Rafter, "Crime, Film and Criminology," 415.

55. Rafter, *Shots in the Mirror*, 48.

56. Rafter, "Crime, Film and Criminology," 403–420.

57. Ibid.,

58. Lichter and Lichter, *Prime Time Crime*.

59. Thomas, "The Psychology of Yellow Journalism," 491.

60. *Sourcebook of Criminal Justice Statistics— 2000*. "Table 2.42 Attitudes toward the Causes of Crime in the United States," and "Table 2.45: Respondents Perceptions about the Primary Cause of Gun Violence."

61. Sasson, *Crime Talk*, 161.

62. Sparks and Sparks list five theoretical groups: catharsis, priming, arousal, desensitization, and cultivation as potential violent media effect mechanisms ("Effects of Media Violence," 278–280). For a recent review of the media violence debate, see Boyle, *Media and Violence: Gendering the Debates*.

63. Recent reviews of this research are offered by Ferguson, "Media Violence: Miscast Causality," 446–447; Freedman, "Media Violence and Its Effect on Aggression;" Grimes, Anderson and Bergen, *Media Violence and Aggression*; Gunter, "Media Violence: Is There a Case for Causality," 1061–1122; Huesmann, "The Impact of Electronic Media Violence," 6–13;

Huesmann and Taylor, "The Role of Media Violence in Violent Behavior," 393–415; and Murray, "Media Violence: The Effects Are Both Real and Strong," 1212–1230.

64. The original 1961 reference was to television by Schramm, Lyle and Parker, *Television in the Lives of Our Children*.

65. See, for example Heath, Bresolin, and Rinaldi, "Effects of Media Violence on Children;" and Wilson, Kunkel, Linz, Apotter, Donnerstein, Smith, Blumenthal and Gray, "Violence in Television Programming Overall," 3–267.

66. Anderson, "The Production of Media Violence and Aggression Research," 1260–1279; Browne and Hamilton-Giachritsis, "The Influence of Violent Media on Children and Adolescents," 701–710; Pennell and Browne, "Film Violence and Young Offenders," 13–28.

67. Wilson and Herrnstein, *Crime and Human Behavior*, 343.

68. Huesmann and Taylor, "The Role of Media Violence," 394; Gunter, "Media Violence," 1110–1113.

69. Huesmann, Moise-Titus, Podolski, and Eron, "Longitudinal Relations between Children's Exposure to TV Violence and Their Aggressive and Violent Behavior," 210; Johnson, Cohen, Smailes, Kasen and Brook, "Television Viewing and Aggressive Behavior During Adolescence and Adulthood," 2468–2471.

70. Coyne, "Does Media Violence Cause Violent Crime," 205–211; Savage, "Does Viewing Violent Media Really Cause Criminal Violence," 99–128; Savage, "The Role of Exposure to Media Violence in the Etiology of Violent Behavior," 1123–1136.

71. Heath, Wharton, Del Rosario, Cook, and Calder, "Impact of the

Introduction of Television on Crime in the United States," 474.

72. Browne & Hamilton-Giachritsis, "The Influence of Violent Media on Children and Adolescents," 701–710; Coyne, "Does Media Violence Cause Violent Crime," 205–211; Huesman and Taylor, "The Role of Media Violence in Violent Behavior," 393–415; Savage, "Does Viewing Violent Media Really Cause Criminal Violence," 99–128; Savage, "The Role of Exposure to Media Violence in the Etiology of Violent Behavior," 1123–1136; Savage and Yancey, "The Effects of Media Violence Exposure on Criminal Aggression," 772–791.

73. Bleyer, *Main Currents in the History of American Journalism*.

74. Papke, *Framing the Criminal*, 171–172.

75. Hays, *President's Report to the Motion Picture Producers and Distributors' Association*.

76. Surette, "Self-reported Copycat Crime among a Population of Serious Violent Juvenile Offenders," 46–69.

77. Cook, Kendzierski, and Thomas, "The Implicit Assumptions of Television Research;" Canter, Sheehan, Alpers, and Mullen, "Media and Mass Homicides."

78. Gunter, "Media Violence: Is There a Case for Causality," 1066.

79. Sadistic fantasy, often supplemented by various media content (print, films, video games, Internet sites, pornography), has been reported as a precursor to juvenile sexual homicides (see Bailey, "Fast Forward to Violence," 6; and Meyers, *Juvenile Sexual Homicide*, 163–164) and a media role in the killing of children by strangers (see Wilson, "Stranger Child-murder," 49–59).

80. Pease and Love, "The Copy-Cat Crime Phenomenon."

81. Heller and Polsky, *Studies in Violence and Television*, 151–152.

82. "Self-reported Copycat Crime among a Population of Serious Violent Juvenile Offenders," 46.

83. Curtis, "Gabriel Tarde," 142–157; Vine, "Gabriel Tarde." 292–304.

84. Tarde, *Penal Philosophy,* 340. Research on the diffusion of riots from large to small cities has has supported Tarde's ideas while including the impact of modern mass media. See Myers, "The Diffusion of Collective Violence: Infectiousness, Susceptibility, and Mass Media Networks," 172-208.

85. Daniel Glazer's 1956 article re-introduced media as a concept worthy of study to criminology (Glaser, "Criminality Theories and Behavioral Images," 433–444).

86. Akers, *Social Learning and Social Structure*; Bandura, *Aggression: A Social Learning Analysis*.

87. Berkowitz, "Some Effects of Thoughts on Anti- and Prosocial Influences of Media Events;" see also Berkowitz and Rogers, "A Priming Effect Analysis of Media Influences."

88. Dijksterhuis and Bargh, "The Perception- behavior Expressway;" Roskos-Ewoldsen, Roskos-Ewoldsen, and Carpentier, "Media Priming: A Synthesis."

89. Jo and Berkowitz, "A Priming Effect Analysis of Media Influences," 46.

90. Huesmann, "The Role of Social Information Processing and Cognitive Schema," 73–109.

91. Claxton, "Joining the Intentional Dance;" Goldman, "Imitation, Mind Reading and Simulation;" Huesmann, "Psychological Process Promoting the Relation," 131.

92. Huesmann, "Psychological Process Promoting the Relation," 130.

93. Mazur, "Bomb Threats and the Mass Media."

94. Gunter, "Media Violence: Is There a Case for Causality," 1097.

95. Shrum, "Media Consumption and Perceptions of Social Reality," 69-95; Petty, Priester and Brinol, "Mass Media Attitude Change," 155–198.

96. Green and Brock, "The Role of Transportation in the Persuasiveness of Public Narratives," 701–721.

97. Slater and Rouner, "Entertainment-education and Elaboration Likelihood," 173–191.

98. Ibid., 185.

99. Surette, "Self-reported Copycat Crime among a Population of Serious Violent Juvenile Offenders." In addition, few differences have been found between juvenile offenders and nonoffenders in media consumption and use. See Bandura, *Aggression: A Social Learning Analysis*; Hagell and Newburn, *Young Offenders and the Media*.

100. Sacco, *When Crime Waves*.

101. As cited in Alexander, "Terrorism and the Media," 161.

102. For a specific example of the complicated relationship between the media and terrorism, see Hayes, "Political Violence, Irish Republicanism and the British Media."

103. Surette, Hansen, and Noble, "Measuring Media Oriented Terrorism;" Tuman, *Communicating Terror*; and Weimann and Winn, *The Theater of Terror: Mass Media and International Terrorism*, 47.

104. Tuman, *Communicating Terror*.

105. See Paletz and Schmid, *Terrorism and the Media*, for an overview.

106. Livingstone, *The War Against Terrorism*, 62.

107. Weimann and Winn, *The Theater of Terror*, 57.

108. Poland, *Understanding Terrorism*, 47; and Weimann and Winn, *The Theater of Terror*.

109. Schmid and de Graaf, *Violence as Communication*; and Weimann and Winn, *The Theater of Terror*.

110. Chermak and Gruenewald, "The Media's Coverage of Domestic Terrorism," 428–461.

111. Holden, "The Contagiousness of Aircraft Hijacking," 874–904.

112. Surette, Hansen and Noble, "Measuring Media Oriented Terrorism," 363.

113. Nacos, *Mass-Mediated Terrorism*; Ross, "Deconstructing the Terrorism-news Media Relationship," 215–225.

114. Courtwright, *Violent Land*. A wry comment on the level of violence in pre–mass media society in the United States is provided by the *Salt Lake Desert News* in the 1860s: "The place is rapidly becoming civilized. Several men having been killed there already" (as cited in Ambrose, *Nothing Like It in the World*, 337).

Chapter 4

1. Wilson, *Cop Knowledge*.

2. Gorelick, "Join Our War."

3. Rafter, *Shots in the Mirror*.

4. Inciardi and Dee, "From the Keystone Cops to Miami Vice."

5. Reiner, "Keystone to Kojak."

6. Stark, "Perry Mason Meets Sonny Crockett," 239.

7. See Blumer, *The Movies and Conduct*; Blumer, and Hauser, *Movies, Delinquency, and Crime*; Charter, *Motion Pictures and Youth: A Summary*; Dale, *Children's Attendance at Motion Pictures*; Holaday and Stoddard, *Getting Ideas from the Movies*; Peterson and Thurstone, *Motion Pictures and the Social Attitudes of Children*; and Shuttleworth

and May, *The Social Conduct and Attitudes of Movie Fans*. For a summary of the Payne Fund studies, see chapter 2 in Lowery, and DeFleur, *Milestones in Mass Communication Research*.

8. Hays, *President's Report to the Motion Picture Producers and Distributors' Association*.

9. Wilson, *Cop Knowledge*, 91.

10. Ibid., 118.

11. *Dirty Harry*, 1971. Director Don Siegel, Warner Brothers.

12. The discussion on cop narratives draws on ideas from Wilson, *Cop Knowledge*. In a similar vein, Reiner (*The Politics of the Police*, 150–152) offers twelve ideal type models of law enforcement stories found in the media.

13. See Hale, "Keeping Women in Their Place," 159-179 for an analysis of the portrait of policewomen in commercial films from 1972 thru 1996.

14. Wilson, *Cop Knowledge*, 134.

15. Wilson, *Cop Knowledge*, 134; and Eschholz, Mallard, and Flynn, "Images of Prime Time Justice."

16. Brown and Benedict, "Perceptions of the Police;" Mawby, "Completing the 'Half-Formed Picture'? Media Images of Policing." See also Lawrence, *The Politics of Force*, 15; Payne, *Brutal Cops, News Coverage*, 1–10.

17. *Bad Boys* (1993) by Inner Circle, Atlantic Records.

18. Donovan, "Armed with the Power of Television."

19. Doyle, *Arresting Images*.

20. Kooistra, Mahoney, and Westervelt, "The World of Crime According to 'COPS,'" Table 2: Index Crimes on "COPS" and in the UCR (1994), 148.

21. Ibid., 153.

22. Cavender, "In the Shadow of Shadow."

23. Sherwin, *When Law Goes Pop*, 184–185.

24. Doyle, "Cops: Television Policing as Policing Reality."

25. Hallett and Powell, "Backstage with COPS."

26. Robbers, *Blinded by Science*, 88.

27. Cavender and Deutsch, "CSI and Moral Authority," 67–81; Tyler, "Viewing CSI and the Threshold of Guilt," 1073.

28. Tyler, "Viewing CSI and the Threshold of Guilt," 1054.

29. Dutelle, *The CSI Effect and Your Department*, 113–114; Robbers, "Blinded by Science," 92.

30. Gillis, "New Crime Shows Educate Criminals."

31. Cavender and Deutsch, "CSI and Moral Authority," 77; Tyler, "Viewing CSI and the Threshold of Guilt," 1068-1073; Roane, "The CSI Effect," 48. Podlas ("The CSI Effect," 463) points out that "the few times a CSI effect has found its way into a criminal trial, it was the prosecution who attempted to exploit its mythology to obtain a conviction."

32. Podlas, "The CSI Effect," 429–465; Shelton, "The CSI Effect: Does It Really Exist?;" Tyler, "Viewing CSI and the Threshold of Guilt," 1050–1085.

33. Shelton, "The CSI Effect: Does It Really Exist?," 5. Podlas ("The CSI Effect") reports similar lack of effects on verdicts.

34. Robbers, "Blinded by Science," 87.

35. Mopas, "Examining the CSI Effect Through an ANT Lens," 110–117; Podlas, "The CSI Effect," 442.

36. Perlmutter, *Policing the Media*.

37. Lenz, *Changing Images of Law*.

38. Lichter and Lichter, *Prime Time Crime*. Reiner, Livingstone, and Allen ("No More Happy Endings?," 115–116) found a decline in civilian heroes

in films over the latter half of the twentieth century.

39. The Chevalier C. Auguste Dupin, an American amateur detective living in France, appeared in three stories: "The Murders in the Rue Morgue," "The Mystery of Marie Roget," and "The Purloined Letter." He is described in the *Oxford Companion to Crime and Mystery Writing* (Herbert, 126): "Dupin is an isolated figure. Well aware of his intellectual superiority, Dupin is particularly contemptuous of the unimaginative methods of the police."

40. Leishman and Mason, *Policing and the Media*, 70, 74. Lenz (*Changing Images of Law*) has put forth the notion that recent media reflects a transition in society away from conservative crime control policies.

41. Price, Merrill, and Clause, "The Depiction of Guns on Prime Time Television."

42. Reiner, "Media Made Criminality," 392.

Chapter 5

1. Sherwin, *When Law Goes Pop,* ix.

2. Robinson (*Justice Blind?,* 133) characterizes the content of the media as constructing due process protections as if they were a cause of crime in the United States.

3. Tyler, "Viewing CSI and the Threshold of Guilt," 1074.

4. Rafter, "American Criminal Trial Films," 9.

5. Asimow and Mader, *Law and Popular Culture*, chapter 2; Stark, "Perry Mason Meets Sonny Crockett;" Surette, "Media Trials."

6. Asimow and Mader, *Law and Popular Culture*.

7. Stark, "Perry Mason Meets Sonny Crockett," 275.

8. Lichter and Lichter, *Prime Time Crime;* Rafter, "American Criminal Trial Films," 9.

9. Greenfield and Osborn, "Film Lawyers;" Stark, "Perry Mason Meets Sonny Crockett."

10. Lenz, *Changing Images of Law.*

11. Rafter, *Shots in the Mirror.*

12. Bailey, Pollock, and Schroeder, "The Best Defense."

13. Carpenter, Lacy, and Fico, "Network News Coverage of High-profile Crime," 901–916.

14. Fox, Sickel, and Steiger (*Tabloid Justice*) discuss the impact of media trials under their related tabloid justice concept.

15. Carpenter, Lacy, and Fico, "Network News Coverage of High-profile Crime," 901–916; Valier, *Crime and Punishment in Contemporary Culture.* Andie Tucher ("Framing the Criminal," 908) cites an 1836 New York trial of a teenage clerk for the murder of a prostitute as the first media circus trial in America due to extensive coverage in the New York penny press.

16. Barber, *News Cameras in the Courtroom,* 112–114; Carpenter, Lacy, and Fico, *Network News Coverage of High-profile Crime,* 901–916; Nasheri, *Crime and Justice in the Age of Court TV.*

17. Fox, Sickel, and Steiger, *Tabloid Justice.*

18. Mathiesen, Prison on Trial, 66–67.

19. Estes v. Texas, 381 U.S. 532, at 570 (1965).

20. Altheide and Snow, *Media Worlds in the Postjournalism Era.*

21. Fox, Sickel, and Steiger, *Tabloid Justice.*

22. Hariman, "Performing the Laws: Popular Trials and Social Knowledge," 23.

23. Surette, "Media Trials."

24. David Papke (*Framing the Criminal,* 22) reports that similar themes existed

in the 1830s. Popular pamphlets portrayed crime within two long-standing themes—the rogue (a semi-hero who commits property fraud) and the fiend (a diabolical, frenzied villain). This period saw the creation of a new theme—the fiendish rogue. An example from the early part of the twentieth century is the 1913 Leo Frank case involving the strangulation of a fourteen-year-old female factory worker in Georgia. As was common in such cases, coverage was heavily biased against the defendant. An Atlanta paper was typical: "Our little girl—ours by the Eternal God! has been pursued to a hideous death and bloody grave by this filthy, perverted Jew of New York." The commutation of Frank's sentence from death to life imprisonment led to Georgia's governor being driven out of office. A year after his conviction, Frank was taken from a prison farm by a band of men, driven 125 miles to the scene of the murder, and lynched.

25. Like many things in life, it appears that being rich and famous and accused of a crime is double-edged. Access to a top-notch defense assures that your case will follow strict due process procedures and that every step in the criminal justice process will be exercised. It wasn't the race card that helped O. J. Simpson in his criminal trial, it was the money card. The rich can depend on a strong, aggressive defense. The poor are much more likely to plea bargain and be adjudicated guilty. However, if you are rich and famous and are found guilty, you are likely to receive a stern sentence. Judges and the state do not want to appear to be favoring rich guilty defendants. Contrary to usual sentencing practices, this appears to be especially true for female defendants of late. Leona Helmsley, Patty Hearst, and Martha Stewart all received jail time as first offenders. In sum, money and fame help you avoid guilty verdicts, but if you are found guilty, you are more likely to be made an example of.

26. Sherwin, *When Law Goes Pop.*

27. Drucker, "The Televised Mediated Trial."

28. Surette, "Media Echoes."

29. Loften, *Justice and the Press,* 138; M. K. Wisehart ("Newspapers and Criminal Justice") makes the earliest historical references to echolike effects from media coverage in 1922.

30. Kaplan and Skolnick, *Criminal Justice,* 467–468.

31. Surette, "Media Echoes."

32. Marcus, "The Media in the Courtroom," 276.

33. 62 A.B.A. Rep, 1134–1135 (1937) cited by Kirtley, "A Leap Not Supported by History."

34. In a case important in Texas due to Estes's political associations, Texas financier Billie Sol Estes was accused of a salad-oil swindle. Cameramen crowded into a tiny courtroom and seriously disrupted the proceedings. After the trial, which was televised despite his objection, Estes appealed his conviction, arguing that the presence of television cameras denied him a fair trial. The Supreme Court agreed and reversed the decision, reversing its own decision sixteen years later in Chandler v. Florida.

35. Estes v. Texas, at 538 and 544.

36. Florida policeman Noel Chandler was tried and convicted with another police officer for a series of burglaries. The case received a large amount of regional media attention and was televised over Chandler's objection as part of a Florida pilot program for televising judicial proceedings. The Supreme Court held that if other constitutional due process guarantees are met, a state could provide for

television coverage of a criminal trial over the objection of defendants.

37. "Public Confidence in Selected Institutions, 1973–1996," Table 2.9.

38. Examples include the 1992 Los Angeles riots following the not guilty verdict for the police officers involved in the Rodney King beating; the 1980 Miami riots following the acquittal of police officers charged in the beating death of black motorist Edward McDuffie; and the 1993 acquittal of police officer William Lozano in the shooting death of a black motorcyclist.

39. United States v. Burr, cited in Marcus, "The Media in the Courtroom," 237.

40. United States v. Burr, 25 F. Case 49, 49. (1807).

41. "Trial by Media," U.S. Press.

42. For an overview and discussion of the research and issues associated with pretrial publicity and fair trials, see Bruschke and Loges, *Free Press vs. Fair Trials.* They note a discrepancy between laboratory research, which generally concludes that pretrial publicity biases trials, and field research, which reports that such effects are not common and occur only when the publicity is excessive and includes persuasive information and when trial evidence is inconclusive.

43. Bruschke and Loges (*Free Press vs. Fair Trials,* 137) argue that combinations of reactive judicial remedies appear to be effective and that pretrial publicity will only bias a trial outcome in rare circumstances.

44. Tyler, "Viewing CSI and the Threshold of Guilt," 1062.

45. The Reporters Committee for Freedom of the Press, downloaded December 2009 from www.rcfp.org/privilege

46. Kirtley, "Shield Laws and Reporter's Privilege," 164.

47. Dalglish, "Protecting Reporters Who Protect Sources," 30–32; Fargo, "Analyzing Federal Shield Law Proposals," 35–82.

48. Kirtley, "Shield Laws and Reporter's Privilege," 170.

49. Sherwin, When Law Goes Pop, 219.

50. An outgrowth of the dominance of visuals discussed by Valverde (*Law and Order,* chapter 9) is the legal dilemma involved in the release or withholding of "gruesome pictures" from crime scenes.

51. Sherwin, *When Law Goes Pop,* 34–35. Amy Fisher, the seventeen-year-old "Long Island Lolita" who shot the wife of her thirty-eight-year-old boyfriend, Joey Buttafuoco, in 1992 became a tabloid legend. She was released from prison in 1999.

52. Fox, Sickel, and Steiger, *Tabloid Justice.*

53. Lenz, *Changing Images of Law.*

54. Fox, Sickel, and Steiger, *Tabloid Justice,* 188, 201.

Chapter 6

1. Freeman, *Popular Culture and Corrections,* 208; Kieby, "Prison Life Through a Lens," 22–23; Levenson, "Inside Information: Prisons and the Media," 14–15.

2. Graber, *Crime News and the Public*; and Roberts and Stalans, *Public Opinion, Crime, and Criminal Justice.*

3. Marsh, "A Comparative Analysis of Crime Coverage in Newspapers," 76.

4. Freeman, *Popular Culture and Corrections.* 47.

5. The most successful television show based on corrections was the HBO network program *Oz,* which aired from 1997 to 2003.

6. Mason, "The Screen Machine," 279–280; O'Sullivan, "Representations of Prison in Nineties Hollywood Cinema," 317–334; Schauer,

"Masculinity Incarcerated," 28–42; and Wilson and O'Sullivan, *Images of Incarceration*. Bennett ("The Good, the Bad and the Ugly," 97–115 presents a unique take on the prison film study by exploring how prison films have depicted the relationship between the media, crime, and punishment.

7. Cheatwood, "Prison Movies;" and Freeman, "Public Perception and Corrections."

8. Rafter, *Shots in the Mirror*, 127.

9. Cheatwood, "Prison Movies." For a critique of Cheatwood's typology, see Mason, "The Screen Machine," 284–288.

10. Mason, "Prison Decayed," 607.

11. Ibid., 621.

12. For a discussion of British television programs about corrections, see Mason, "Watching the Invisible;" and Wilson and O'Sullivan, *Images of Incarceration*.

13. Mason, *Captured by the Media*; Mason, "Lies, Distortion and What Doesn't Work," 251–267; Russell, "Tabloid Tactics," 32–33.

14. Chermak "Police Courts and Corrections in the Media," 96.

15. Doyle and Ericson, "Breaking into Prison." See also Lotz, *Crime and the American Press*.

16. For example, Andrew Hochstetler ("Reporting of Executions in U.S. Newspapers," 8) provides evidence that the backwards law of media content extends to coverage of death row so that the more sensational cases receive the most coverage. A small body of research has also examined the portrait of capital punishment in films. See Garland, *The Culture of Control*; Greer, "Delivering Death," 84–102; Harding, "Celluloid Death," 1167–1179; Sarat, "Death Row, Aisle Seat," 1–3; Sarat, *When the State Kills*.

17. This was found to be true for the 1970s by Jacobs and Brooks, "The Mass Media and Prison News;" and for the 1990s by Doyle and Ericson, "Breaking into Prison," 157–158.

18. Mason, "Misinformation, Myth and Distortion," 481–496.

19. One counter balance to this is the coverage that efforts to free wrongly convicted inmates will periodically garner. See www.InnocenceProject. org. When they do result in a prisoner's release the accompanying news coverage contributes to the general negative view of corrections, as well as the police and courts. In these cases, by portraying them as locking up the wrong people.

20. Chermak, *Victims in the News*.

21. Campbell, "Journalists Should Demand Prison Access," 34.

22. Doyle and Ericson, "Breaking into Prison," 167.

23. Ibid., 183.

24. Ibid., 183–184.

25. An exception to this pattern of negative sexually focused coverage is reported for the coverage of the imprisonment of Martha Stewart. See Cecil, "Doing Time in Camp Cupcake," 142–160.

26. Freeman, *Popular Culture and Corrections*, 114–115.

27. Bennett, "The Good, the Bad and the Ugly," 112; Mason, "Prison Decayed," 616.

28. Ciasullo, "Containing Deviant Desire," 195–223.

29. Britton, *At Work in the Iron Cage*; Ciasullo, "Containing Deviant Desire," 197; Clowers, "Dykes, Gangs, and Danger," 28.

30. Clowers, "Dykes, Gangs, and Danger," 28.

31. Cecil, Looking Beyond Caged Heat, 321; Cecil, Dramatic portrayals of violent women, 243–258.

32. Cecil, "Looking Beyond Caged Heat," 321; Freeman, *Popular Culture and Corrections*, 46.

33. Cecil, "Looking Beyond Caged Heat," 322.

34. Freeman, *Popular Culture and Corrections*, 46. See also Wilson and O'Sullivan, *Images of Incarceration*.

35. Mason, "Prison Decayed," 616.

36. Davis, *Are Prisons Obselete?*, cited by Mason, "Prison Decayed," 616.

37. Mathiesen, "Television, Public Space and Prison Population," 39.

38. Bennett, "The Good, the Bad and the Ugly," 99.

39. *Ibid.*, 112.

40. Mason, "Prison Decayed," 609; Mathiesen, *Prisons on Trial*; Zaner, "The Screen Test," 64; see also Getty, "Media Wise," 126–131.

Chapter 7

1. Research on media effects on public attitudes began in the 1930s with a set of research projects collectively called the Payne Fund studies. Among other findings, this early research reported that films such as *Birth of a Nation*—a sympathetic and romantic portrayal of the creation of the Ku Klux Klan—could generate unfavorable attitudes toward blacks among viewers. Although the effects eventually wore off, they were found to persist for a significant period of time (up to eight months).

2. National Institute of Mental Health, *Television and Behavior*, 90.

3. Lindesmith, *The Addict and the Law*.

4. Other movies in which illegal drugs are shown positively include *The Forty Year Old Virgin*, *Harold and Kumar Go To White Castle*, and *Dazed and Confused*.

5. American Association of Advertising Agencies, *What We've Learned About Advertising*.

6. Black, *Changing Attitudes Toward Drug Use*; and O'Keefe et al., *Taking a Bite Out of Crime*.

7. Surette, "Methodological Problems in Determining Media Effects on Criminal Justice."

8. Weinstein, "Cross-Hazard Consistencies."

9. See O'Keefe and Reid, "Media Public Information Campaigns and Criminal Justice Policy;" and O'Keefe, Rosenbaum, Lavrakas, Reid, and Botta, *Taking a Bite Out of Crime*.

10. Rosenbaum, Lurigio, and Lavrakas, *Crime Stoppers*, 110.

11. Rosenbaum, Lurigio, and Lavrakas, "Enhancing Citizen Participation and Solving Serious Crime," 417.

12. An assessment of a Florida program's "crime of the week" and "most wanted" cases for the first two years of operation revealed that the types of crime portrayed most often were violent crimes; nonviolent crimes were rarely portrayed, and homicides were the single most popular crime shown. On the whole, the program portrayed criminality as an attribute of a young, violent, dangerous class of criminals composed mostly of minorities. Crime was portrayed as largely stranger-to-stranger, injurious or fatal encounters in which handguns had a dominant role. See Surette, "The Mass Media and Criminal Investigations." Yvonne Jewkes (*Media and Crime*, 155–161) found that in Britain nearly all of the crimes shown on *Crimewatch UK* conform to news values of predatory violence, particularly against women and children.

13. Pfuhl, "Crimestoppers," 519.

14. Lavrakas, Rosenbaum, and Lurigio, "Media Cooperation with Police."

15. Rheingold, Campbell, Self-Brown, de Arellano, Resnick, and Kilpatrick, "Prevention of Child Sexual Abuse," 352–363; Santa and Cochran, "Does

the Impact of Anti-drinking and Driving," 109–129.

16. Surette and Terry, "Videotaped Misdemeanor First Appearances."

17. Marx, "Electric Eye in the Sky," 228.

18. Surette and Terry, "Video in the Misdemeanor Court."

19. Grant, "The Videotaping of Police Interrogations in Canada."

20. Patton, "Caught," 125, quoted by Stephen Graham in "Toward the Fifth Utility?," 89.

21. The looping of media content moves some surveillance images into newscasts so that the more entertaining and newsworthy scenes are shown to a mass audience.

22. The effectiveness of CCTV systems for reducing terrorist acts has been called into question however. See Fussey, "Observing Potentiality in the Global City," 171–192.

23. Norris, McCahill, and Wood ("The Growth of CCTV," 110) credit the first large scale open public space CCTV system as opening in England in 1985.

24. Haggerty and Gozso, "Seeing Beyond the Ruins," 169–187.

25. Williams, "Effective CCTV and the Challenge," 97–107.

26. Gill and Loveday, "What Do Offenders Think about CCTV?," 17–25. See also Allard, Wortley, and Stewart, "The Effect of CCTV on Prisoner Misbehavior," 404–422.

27. Hier, Greenberg, Walby, and Lett, "Media, Communication and the Establishment," 734; Sutton and Wilson, "Open-street CCTV in Australia," 310–322; Webster, "The Evolving Diffusion, Regulation and Governance," 230–250.

28. Warren and Brandeis, "The Right to Privacy," 195: "Recent inventions and business methods call attention to the next step which must be taken for the protection of the person, and for securing to the individual what Judge Cooley calls the right 'to be let alone.' Instantaneous photographs and newspaper enterprise have invaded the sacred precincts of private and domestic life; and numerous mechanical devices threaten to make good the prediction that 'what is whispered in the closet shall be proclaimed from the house-tops.'"

29. Fussey ("Beyond Liberty, Beyond Security," 121) estimates one camera for every 14 Britains. See also Norris and Armstrong, *The Maximum Surveillance Society*, 39, quoting a 1997 assessment offered in an article in the British newspaper *The Economist*: "Britain is leading the world in CCTV technology and its use. Precise figures are not available, but it appears that Britain now has more electronic eyes per head of population than any other country in the world, one-party states included ("The All-Seeing Eye," 52). See also Wardell, "4.2 Million Cameras Keep Eye on British."

30. Chris Horne ("The Case for: CCTV Should Be Introduced") states that one of the first systems was installed in 1961 in Cumbernauld, England. Norris and Armstrong (*The Maximum Surveillance Society*, 18) state that the first systems were launched in English retail stores in 1967. Chris Williams ("Police Surveillance and the Emergence of CCTV in the 1960s," 14) places the first police use of a CCTV system in Liverpool, England, in 1964.

31. Borg, "The Structure of Social Monitoring in the Process of Social Control," 287–288.

32. Wardell, "4.2 Million Cameras Keep Eye on British," "Britain Is 'Surveillance Society.'"

33. Newburn and Hayman, *Policing, Surveillance and Social Control*. Of course, the traditional criminal justice

system's inability to deal with crime is a mainstay of the entertainment media's content.

34. Goold, *CCTV and Policing*, 34–35.

35. Marx, *Undercover*; Fussey, "Observing Potentiality in the Global City," 173; Hier, Greenberg, Walby, and Lett, "Media, Communication and the Establishment," 734.

36. Norris, McCahill, and Wood, "The Growth of CCTV," 110–135.

37. Graham, "The Eyes Have It."

38. Fussey, "Beyond Liberty, Beyond Security," 120–135.

39. "The All-Seeing Eye," 52.

40. Bloss, "Escalating U.S. Police Surveillance after 9/11," 213.

41. Marx, *Undercover*.

42. Short and Ditton, *Does Closed Circuit Television Prevent Crime?* and "Seen and Now Heard."

43. Welsh and Farrington, "Evidence-Based Crime Prevention," 21.

44. Ratcliffe, Taniguchi, and Taylor, The Crime Reduction Effects of Public CCTV Cameras."

45. For research reviews see Gill, *CCTV*; Goold, *CCTV and Policing*; and Welsh and Farrington, "Crime Prevention Effects of Closed Circuit Television;" Welsh and Farrington, "Public Area CCTV and Crime Prevention."

46. For a general discussion of CCTV related issues see Lyon, *Theorizing the Panopticon and Beyond*.

47. Surette, "The Thinking Eye," 152.

48. Williams, "Effective CCTV," 104. See also Lomell, "Targeting the Unwanted," 3472–3561; Smith, "Behind the Screens," 376–395.

49. Surette, "CCTV and Citizen Guardianship Suppression," 100–125.

50. Hentschel, "Making (In)Visible," 300.

51. Brown, *CCTV in Town Centres*; Burrows, "Closed Circuit Television and Crime on the London Underground;" and Welsh and Farrington, "Crime Prevention Effects of Closed Circuit Television."

52. Tilley, "Understanding Car Parks, Crime and CCTV."

53. The Supreme Court's legal reasoning is summarized in United States v. Knotts 368 U.S. 276, 281–82 (1983): "A person traveling in an automobile on public thoroughfares has no reasonable expectation of privacy in his movements from one place to another. When [an individual] traveled over the public streets he voluntarily conveyed to anyone who wanted to look the fact that he was traveling over particular roads in a particular direction, and the fact of his final destination when he exited from public roads onto private property."

54. Sechrest, Liquori, and Perry, "Using Video Technology in Police Patrol."

55. Jefferis, Kaminski, Holmes, and Hanley, "The Effect of a Videotaped Arrest on Public Perceptions of Police Use of Force," 381; Weitzer, "Incidents of Police Misconduct and Public Opinion."

56. Parrish, "Police and the Media," 25.

57. Hentschel, "Making (In)Visible," 294.

58. "Americans OK with Video Scrutiny," CBS News Poll.

59. Fussey, "Observing Potentiality in the Global City," 171–192.

60. Surette, "The Thinking Eye," 152.

61. Allard, Wortley, and Stewart, "The Effect of CCTV on Prisoner Misbehavior," 404–422; Newburn and Hayman, *Policing, Surveillance and Social Control*.

62. Young, *The Exclusive Society*, 192.

Chapter 8

1. See Packer, *The Limits of the Criminal Sanction*.

2. Tajgman, "From Estes to Chandler," 509.

3. Altheide, "The Mass Media, Crime and Terrorism," 982–997; Hron, "Torture Goes Pop!," 22–30.

4. Mason, "Misinformation, Myth and Distortion," 491.

5. Roberts and Doob, "News Media Influences on Public Views on Sentencing," citing Canadian Sentencing Commission, *Sentencing in the Media.*

6. Iyengar, *Is Anyone Responsible?*

7. Graber, *Crime News and the Public.*

8. Beckett and Sasson, *The Politics of Injustice.*

9. Barrile, "Television and Attitudes about Crime;" Graber, *Crime News and the Public*, 73; and Sasson, *Crime Talk.*

10. Christie, "The Ideal Victim."

11. Altheide, *Creating Fear*, 146.

12. Sotirovic, "Affective and Cognitive Processes as Mediators of Media Influences on Crime-Policy Preferences," 311.

13. Rennie, *The Search for Criminal Man.*

14. McCombs, *Setting the Agenda.*

15. Lasorsa and Wanta, "Effects of Personal, Interpersonal and Media Experiences on Issue Saliences;" and Protess, Cook, Doppelt, Ettema, Gordon, Leff, and Miller, *The Journalism of Outrage.*

16. Rogers and Dearing, "Agenda-Setting Research."

17. Gerbner, Gross, Morgan, and Signorielli, "Growing Up with Television;" and Morgan and Shanahan, "Two Decades of Cultivation Research."

18. See, for example, Hirsch, "The 'Scary World,'" and "On Not Learning from One's Own Mistakes."

19. Grabe and Drew, "Crime Cultivations," 167; Hetsroni and Tukachinsky, "Television-world Estimates, Real-world Estimates," 134.

20. Banks, "Spaces of (in)security," 169–187.

21. Dowler, "Media Consumption and Public Attitudes toward Crime and Justice," 116. Valerie Callanan (*Feeding the Fear of Crime*), for example, found that in California heavy consumers of crime-related media are more fearful of crime, more likely to believe crime is increasing, more likely to rate crime as a serious problem, more likely to believe the world is "just," less likely to support rehabilitation, and much more likely to support three strikes sentencing.

22. Chadee and Ditton, "Fear of Crime and the Media," 322–332.

23. Heath and Petraitis, "Television Viewing and Fear of Crime." Specific media effects are discussed by Weitzer and Kubrin ("Breaking News," 516–518).

24. Sparks and Ogles, "The Difference Between Fear of Victimization and the Probability of Being Victimized."

25. See Ditton, Chadee, Farrall, Gilchrist, and Bannister, "From Imitation to Intimidation, 595–610; Eschholz, Chiricos, and Gertz, "Television and Fear of Crime;" and Lane and Meeker, "Ethnicity, Information Sources, and Fear of Crime."

26. Mason, "Misinformation, Myth and Distortion," 491.

27. Gillespie, McLaughlin, Adams, and Symmonds, *Media and the Shaping of Public Knowledge.*

28. Green, "Public Opinion versus Public Judgment," 132; Allen, "There Must Be Some Way of Dealing with Kids," 5.

29. Green, "Public Opinion versus Public Judgment," 141; Griffin and Miller, "Child Abduction, AMBER Alert, and Crime Control Theater,"159–175.

30. Surette, "Media Echoes."

31. Sacco and Silverman, "Selling Crime Prevention."

32. For example, Snell, Bailey, Carona, and Mebane ("School Crime Policy Changes," 208) report that highly publicized school crimes impact school policy decisions to install metal detectors and video cameras in distant states.

33. Green, "Public Opinion versus Public Judgment," 141.

34. Raney and Bryant ("Moral Judgment and Crime Drama," 402–415) argue that crime dramas contain implied pro and con statements about justice policies. The greater the enjoyment of the drama, the more likely an effect on judgments and support of those justice policy statements will appear.

35. Pfeiffer, Windzio, and Kleimann, "Media Use and Its impacts," 259–285.

36. Green, "Public Opinion versus Public Judgment," 144.

37. Altheide, "The Mass Media, Crime and Terrorism," 982-997; Fussey, "Beyond Liberty, Beyond Security," 124; Goidel, Freeman, and Procopio, "The Impact of Television Viewing on Perceptions of Juvenile Crime," 119–139; Ruddell and Decker, "Kids and Assault Weapons," 45–63.

38. Dardis, Baumgartner, Boydstun, De Boef, and Shen, "Media Framing of Capital Punishment," 15–16.

39. Mason, "Prison Decayed," 607-626; Mason, "Misinformation, Myth and Distortion," 491.

40. Reiner, "Media Made Criminality," 403.

41. Kupchik and Bracy, "The News Media on School Crime and Violence: Constructing Dangerousness and Fueling Fear," 152.

42. Altheide, *Creating Fear*, 137.

43. Bennett, *News*, 96.

Chapter 9

1. Sotirovic, "Affective and Cognitive Processes as Mediators of Media Influences on Crime-Policy Preferences," 313.

2. Gorelick, "Join Our War," 429.

3. Surette, Hansen, and Nobel, "Measuring Media Oriented Terrorism."

4. Manning, "Media Loops."

5. Penfold, "The Star's Image, Victimization and Celebrity Culture," 289.

6. For example, the success of the reality show *Survivor* resulted in a spate of copycat reality shows.

7. Mathiesen, "The Eagle and the Sun."

8. Grabe and Drew, "Crime Cultivations," 167.

9. Rushkoff, "Media: It's the Real Thing."

10. Meyrowitz, *No Sense of Place*, 319.

11. Valier, *Crime and Punishment in Contemporary Culture.* 149–150.

12. Richmond, "Can You Find Me Know," 283–319; Valier, *Crime and Punishment in Contemporary Culture*, 149.

13. Thomas, *Social Behavior and Personality*, 81.

14. Rapping, *Law and Justice as Seen on TV.*

15. Poyntz, "Homey I Shot the Kids," 8.

References

Adoni, H., and S. Mane. 1984. "Media and the Social Construction of Reality." *Communication Research 11*(3): 323–340.

Akers, R. L. 1998. *Social Learning and Social Structure: A General Theory of Crime and Deviance*. Athens, GA: Northeastern University Press.

Alexander, Y. 1979. "Terrorism and the Media: Some Considerations." In *Terrorism: Theory and Practice*, eds. Y. Alexander, D. Carlton, and P. Wilkinson, 159–174. Boulder, CO: Westview Press.

Allard, T., R. Wortley, and A. Stewart. 2008. "The Effect of CCTV on Prisoner Misbehavior." *The Prison Journal 88*(3): 404–422.

Allen, J., S. Livingstone, and R. Reiner. 1998. "True Lies: Changing Images of Crime in British Postwar Cinema." *European Journal of Communication 13*(1): 53–75.

Allen, R. 2002. "There Must Be Some Way of Dealing with Kids: Young Offenders, Public Attitudes and Policy Change." *Youth Justice 2*(1): 3–13.

Altheide, D. 2002. *Creating Fear*. Hawthorne, NY: Aldine de Gruyter.

Altheide, D. 2006. "The Mass Media, Crime and Terrorism." *Journal of International Criminal Justice 4*: 982–997.

Altheide, D., and R. Snow. 1991. *Media Worlds in the Postjournalism Era*. Hawthorne, NY: Aldine de Gruyter.

Ambrose, S. 2000. *Nothing Like It in the World*. New York: Simon & Schuster.

American Association of Advertising Agencies. 1990. *What We've Learned about Advertising from the Media-Advertising Partnership for a Drug-Free America*. New York: Author.

"Americans OK with Video Scrutiny." 2002. New York: CBS News Poll (April 21).

Anderson, C., D. Gentile, and K. Buckley. 2007. *Violent Video Game Effects on Children and Adolescents: Theory, Research, and Public Policy*. New York: Oxford University Press.

Anderson, C. 2004. "An Update on the Effects of Playing Violent Video Games." *Journal of Adolescence 27*(1): 113–122.

Anderson, J. 2008. "The Production of Media Violence and Aggression Research: A Cultural Analysis." *American Behavioral Scientist 51*(8): 1260–1279.

Arendt, S. 2007. "Teens Kill Child While Acting out Mortal Kombat." *Wired* Downloaded from http://www.wired.com/gamelife/2007/12/drunk-teens-kil

Armour, R. 1980. *Film*. Westport, CT: Greenwood Press.

Asimow, M., and S. Mader. 2004. *Law and Popular Culture*. New York: Peter Lang.

Brants, K., and P. Neijens. 1998. "The Infotainment of Politics." *Political Communication* 15(2): 149–164.

Bailey, S., A. Carona, and D. Mebane. 2002. "School Crime Policy Changes: The Impact of Recent Highly-Publicized School Crimes." *American Journal of Criminal Justice* 26(2): 280–285.

Bailey, F., and D. Hale, 2004 *Blood on Her Hands: Women Who Murder*. Belmont, CA: Wadsworth.

Bailey, F., J. M. Pollock, and S. Schroeder. 1998. "The Best Defense: Images of Female Attorneys in Popular Films." In *Popular Culture, Crime and Justice*, eds. F. Bailey and D. Hale, 180–195. Belmont, CA: Wadsworth.

Bailey, S. M. 1993. "Fast Forward to Violence." *Criminal Justice Matters* 11: 1, 6–7.

Ball, M. 1981. *The Promise of American Law*. Athens, GA: University of Georgia Press.

Bandura, A. 1973. *Aggression: A Social Learning Analysis*. Englewood Cliffs, NJ: Prentice-Hall.

Banks, M. 2005. "Spaces of (In)security: Media and Fear of Crime in a Local Context." *Crime Media Culture* 1(2): 169–187.

Barber, S. 1987. *News Cameras in the Courtroom*. Norwood, NJ: Ablex.

Barrile, L. 1984. "Television and Attitudes about Crime: Do Heavy Viewers Distort Criminality and Support Retributive Justice?" In *Justice and the Media*, ed. Ray Surette, 141–158. Springfield, IL: Thomas.

Beckett, K., and T. Sasson. 2000. *The Politics of Injustice: Crime and Punishment in America*. Thousand Oaks, CA: Pine Forge Press.

Bennet, W. L. 1996. *News: The Politics of Illusion*. New York: Longman.

Bennett, J. 2006. "The Good, the Bad and the Ugly: The Media in Prison Films." *The Howard Journal* 45(2): 97–115.

Berger, J. 2009. "Giuliani Criticizes Terror Trials in New York." *The New York Times*, November 16. Downloaded January 26, 2010 from http://www.nytimes.com/.

Berkowitz, L. 1984. "Some Effects of Thoughts on Anti- and Prosocial Influences of Media Events: A Cognitive-Neoassociation Analysis." *Psychological Bulletin* 95: 410–417.

Berkowitz, L., and K. Rogers. 1986. "A Priming Effect Analysis of Media Influences." In *Perspectives on Media Effects*, eds. J. Bryant and D. Zillman, 57–81. Hillsdale, NJ: Erlbaum.

Best, J. 1991. *Images of Issues: Typifying Contemporary Social Problems*. New York: Aldine de Gruyter.

Best, J. 2001. "The Diffusion of Social Problems." In *How Claims Spread: Cross- National Diffusion of Social Problems*, ed. J. Best, 1–18. New York: Aldine de Gruyter.

Best, J., and M. Hutchinson. 1996. "The Gang Initiation Rite as a Motif in Contemporary Crime Discourse." *Justice Quarterly* 13: 383–404.

Bing, R. 2010. *Race, Crime, and the Media*. New York: McGraw Hill.

Black, G. 1988. *Changing Attitudes Toward Drug Use: Executive Summary and Statistical Report*. Rochester, NY: Partnership for a Drug-Free America.

Bleyer, W. 1927. *Main Currents in the History of American Journalism*. Boston: Houghton Mifflin.

Bloss, W. 2007. "Escalating U.S. Police Surveillance after 9/11: An Examination of Causes and Effects." *Surveillance and Society* 4(3): 208–228.

Blumer, H. 1933. *The Movies and Conduct.* New York: Macmillan.

Blumer, H., and P. Hauser. 1933. *Movies, Delinquency, and Crime.* New York: Macmillan.

Bond-Maupin, L. 1998. "'That Wasn't Even Me They Showed': Women as Criminals on *America's Most Wanted.*" *Violence Against Women* 4(1): 30–44.

Borg, M. 1997. "The Structure of Social Monitoring in the Process of Social Control." *Deviant Behavior* 18: 273–293.

Bortner, M. A. 1984. "Media Images and Public Attitudes toward Crime and Justice." In *Justice and the Media*, ed. R. Surette, 15–30. Springfield, IL: Thomas.

Boyle. K. 2005. *Media and Violence: Gendering the Debates.* Thousand Oaks, CA: Sage.

Brants, K., and P. Neijens. 1998. "The Infotainment of Politics." *Political Communication* 15: 149–164.

"Britain Is 'Surveillance Society.'" BBC News. Downloaded Jan 13, 2010 from http://news.bbc.co.uk/2/hi/uk_news/6108496.stm

Britton, D. M. 2003. *At Work in the Iron Cage: The Prison as Gendered Organization.* New York: New York University Press.

Broe, D. 2003. "Class, Crime, and Film Noir." *Social Justice* 30(1): 22–41.

Brown, B. 1995. *CCTV in Town Centres: Three Case Studies. Police Research Group Crime Detection and Prevention Series*, paper no 68. London: Home Office Police Department.

Brown, B., and W.R. Benedict. 2002. "Perceptions of the Police." *Policing* 25(3): 543–580.

Browne, K., and C. Hamilton-Giachritsis. 2005. "The Influence of Violent Media on Children and Adolescents: A Public-health Approach." *Lancet* 365: 701–710.

Bruschke, J., and W. Loges. 2004. *Free Press vs. Fair Trials.* Mahwah, NJ: Erlbaum.

Burns, R. 2007. "Media Portrayal of White-Collar Crime." In *Encyclopedia of White-Collar Crime,* eds. J. Gerber and E. Jensen, 182–184. Westport, CT: Greenwood Press.

Burrows, J. 1980. "Closed Circuit Television and Crime on the London Underground." In *Designing Out Crime,* eds. R. Clarke and P. Mayhew, 75–83. London: H. M. Stationery Office for Home Office Research Unit.

Callanan, V. 2005. *Feeding the Fear of Crime: Crime-related Media and Support for Three Strikes.* New York: LFB Scholarly Publishing LLC.

Campbell, J. 2007. "Journalists Should Demand Prison Access." *Quill* 95(4): 34.

Canter, C., P. Sheehan, P. Alpers, and P. Mullen. 1999. "Media and Mass Homicides." *Archives of Suicide Research* 5: 283–290.

Carpenter, S., S. Lacy, and F. Fico. 2006. "Network News Coverage of High-profile Crime during 2004: A Study of Source Use and Reporter Context." *Journalism and Mass Communication Quarterly* 83(4): 901–916.

Carrabine, E. 2008. *Crime, Culture and the Media.* Cambridge, UK: Polity Press.

Cavalli, E. 2007. "Chinese Teen Burns Classmate, Blames World of Warcraft." *Wired.* http://www.wired.com/gamelife/2007/12/chinese-teen-bu/

Cavender, G. 1998. "In the Shadow of Shadows: Television Reality Crime Programming." In *Entertaining Crime: Television Reality Programs,* ed. M. Fishman and G. Cavender, 79–94. New York: Aldine de Gruyter.

Cavender, G. 2004. "In Search of Community on Reality TV." In *Understanding Reality*, eds. S. Homes and D. Jermyn, 154–172. New York: Routledge.

Cavender, G., and M. Fishman. 1998. "Television Reality Crime Programs: Context and History." In *Entertaining Crime: Television Reality Programs*, eds. M. Fishman and G. Cavender, 3–15. New York: Aldine De Gruyter.

Cavender, G., and A. Mulcahy. 1998. "Trial by Fire: Media Constructions of Corporate Deviance." *Justice Quarterly 15*: 697–717.

Cavender, G., and S. Deutsch. 2007. "CSI and Moral Authority: The Police and Science." *Crime Media Culture 31*(1): 67–81.

Cecil, D. 2007. "Doing Time in Camp Cupcake: Lessons Learned from Newspaper Accounts of Martha Stewart's Incarceration." *Journal of Criminal Justice and Popular Culture, 14*(2): 142–160.

Cecil, D. 2007. "Dramatic Portrayals of Violent Women: Female Offenders on Prime Time Crime Dramas." *Journal of Criminal Justice and Popular Culture 14*(3): 243–258.

Cecil, D. 2007. "Looking Beyond Caged Heat: Media Images of Women in Prison." *Feminist Criminology 2*(4): 304–326.

Chadee, D., and J. Ditton. 2005. "Fear of Crime and the Media: Assessing the Lack of Relationship." *Crime Media Culture 1*(3): 322–332.

Chandler v. Florida, 101 S. Ct. 1981.

Charter, W. 1933. *Motion Pictures and Youth: A Summary*. New York: Macmillan.

Cheatwood, D. 1998. "Prison Movies: Films about Adult, Male, Civilian Prisons; 1929–1995." In *Popular Culture, Crime, and Justice*, eds. F. Bailey and D. Hale, 209–231. Belmont, CA: Wadsworth.

Cheatwood, D. 2001. "Early Images of Crime and Criminal Justice: Commercial Radio from 1929 to 1962." Paper presented at the American Society of Criminology, Atlanta, GA.

Chermak, S. 1995. *Victims in the News*. Boulder, CO: Westview Press.

Chermak, S. 1998. "Police, Courts, and Corrections in the Media." In *Popular Culture, Crime and Justice*, eds. F. Bailey and D. Hale, 87–99. Belmont, CA: Wadsworth.

Chermak, S., and J. Gruenewald. 2006. "The Media's Coverage of Domestic Terrorism." *Justice Quarterly 23*(4): 428–461.

Chibnall, S. 1980. "Chronicles of the Gallows: The Social History of Crime Reporting." In *The Sociology of Journalism and the Press*, ed. H. Christian, 179–217. Lanham, MD: Rowman & Littlefield.

Chibnall, S. 1981. "The Production of Knowledge by Crime Reporters." In *The Manufacture of News*, eds. S. Cohen and J. Young, 75–97. Thousand Oaks, CA: Sage.

Christie, N. 1986. "The Ideal Victim." In *From Crime Policy to Victim Policy: Reorienting the Justice System*, ed. E. A. Fattah, 17–30. New York: St. Martin's Press.

Ciasullo, A. 2008. "Containing Deviant Desire: Lesbianism, Heterosexuality and the Women-in-prison Narrative." *Journal of Popular Culture 41*(2): 195–223.

Claxton, G. 2005. "Joining the Intentional Dance." In *Perspectives on Imitation: From Neuroscience to Social Science*. Vol. 2 Imitation, Human Development, and Culture, eds. S. Hurley and N. Chater, 193–196. Cambride, MA: MIT Press.

Clowers, M. 2001. "Dykes, Gangs, and Danger: Debunking Popular Myths about Maximum Security Life." *Journal of Criminal Justice and Popular Culture 9*(1): 22–30.

Cohen, S., and J. Young. 1981. *The Manufacture of News.* Thousand Oaks, CA: Sage.

Cole, J. 1996. *The UCLA Television Violence Monitoring Report.* Los Angeles: UCLA Center for Communication Policy.

Coleman, J. 2006. *The Criminal Elite.* New York: Worth Publishers.

Conrich, I. 2003. "Mass Media/Mass Murder: Serial Killer Cinema and the Modern Violated Body." In *Criminal Visions: Media Representations of Crime and Justice*, ed. P. Mason, 156–171. Devon, UK: Willan.

Cook, T., D. Kendzierski, and S. Thomas. 1983. "The Implicit Assumptions of Television Research: An Analysis of the 1982 NIMH Report on Television and Behavior." *Public Opinion Quarterly* 47: 161–201.

Courtwright, D. 1996. *Violent Land: Single Men and Social Disorder from the Frontier to the Inner City.* Cambridge: Harvard University Press.

Coyne, S. 2007. "Does Media Violence Cause Violent Crime?" *European Journal of Criminal Policy Research* 13: 205–211.

Curran, J. 1982. "Communications, Power and Social Order." In *Culture, Society and the Media*, eds. M, Gurevitch, T. Bennett, J. Curran, and J. Woollacott, 202–235. London: Methuen.

Curtis, J. 1953. "Gabriel Tarde." In *Social Theorists,* ed. C. Mihanovich, 142–157. Milwaukee, WI: Bruce Publishing.

Dale, E. 1935. *Children's Attendance at Motion Pictures.* New York: Macmillan.

Dalglish, L. 2005. "Protecting Reporters Who Protect Sources. *Nieman Reports* 59(2): 30–32.

Dardis, F., F. Baumgartner, A. Boydstun, S. De Boef, and F. Shen. 2008. "Media Framing of Capital Punishment and Its Impact on Individuals' Cognitive Responses." *Mass Communication and Society 11*: 115–140.

Davis, A. 2003. *Are Prisons Obselete?* London: Open Media.

DeFleur, M., and S. Ball-Rokeach. 1975. *Theories of Mass Communication.* New York: McKay.

Dijksterhuis, A., and J. Bargh. 2001. "The Perception–Behavior Expressway: Automatic Effects of Social Perception on Social Behavior." In *Advances in Experimental Social Psychology*, vol *30*, ed. M. Zanna, 1–40. New York: Academic Press.

Ditton, J., D. Chadee, S. Farrall, E. Gilchrist, and J. Bannister. 2004. "From Imitation to Intimidation." *British Journal of Criminology* 44(4): 595–610.

Dixon, R., and K. Maddox. 2005. "Skin Tone, Crime News, and Social Reality Judgments: Priming the Stereotype of the Dark and Dangerous Black Criminal." *Journal of Applied Social Psychology 38*: 1555–1570.

Dixon, T., C. Azocar, and M. Casas. 2003. "The Portrayal of Race and Crime on Television Network News." *Journal of Broadcasting and Electronic Media 47*: 495–520.

Dixon, T. 2008. "Crime News and Radicalized Beliefs: Understanding the Relationship Between Local News Viewing and Perceptions of African Americans and Crime." *Journal of Communication 58*: 106–125.

Dixon, T., and D. Linz. 2000. "Overrepresentation and Underrepresentation of Victimization on Local Television News." *Communication Research 27*: 547–573.

Dominick, J. 1978. "Crime and Law Enforcement in the Mass Media." In *Deviance and Mass Media*, ed. C. Winick, 105–128. Thousand Oaks, CA: Sage.

Donovan, P. 1998. "Armed with the Power of Television: Reality Crime Programming and the Reconstruction of Law and Order in the United States." In *Entertaining Crime*, eds. M. Fishman and G. Cavender, 117–140. New York: Aldine de Gruyter.

Dowler, K. 2003. "Media Consumption and Public Attitudes toward Crime and Justice: The Relationship Between Fear of Crime, Punitive Attitudes, and Perceived Police Effectiveness." *Journal of Criminal Justice and Popular Culture* 10(2): 109–126.

Dowler, K. 2004. "Comparing American and Canadian Local Television Crime Stories: A Content Analysis" *Canadian Journal of Criminology and Criminal Justice* 46(5): 573–596.

Dowler, K., T. Fleming, and S. Muzzatti. 2006. "Constructing Crime: Media Crime and Popular Culture." *Canadian Journal of Criminology and Criminal Justice* 48(6): 837–850.

Doyle, A. 1998. "Cops: Television Policing as Policing Reality." In *Entertaining Crime*, eds. M. Fishman and G. Cavender, 95–116. New York: Aldine de Gruyter.

Doyle, A. 2003. *Arresting Images: Crime and Policing in Front of the Television Camera*. Toronto: University of Toronto Press.

Doyle, A., and R. Ericson. 1996. "Breaking into Prison: News Sources and Correctional Institutions." *Canadian Journal of Criminology* 38: 155–190.

Drechsel, R. 1983. *News Making in the Trial Courts*. White Plains, NY: Longman.

Drucker, S. 1989. "The Televised Mediated Trial: Formal and Substantive Characteristics." *Communication Quarterly* 37: 305–318.

Duffy, S. 2002. *Closing the Net: How They Cracked the Case*, CNN, October 25, Posted: 8:28 AM EDT downloaded from //archives.cnn.com/2002/US/ South/10/24/sniper.case.cracked/index.html

Dutelle, A. 2006. "The CSI Effect and Your Department." *Law & Order* 54(5): 113–114.

Duwe, G. 2000. "Body-Count Journalism: The Presentation of Mass Murder in the News Media." *Homicide Studies* 4(4): 364–399.

Ericson, R., P. Baranek, and J. Chan. 1987. *Visualizing Deviance*. Toronto: University of Toronto Press.

Ericson, R., P. Baranek, and J. Chan. 1989. *Negotiating Control: A Study of News Sources*. Toronto: University of Toronto Press.

Ericson, R., P. Baranek, and J. Chan. 1991. *Representing Law and Order: Crime, Law, and Justice in the News Media*. Toronto: University of Toronto Press.

Eschholz, S., T. Chiricos, and M. Gertz. 2003. "Television and Fear of Crime: Program Types, Audience Traits and the Mediating Effect of Perceived Neighborhood Racial Composition." *Social Problems* 50(3): 395–415.

Escholz, S., M. Mallard, and S. Flynn. 2004. "Images of Prime Time Justice: A Content Analysis of *NYPD Blue* and *Law & Order*." *Journal of Criminal Justice and Popular Culture* 10(3): 161–180.

Estes v. Texas, 381 U.S. (1965).

Fargo, A. L. 2006. "Analyzing Federal Shield Law Proposals: What Congress Can Learn from the States." *Communication Law and Policy* 11(1): 35–82.

Ferguson, C. J. 2002. "Media Violence: Miscast Causality." *American Psychologist* 57: 446–47.

Ferrel, J. 1998. "Criminalizing Popular Culture." In *Popular Culture, Crime, and Justice*, eds. F. Bailey and D. Hale, 71–83. Belmont, CA: Wadsworth.

Fisher, J. 1997. *Killer Among Us: Public Reactions to Serial Murder*. Westport, CT: Praeger

Fishman, M., and G. Cavender. 1998. *Entertaining Crime: Television Reality Programs.* New York: Aldine de Gruyter.

Flew, T. 2002. *New Media: An Introduction,* South Melbourne, Australia: Oxford University Press.

Foucault, M. 1972. *The Archaeology of Knowledge.* London: Tavistock Press.

Fox, R., R. van Sickel, and T. Steiger. 2007. *Tabloid Justice.* Bolder, CO: Lynne Rienner Pub.

Franklin, B. 2006. *Local Journalism and Local Media: Making the Local News.* London: Routledge.

Fleming, P., and S. Zyglidopoulos. 2009. *Charting Corporate Corruption.* Northampton, MA: Edward Elgar Pub.

Freedman, J. 2002. *Media Violence and Its Effect on Aggression.* Toronto: University of Toronto Press.

Freeman, R. 1998. "Public Perception and Corrections: Correctional Officers as Smug Hacks." In *Popular Culture, Crime, and Justice,* eds. F. Bailey and D. Hale, 196–208. Belmont, CA: Wadsworth.

Freeman, R. 2000. *Popular Culture and Corrections.* Lanham, MD: American Correctional Association.

Friedrichs, D. 2004. *Trusted Criminals: White Collar Crime in Contemporary Society.* Belmont, CA: Thomson.

Fussey, P. 2007. "Observing Potentiality in the Global City." *International Criminal Justice Review* 17(3): 171–192.

Fussey, P. 2008. "Beyond Liberty, Beyond Security: The Politics of Public Surveillance." *British Politics* 3: 120–135.

Gans, H. 1979. *Deciding What's News.* New York: Pantheon.

Garland, D. 2001. *The Culture of Control.* Oxford, UK: Oxford University Press.

Geis, G. 2007. *White-Collar and Corporate Crime.* Upper Saddle River, NJ: Pearson Prentice-Hall.

Gerber, J., and E. Jensen. 2007. *Encyclopedia of White-Collar Crime.* Westport CT: Greenwood Press.

Gerbner, G., L. Gross, M. Morgan, and N. Signorielli. 1994. "Growing Up with Television: The Cultivation Perspective." In *Media Effects,* eds. B. Jennings and D. Zillman, 17–41. Hillsdale, NJ: Erlbaum.

Gergen, K. 1985. "Social Constructionist Inquiry: Context and Implications." In *The Social Construction of the Person,* eds. K. Gergen and K. Davis, 3–18. New York: Springer-Verlag.

Gerstein, J. 2009. *New York Terrorist Trial Raises Stake.* November 13, Downloaded January 23, 2010 from http://www.politico.com/new/stories/1109/29486.html.

Getty, C. 2001. "Media Wise." *Corrections Today* 63(7): 126–131.

Gill, M. 2003. *CCTV.* Leicester, UK: Perpetuity Press.

Gill, M., and K. Loveday. 2003. "What Do Offenders Think about CCTV?" *Crime Prevention and Community Safety* 5(3): 17–25.

Gillespie, M., E. McLaughlin, S. Adams, and A. Symmonds. 2003. *Media and the Shaping of Public Knowledge and Attitudes Towards Crime and Punishment.* London: Esmee Fairbairn Foundation. Downloaded April 6, 2010 from http://www.Rethinking.org.uk/latest/pdf/briefing4.pdf.

Gilliam, F., and S. Iyengar. 2000. "Prime Suspects: The Influence of Local Television News on the Viewing Public." *American Journal of Political Science* 44(3): 560–573.

Gillis, C. 2005 (November 7) "New Crime Shows Educate Criminals." *Maclean's Magazine.* Downloaded from www.thecanadianencyclopedia.com/index.cfm? PgNm=TCE& Params=M1ARTM0012851

Gladwell, M. 2005. *Blink.* New York: Little, Brown

Glaser, D. 1956. "Criminality Theories and Behavioral Images." *American Journal of Sociology 61*(5): 433–444.

Goff, C. 2001. "The Westray Mine Disaster: Media Coverage of a Corporate Crime in Canada." In *Contemporary Issues in Crime and Criminal Justice*, eds. H. N. Potell and D. Schichor, 195–217. Upper Saddle River, NJ: Prentice-Hall.

Goidel, R., C. Freeman, and S. Procopio. 2006. "The Impact of Television Viewing on Perceptions of Juvenile Crime." *Journal of Broadcasting and Electronic Media, 50*(1): 119–139.

Goldman, A. 2005. "Imitation, Mind Reading, and Simulation." In *Perspectives on Imitation: From Neuroscience to Social Science.* Vol. 2, Imitation, Human Development, and Culture, eds. S. Hurley and N. Chater, 79–94. Cambride, MA: MIT Press.

Goold, B. 2004. *CCTV and Policing.* Oxford, UK: Oxford University Press.

Gordon, M., and L. Heath. 1981. "The News Business, Crime, and Fear." In *Reactions to Crime*, ed. D. Lewis, 227–247. Thousand Oaks, CA: Sage.

Gorelick, S. 1989. "Join Our War: The Construction of Ideology in a Newspaper Crimefighting Campaign." *Crime and Delinquency 35*: 421–436.

Gorn, E. 1992. "The Wicked World: The National Police Gazette and Gilded-Age America." *Media Studies Journal 6*: 3–4.

Grabe, M., and D. Drew. 2007. "Crime Cultivations: Comparisons across Media Genres and Channels." *Journal of Broadcasting and Electronic Media 51*(1): 147–171.

Graber, D. 1980. *Crime News and the Public.* New York: Praeger.

Graber, D. 1994. "The Infotainment Quotient in Routine Television News: A Director's Perspective." *Discourse and Society 5*: 483–509.

Graham, S. 1999. "The Eyes Have It—CCTV as the 'Fifth Utility'." *Town and Country Planning 68*: 312–315.

Grant, A. 1990. "The Videotaping of Police Interrogations in Canada." In *The Media and Criminal Justice Policy*, ed. R. Surette, 265–276. Springfield, IL: Thomas.

Green, D. 2005. "Public Opinion versus Public Judgment about Crime." *British Journal of Criminology 46*: 131–154.

Green, M., and T. Brock. 2000. "The Role of Transportation in the Persuasiveness of Public Narratives. *Journal of Personality and Social Psychology 79*(3): 701–721.

Greenfield, S., and G. Osborn. 2003. "Film Lawyers: Above and Beyond the Law." In *Criminal Visions: Media Representations of Crime and Justice*, ed. P. Mason, 238–253. Devon, UK: W. H. A.

Greer, C. 2003. *Sex Crime and the Media.* Cullompton, UK: Willan.

Greer, C. 2006. "Delivering Death: Capital Punishment, Botched Executions and the American News Media." In *Captured by the Media: Prison Discourse in Popular Culture*, ed. P. Mason, 84–102. Cullompton, UK: Willan.

Greer, C. 2009. *Crime and Media: A Reader.* London, UK: Routledge.

Grey, S., and D. Carvajal. 2007. "Secret Prisons in 2 Countries Held Qaeda Suspects, Report Says." *The New York Times.* June 8: A12. Downloaded January 19, 2010 from http:// proquest.umi.com/.

Griffin, T., and M. Miller. 2008. "Child Abduction, AMBER Alert, and Crime Control Theater." *Criminal Justice Review 33*(2): 159–176.

Grimes, T., J. Anderson, and L. Bergen. 2008. *Media Violence and Aggression: Science and Ideology.* Thousand Oaks, CA: Sage.

Grochowski, T. 2006. "Running in Cyberspace." *Television and New Media* 7(4): 361–382.

Grodal, T. 2003. "Stories for Eye, Ear and Muscles." In *The Video Game Theory Reader*, eds. M. Wolf and B. Perron, 129–155. New York: Routledge.

Grodal, T. 2003. "Video Games and the Pleasures of Control." In *Media Entertainment*, eds. D. Zillmann and P. Vorderer, 197–212. Mahwah, NJ: Erlbaum.

Gunter, B. 2008. "Media Violence: Is There a Case for Causality?" *American Behavioral Scientist* 51(8): 1061–1122.

Hagell, A., and T. Newburn. 1994. *Young Offenders and the Media: Viewing Habits and Preferences*. London: Policy Studies Institute.

Haggerty, K., and A. Gozso. 2005. "Seeing Beyond the Ruins: Surveillance as a Response to Terrorist Threats." *Canadian Journal of Sociology* 30(2), 169–187.

Hale, D. 1998. "Keeping Women in Their Place: An Analysis of Policewomen in Video, 1972–1996. In *Popular Culture, Crime and Justice.*, eds. F. Bailey and D. Hale, 159–179. Belmont, CA: Wadsworth.

Hall, S., C. Chritcher, T. Jefferson, J. Clarke, and B. Roberts. 1981. "The Social Production of News: Mugging in the Media." In *The Manufacture of News*, eds. S. Cohen and J. Young, 335–367. Thousand Oaks, CA: Sage.

Hallett, M., and D. Powell. 1995. "Backstage with COPS: The Dramaturgical Reification of Police Subculture in American Crime Infotainment." *American Journal of Police* 14(1): 101–129.

Hamm, M. 2008. "Prisoner Radicalization: Assessing the Threat in U.S. Correctional Institutions." *NIJ Journal* 261:14-19. Washington, DC: National Institute of Justice.

Harding R. 1996. "Celluloid Death: Cinematic Depictions of Capital Punishment." *University of San Francisco Law Review 30*(4): 1167–1179.

Hariman, R. 1990. "Performing the Laws: Popular Trials and Social Knowledge." In *Popular Trials: Rhetoric, Mass Media, and the Law*, ed. R. Hariman, 17–30. Tuscaloosa: University of Alabama Press.

Hayes, M. 2003. "Political Violence, Irish Republicanism and the British Media: Semantics, Symbosis and the State." In *Criminal Visions: Media Representations of Crime and Justice*, ed. P. Mason, 133–155. Devon, UK: Willan.

Hays, W. H. 1932. *President's Report to the Motion Picture Producers and Distributors' Association*. Washington, DC: U.S. Government Printing Office.

Heath, L., L. Bresolin, and R. Rinaldi. 1969. "Effects of Media Violence on Children: A Review of the Literature." *Archives of General Psychiatry 46*: 376–379.

Heath, L., and J. Petraitis. 1987. "Television Viewing and Fear of Crime: Where Is the Mean World?" *Basic and Applied Social Psychology* 8: 97–123.

Heller, M., and S. Polsky. 1976. *Studies in Violence and Television*. New York: American Broadcasting Company.

Hennigan, K., L. Heath, J. D. Wharton, M. Del Rosario, T. Cook, and B. Calder. 1982. "Impact of the Introduction of Television on Crime in the United States." *Journal of Personality and Social Psychology 42*: 461–477.

Hentschel, C. 2007. "Making (In)Visible: CCTV, Living Cameras, and Their Objects in a Post-Apartheid Metropolis, *International Criminal Justice review* 17(4): 289–303.

Herbert, R. 1999. *Oxford Companion to Crime and Mystery Writing*. Oxford, UK: Oxford University Press.

Hersh, S. 2004. *Chain of Command: The Road from 9/11 to Abu Ghraib*. New York: Harper Collins.

Hetsroni, A., and R. Tukachinsky. 2006. "Television-world Estimates, Real-world Estimates, and Television Viewing: A New Scheme for Cultivation." *Journal of Communication* 56: 133–156.

Hickey, E. 2004. *Serial Murderers and Their Victims.* Belmont, CA: Wadsworth.

Hier, S., J. Greenberg, K. Walby, and D. Lett. 2007. "Media, Communication and the Establishment of Public Camera Surveillance Programmes in Canada." *Media, Culture and Society* 29(5): 727–751.

Hirsch, P. 1980. "The 'Scary World' of the Nonviewer and Other Anomalies." *Communications Research* 7: 403–456.

Hirsch, P. 1981. "On Not Learning from One's Own Mistakes: A Reanalysis of Gerbner et al.'s Findings on Cultivation Analysis, Part II." *Communications Research* 8: 3–37.

Hochstetler, A. 2001. "Reporting of Executions in U.S. Newspapers." *Journal of Crime and Justice* 24(1): 1–11.

Holaday, P., and G. Stoddard. 1933. *Getting Ideas from the Movies.* New York: Macmillan.

Holden, R. 1986. "The Contagiousness of Aircraft Hijacking." *American Journal of Sociology* 91(4): 874–904.

Horne, C. 1996. "The Case for: CCTV Should Be Introduced." *International Journal of Risk, Security and Crime Prevention* 1(4): 317–326.

Hron, M. 2008. "Torture Goes Pop!" *Peace Review* 20(1): 22–30.

Huesmann, L. R. 1986. "Psychological Process Promoting the Relation Between Exposure to Media Violence and Aggressive Behavior by the Viewer." *Journal of Social Issues* 42(3): 125–139.

Huesmann, L. R. 2007. "The Impact of Electronic Media Violence: Scientific Theory and Research." *Journal of Adolescent Health* 41: 6–13.

Huesmann, L. R. 1998. "The Role of Social Information Processing and Cognitive Schema in the Acquisition and Maintenance of Habitual Aggressive Behavior." In *Human Aggression,* eds. R. Geen and E. Donnerstein, 73–109. New York: Academic Press.

Huesmann, L. R., and L. Taylor. 2006. "The Role of Media Violence in Violent Behavior." *Annual Review Public Health* 27: 393–415.

Huesmann, L. R., J. Moise-Titus, C. Podolski, and L. Eron. 2003. "Longitudinal Relations Between Children's Exposure to TV Violence and Their Aggressive and Violent Behavior in Young Adulthood: 1977–1992." *Developmental Psychology* 39(1): 201–221.

Hughes, H. 1940. *News and the Human Interest Story.* Chicago: University of Chicago Press.

Hunter, S. 1988. "Terrorists in Prison: Security Concerns and Management Strategies." *Corrections Today* 50(4): 30, 32, 34.

Ibarra, P., and J. Kitsuse. 1993. "Vernacular Constituents of Moral Discourse: An Interactionist Proposal for the Study of Social Problems." In *Reconsidering Social Construction,* eds. J. Holstein and G. Miller, 25–58. New York: Aldine de Gruyter.

Inciardi, J. and J. Dee. 1987. "From the Keystone Cops to Miami Vice: Images of Policing in American Popular Culture." *Journal of Popular Culture* 21: 84–102.

Innes, M. 2003. "'Signal Crimes': Detective Work, Mass Media and Constructing Collective Memory." In *Criminal Visions: Media Representations of Crime and Justice,* ed. P. Mason, 13–32. Cullompton, UK: Willan.

Innes, M. 2004. "Signal Crimes and Signal Disorders: Notes on Deviance as Communicative Action." *British Journal of Sociology* 55(3): 335–355.

Isaacs, N. 1961. "The Crime of Crime Reporting." *Crime and Delinquency* 7: 312–320.

Iyengar, S. 1991. *Is Anyone Responsible? How Television Frames Political Issues.* Chicago: University of Chicago Press.

Jacobs, J., and H. Brooks. 1983. "The Mass Media and Prison News." In *New Perspectives on Prisons and Imprisonment,* ed. James B. Jacobs, 106–115. Ithaca, NY: Cornell University Press.

Jarvis, B. 2007. "Monsters Inc.: Serial Killers and Consumer Culture." *Crime Media Culture 3:* 326–344.

Jefferis, E., R. Kaminski, S. Holmes, and D. Hanley. 1997. "The Effect of a Videotaped Arrest on Public Perceptions of Police Use of Force." *Journal of Criminal Justice 25*(5): 381–395.

Jenkins, P. 1994. *Using Murder: The Social Construction of Serial Murder.* Hawthorne, NY: Aldine De Gruyter.

Jenkins, P. 1998. *Moral Panic: Changing Concepts of the Child Molester in Modern America.* New Haven, CT: Yale University Press.

Jewkes, Y. 2004. *Media and Crime.* London, UK: Sage.

Jo, E., and L. Berkowitz. 1994. "A Priming Effect Analysis of Media Influences: An Update." In *Media Effects Advances in Theory and Research,* eds. J. Bryant and D. Zillman. Hillsdale, NJ: Erlbaum.

Johnson, J., P. Cohen, E. Smailes, S. Kasen, and J. Brook. 2002. "Television Viewing and Aggressive Behavior during Adolescence and Adulthood." *Science 295:* 2468–2471.

Johnston, J., D. Hawkins, and A. Michner. 1994. "Homicide Reporting in Chicago Dailies." *Journalism Quarterly* 71: 860–872.

Jones, E. T. 1976. "The Press as Metropolitan Monitor." *Public Opinion Quarterly 40:* 239–244.

Kaplan, J., and J. Skolnick. 1982. *Criminal Justice.* Mineola, NY: Foundation Press.

Kieby, D. 2003. "Prison Life Through a Lens." *Prison Service News 215:* 22–23.

Kiousis, S. 2002. "Interactivity: A Concept Explication." *New Media and Society 4*(3): 355–383.

Kirtley, J. 1990. "Shield Laws and Reporter's Privilege—A National Assessment." In *The Media and Criminal Justice Policy,* ed. R. Surette, 163–176. Springfield, IL: Thomas.

Kirtley, J. 1995. "A Leap Not Supported by History: The Continuing Story of Cameras in the Federal Courts." *Government Information Quarterly 12:* 367–389.

Kooistra, P., J. Mahoney, and S. Westervelt. 1998. "The World of Crime According to Cops." In *Entertaining Crime: Television Reality Programs,* eds. M. Fishman and G. Cavender, 141–158. New York: Aldine de Gruyter.

Kupchik, A., and N. Bracy. 2009. "The News Media on School Crime and Violence: Constructing Dangerousness and Fueling Fear." *Youth Violence and Juvenile Justice 7:* 136–155.

Lackey, C. 2001. "Visualizing White-Collar Crime Generic Imagery in Popular Film." *Visual Sociology 16*(2): 75–93.

Lane, J., and J. Meeker. 2003. "Ethnicity, Information Sources, and Fear of Crime." *Deviant Behavior 24:* 1–26.

Langer, G. 2004. *Legacy of Suspicion.* New York: ABC News Poll, July.

Lasorsa, D., and W. Wanta. 1990. "Effects of Personal, Interpersonal and Media Experiences on Issue Saliences." *Journalism Quarterly 67:* 804–813.

Latanya, A. C., and N. Abeles. 2009. "Ethics, Prisoner Interrogation, national Security, and the Media." *Psychological Services 6*(1): 11–21.

Lavrakas, P., D. Rosenbaum, and A. Lurigio. 1990. "Media Cooperation with Police: The Case of Crime Stoppers." In *Media and Criminal Justice Policy*, ed. R. Surette, 225–242. Springfield, IL: Thomas.

Lawrence, R. 2000. *The Politics of Force: Media and the Construction of Police Brutality*. Berkeley, CA: University of California Press.

Leishman, F., and P. Mason. 2003. *Policing and the Media: Facts, Fictions, and Factions*. Devon, UK: Willan.

Leitch, T., 2002. *Crime Films*. Cambridge, UK: Cambridge University Press.

Lenz, T. 2003. *Changing Images of Law in Film and Television Crime Stories*. New York: Peter Lang.

Levenson, J. 2001. "Inside Information: Prisons and the Media." *Criminal Justice Matters* 43: 14–15.

Levi, M. 2001. "White-Collar Crime in the News." *Criminal Justice Matters* 43: 24–25.

Levi, M. 2006. "The Media Construction of Financial White-collar Crimes." *British Journal of Criminology* 46: 1037–1057.

Levi, M. 2008. "Measuring the Impact of Fraud in the UK." *British Journal of Criminology* 48: 293–318.

Levi, M. 2009. "Suite Revenge: The Shaping of Folk Devils and Moral Panics about White-Collar Crime." *British Journal of Criminology* 49(1): 48–67.

Levi, M., and A. Pithouse. 2006. *White Collar Crime and Its Victims: The Social and Media Construction of Business Fraud*. Oxford: Clarendon Press.

Levi, M., and J. Burrows. 2008. "Measuring the Impact of Fraud in the UK." *British Journal of Criminology* 48: 292–318.

Lichter, L. S., and S. R. Lichter. 1983. *Prime Time Crime*. Washington, DC: Media Institute.

Lichter, S. R., L. S. Lichter, and S. Rothman. 1994. *Prime Time*. Washington, DC: Regnery.

Lindesmith, A. 1965. *The Addict and the Law*. Bloomington: Indiana University Press.

Lindlof, T. 1988. "Media Audiences as Interpretive Communities." In *Communication Yearbook 11*, ed. J. Anderson, 81–107. Newbury Park, CA: Sage.

Ling, R., and S. Campbell. 2010. *The Reconstruction of Space and Time: Mobile Communication Practices*. Piscataway, NJ: Transaction Press.

Lippmann, W. 1922. *Public Opinion*. New York: Macmillan.

Lipschultz, J., and M. Hilt. 2002. *Crime and Local Television News: Dramatic, Breaking, and Live from the Scene*. Mahwah, NJ: Erlbaum.

Lister, M., J. Dovey, S. Giddings, I. Grant, and K. Kelly. 2003. *New Media: A Critical Introduction*, New York: Routledge.

Livingstone, N. 1982. *The War against Terrorism*. Lexington, MA: Heath.

Loften, J. 1966. *Justice and the Press*. Boston, MA: Beacon Press.

Lomell, H. 2004. "Targeting the Unwanted: Video Surveillance and Categorical Exclusion in Oslo, Norway?" *Surveillance and Society* 2(2/3): 3472–3561.

Lotz, R. 1991. *Crime and the American Press*. New York: Praeger.

Lowery, S., and M. De Fleur. 1983. *Milestones in Mass Communication Research*. White Plains, NY: Longman.

Lynch, M., P. Stretesky, and P. Hammond. 2000. "Media Coverage of Chemical Crimes, Hillsborough County, Florida, 1987–97." *British Journal of Criminology* 40: 112–126.

Lyon D. 2006. *Theorizing the Panopticon and Beyond*. Cullompton, UK: Willan Pub.

Mann, C., and M.. Zatz. 2002. *Images of Color Images of Crime: Readings.* Los Angeles, CA: Roxbury Publishing.

Manning, P. 1998. "Media Loops." In *Popular Culture, Crime and Justice,* eds. F. Bailey and D. Hale, 25–39. Belmont, CA: Wadsworth.

Marcus, P. 1982. "The Media in the Courtroom: Attending, Reporting, Televising Criminal Cases." *Indiana Law Journal* (Spring): 235–287.

Marsh, H. 1991. "A Comparative Analysis of Crime Coverage in Newspapers in the United States and Other Countries from 1960 to 1989: A Review of the Literature." *Journal of Criminal Justice 19*: 67–80.

Martens, F., and M. Cunningham-Niederer. 1985. "Media Magic, Mafia Mania." *Federal Probation 49*(2): 60–68.

Marx, G. 1988. *Undercover: Police Surveillance in America.* Berkeley: University of California Press.

Marx, G. 1996. "Electric Eye in the Sky: Some Reflections on the New Surveillance and Popular Culture." In *Computers, Surveillance, and Privacy,* eds. D. Lyon and E. Zureik, 193–233. Minneapolis: University of Minnesota Press.

Mason, P. 2000. "Watching the Invisible: Televisual Portrayal of the British Prison 1980–1990." *International Journal of the Sociology of Law 28*: 33–44.

Mason, P. 2003. "The Screen Machine: Cinematic Representations of Prison." In *Criminal Visions: Media Representations of Crime and Justice,* ed. P. Mason, 278–297. Devon, UK: Willan.

Mason, P. 2006. *Captured by the Media; Prison Discourse in Popular Culture.* Cullompton, UK: Willan.

Mason, P. 2006. "Prison Decayed: Cinematic Penal Discourse and Populism 1995-2005." *Social Semiotics 16*(4): 607–626.

Mason, P. 2006. "Lies, Distortion and What Doesn't Work: Monitoring Prison Stories in the British Media." *Crime, Media Culture 2*(3): 251–267.

Mason, P. 2007. "Misinformation, Myth and Distortion: How the Press Construct Imprisonment in Britain." *Journalism Studies 8*(3): 481–496.

Mathiesen, T. 1987. "The Eagle and the Sun: On Panoptical Systems and Mass Media in Modern Society." In *Transcarceration: Essays in the Sociology of Social Control,* eds. J. Lowman, R. Menzies, and T. S. Palys, 59–76. Brookfield, VT: Gower.

Mathiesen, T. 1990. *Prison on Trial: A Critical Assessment.* Belmont, CA: Sage.

Mathiesen, T. 2000. *Prisons on Trial.* Winchester, UK: Waterside Press.

Mathiesen, T. 2001. "Television, Public Space and Prison Population." *Punishment and Society 3*(1): 35–42.

Mawby, R. 2003. "Completing the 'Half-Formed Picture'? Media Images of Policing." In *Criminal Visions: Media Representations of Crime and Justice,* ed. P. Mason, 214–237. Devon, UK: Willan.

Mawby, R., and J. Brown. 1984. "Newspaper Images of the Victim: A British Study." *Victimology 9*(1): 82–94.

Maxson, C., K. Hennigan, and D. Sloane. 2003. *Factors That Influence Public Opinion of the Police.* Washington, DC: National Institute of Justice.

Mazur, A. 1982. "Bomb Threats and the Mass Media: Evidence for a Theory of Suggestion." *American Sociological Review 47*: 407–411.

McCombs, M. 2004. *Setting the Agenda: The Mass Media and Public Opinion.* Cambridge, UK: Polity Press.

Meyers, M. 1994. "News of Battering." *Journal of Communication 44*: 47–63.

Meyers, M. 1996. *News Coverage of Violence Against Women.* Thousand Oaks, CA: Sage.

Meyers, W. 2002. *Juvenile Sexual Homicide.* New York: Academic Press.

Meyrowitz, J. 1985. *No Sense of Place.* New York: Oxford University Press.

Miller, M., T. Griffin, S. Clinkinbeard, and R. Thomas. 2009. "The Psychology of AMBER Alert: Unresolved Issues and Implications." *Social Science Journal 42*: 111–123.

Minnebo, J. 2006. "The Relation Between Psychological Distress, Television Exposure, and Television-viewing Motives in Crime Victims." *Media Psychology 8*(2): 65–93.

Mopas, M. 2007. "Examining the CSI effect through an ANT lens." *Crime Media Culture 31*(1): 110–117.

Morgan, M., and J. Shanahan. 1997. "Two Decades of Cultivation Research: An Appraisal and Meta-Analysis." *Communication Yearbook 20*: 1–45.

Murray, J. 2008. "Media Violence: The Effects are Both Real and Strong." *American Behavioral Scientist 51*(8): 1212–1230.

Myers, D. 2000. "The Diffusion of Collective Violence: Infectiousness, Susceptibility, and Mass Media Networks." *American Journal of Sociology. 106*(1): 173–208.

Nacos, B. 2007. *Mass-Mediated Terrorism.* Lanham, MD: Rowan and Littlefield.

Nasheri, H. 2002. *Crime and Justice in the Age of Court TV.* New York: LFB Scholarly Publishing LLC.

National Institute of Mental Health. 1982. *Television and Behavior: Ten Years of Scientific Progress and Implications for the Eighties.* Vol. *1.* Summary Report. Rockville, MD: U.S. Government Printing Service.

Newburn, T. 1994. *Young Offenders and the Media: Viewing Habits and Preferences.* London: Policy Studies Institute.

Newburn, T., and S. Hayman. 2002. *Policing, Surveillance and Social Control: CCTV and Police Monitoring of Suspects.* Portland, UK: Willan.

Nichols, L. 1999. "White-Collar Cinema: Changing Representations of Upper World Deviance in Popular Films." *Perspectives on Social Problems 11*: 61–84.

Norris, C., and G. Armstrong. 1999. *The Maximum Surveillance Society: The Rise of CCTV.* Oxford, UK: Berg.

Norris, C., M. McCahill, and D. Wood. 2004. "The Growth of CCTV: A Global Perspective on the International Diffusion of Video Surveillance in Publicly Accessible Space." *Surveillance and Society 2*(2/3): 110–135.

Nyberg, A. 1998. "Comic Books and Juvenile Delinquency: A Historical Perspective." In *Popular Culture, Crime, and Justice,* eds. F. Bailey and D. Hale, 71–70. Belmont, CA: Wadsworth.

Oberdorfer, D. 1977. *TET!* Baltimore, MD: Johns Hopkins University Press.

O'Keefe, G., and K. Reid. 1990. "Media Public Information Campaigns and Criminal Justice Policy: Beyond McGruff." In *Media and Criminal Justice Policy,* ed. R. Surette, 209–224. Springfield, IL: Thomas.

O'Keefe, G., D. Rosenbaum, P. Lavrakas, K. Reid, and R. Botta. 1996. *Taking a Bite Out of Crime.* Thousand Oaks, CA: Sage.

O'Sullivan, S. 2001. "Representations of Prison in Nineties Hollywood Cinema: From Con Air to the Shawshank Redemption". *Howard Journal of Criminal Justice 40*(4): 317–334.

Oliver, M. 1994. "Portrayals of Crime, Race, and Aggression in Reality Based Police Shows: A Content Analysis." *Journal of Broadcasting & Electronic Media 38*: 179–192.

Packer, H. 1968. *The Limits of the Criminal Sanction.* Stanford, CA: Stanford University Press.

Paletz, D., and A. Schmid. 1992. *Terrorism and the Media*. Newbury Park, CA: Sage.

Papke, D. 1987. *Framing the Criminal*. Hamden, CT: Archon Books.

Parks, M. R., and L. D. Robers. 1998. "Making MOOsic: The Development of Personal Relationships Online and a Comparison to Their Off-line Counterparts." *Journal of Social and Personal Relationships 15*(4): 517–537.

Parrish, P. 1993. "Police and the Media." *FBI Law Enforcement Bulletin 62*(9): 24–25.

Patton, P. 1995. "Caught." *Wired* (January): 125–130.

Payne, G. 2007. "Brutal Cops, News Coverage, and Public Perceptions of Law enforcement: An Experimental Investigation of Reality Construction." *Journal of Humanities and Social Sciences 1*(2): 1–10.

Pease, S., and C. Love. 1984. "The Copy-Cat Crime Phenomenon." In *Justice and the Media*, ed. R. Surette, 199–211. Springfield, IL: Thomas.

Penfold, R. 2004. "The Star's Image, Victimization and Celebrity Culture." *Punishment and Society 6*(3): 289–302.

Pennell, A., and K. Browne. 1998. "Film Violence and Young Offenders." *Aggression and Violent Behvaior 4*(1): 13–28.

Perlmutter, D. 2000. *Policing the Media: Street Cops and Public Perceptions of Law Enforcement*. Thousand Oaks, CA: Sage.

Peterson, R., and L. L. Thurstone. 1933. *Motion Pictures and the Social Attitudes of Children*. New York: Macmillan.

Petty, R., J. Priester, and P. Brinol. 2002. "Mass Media Attitude Change: Implications of the Elaboration Likelihood Model of Persuasion."In *Media Effects: Advances in Theory and Research*, eds. J. Bryant and D. Zillmann, 155–198. Mahwah, NJ: Erlbaum Publishers.

Pfeiffer, C., M. Windzio, and M. Kleimann. 2005. "Media Use and Its Impacts on Crime Perception, Sentencing Attitudes and Crime Policy." *European Journal of Criminology 2*(3): 259–285.

Pfuhl, E. 1992. "Crimestoppers: The Legitimation of Snitching." *Justice Quarterly 9*(3): 505–528.

Podlas, K. 2006. "The CSI Effect: Exposing the Media Myth." *Media and Entertainment Law Journal 16*: 429–465.

Poland, J. 1988. *Understanding Terrorism*. Englewood Cliffs, NJ: Prentice Hall.

Potter G., and V. Kappeler. 2006. *Constructing Crime*. Prospects Heights, IL: Waveland.

Powell, A. 2009. "Wendy's Vandalism Prank on West Bank Leads to Arrest of Texas Teenager." *New Orleans Metro Crime and Court News*. http://www.nola.com/crime/index.ssf/2009/09/jpso_announces_arrest_in_broke.html

Poyntz, S. 1997. "Homey, I Shot the Kids: Hollywood and the War on Drugs." *Emergency Librarian 25*(2): 3–9.

Price, J., E. Merrill, and M. Clause. 1992. "The Depiction of Guns on Prime Time Television." *Journal of School Health 62*(1): 15–19.

Priest, D. 2005. "CIA Holds Terror Suspects in Secret Prisons." *The Washington Post*, Wednesday, Nov. 2. Downloaded January 20, 2010 from http://www.Washingtonpost.com/.

Pritchard, D. 1985. "Race, Homicide and Newspapers." *Journalism Quarterly 62*: 500–507.

Pritchard, D., and K. Hughes. 1997. "Patterns of Deviance in Crime News." *Journal of Communication 47*(3): 49–67.

Protess, D., F. Cook, J. Doppelt, J. Ettema, M. Gordon, D. Leff, and P. Miller. 1991. *The Journalism of*

Outrage: Investigative Reporting and Agenda Building in America. New York: Guilford Press.

"Public Confidence in Selected Institutions, 1973–1996." 1996. *Sourcebook of Criminal Justice Statistics 1995*, Table 2.9. Washington, DC: Bureau of Justice Statistics.

Quinney, R. 1970. *The Social Reality of Crime.* Boston: Little, Brown and Co.

Rafter, N. 2000. *Shots in the Mirror: Crime Films and Society.* Oxford, UK: Oxford University Press.

Rafter, N. 2001. "American Criminal Trial Films: An Overview of Their Development, 1930–2000." *Journal of Law and Society* 28(1): 9–24.

Rafter, N. 2007. "Crime, Film and Criminology: Recent Sex-crime Movies." *Theoretical Criminology* 11(3): 403–420.

Raney, A., and J. Bryant. 2002. "Moral Judgment and Crime Drama: An Integrated Theory of Enjoyment." *Journal of Communication* 52(2): 402–415.

Rapping, E. 2003. *Law and Justice as Seen on TV.* New York: New York University Press.

Rebovich, D., and J. Kane. 2002. "An Eye for an Eye in the Electronic Age: Gauging Public Attitude Toward White Collar Crime and Punishment." *Journal of Economic Crime Management* 1(2): 1–19.

Reinarman, C. 1988. "The Social Construction of an Alcohol Problem: The Case of Mothers against Drunk Drivers and Social Control in the 1980s." *Theory and Society* 17: 91–120.

Reiner, R. 1981. "Keystone to Kojak: the Hollywood Cop." In *Cinema, Politics and Society in America*, eds. P. Davies and B. Neve, 196–220. New York: St. Martin's Press.

Reiner, R. 2000. *The Politics of the Police.* Oxford, UK: Oxford University Press.

Reiner, R. 2002. "Media Made Criminality: The Representation of Crime in the Mass Media." In *The Oxford Handbook of Criminology*, eds. M. Maguire, R. Morgan, and R. Reiner, 376–416. Oxford, UK: Oxford University Press.

Reiner, R., S. Livingstone, and J. Allen. 2000. "No More Happy Endings?" In *Crime, Risk and Insecurity*, eds. T. Hope and R. Sparks, 107–125. London: Routledge.

Reiner, R., S. Livingstone, and J. Allen. 2003. "From Law and Order to Lynch Mobs: Crime News since the Second World War." In *Criminal Visions: Media Representations of Crime and Justice*, ed. P. Mason, 13–32. Devon, UK: Willan.

Rennie, Y. 1978. *The Search for Criminal Man.* New York: Lexington Books.

Rennison, M. 2003. *Intimate Partner Violence, 1993–2001.* Washington DC: U.S. Dept. of Justice.

Rentschler, C. 2007. "Victims' Rights and the Struggle over Crime in the Media." *Canadian Journal of Communication* 32(2): 219–239.

Rheingold, A., C. Campbell, S. Self-Brown, M. de Arellano, H. Resnick, and D. Kilpatrick. 2007. "Prevention of Child Sexual Abuse: Evaluation of a Community Media Campaign." *Child Maltreatment* 12(4): 352–363.

Richmond, D. 2007. "Can You Find Me Now: Tracking the Limits on Government Access to Cellular GPS Location Data. *Communication Law Conspectus* 16(1): 283–319.

Roane, K. 2005, April. "The CSI Effect." *U.S. News & World Report* 138(15): 48–54.

Robbers, M. 2008. "Blinded by Science: The Social Construction of Reality in Forensic Television Shows and Its Effect on Criminal Jury Trials." *Criminal Justice Policy Review* 19(1): 84–102.

Roberts, J., and A. Doob. 1990. "News Media Influences on Public Views on Sentencing." *Law and Human Behavior* 14(5): 451–468.

Robinson, M. 2005. *Justice Blind?* Upper Saddle River, NJ: Pearson Prentice-Hall.

Rogers, E. 2003. *Diffusion of Innovations.* New York: Free Press.

Rogers, E., and J. Dearing. 1988. "Agenda-Setting Research: Where Has It Been, Where Is It Going?" In *Communication Yearbook 11*, ed. J. A. Anderson, 555–594. Thousand Oaks, CA: Sage.

Rome, D. 2004. *Black Demons: The Media's Depiction of the African American Male Criminal Stereotype.* Westport, CT: Praeger.

Rosenbaum, D., A. Lurigio, and P. Lavrakas. 1986. *Crime Stoppers: A National Evaluation of Program Operations and Effects.* Evanston, IL: Center for Urban Affairs and Policy Research, Northwestern University.

Rosenbaum, D., A. Lurigio, and P. Lavrakas. 1989. "Enhancing Citizen Participation and Solving Serious Crime: A National Evaluation of Crime Stoppers Programs." *Crime and Delinquency 35*: 401–420.

Roshier, B. 1981. "The Selection of Crime News in the Press." In *The Manufacture of News*, eds. S. Cohen and J. Young, 40–51. Thousand Oaks, CA: Sage.

Roskos-Ewoldsen, D., B. Roskos-Ewoldsen, R. Francesca, and D. Carpentier. 2002. "Media Priming: A Synthesis." In *Media Effects: Advances in Theory and Research*, eds. B. Jennings and D. Zillmann, 97–120. Mahwah, NJ: Erlbaum.

Ross, J. 2007. "Deconstructing the Terrorism-news Media Relationship." *Crime, Media Culture 3*: 215–225.

Ruddell, R., and S. Decker. 2005. "Kids and Assault Weapons; Social Problem or Social Construction?" *Criminal Justice Review 30*(1): 45–63.

Rushkoff, D. 1994. "Media: It's the Real Thing." *NPQ* (Summer): 4–15.

Russell, L. 2005. "Tabloid Tactics: Pushing Prison Reduction". *Criminal Justice Matters 59*: 32–33.

Sacco, V., and R. Silverman. 1981. "Selling Crime Prevention: The Evaluation of a Mass Media Campaign." *Canadian Journal of Criminology 23*: 191–201.

Sacco, V. 2005. *When Crime Waves.* Thousand Oaks, CA: Sage.

Sacco, V., and Kennedy, B. 1996. *The Criminal Event: An Introduction to Criminology.* Belmont, CA: Wadsworth.

Santa, A., and B. Cochran. 2008. "Does the Impact of Anti-drinking and Driving Public Service Announcements Differ Based on Message Type and Viewer Characteristics?" *Journal of Drug Education 38*(2): 109–29.

Sarat, A. 2000. "Death Row, Aisle Seat." *The American Prospect 11*(7): 1–3.

Sarat, A. 2002. *When the State Kills: Capital Punishment and the American Condition.* Princeton, NJ: Princeton University Press.

Sasson, T. 1995. *Crime Talk.* Hawthorne, NY: Aldine de Gruyter.

Savage, J. 2004. "Does Viewing Violent Media Really Cause Criminal Violence? A Methodological Review." *Aggression and Violent Behavior 10*: 99–128.

Savage, J. 2008. "The Role of Exposure to Media Violence in the Etiology of Violent Behavior." *American Behavioral Scientist 51*(8): 1123–1136.

Savage, J., and C. Yancey. 2008. "The Effects of Media Violence Exposure on Criminal Aggression: A Meta-Analysis." *Criminal Justice and Behavior 35*(6): 772–791.

Schank, R., and R. Abelson. 1977. *Scripts, Plans, Goals, and Understanding.* Mahwah, NJ: Erlbaum.

Schauer, T. 2004. "Masculinity Incarcerated: Insurrectionary Speech and Masculinity." *Journal for Crime, Conflict and Media Culture* 1(3): 28–42.

Schechter, H. 2003. *The Serial Killer Files*. New York: Ballantine.

Schlesinger, P., H. Tumber, and G. Murdock. 1991. "The Media Politics of Crime and Criminal Justice." *British Journal of Sociology* 42: 397–420.

Schmid, A., and J. de Graaf. 1982. *Violence as Communication*. Thousand Oaks, CA.: Sage.

Schramm, W., J. Lyle, and E. B. Parker. 1961. *Television in the Lives of Our Children*. Stanford, CA: Stanford University Press.

Schwartz, J. 2009. "As Jurors Turn to Google and Twitter, Mistrials are Popping Up." *New York Times*, Wed., March 18: A1, A18.

Sechrest, D., W. Liquori, and J. Perry. 1990. "Using Video Technology in Police Patrol." In *The Media and Criminal Justice Policy*, ed. R. Surette, 255–264. Springfield, IL: Thomas.

Self, R. 2007. "Stewart, Martha." In *Encyclopedia of White-Collar Crime*, eds. J. Gerber and E. Jenson, 270–271. Westport, CT: Greenwood Press.

Shaaber, M. 1929. *Some Forerunners of the Newspaper in England*. Philadelphia: University of Pennsylvania Press.

Shaheen, J. 2001. *Reel Bad Arabs*. New York: Olive Branch Press.

Shelly, J., and C. Ashkins. 1981. "Crime, Crime News, and Crime Views." *Public Opinion Quarterly* 45: 492–506.

Shelton, D. 2006. "The CSI Effect: Does It Really Exist?" *National Institute of Justice Journal 259*: 1–6.

Sherizen, S. 1978. "Social Creation of Crime News." In *Deviance and Mass Media*, ed. C. Winick, 203–224. Thousand Oaks, CA: Sage.

Sherry, J. L. 2001. "The Effects of Violent Video Games on Aggression: A Meta Analysis." *Human Communication Research* 27(33): 409–432.

Sherwin, R. 2000. *When Law Goes Pop: The Vanishing Line Between Law and Popular Culture*. Chicago, IL: University of Chicago Press.

Shichor, D., and D. Sechrest. 1996. *Three Strikes and You're Out: Vengeance as Public Policy*. Thousand Oaks, CA: Sage.

Shipley, W., and G. Cavender. 2001. "Murder and Mayhem at the Movies." *Journal of Criminal Justice and Popular Culture* 9(1): 1–14.

Shoemaker, P. 1991. *Gatekeeping*, Thousand Oaks, CA: Sage.

Short, E., and J. Ditton. 1996. *Does Closed Circuit Television Prevent Crime?* Monograph of The Scottish Office Central Research Unit, Edinburgh, Scotland.

Shrum L. J. 2002. "Media Consumption and Perceptions of Social Reality: Effects and Underlying Processes." In *Media Effects: Advances in Theory and Research*, eds. J. Bryant Jennings and D. Zillmann, Dolf, 69–95. Mahwah, NJ: Erlbaum.

Shuttleworth, F., and M. May. 1933. *The Social Conduct and Attitudes of Movie Fans*. New York: Macmillan.

Sigal, L. 1973. *Reporters and Officials*. Lexington, MA: Heath.

Simpson, P. 2000. *Psycho Paths: Tracking the Serial Killer through Contemporary American Film and Fiction*. Carbondale, IL: Southern Illinois University Press.

Slater, M., and D. Rouner. 2002. "Entertainment-education and Elaboration Likelihood: Understanding the Processing of Narrative Persuasion." *Communication Theory* 12(2): 173–191.

Smith, D. 2004. "Behind the Screens: Examining Construction of Deviance and Information Practices Among CCTV Control Rook Operators in the UK." *Surveillance Society* 2(2/3): 376–395.

Snider, L. 2008. "Corporate Economic Crimes." In *Corporate and White-Collar Crime,* eds. J. Minkes and L. Minkes, 39–60. Los Angeles, CA: Sage.

Sorenson, S., J. Peterson-Manz, and R. Berk. 1998. "News Media Coverage and the Epidemiology of Homicide." *American Journal of Public Health* 88(10): 1510–1514.

Sotirovic, M. 2001. "Affective and Cognitive Processes as Mediators of Media Influences on Crime-Policy Preferences." *Mass Communication & Society* 4(3): 311–329.

Sparks, G., and C. Sparks. 2002. "Effects of Media Violence." In *Media Effects: Advances in Theory and Research*, ed. J. Bryant and D. Zillman, 269–285. Mahwah, NJ: Erlbaum.

Sparks, G., and R. Ogles. 1990. "The Difference Between Fear of Victimization and the Probability of Being Victimized: Implications for Cultivation." *Journal of Broadcasting and Electronic Media* 34(3): 351–358.

Sparks, R. 1992. *Television and the Drama of Crime*. Buckingham, UK: Open University Press.

Spector, M., and J. Kitsuse. 1987. *Constructing Social Problems.* Hawthorne, NY: Aldine de Gruyter.

Stark, S. 1987. "Perry Mason Meets Sonny Crockett: The History of Lawyers and the Police as Television Heroes." *University of Miami Law Review 42*: 229–283.

Stark, S. 1997. *Glued to the Set.* New York: Dell.

Stephenson-Burton, A. 1995. "Through the Looking-Glass: Public Images of White Collar Crime." In *Crime and the Media*, eds. D. Kidd-Hewitt and R. Osborne, 131–163. London: Pluto.

Stevens, J., and H. Garcia. 1980. *Communication History*. Thousand Oaks, CA: Sage.

Sumser, J. 1996. *Morality and Social Order in Television Crime Drama.* Jefferson, NC: McFarland.

Surette, R. 1986. "The Mass Media and Criminal Investigations: Crime Stoppers in Dade County, Florida." *Journal of Justice Issues 1*(1): 21–38.

Surette, R. 1989. "Media Trials." *Journal of Criminal Justice 17*: 293–308.

Surette, R. 1992. "Methodological Problems in Determining Media Effects on Criminal Justice: A Review and Suggestions for the Future." *Criminal Justice Policy Review 6*(4): 291–310.

Surette, R. 1998. "Some Unpopular Thoughts about Popular Culture." In *Popular Culture, Crime and Justice*, ed. F. Bailey and D. Hale, xiv–xxiv. Belmont, CA: Wadsworth.

Surette, R. 1999. "Media Echoes: Systemic Effects of News Coverage." *Justice Quarterly 16*: 601–631.

Surette, R. 2002. "Self Reported Copy Cat Crime among a Population of Serious Violent Juvenile Offenders." *Crime and Delinquency 48*(1): 46–69.

Surette, R. 2005. "The Thinking Eye: Pros and Cons of Second Generation CCTV Surveillance Systems." *Policing 28*(1) 152–173.

Surette, R. 2006. "CCTV and Citizen Guardianship Suppression: A Questionable Proposition." *Police Quarterly 9*(1): 100–125.

Surette, R., and C. Otto. 2002. "A Test of a Crime and Justice Infotainment Measure." *Journal of Criminal Justice* 30(5): 443–453.

Surette, R., and C. Terry. 1984. "Videotaped Misdemeanor First Appearances: Fairness from the Defendant's Perspective." In *Justice and the Media*, ed. R. Surette, 305–320. Springfield, IL: Thomas.

Surette, R., and C. Terry. 1985. "Video in the Misdemeanor Court: The South Florida Experience." *Judicature 69*(1): 13–19.

Surette, R., K. Hansen, and G. Noble. 2009. "Measuring Media Oriented Terrorism." *Journal of Criminal Justice* 37: 360–370.

Sutton, A., and D. Wilson. 2004. "Open-street CCTV in Australia: Politics and Expansion." *Surveillance and Society* 2(2/3): 310–322.

Tajgman, D. 1981. "From Estes to Chandler: The Distinction Between Television and Newspaper Trial Coverage." *Communication/Entertainment Law Journal 3*: 503–541.

Tarde, G. 1912. *Penal Philosophy*. Translated R. Howell (1912 by Little, Brown, and Co.). Reprinted 1968. Montclair, NJ: Patterson Smith

"The All-Seeing Eye." 1997. *The Economist 342*: 79–99 (January 11).

Thomas, W. I. 1908. "The Psychology of Yellow Journalism." *American Magazine 65*: 491–496.

Thomas, W. I. 1951. *Social Behavior and Personality*. Chicago: University of Chicago Press.

Thompson, C., R. Young, and R. Burns. 2000. "Representing Gangs in the News: Media Constructions of Criminal Gangs." *Sociological Spectrum* 20: 409–432.

Tilley, N. 1993. "Understanding Car Parks, Crime and CCTV: Evaluation Lessons from Safer Cities." *Police Research Group Crime Detection and Prevention Series*, paper no. 42. London: Home Office.

Tombs, S. 2008. "Corporations and Health and Safety." In *Corporate and White-Collar Crime*, eds. J. Minkes and L. Minkes, 18–38. Los Angeles, CA: Sage.

Tombs, S., and Whyte, D. 2001. "Reporting Corporate Crime Out of Existence." *Criminal Justice Matters 43*: 22–23.

"Trial by Media." 1984. *U.S. Press 10*(30): 4.

Tucher, A. 1999–2000. "Framing the Criminal: Trade Secrets of the Crime Reporter." *New York Law School Review 6*(3–4): 905–913.

Tuchman, G. 1973. "Making News by Doing Work." *American Journal of Sociology 79*: 110–131.

Tuchman, G. 1978. *Making News: A Study in the Construction of Reality*. New York: Free Press.

Tuman, J. 2003. *Communicating Terror: The Rhetorical Dimensions of Terrorism*. Thousand Oaks, CA: Sage.

Tunnel, K. 1998. "Reflections on Crime, Criminals, and Control in News-magazine Television Programs." In *Popular Culture, Crime, and Justice*, eds. F. Bailey and D. Hale, 111–122. Belmont, CA: Wadsworth.

Tyler, T. 2006. "Viewing CSI and the Threshold of Guilt: Managing Truth and Justice in Reality and Fiction." *Yale Law Journal 115*(5): 1050–1085.

United States v. Burr, 25F, Cas 49 (C.C.D. Va. 1807) No. 14692g.

Useem, B., and O. Clayton. 2009. "Radicalization of U.S. Prisoners." *Criminology and Public Policy 8*(3): 561–592.

Valier, C. 2004. *Crime and Punishment in Contemporary Culture*. New York: Routledge.

Valverde, M. 2006. *Law and Order: Images, Meanings, Myths*. New Brunswick, NJ: Rutgers University Press.

"Video Game 'Sparked Hammer Murder.'" 2004. CNN.com. Downloaded from http://www.cnn.com/2004/WORLD/europe/07/29/uk.manhunt/

Vine, M. 1973. "Gabriel Tarde." In *Pioneers in Criminology*, ed. H. Mannheim, 292–304. Montclair, NJ: Patterson Smith.

Vogt, E. 2007. *Terrorists in Prison: The Challenge Facing Corrections*. Inside Homeland Security. Downloaded January 26, 2010 from http://www.nicic.org/Library/022793

Wardell, J. 2004. "4.2 Million Cameras Keep Eye on British." *Orlando Sentinel* (August 15): B2.

Wardle, C. 2006. ""It Could Happen to You": The Move Towards 'Personal' and 'Societal' Narratives in Newspaper Coverage of Child Murder, 1993–2000." *Journalism Studies* 7(4): 515–533.

Warr, M. 1991. "America's Perceptions of Crime and Punishment." In *Criminology: A Contemporary Handbook*, ed. J. F. Sheley. Belmont, CA: Wadsworth.

Warren, S. D., and L. D. Brandeis. 1890. "The Right to Privacy." *Harvard Law Review* 4(5): 193–220.

Wasserman, E. 1995. "No Big Deal: O. J. Just Another 'Trial of the Century.'" *Miami Herald* (July 18): 1A, 10A.

Webster, C. 2004. "The Evolving Diffusion, Regulation and Governance of Closed Circuit Television in the UK." *Surveillance and Society* 2(2/3): 230–250.

Weimann, G., and C. Winn. 1994. *The Theater of Terror: Mass Media and International Terrorism*. White Plains, NY: Longman.

Weinstein, N. 1987. "Cross-Hazard Consistencies: Conclusions about Self-Protective Behaviour." In *Taking Care: Understanding and Encouraging Self-Protective Behavior*, ed. N. Weinstein, 325–336. New York: Cambridge University Press.

Weiser, G. 2009. "Secret C.I.A. Jails an Issue in Terror Case." *The New York Times*, July 2: A 20. Downloaded January 25, 2010 from http://proquest.umi.com/.

Weitzer, R., and C. Kubrin. 2004. "Breaking News: How Local TV News and Real-World Conditions Affect Fear of Crime." *Justice Quarterly* 21(3): 497–520.

Weitzer, R. 2002. "Incidents of Police Misconduct and Public Opinion." *Journal of Criminal Justice* 30: 397–408.

Welsh, B., and D. Farrington. 2002. *Crime Prevention Effects of Closed Circuit Television: A Systematic Review*. Home Office Research Study 252. London: Home Office.

Welsh, B., and D. Farrington. 2004. "Evidence-Based Crime Prevention: The Effectiveness of CCTV." *Crime Prevention and Community Safety* 6: 21–33.

Whitaker, J., and B. Bushman. 2009. "A Review of the Effects of Violent Video Games on Children and Adolescents." *Washington & Lee Law Review*, Summer 66: 1033–1051.

Wilbanks, W. 1984. *Murder in Miami: An Analysis of Homicide Patterns and Trends in Dade County* (Miami) Florida. 1917–1983. New York: University Press of America.

Williams, C. 2003. "Police Surveillance and the Emergence of CCTV in the 1960s." In *CCTV*, ed. M. Gill, 9–22. Leicester, UK: Perpetuity.

Williams, D. 2007. "Effective CCTV and the Challenge of Constructing Legitimate Suspicion Using Remote Visual Images." *Journal of Investigative Psychology and Offender Profiling* 4: 97–107.

Williams, K., and C. Johnstone. 2000. "The Politics of the Selective Gaze: Closed Circuit Television and the Policing of Public Space." *Crime, Law and Social Change* 34: 183–210.

Wilson, B., D. Kunkel, D. Linz, J. Potter, E. Donnerstein, S. Smith, E. Blumenthal, and T. Gray. 1997. "Violence in Television Programming Overall: University of California, Santa Barbara Study, Part I.: In *National Television Violence Study*: Vol. 1. Newbury Park, CA: Sage.

Wilson, C. 2000. *Cop Knowledge*. Chicago, IL: University of Chicago Press.

Wilson, P. 1987 "'Stranger' Child-murder: Issues Relating to Causes and Controls." *International Journal of offender Therapy and Comparative Criminology* 31: 49–9.

Wilson, D., and S. O'Sullivan. 2004. *Images of Incarceration: Representations of Prison in Film and Television Drama*. Winchester, UK: Waterside Press.

Wilson, J. Q., and R. Herrnstein. 1985. *Crime and Human Behavior.* New York: Simon & Schuster.

Wisehart, M. K. [1922] 1968. "Newspapers and Criminal Justice." In *Criminal Justice in Cleveland*, eds. R. Pound and F. Frankfurter, 515–555. Montclair, NJ: Patterson Smith.

"Woman Arrested for Killing Virtual Reality Husband." 2008. CNN.com/technology. Downloaded from http://www.cnn.com/2008/TECH/ptech/10/23/avatar.murder.japan.ap/index.html.

Wright, J., F. Cullen, and M. Blankenship. 1995. "The Social Construction of Corporate Violence: Media Coverage of the Imperial Food Products Fire." *Crime & Delinquency 41*: 20–6.

Wykes, M. 2007. "Constructing Crime: Culture, Stalking, Celebrity and Cyber." *Crime, Media, Culture 3*(2): 158–174.

Young, J. 1999. *The Exclusive Society.* Thousand Oaks, CA: Sage.

Zaner, L. 1989. "The Screen Test: Has Hollywood Hurt Corrections' Image?" *Corrections Today 51*: 64–66, 94, 95, 98.

Zgoba, K., M. Dalessandro, B. Veysey, and P. Witt. 2008. *Megan's Law: Assessing the Practical and Monetary Efficacy.* Rockville, MD: National Institute of Justice/NCJRS. Downloaded Jan 15, 2010 from http://www.ncjrs.gov/App/publications/abstract.aspx?ID=247350

Index

Page numbers in bold denote pages where the terms are defined; followed by b indicate a boxed item; followed by f indicate figures; followed by t indicate a table.

A

abuse of power media trials,
    112, 115t
Adam Walsh Child Protection and Safety
    Act, 3
advertising, 16
Al-Qaeda, 43b, 114t
Altheide, David, 197
Amber alerts, 3f
American Focus on Satanic
    Crime, 37b
announcement effect, 159
anticipatory effect, 194
anti-crime ad programs, 156–159
    three basic types, 158t
    twenty-first-century crime, media
        and justice, 202–204
    Web Sites, 162b
Arbuckle, Fatty, 24
Armstrong, Gary, 173b
Asimow, Michael, 131
Attorneys
    crime-fighting, 107
    female, portrait of,
        108–109
    portrait of, 106–108
authority and control corrections films,
    137

B

backwards law, 182–184
    corrections, 136
    courts, 107, 128b
Bailey, Frankie, 28, 131, 154
bandit heroes, 12
Barak, Gregg, 36b, 51
beat system, 18
Beckett, Katherine, 199
beliefs and attitudes, 190–191
Bergman Paul, 131
Berkowitz, Leonard, 74
Best, Joel, 45, 51
big brother, 168, 174–175
blocked opportunities frame, 38t–39
books with criminal justice themes
    Bobbsy Twins, 100
    Hardy Boys, 100
    The Lost World, 151
    New Centurions, 901
    Revolutionary War Science, 70
    Tom Sawyer, 100
books with social construction themes
    Blink, 29
    The Jungle, 60
    Public Opinion, 29
Borden, Lizzie, 113
Botta, Renee, 179

Boyle, Karen, 82
Brandeis, William, 168
Bruschke, Jon, 131
Burr, Aaron, 119, 120
business and professional criminals, 64–65

C

Cagney, James, 88
Callanan, Valerie, 199
camera surveillance, 172b–173b, 175–176
Carlie's Law, 3
case processing and technology, 163–166
cathartic effect, 67–68
Cavender, Gray, 94
CCTV (closed circuit television), 168–172
celebrity crime, 188b
Chandler v. Florida, 118, 119
change of venue, 123b
Chaplin, Charlie, 86
Cheatwood, Derral, 136
Chermak, Steven, 140–141
citizen-cooperation ads, 160–163
citizen soldiers, 99–100
    private citizens, 99–100
    private investigators (PIs), 99
    professional crime soldiers versus,
        101–103
claims, 34–37
    factual, 4–5, 34–36
    interpretative, 36
    from politicians, 36b
claims makers, 34–37
Clinton, President Bill, 39
closed circuit television (CCTV). See
        CCTV (closed circuit television)
Columbine school shootings, 40, 42
comic books, 6, 8–10
    Dick Tracy, 89
commercial movies, 135f
commodification, 22
contempt of court, 122–123
continuance, 123b
conversational reality, 48–49
    defined, **48**
cops, 90–92
cops narrative, 97
copycat crime, 70–77
    aggregate model phases, 76f
    individual level model, 75f

correctional
    horrors, 144
    infotainmemt and television, 138–140
    institutions, 150
    sources, 135–148, 145b
corrections
    historical perspective, 132–135
    infotainment, 138–140
    news of, 140–148, 152b
    portraits and stereotypes, 148–150
    primitive "lost world", 151–152
    television, 138–140
    television news, 140–148
correspondents, self-labeled, 22
counterproductive effects, 194
courtroom cameras, 111, 113, 117,
        118–119
CourtTV, 128b–129b
courtroom films, 106–108
courts, as entertainment, 126–130
crime, as a technology problem, 187–188,
        199
crime, chase, capture, 20, 93t
crime control
    benefits and concerns of, 171–174
    case processing and technology,
        163–166
    citizen-cooperation ads, 160–163
    history and issues, 167–171
    judicial system use, 163–165
    law enforcement use, 165–166
    media and, 155–163
    1984 icon, 176–178, 175–176
    police and public safety, 174–176
    public service announcement (PSAs),
        156–159
    surveillance, 166–178
    victimization-reduction ads, 159–160
crime news, 7t, 16–19
crime realities, 18, 26
crimes, 57–58
Crime Stoppers, 158t, 160
crime thrillers, 6
criminal justice policy, 196f, 180–199
criminals, 53–54
criminogenic infotainment, 79–81
criminogenic media, 66–79
    copycat crime, 70–77
    media and criminal behavior, 69–70
    violent media and aggression, 67–69

criminological theories, 61–64
  biological, 61
  overview, 52
  political, 63–64
  psychological, 61–62
  rational choice, 61
  sociological, 61–62
Croteau, David, 218
CSI: Crime Scene Investigations effect, 95–97

D

D. C. snipers, 62b
detective Dupin, 100
detective thrillers, 6
diffusion, 172–173
digital interactive media, 13–15
digital manipulation of visual images, 164
dime novels, 6, 7t, 12, 52
displacement, 172
Donovan, Pamela, 93
Doyle, Aaron, 93, 143
Doyle, Arthur, 151
driving under the influence (DUI), 45–46, 159
due process, 94, 95, 98t, 118, 181

E

Easy E,
echo effect, 194
Enron, 58
entertainment, 15–16
episodic format, 183–184
Ericson, Richard, 143
Estes v. Texas, 110–111, 117–118
evil stranger media trials, 113, 116t
experienced reality, 31
exposure, 10

F

Facebook fugitive, 152b
faulty system frame, 38–39
FBI (Federal Bureau of Investigation)
  annual justice report, 48–49
  Crime Index, 58
  Narcotics, 157
fear of crime, 57, 81, 119, 151, 189

film
  historical crime themes, 12–13
film noir, 99
films with criminal justice themes
  20,000, Years in Sing Sing, 136
  48 Hours, 145b
  Aliens, 137
  Badlands, 82
  Cool Hand Luke, 132, 137
  Dirty Harry, 90, 91, 101
  Escape from Alcatraz, 136
  Escape from New York, 137
  Great Train Robbery, 53
  Half-Baked, 158
  Henry: Portrait of a Serial Killer, 82
  Holes, 137
  I Am A Fugitive from a Chain Gang, 2, 136
  JFK, 5
  Monster, 82
  Murder in the Heartland, 82
  Natural Born Killers, 199
  Police Academy, 86
  Psycho, 61
  Raiders of the Lost Ark, 187
  Red Dawn, 187
  Reefer Madness, 157
  Riot in Cell Block , 136
  Robin Hood, 65
  Scared Straight, 140
  Silence of the Lambs, 2, 82
  Super Trooper, 86
  The Big House, 136
  The Birdman of Alcatraz, 136
  The Shawshank Redemption, 137, 153
  The Stranger Beside Me, 82
  Titticut Follies, 140
  To Kill a Mockingbird, 23
films with psychological theories
  Psycho, 62
films with white-collar crime themes
  Catch Me If You Can, 60
  Erin Brockovich, 60
  Wall Street, 60
first amendment, 121, 122b, 211
Fisher, Amy, 127
Fishman, Mark, 104
Forensic effect, 95–97
frames, 37–40
  defined, **37**

frames (*continued*)
　influence on crime and justice
　　policy, 40
freedom and release corrections films,
　137–138
Freedom of Information Act (1966), 125
Freeman, Robert, 144, 154
Freud, Sigmund, 61–62
front-end loaded, 86, 95, 144, 182

G

gatekeeper, 18–19
Gerbner, George, 190
Gergen, Kenneth, 51
Gest, Ted, 199
Gladwell, Malcolm, 29–30
g-men, 87–90
good cop/bad cop frame, 84–86
Goold, Benjamin, 173b, 179
Government information, 125
Government in Sunshine Act (1976), 125
Grand Theft Auto, copycat crime, 72b
Grant, Barry, 82
Grant, Hugh, 188
guns, portrayal of, 102–103

H

Hale, Donna, 28, 154
Hatty, Suzanne, 44b
Hauptmann, Bruno, 24, 11f, 116t, 117.
　See also Lindbergh baby kidnapping
Haymarket Square bombing, 70
Hays Code, 88b
Hays Commission, 70, 88
Hearst, Patty, 24, 115t
Heller, Melvin, 71
Hennigan, Karen, 69–70
heroic inmates, 149
Hilton, Paris, 139b–140b
Hinckley, John, 74, 133
Hindenberg, 10
Homeland Security Act of 2002, 125
Hoynes, William, 218

I

ideal heroes, 185
ideal offenders, 185

ideal victims, 185b
imitation, 146, 70, 73–77. *See also* copycat
　crime
immanent justice, 186–187
　defined, **186**
incarceration rates, 133b
infotainment, 19–21
　as content, 15
　and courts, 105–106
　criminogenic, 79–81
　defined, **19**
　history of, 7t
　and media trials, 23–24
　television, 138–140
　and terrorism, 77–79
　and police, 92–95
institutions, 150
Inspector Clouseaus, 86
interactivity, 13–15
Internet news Web sites, 21–22

J

Jackson, Michael, homicide case, 23f
Jenkins, Phillip, 37b, 44b, 55
Jewkes, Yvonne, n.
Jessica's Law, 3
judicial mechanisms to control publicity,
　121–125
　proactive, 121–122
　reactive, 121–122, 123b
judicial system, and crime control,
　163–165
juror expectations, 95–97
jury instructions, 123b
justice policy
　backwards law, 182–184
　beliefs and attitudes, 190–191
　celebrity crime, 188b
　ecology of, 184–186
　immanent rules, 186–187
　media construction and, 180–181
　memorial, 185b
　policies, 191–195
　process chart, 197f
　public agenda, 189–190
　real-world crime, 188–189
　Relationship models, 193b
　research and, 189–195
　social construction of, 195–198

technology and, 187–189
tenets, 181–187
Three Strikes, 192b
juveniles armed with assault rifles, 44

K

Kappeler, Victor, 51
Katzenbach, Nicholas B,. 39
Keystone Kops, 86–87
King, Rodney, 28, 42, 46–48
Kitsuse, John, 51
Klaas, Polly, 2
Knox, Amanda, 124b
Kooistra, Paul, 93

L

lampooned police, 86–87
Lavrakas, Paul, 179
law enforcement, 84–86
    and crime control, 165–166
Lawrence, Regina, 104
Lee, Ivy, 34
legal versus factual guilt, 121, 181
legends
    Al Capone, 86
    Bonnie and Clyde, 86
    Eliot Ness, 86
    James, Jesse, 86
    Wild Bill Hickok, 86
Leishman, Frank, 104
Leitch, Thomas, 213
Lichter, Linda, 100, 108
Lichter, Robert and Linda, 100, 108
Lindbergh baby kidnapping, 10, 110f.
    See also Hauptmann, Bruno
linkage, 36, 37b
Lippman, Walter, 29
Loges, William,
looping, 5, 131
Love Canal, 58

M

Malvo, Lee, 62b
manipulative model, 17
mainstreaming, 190
Marighella, Carlos, 77
market model, 17

Mason, Paul, 104, 154
Mazur, Allen, 74
McGruff, Crime Dog, 160
McVeigh, Timothy, 116t
media
    and crime control, 155–163
    and criminal behavior, 69–70
    and criminal justice, 1–4
    and criminality, 64–66
    and justice policy, 180–181
    and social reality construction, 32
media, merging of content types, 13–24
media messages, 200–209b
mediated criminal justice, 213–215
media criminogenic effects, 66–79
media effect models, 203–204
media oriented terrorist event (MOTE),
    77–79
    defined, **78**
mediated reality, 207
media trials, 23–24, 109–119
    defined, **23**
    effects of, 110–114
    examples, 115t–116t
    judicial news and entertainment,
        114–117
    live television, 117–119
media trials, example of
    Arbuckle, Fatty, 24
    Beecher, Henry Ward, 109
    Borden, Lizzie, 109
    Bryant, Kobe, 116t
    Bundy, Ted, 116t
    Clinton Impeachment, 115t
    Dahmer, Jeffery, 113
    Hauptmann, Bruno, 24
    Hearst, Patty, 24
    King, Rodney, 42, 46–48
    Leopold and Loeb, 115
    McVeigh, Timothy, 116t
    Peterson, Scott, 116t
    Rosenberg, Julius and Ethel, 24
    Sacco and Vanzetti, 24
    Sheppard, Sam, 115t
    Simpson, O.J., 38t–42, 112
    Smith, William Kennedy, 128b
    Wuornos, Aileen, 82
    Yousef, Ramzi, 116t
media violence frame, 39–40
media weapons cult, 102

mediated experience, 24–27
    defined, **24**
mediated reality, 25, 207–209
Megan's law, 2, 185b
memorial criminal justice policies, 2, 185b
Meyrowitz, Joshua, 28
Missing Broadcast Emergency Response
    Alter. *See* AMBER alert
mistrials, 208
modeling personality, 203f
Mohammad, D.C. sniper, 62b
Moore, Devin, 72
moral crusades, 190
Moran, Jade, 179
Most, Johann, 70
Most Wanted ads, 160–161f
Mothers Against Drunk Driving (MADD),
    46
multimedia web, 10
Munich Olympics, 79

N

NASA space program, 138
narratives, 41–42
    defined, **41**
    factual, 97
    fictional, 97
    persuasion, 74–75
narrowcasting, 8t, 13
Nasheri, Hedieh, 129b, 131
nature of confinement corrections films,
    136
negligible cause models, 203–204
new media, 152b, 207–208
news, 16–19
news formats, 22
newsmagazines, 21–22
newsworthiness, 17
1972 Olympics, 79
1984, as icon, 175–178
Norris, Clive, 173, 179

O

Obama, President, 36b
O'Keefe, Garrett, 179
on-demand media, 13
O'Neal, Tatum, 188b
organizational model, 17

ownership, 43–44
    and the media, 44b

P

Packer, Herbert, 181
Palestine Liberation Organization, 79
Patriot Act of 2001, 125
Payne Foundation, 70
Payne Fund research, 88
Penny Press, 6–7t, 109, 133f
    New York Sun, 6
Perlmutter, David, 99t, 104, 104
Personal digital assistant devices, 2
Poe, Edgar Allan, 100
police and public safety, 174–176
police media narratives, 97–99t
police procedurals, 87–90
police reality programs, 93–95
policewomen, 108–109
policy crusades, 194
Polsky, Samuel, 71
Potter, Gary, 51
ponzi schemes, 58
psychotic killers, 113, 116t
predator criminals, 54–55
    defined, **54**
    media portrait, 56f
prejudicial publicity, 120f
pretrial publicity, 119–126
    judicial mechanisms to deal with,
        121–125
    overview, 118–121
primary cause models, 203f
priming, 73
print media, 6–10
prison films, 135–138
prisoners, 149–150
    female, 149, 153
Privacy Act (1974), 125
private citizens, 99–100
private investigators (PIs), 99
privileged conversation, 135
professional crime soldiers, 86–88
    citizen soldiers versus, 101–103
    cops, 92
    difference between media and real cops,
        98t–99t
    g-men, 87–90
    as infotainment, 82–95

lampooned police, 86–87
  media portrayal, 95–97
  police and the media, 97–99t
profiling, 172b
prosocial television, 156
psychopathic supermale criminals, 64
public access, 206–207
public agenda, 189–190
publications, suggested, 28
public crusades, 8t
public information officers (PIOs), 18
public safety and police, 174–176
public service announcements (PSAs),
    156–159
pursuit of justice corrections films,
    136–137

R

Racist system frame, 38t–39
radio, 7t, 10–12, 24
Radio Noir programs, 11
radio program detectives
  Nick Carta, 11
  Philip Marlowe, 11
radio program with criminal justice themes
  Dragnet, 89
  Gang Busters, 11
  Sherlock Holmes, 11
  The Shadow, 11
  True Detective, 11
  War of the Worlds, 11
Rafter, Nicole, 136
readings, suggested, 28, 51, 82–83, 104,
    131, 154, 179, 199, 218
Reagan, President, 74
reality crime shows, 22–23
  Americas' Most Wanted, 11
  COPS, 20, 92–93
real-world crime, 188–189
Reid, Kathaleen, 179
reciprocal feedback model, 204f
relationship models, 193b–194
Reporters, 125–126
  privileged conversation, 125–126
  self-labeled, 22
road rage, 45
Robin Hood, 65, 99
Rome, Dennis, 83
Rosenbaum, Dennis, 179

S

Sacco, Vincent, 24, 218
Sasson, Theodore, 38
satanic cults, 37b
Scopes "monkey" trial, 10
scripts, 73
Sechrest, Dale, 199
September terrorist attacks (911), 42–43b,
    79, 116t, 146b–147b, 171
Sequestration, 123b
serial killers
  Bundy, Ted, 82, 116t
  Dahmer, Jeffery, 113
  Gacy, John Wayne, 113
  Lucus, Henry Lee, 82
  Starkweather, Charles, 82
  Wuornos, Aileen, 82
sex offender database, 3f
Sherwin, Richard, 127, 131
Shichor, David, 199
shield laws, 125–126
Simpson, O.J., 38t, 40, 42
Simpson, Philip, 83
sinful rich media trials,
    112–113, 115t–116t
sixth amendment, 122b
smug hack corrections, 150
social breakdown frame, 38t–39
social constructionism, 29–48
  concepts of, 34–44
  constructed reality, 32
  criminal justice policy, 48–50
  defined, **30**
  diagram, 33f
  justice policy, 195–198
  and media, 32–34
  overview, 29–30
  process in action, 44–48
  social knowledge, 30–34
  stages of, 32–34
socially constructed reality, process in
    action, 44–48
  defined, **32**
social knowledge, 30–34
soldiers, 85
sound media, 10–11
Spector, Malcom, 51
Stewart, Martha, 58, 59b
stimulating effect, 67–68

Sumser, John, 83
surveilliance, 166–178
    challenges to, 173
    effect, 167, 168f
    history of, 167–171
    twenty-first-century crime, media and
        justice, 211–213
symbolic crimes, 42–43
    Columbine school shootings, 40, 42
    construction formula, 43
    defined, **32**
    King, Rodney, 42, 46–48
    Klaas, Polly, 42
    9/11 terrorist attacks, 43b, 79
symbolic reality, 31–32

T

Tarde, Gabriel, 73
technology, 187–189
Teapot Dome scandal, 58
television, 12–13
    crime stories by criminal justice stage,
        141t
    violent content, 68, 202
television crime and justice infotainment
        program titles
    Americas' Most Wanted, 156
    COPS, 20, 92–93
    Inside American Jail, 138
    Intervention, 138
    Parole Board, 138
    Street Time, 138
    Wanted: Dead or Alive, 156
television entertainment program titles
    60 Minutes, 22
    Barney Fife, 86
    CSI: Crime Scene Investigations, 96b
    Dragnet, 11, 89f–90
    Law and Order, 129b
    Murder She Wrote, 100
    Oz, 129
    Police Story, 90
    Scooby-Doo, 100
    Sesame Street, 156
    The Practice, 129
terrorism, 77–80
    corrections and the media, 146b–147b
    crime fighting, as entertainment, 102b
        See also media oriented terrorist event

thematic format, 193
thematic news, 183
Thomas, W. I., 213
Three Mile Island, 58
Three Strikes and You're Out, 192b
trash-TV talk shows, 22
true crime books, 92
Tuman, Joseph, 83
twenty-first-century crime, media, and justice
    anticrime efforts, 202–204
    applications of, 215–217
    claims of, 201–202
    competing models of, 203f
    courts as entertainment, 126–130
    crime realities, 18, 26
    future reality of, 209–213
    media messages, 200–209b
    mediated criminal justice, 213–215
    mediated reality, 207
    postulates of, 204–206
    public access, 206–207
    reciprocal feedback model, 204f
    spectacles of, 209–211
    surveillance and, 211–213
    twitter and trials, 208b
    virtual reality, 209b
    YouTube and, 214b
twitter and trials, 208b
2001 World Trade Center attacks, 207

U

ultraviolence, 102
United Kingdom, and surveillance,
    169b–170b

V

victim and heroic criminals, 65
victimization-reduction ads, 159–160
victim rights, 4
victims of crime, 55–57
video lineup, 166, 178
video mug book, 166
videotaped interrogation, 165–166
violent media and aggression, 67–69
violent media frame, 38t–40
voir dire, 123b
virtual reality, 209b
visual media, 11–13

W

War, 85
Warren Commission Report, 5
Warren, Earl, 111
Web sites, 21–22
Weimann, Gabriel, 218
Wells, Orson, 10
Western outlaws, 12
What's Your Neighbor Hiding? 211
white-collar crime, 58–61
whodunit effect, 95–96b
Wilson, Christopher, 104

Wilson, D., 154
Wolf, Michael, 218
Woods, Tiger, 35b, 207
WorldCom, 58
worldview cultivation, 190
World Wide Web, 25

Y

yellow journalism, 7t, 17
YouTube and, 214b